Knowing God
through Journey and Pilgrimage

Knowing God through Journey and Pilgrimage

A Scriptural Study of Journey, Jesus' Pilgrimages, and Their Significance to the Feasts of Passover, Pentecost, and Tabernacles

SEUNG YEAL LEE

WIPF & STOCK · Eugene, Oregon

KNOWING GOD THROUGH JOURNEY AND PILGRIMAGE
A Scriptural Study of Journey, Jesus' Pilgrimages, and Their Significance to the
Feasts of Passover, Pentecost, and Tabernacles

Copyright © 2011 Seung Yeal Lee. All rights reserved. Except for brief quotations in critical publications or reviews, no part of this book may be reproduced in any manner without prior written permission from the publisher. Write: Permissions, Wipf and Stock Publishers, 199 W. 8th Ave., Suite 3, Eugene, OR 97401.

Scripture quotations, unless otherwise stated, are taken from Holy Bible, New International Version,® NIV.® Copyright© 1973, 1978, 1984 by Biblica, Inc.™ Used by permission of Zondervan. All rights reserved worldwide. www.zondervan.com

"BWHEBB, BWHEBL, BWTRANSH [Hebrew]; BWGRKL, BWGRKN, and BWGRKI [Greek] Postscript® Type 1 and TrueTypeT fonts Copyright © 1994-2009 BibleWorks, LLC. All rights reserved. These Biblical Greek and Hebrew fonts are used with permission and are from BibleWorks, software for Biblical exegesis and research."

Wipf & Stock
An Imprint of Wipf and Stock Publishers
199 W. 8th Ave., Suite 3
Eugene, OR 97401

www.wipfandstock.com

ISBN 13: 978-1-60899-819-7

Manufactured in the U.S.A.

Contents

Preface / vii
Acknowledgments / ix
Introduction / xi
Abbreviations / xv

1. Pilgrims and Disciples, Mixed Metaphors? / 1
2. Pilgrimage as a Paradigm for the People of God / 46
3. Jesus and the First Two Passover Pilgrimages / 87
4. Jesus and the Tabernacles Pilgrimage / 117
5. Jesus and the Final Passover Pilgrimage (John 12–19; Luke 9–19) / 143
6. Jesus and the Pentecost Pilgrimage / 167
7. Summary of Conclusions / 199

Appendix: Pilgrimage in Other Ancient Texts / 209
Bibliography / 237
Index of Names and Subjects / 253

Preface

THE HEBREW/CHRISTIAN SCRIPTURES INCLUDE many allusions to pilgrimage customs and practices, yet the information is scattered and requires a considerable amount of reconstruction. The fact that the six-volume *Anchor Bible Dictionary* contains no article on "pilgrimage" is symptomatic of this neglect. Thus this study is an attempt to rectify this need. It is posited that the pilgrimage paradigm, including the journey motif, has influenced the thought patterns of the writers of both the OT and NT.

Chapter 1 deals with the Creation and patriarchal narratives, examining how the pilgrimage (journey) paradigm relates to discipleship. The dispute regarding source criticism and redactional meaning is largely irrelevant for my task. Each text is to be understood within the narrative's meaning and plot.

Chapter 2, reviewing the history of the people of God, shows that together with the exile and restoration, the Exodus establishes the significance of pilgrimage as a paradigm for Israel that eventually shapes Judaism.

Chapters 3 to 6 follow Jesus' journey to Jerusalem on the three feasts of pilgrimage in Luke-Acts and John and their relevance to the way he revealed himself, and taught his disciples. Jesus' teaching on the way to Jerusalem is examined in the context of the pilgrimage paradigm to evaluate if the feasts are significant for Jesus' self-understanding and his teaching.

The study concludes that the three feasts of pilgrimage have developed their own characters and meanings for the momentous events in the history of Israel, and both Luke-Acts and John reflect the significance of the pilgrimage paradigm for Jesus' concern for revealing himself as the Pilgrim, the Suffering Messiah, the temple, the Way, and the hope for the *Parousia* (Second Coming of Christ), and training his disciples in a physical and eschatological sense of pilgrimage to Jerusalem.

Acknowledgments

MY UTMOST THANKS GO to God who has called me as I now am despite my weakness and unfaithfulness in my daily walk with the Lord. This body of work is literally a form of offering my growing faithfulness to the Lord.

I would like to thank Dr. Tom Holland for first encouraging me to write this thesis and for his continued support during its progress. My gratitude extends to Professor D. P. Davies and Dr. Eryl Davies for their kind guidance and encouragement. Special appreciation goes to Dr. Won Suk Ma for his clear guidance and kind encouragement for this work to be published and for my journey as a missionary.

My greatest thanks are also reserved for all family and friends who have generously supported me with prayer, finances, and encouragement in the Lord, particularly Kyung-Ja Choi, my mother-in-law, for her continual encouragement. I am also indebted to Howard David who polished up my English and Marcus Hobson, the librarian of Wales Evangelical School of Theology, from whose hands I have gained access to a number of books that are useful and even crucial to my study.

The work could not have been accomplished without my wife, Sarah, for her labor in bearing many responsibilities with patience and understanding. Sarah has borne so much to enable me to make this long journey. I owe her more than can ever be expressed. To Joseph, Samuel, and Daniel, who saw less of their father, I promise not to undertake another doctorate.

Soli Deo gloria

Introduction

A PERSONAL PILGRIMAGE

ON RETIRING FROM THE army in Korea, I organized a praise and worship band and committed myself to the role of worship leader. This was followed by graduation from university after which I established a small frozen food factory in order to provide for the ministry to which I felt called. I spent six years working in the business. The experience in these two different fields had a profound effect upon my life. It was during this time that I became interested in the meaning of the Year of Jubilee and felt a deep sense of God's call to follow him in a literal sense. This led to a change of abode for my future sphere of Christian service, resulting in a degree in theology gained in the U.K. Thus my journey with the pilgrimage paradigm began when I came to Britain, leaving behind the culture in which I had been brought up. This change of abode combined with the study of missiology at the college has opened my eyes both cross-culturally and missiologically. It was in the early part of this training that the geographical dimension of Jesus' salvation ministry began to fascinate me.

During the first year of my undergraduate studies, given an opportunity to preach for the first time in the U.K, this fascination led me to focus on the Year of Jubilee in Leviticus. The second time I preached I asked the question, "Why did God choose Nazareth in Galilee for the salvation ministry?" In one sense it began when I first encountered Josephus in preparing the second sermon. It was purely by chance that my initial interest in Galilee coincided with what Josephus described in relation to the people in Galilee. Since then, an ongoing curiosity and searching for the truth in relation to these two subjects has remained with me, becoming an inspiration for my thesis and, ultimately, this book. (The first subject for preaching has become the last section of the last chapter, and the second preaching an insight into seeing the meaning of the journey motif, including Jesus' pilgrimages to Jerusalem.) As I was initiated and encouraged by Dr. Tom Holland to establish the pilgrimage paradigm, a further development in my thinking took place and became more clearly focused during the course of this study.

METHODOLOGY

Within Christianity pilgrimage has been a long held tradition dating back to the very origins of Christianity.[1] There are various historical accounts of pilgrimage. However, it has not yet come to theological prominence. Theological analyses are rare.[2] Characteristically enough, neither the *Anchor Bible Dictionary* nor the *Theological Dictionary of the New Testament* by Gerhard Kittel has even one single article on pilgrimage. It is also true that the Bible lacks a technical term for pilgrimage.[3]

The Bible, nevertheless, contains many allusions to the concept of pilgrimage including the journey motif, but the scattered information requires a considerable amount of reconstruction. Thus this study is extensive, rather than intensive in its analysis. Having realized that we should not base our argument on a single piece of evidence, ignoring other evidence, the method used here is to think of the Bible as a gradual revelation, reconstructing the scattered information. The study of biblical history gives us the understanding of God and his revelation as a gradual process.

With the pilgrimage paradigm setting as a major criterion for our selection of the three pilgrimage feasts, the journey motif constitutes an essential literary context for the present assessment of each narrative.

---

1. Pilgrimage is not confined to Christianity. It is central to Islam. It is a phenomenon among other religions too.

2. It is fortunate that there is a book recently published for the contours of a Christian theology of pilgrimage for today. See Bartholomew and Hughes, *Christian Theology of Pilgrimage*.

3. In later development παροικίας and παρεπιδήμοις or their cognates are used independently (1 Pet 1:1, 17) and in Old Testament quotations (Heb 11:13; 1 Pet 2:11). By New Testament times it is probably true to say that the παροικίας not only resided longer in a place than the παρεπιδήμοις but also that he was more fully incorporated into the civic life and fiscal obligations of his adopted community. The strangers and pilgrims of Hebrews 11:13 translates the Greek beautifully. See Finlayson, "Pilgrimage," 998.

The dispute regarding source criticism, redactional meaning, or literary criticism is largely irrelevant for my task. Each narrative is to be assessed within its context, meaning, and plot. At the start of the journey the prospect of the paradigm is limited and fragmented, but in terms of the whole what we see along the way will reach the pinnacle and recognize a panoramic view from the top. This work is thus an attempt to discover and paint the whole picture, not part of it. Having identified the passages in the Old Testament and other ancient texts that contain the pilgrimage paradigm, the entirety of this work intends to capture a comprehensive vision of what Luke-Acts and the Fourth Gospel endeavor to convey in the context of the three pilgrimage feasts. The whole observation displays the characteristics of the pilgrimage paradigm in terms of the journey motif, the walk and way metaphor, and the knowing God motif.

In the formulation of the history of Israel, Creation, together with Abraham and Jacob, had decisive significance for the historical interpreter. For Israel Creation is the calling from God to grasp the reality of God as the Creator and that of mankind as his creatures and homeless on this earth, yearning for a return to the Edenic state, *being with God* as the final destination of pilgrimage. Through the journey framework God had guided Abraham and Jacob in their lives and led Israel as a nation to the promised land. Again, God brought a similar framework and process—being carried away to Babylon, sojourn in Babylon, and the return to the promised land—for his idolatrous people to know who he was and to come back to him. Thus the exile and restoration for Israel were not just a physical movement, but also a pilgrimage of faith and the working of God that enabled the people to recognize their identity before him.

Jewish literature from the Second Temple period that contains many allusions and information for pilgrimage customs and practices also spells out how deeply the pilgrimage practice in relation to the three pilgrimage feasts was embedded in the everyday life of the Israelites. In the New Testament the public ministry of Jesus is thus portrayed in terms of his repeated pilgrimages to Jerusalem leading to the cross and the ascension to God. This thesis represents Jesus' self-understanding in relation to the three pilgrimage feasts by analyzing the proposition that the pilgrimage paradigm, including the journey motif, has influenced the thought patterns of the writers of both the OT and NT.

For this task Luke-Acts and the Fourth Gospel in the New Testament are chosen, because of the similarity between them with regard to the common literary pattern of journey to Jerusalem in relation to the pilgrimage feasts. Although it is still difficult to explain how both traditions developed the encompassing narrative situation of Jesus' pilgrimages to Jerusalem, the fact that Luke and John share a number of agreements against Matthew and Mark and that a considerable number of contacts did exist between Luke-Acts and the Judean narratives of John, would provide a good basis for establishing the pilgrimage paradigm in both traditions.[4]

Finally, Jesus' pilgrimage to Jerusalem is scrutinized on the basis of the meaning and content of each pilgrimage. While the Feast of Passover was historicized in remembrance of the Exodus event, the Feast of Tabernacles was associated with the wilderness wandering of Israel, and the Feast of Pentecost with the events of Mount Sinai and with the patriarchs. Although some of the original ideas have remained right down to the Second Temple period, all these symbols and rites of each feast were gradually reinterpreted in the context of the evolving history of the Israelites. In Jesus' pilgrimages the feasts were imbued with new meaning and with further significance.

---

4. F. Lamar Cribbs summarizes the similarity between them. (1) Luke omits a number of Matthean/Markan details, phrases, or passages that are in disagreement with the information contained in comparable passages in John (e.g., compare Matt 6:13/Mark 8:27 with John 6:24; Matt 17:9–13/Mark 9:9–13 with John 1:21; Matt 21:8/Mark 11:8 with John 12:13; Matt 21:9/Mark 11:10 with John 12:13b; Matt 26:35/Mark 14:31 with John 13:37–38; Matt 26:56/Mark 14:50 with John 18:15; Matt 26:65–66/Mark 14:63–65 with John 18:19–24; Matt 26:74/Mark 14:71 with John 18:26–27; or Matt 27:14/Mark 15:5 with John 18:33–38 and the parallel sections of Luke), and in several instances Luke substitutes his own version of an event (e.g., 5:1–11; 7:36–50; 22:31–34; 23:6–12; 24:13–53) at precisely those places in his narrative where John is found to be in disagreement with Matthew/Mark. (2) A number of close verbal parallels also exist between Luke and John (e.g., Luke 3:l6a, b, d = John l:26a, b, 27b; Luke 7:38b = John 12:3b; Luke 22:3 = John 13:27; Luke 22:34 = John 13:38; Luke 22:58b = John 18:17b; Luke 22:67 = John 10:24–25; Luke 22:70b = John 18:37b; Luke 23:3 = John 18:33; Luke 23:4 = John 18:38b; Luke 23:53 = John 19:41; Luke 24:la = John 20:la; Luke 24:2 = John 20:lc; Luke 24:36 = John 20:19c). See Cribbs, "St. Luke and the Johannine Tradition," 447–49; cf. Parker, "Two Editions of John," 303–14.

Abbreviations

ABD	*Anchor Bible Dictionary*. Edited by David Noel Freedman. 6 vols. New York, 1992
Abraham	Philo, *On the Life of Abraham*
Ag. Ap.	Josephus, *Against Apion*
AJSL	*American Journal of Semitic Languages and Literature*
Ant.	Josephus, *Jewish Antiquities*
b.	Babylonian Talmud
Bar	Baruch
BAR	*Biblical Archaeology Review*
BSac	*Bibliotheca sacra*
BZNW	Beihefte zur Zeitschrift für die neutestamentliche
CBQ	*Catholic Biblical Quarterly*
CD	Cairo Genizah copy of the *Damascus Document*
CTJ	*Calvin Theological Journal*
Decalogue	Philo, *On the Decalogue*
DJG	*Dictionary of Jesus and the Gospels*. Edited by J. B. Green and S. McKnight. Downer's Grove, 1992
DOT	*Dictionary of the Old Testament: Pentateuch.* Edited by David W. Baker and T. Desmond Alexander. Leicester, 2003
DRev.	*Downside Review*
EncJud	Encyclopaedia Judaica. 16 vols. Jerusalem, 1972
ER	*Ecumenical Review*
1–2 Esd	1–2 Esdras
ExpTim.	*Expository Times*
FRLANT	Forschungen zur Religion und Literatur des Alten und Neuen Testaments

GOTR	Greek Orthodox Theological Review
Hag.	Hagiga
HTR	Harvard Theological Review
HUCA	Hebrew Union College Annual
IDBSup	Interpreter's Dictionary of the Bible: Supplementary Volume. Edited by Keith R. Crim. Nashville, 1976
JBL	Journal of Biblical Literature
JETS	Journal of the Evangelical Theological Society
JRS	Journal of Roman Studies
JSNT	Journal for the Study of the New Testament
JSOT	Journal for the Study of the Old Testament
JTS	Journal of Theological Studies
JTSA	Journal of Theology for Southern Africa
Jub.	Jubilees
J.W.	Josephus, *The Jewish War*
L.A.B.	*Biblical Antiquities*
Life	Josephus, *The Life*
LXX	Septuagint
1–2 Macc	1–2 Maccabees
Midr.	Midrash
Migration	Philo, *On the migration of Abraham*
m.	Mishnah
NIDOTTE	New International Dictionary of the Old Testament Theology and Exegesis. Edited by W. A. VanGemeren. 5 vols. Grand Rapids, 1997
NovT	Novum Testamentum
NT	New Testament
NTS	New Testament Studies
OT	Old Testament
Pesah.	Pesahim
POxy	Oxyrhynchus papyri
Providence 1, 2	Josephus, *On Providence 1, 2*
PRSt	Perspectives in Religious Studies
Pseudo-Philo	L.A.B.
1QH	Hymns of Thanksgiving
1QS	Rule of the Community (Manual of Discipline)
Rewards	Philo, *On Rewards and Punishments*

RTR	*Reformed Theological Review*
ResQ.	*Restoration Quarterly*
SE	*Studia evangelica*
SEA	*Svensk exegetisk arsbok*
SJT	*Scottish Journal of Theology*
Spec. Laws 1, 2, 3, 4	Josephus, *On the Special Laws* 1, 2, 3, 4
t.	Tosefta
TDNT	*Theological Dictionary of the New Testament.* Edited by Gerhard Kittel and Gerhard Friedrich. Translated by Geoffrey W. Bromiley. 10 vols. Grand Rapids, 1964–1976
TDOT	*Theological Dictionary of the Old Testament.* Edited by G. Johannes Botterweck, Helmer Ringgren et al. Translated by J. T. Willis, Geoffrey W. Bromiley et al. 15 vols. Grand Rapids, 1974–2006
T. Levi	*Testament of Levi*
Tob	Tobit
TS	*Theological Studies*
VE	*Vox evangelica*
Virtues	Philo, *On the Virtues*
VT	*Vetus Testamentum*
WTJ	*Westminster Theological Journal*
WUNT	Wissenschaftliche Untersuchungen zum Neuen Testament
y.	Palestinian or Jerusalem Talmud

1

Pilgrims and Disciples, Mixed Metaphors?

THE CREATION STORY PLAYS a significant role in the biblical canon, not because it comes first in the whole Bible, but because it lays the foundations for understanding the other books of the Bible.[1] Thus many different dimensions (full of symbols and imagery) can be traced in the themes and tones of the account. Having appreciated that we might diminish what is given when the story is focused too closely on any single meaning or intent, we shall discuss Genesis chapters 2 and 3, showing how a pilgrimage and discipleship perspective develops as the account unfolds.[2]

---

1. James Barr claims that the place of Creation as the starting-point should be emphasized. "It was surely a great mistake to say, as Westermann said in the tradition of Gerhard von Rad, that the beginning of the Old Testament is not the beginning of Genesis but the beginning of Exodus . . . The Bible therefore began with a great act of deliverance, and the creation theme was added on later . . . There may have been some tradition-historical basis for this: it is quite true that many old statements emphasize the exodus from Egypt and say nothing about creation. But as a theological picture it derives its apparent strength from the modern Christian idea of the theological priority of redemption over creation and likewise, analogically, from the emphasis on special revelation and the rejection of natural theology . . . the priority of the exodus may thus have considerable importance as a significant stage in the theological development, but if we see the material as a story, the reverse is much more important. The starting-point is all-important. What is said at the beginning sets the stage for that which is to follow." Barr, *Concept of Biblical Theology*, 473.

2. "Loyalty," or possibly "obedience," might be a better word for the Genesis narrative. However, for the consistency of the whole book, the term "discipleship" is used.

ADAMIC PILGRIMAGE

[T]he Lord God formed the man from the dust of the ground... The Lord God took the man and put him in the Garden of Eden to work it and take care of it (Gen 2:7, 15). Adam gave names to the creatures (v. 20), exercising dominion and the perceptibility of thinking.[3] Why is Adam granted this mandate? Because it pleases God that humanity should be his partner in an adventure of voluntary obligation and relationship.[4] God, however, looks at Adam and declares, "It is not good for the man to be alone" (v. 18). Recognizing this, God provides a suitable companion (vv. 21–22), and pronounces the union of man and women (v. 24). They are one. Emphasizing the essential corporate nature of humanity, God blesses their relationship that is to be a reflection of Adam's relationship with God.

Then the man and his wife heard the sound of the Lord God as he was walking in the garden in the cool of the day (Gen 3:8). Emphasis is given to a new act. Before they had not heard and now they do hear. As Umberto Cassuto points out, it is possible that the Lord God had already been walking in the garden prior to this.[5] The words, "as he was walking in the garden," from the Creation account reveals the account of "Yahweh's brief sojourn in the garden"[6] as "an example of Biblical anthropomorphism."[7] F. J. Helfmeyer offers a theological use of "walking הָלַךְ as God's going."

> Yahweh "goes for a stroll," he takes "his daily walk" in the garden when the wind blows through the treetops (cf. 2 5.5:24)—perhaps an answer (etiological?) to the question of the origin and nature of the cooling breeze, but more likely (for J) an expression of the intimate relationship between Yahweh and mankind, for the presentation of which "everything is transposed into human terms."[8]

---

3. Although Adam means "mankind" and "man" in Hebrew, Adam is also the common expression for "to die," namely, "to return to the dust" (Gen 3:19; cf. Job 10:9; 34:15; Ps 104:29). The imagery stresses the bond between humans and the earth and also underlines our frailty, especially our mortality.

4. Barth, *God With Us*, 21.

5. Casssuto, *Commentary on the Book of Genesis*, 1:151.

6. Helfmeyer, "הָלַךְ," 402.

7. Casssuto, *Commentary on the Book of Genesis*, 1:150.

8. Helfmeyer quotes von Rad, Ehrlich, Speiser, and Cassuto. See Helfmeyer, "הָלַךְ," 402.

Gordon Wenham also confirms that the Hebrew term walking הָלַךְ is subsequently used of God's presence in the tabernacle (Lev 26:12; Deut 23:15; 2 Sam 7:6–7), emphasizing the relationship between the garden and the later shrines.[9] *The Lord God called to the man . . . He answered* (Gen 3:9–10). God engages man in dialogue. God who is present and active in the world speaks directly only to mankind. The fact that God walked in the garden and engaged man in dialogue clearly indicates that the linkage of Creator and Creation is "relationship," grounded not on coercion but full trust and commitment. Relationship (to be with his God) is the original purpose for mankind. God created Adam to have a trust relationship with him, a corporate relationship with his wife (Gen 2:20), and a stewardship relationship with Creation (Gen 1:27–28).[10] The garden of Eden, therefore, is not only the paradisiacal place of joy and fellowship with God, but also the place where Adam has to implement the relationships that are delegated to the human community of trust, unity, and stewardship.

We may consider further analogies to the garden of Eden and Adam. Having noted that the presence of God in Eden and Ezekiel's identifications of Eden,[11] particularly the ornamentation of the king of Tyre,[12] William Dumbrell believes Genesis 2:9–17 depicts Eden as a garden sanctuary, which gives to the original inhabitant of the garden, Adam, a pronounced priestly/kingly character.[13] The analogies between Adam's role in Eden and the relationship of Israel to Adam are significant for the

---

9. Wenham, *Genesis 1–15*, 76.

10. In Hebrew, "Adam" means "mankind" and "man." Therefore, the relationship with Adam implies God's desire for mankind as a whole. The Hebrew words "to work" (*ābad*) and "take care of" (*shāmar*) literally mean "to serve" and "to guard" respectively. The term "stewardship" well embraces the meaning of the terms "dominion" and "ruling."

11. In Ezekiel 28:13–14, Eden is clearly conceived of as a mountain sanctuary (cf. "holy mount of God," Ezek 28:14; "mount of God," Ezek 38: 16). See Ezekiel 36:33–36, where the garden of Eden, as the symbol of fertility, is a fitting analogy for the land of Palestine about to be restored. Palestine as a whole is conceived of as a divine garden in Ezekiel 47:1–l2.

12. They are likened to the original cherub in the garden (Ezek 28:13) and correspond closely (in the LXX reading) to the precious stones set in the breastplate of the Israelite high priest (Exod 28:17–20). See Dumbrell, "Genesis 2:1–17," 61.

13. Dumbrell, "Genesis 2:1–17," 61. See also Wenham, "Sanctuary Symbolism," 399–404. Wenham points out that the verbs "cultivate" or "work," "serve" (*ābad*) and "guard" (*shāmar*) in Genesis 2:15 are translated elsewhere in the OT as "serving" and "guarding" and can refer to priestly service.

later understanding of Israel's vocation.[14] For Israel, like Adam, is put into a sacred space to exercise "a corporate, royal priestly role"[15] (Exod 19:4–6). The priestly/kingly role of Adam in Eden makes the connections between Eden and the later Jerusalem Temple a strong possibility. The presence of cherubim (Gen 3:24) and the description of the garden as the place where the Lord God walks (Gen 3:8) contribute to understanding this place as a holy tabernacle. When observing the similarities between Eden and the later sanctuaries, it is hardly surprising that the garden of Eden becomes a prototype for the later tabernacle.[16] Dumbrell sums up the point well:

> Eden was the garden of God, and God's presence was the central aspect of the garden. That Eden is customarily understood in the later biblical narratives as the earthly center where God was to be found is clear from Isaiah 51:3, where Eden and the garden of Yahweh are paralleled. As such, Eden is the representation of what the world is to become, as indicated by the fact that the new Jerusalem is presented in terms of the Holy of Holies of the Jerusalem Temple (Rev 21–22; see again Ezek 36:33–36). As part of this association of the garden with the sanctuary, the Jerusalem Temple is pictured as the forthcoming source of life-giving streams for the world (Ezek 47:1–12; cf. Joel 3: 18).[17]

The first man and woman in the garden experienced an incomparable privilege to be able to have a close relationship with God face to face. The experience is not comparable to the limited direct access into God's presence in the tabernacle and later the Jerusalem Temple. The incomparable privilege, however, comes to the end.

She took some and ate it . . . and he ate it . . . But the Lord God called to the man, "Where are you?". . . I was naked, so I hid (Gen 3:6, 9, 10). God did not create humanity infallible. The Creation account in chapters 2 and 3 reveal how mankind becomes sinful by willful disobedience. The first man and woman lost open fellowship with God. *She took some and ate it. . . . and he ate it* (Gen 3:6). Obedience was the response to the relationship with God. By eating of the tree of the knowledge of good and

---

14. Dumbrell, "Genesis 2:1–17," 61.

15. Ibid., 62.

16. Meredith Kline describes the garden of Eden as "the temple-garden of God" and "a microcosmic house of God." See Kline, "Investiture with the Image of God," 39–40.

17. Dumbrell, "Genesis 2:1–17," 60–61.

evil, voluntary partnership with God is, however, vividly altered.[18] When they heard the voice of the Lord God, they hid (Gen 3:8). Since the linkage of Creator and Creation is "relationship" grounded on full trust and commitment, the disobedience of one of the voluntary partners resulted in violating the relationship. *I was naked, so I hid* (Gen 3:10). Fear of the presence of God (v. 8) and a deep sense of shame (v. 7) resulted from willful disobedience. God, nevertheless, remains in relationship with the creatures.[19] The characteristics of the image of God that enable mankind to communicate with God was to be a reflection of the image of God that would remain intact after the entrance of sin (Gen 5:1–2; 9:6).[20]

Where are you? (Gen 3:9) The call from God is challenging the hiding partners, wanting them to ask his forgiveness voluntarily. *The man said, "The woman you put here with me"* . . . *The woman said, "The serpent deceived me, and I ate"* (Gen 3:12–13). Unity between the couple disintegrated; they placed the blame on the other. As they seek to evade their responsibilities, God teaches them to be accountable for their actions.[21] Although sin has led to dissonances in interpersonal relationships, the remark "it is not good for the man to be alone" (Gen 2:18) is every reason to give mankind hope. The only negative phrase of the Creation account[22] confirms a *Mitsein*, "being with."[23] Henri Blocher comments that if the calling of mankind is to be with his God, it is fitting that his

---

18. Why would God test Adam by placing the tree of the knowledge of good and evil in the garden? According to his divine foreknowledge, God knew he would eat of it, but he let the first man and women fall. What is the point of this whole exercise in the end? When God formed Adam and Eve, they were endowed with untested obedience. Therefore, confirming their obedience becomes a necessary trial to make them into free "voluntary partners" (Barth, *God With Us,* 33), the original purpose of God for mankind is to form with him "a voluntary partnership." Disciples are certainly voluntary partners of God. The real purpose of God for Israel was to make them the voluntary partners of God.

19. This point raises a cogent clue to grasp "the image of God" after the entrance of sin, though the meaning of the image of God is still open to much debate.

20. The distinction between the image of God that is lost and the image of God that remains after the entrance of sin is still open to debate as well.

21. Westermann, *Creation,* 97.

22. It is not (לֹא) good. The word לֹא, before an adjective, is more emphatic negation than אֵין (not). Thus Cassuto believes that it is not only the absence of something good, but also a dreadful deficiency. See Cassuto, *Commentary on the Book of Genesis,* 1:126–27.

23. Blocher, *In the Beginning,* 96.

earthly existence should already be characterized by "being with."[24] The constitution of each of us is a summons to community since human life attains its full realization only in community.[25] Walter Brueggemann makes this point clearer.

> [I]t is worth noting that mankind is spoken of as singular ("he created him") and plural ("he created them"). This peculiar formula makes an important affirmation. On the one hand, mankind is a single entity. All human persons stand in solidarity before God. But on the other hand, mankind is a community, male and female. And none is the full image of God alone. Only in community of mankind is God reflected. God is, according to this bold affirmation, not mirrored as an individual but as a community.[26]

This certainty leaves hopeful signs for mankind in shaping the future, though expulsion from the garden becomes necessary.

He must not be allowed to reach out his hand and take also from the tree of life and eat, and live forever. So the Lord God banished him from the Garden of Eden . . . (Gen 3:22–23). The situation moves from the hiding of mankind (3:8–10) to the driving out by God (3:23–24). The Scripture clearly indicates that the reason for the expulsion from the garden was to have mankind separated from the tree of life. Though the meaning of the tree of the knowledge of good and evil is uncertain,[27] from its usage (Gen 2:16; 3:3–7, 21) the tree symbolizes the freedom of choice over good and

---

24. Ibid., 97.

25. Ibid., 96–97, 227. Mutual help is an essential part of human existence. Thus "being with" is the reflection of a deficiency of mankind. Thus mankind desires the help of a partner.

26. Brueggemann, *Genesis*, 33–34.

27. With the Hebrew concept of the terms (knowledge [know], good and evil) and biblical references (2 Sam 19:35; 2 Sam 14:17; 1 Kgs 3:9; Isa 7:15–16; Deut 1:39) several cautious writers have drawn a meaning of the tree of the knowledge of good and evil. Although their interpretations still do not make crystal clear sense, it is worth pondering over John Calvin and Karen Armstrong's comments. Calvin notes, "Not because God would have him to stray like a sheep, without judgment and without choice; but that he might not seek to be wiser than became him, nor by trusting to his own understanding, cast off the yoke of God, and constitute himself an arbiter and judge of good and evil." See Calvin, *Genesis*, 118. Armstrong states, "What Adam and Eve sought from the tree of knowledge was not philosophical or scientific knowledge desired by the Greeks, but practical knowledge that would give them blessing and fulfillment." See Armstrong, *In the Beginning*, 27.

evil.[28] By eating the fruit of the tree, the first man faces the coming of death. Adam and Eve are told that when they eat of the fruit, they will surely die (Gen 2:17; 3:3). Death is the consequence of disobedience. Adam and Eve, however, did not die immediately after their disobedience. So, is this death in the general sense of mortality, or is it death in the final judgment as a punishment? For James Boice the consequence of disobedience is death to God in terms of relationship.[29] For the majority of commentators, including Bruce Birch, the penalty for eating is death—capital punishment—not an ontological change (from being immortal to being mortal).[30] However, some argue that death in Genesis 3:19 is not meant to be a punishment for the man's transgression,[31] but part of the natural order of things and the limitation of the toil of human work.[32] Although it is doubtful that their argument on this issue can be accepted, it is quite possible to maintain that death is not the main focus in the historical drama. Victor Hamilton makes an interesting comment in relation to "original sin."

> Given the OT's emphasis on corporate personality, the sins of the fathers being visited unto subsequent generations, it is perhaps surprising that the OT says virtually nothing about Adam or Eve after Gen. 5. For example, the prophets do not hesitate to draw on the catastrophe at Sodom and Gomorrah to illustrate the consequences of disobedience, but they never use the story of the expulsion from Eden to draw a similar analogy. As a matter of fact, one must wait until Rom 5 and 1 Cor 15 for an extensive discussion of Adam.[33]

As Brueggemann points out, it is not God, but the serpent that has made death a primary issue on the human agenda, transforming it into a terror, which puts everything in question.[34] On this issue, James Barr proposes *a provoking focus shift* to the long-established position of Oscar

---

28. LaSor et al., *Old Testament Survey*, 26.

29. Boice, *Genesis*, 140–43. For Holzinger this (punishment) is twofold; the relationship to the ground that he lives is changed, then he is under sentence of death. See Westermann, *Genesis 1–11*, 266.

30. Birch et al., *Theological Introduction*, 51–52.

31. Westermann, J. Skinner, Gunkel, and L. Köhler.

32. Westermann, *Genesis 1–11*, 267.

33. Hamilton, *Genesis, Chapters 1–17*, 210–11.

34. Brueggemann, *Genesis*, 48.

Cullmann.³⁵ For him the problem that Adam's disobedience created was not that he brought death into the world, but that he brought near to himself the distant possibility of immortality.³⁶ This is, he believes, the only reason why Adam and Eve could not escape from the expulsion from the garden of Eden. His conclusion sounds promising.

> In the Garden of Eden there was the tree of life. The human pair might just have got to that tree, but they did not, because God stopped them; no one was to enter the garden, and the cherubim with flaming sword stood there to guard the gate. Humanity was not fit to come near the tree. Nevertheless the tree remained there in the garden. Later one came to redeem the defect of humanity. Immortality was brought to light.³⁷

The *focus shift* of Barr offers a pivotal clue that the eventual conclusion of life is to live forever with God, the hope of immortality that was on the biblical agenda from the very beginning. This aspect of the Fall now calls our attention to the tree of life. Unlike with the tree of the knowledge of good and evil, many biblical references contribute to understanding the meaning of the tree of life.³⁸ The tree of life appears metaphorically and symbolically in most biblical references. Is the tree of life the source of life, then? The first man is formed from the dust of the ground and has breath in him from God in order that he should live (Gen 2:7). If death were not part of God's plan, the existence of the tree of life would have been meaningless. It is certain that God created mankind mortal. An ontological change (from being immortal to being mortal), therefore, was not expected after the sin of the first couple. This means that mankind, from the beginning, totally depended on "the attentive giving of

---

35. The Fall and its consequences have traditionally been the main focus for the Creation narrative. Barr, however, proposes a radical and significant alternative that the main theme of the Creation account is not the origin of sin, but the possibility of immortality. Therefore, "focus shift" would be an explanatory term for the alternative. See Barr, *Garden of Eden*. In his *Salvation in History*, Cullmann takes Paul's use of Genesis as normative. Barr argues that Paul's handling of the theme of Adam and Eve fits poorly with Genesis and concludes that Hellenistic influence is the main reason for the poor handling of the theme. See Barr, *Garden of Eden*.

36. Barr, *Garden of Eden*, 5–6.

37. Ibid., 116.

38. The tree of life appears not only in the OT (Gen 2:9; 3:22, 24; Prov 3:18; 11:30; 13:12; 15:4), but all of these Proverbs passages should be understood as using the phrase "tree of life" metaphorically, and in Revelation 2 and 22 the tree of life is obviously a symbol.

Yahweh in order to have life" (cf. Ps 104:29–30).[39] The fact that verse 9 emphasizes not the tree of life, but the tree's planter, reinforces the idea that life is from God, not from the tree.[40]

So the Lord God banished him from the Garden of Eden . . . (Gen 3:22–23). Because of the disobedience of the couple and the location of the tree of life the first man and women have to leave the garden. In fact, they are thrown out.[41] However, life outside the garden for humankind is not meant to be without God. If that were the case, life outside the garden would not have existed, for God is the source of life. God still remains in relationship with mankind, leaving hopeful signs for the future. Therefore, life outside the garden is better viewed not as life without God, but as "life away from one's true home."[42] Geographically they are relocated from their home, to live in exile east of Eden. They are homeless on this earth. They are no more than exiles wandering and yearning for a return to the Edenic state, the final destination of pilgrimage. God's presence was the central aspect of the garden. Therefore, *being with God* is the best description of the Edenic state. Christopher Barth offers a valuable comment on expulsion:

> He expels and destroys, so that the stories come down as stern warnings. Yet we are not told that he actually rejects the work of his hands. The curse that is mentioned (Gen 3:14, 17; 4:11) involves a worsening of life's conditions, not total annihilation. Expulsion proves to be a protective measure that guards humanity against final extermination (Gen 3, 4).[43]

God intervenes in the historical drama of mankind as both judge and rescuer. Expulsion from a judge's point of view can also be described

---

39. Brueggemann, *Theology of the Old Testament*, 453.

40. Watson, "Tree of Life," 235.

41. Cassuto and Hamilton explore the meaning of "*salah*." God was concerned that the man might "put forth" (*salah*) his hand; so God expelled or put him out (*salah*) of the garden. The same Hebrew verb designates what man might do and what God did do (although the stem used in verse 22 is Qal and that used in verse 23 is Piel). In these Genesis 3 references the Piel of *salah* means simply "to send (forth)." But since here *salah* parallels *garas*, "to drive out, expel," we are obliged to translate it more strongly than simply "send," hence our choice of expelled. The verb *garas* in the Qal may mean "to drive out" (Exod 34:11) or "to divorce" (Lev 21:7, 14; 22:13). See Cassuto, *Commentary on the Book of Genesis*, 1:173, and Hamilton, *Genesis, Chapters 1–17*, 209.

42. Birch et al., *Theological Introduction*, 51.

43. Barth, *God With Us*, 35.

as *the first journey mankind has ever taken* from a rescuer's point of view. When expulsion is understood as the result of the rescue rather than that of judgment, God's saving grace becomes crystal clear as the historical drama of mankind unfolds. *After he drove the man out, he placed on the east side of the Garden of Eden* (Gen 3:24). In Genesis 2:17 (you will surely die), God warns Adam of what disobedience will result in but later rescues Adam and Eve, placing them on the east side of the garden (3:24). In Genesis 4:6–7 (sin is crouching at your door . . . you must master it) God also alerts Cain before his monstrous murder, the first murder, and later protects him throughout his wanderings (4:15). In Genesis 6:5, the Lord regrets the corrupt earth but preserves Noah, his offspring, and two of all living creatures from the flood. It is certain that the expulsion was God's design to protect and later to train his people, Israel. Thus, the journeys, the Exodus, and experiences of exile that later generations underwent are echoed by the expulsion from the garden.[44] The expulsion of Adam from the garden mirrors later Israelite exiles from the land. It is also possible to find other important resonance within the canonical context.[45]

ABRAHAMIC PILGRIMAGE

The fourteen chapters given to the story of Abraham indicate that he plays the most significant role in the book of Genesis. This is certainly true as regards the origin of Israel. Israel's history, as the Torah sees it, strictly begins only in Egypt or in Palestine. However, the story of God's people goes back to the family of Abraham (cf., e.g., Neh 9:7, Matt 1:1–18), if not that of Seth (Gen 4:25–26).[46] If the Creation story shows that human disobedience results in exile, the Abraham account shows

---

44. When considering that the Creation account (P) served to encourage the despairing exiles by proclaiming that the God of Israel was the Lord of all of life, as opposed to Babylonian claims that the Babylonian gods seemed to be in control of all that was happening, we can clearly appreciate that the text serves as a testimonial assertion and tackles a real historical problem. Thus this point led many scholars to conclude that Genesis was written in light of the Exodus, emphasizing the Egypt connection in it.

45. R. W. L. Moberly sees possible links between Genesis 22 and the paradigmatic story of human disobedience to and alienation from God in Genesis 2–3. For Moberly, Abraham's genuine "fear of God" provides a definitive alternative to the way of Adam and Eve. It also has important resonances with the portrayal of Jesus in Matthew's gospel. See Moberly, *Bible, Theology and Faith*, 97.

46. Goldingay, *Theological Diversity*, 60.

that gaining the land, in a future sense, is dependent on obedience to God. The Abrahamic pilgrimage of hope began on no other basis than the promise of Yahweh (12:1–4). Abraham's biography is structured on "the metaphor of journey as a way of characterizing the life of faith."[47] Thus pilgrimage for Abraham is not just a physical movement, but also a pilgrimage of faith that encompasses *knowing God* and *obedience to God as a consequence of knowing God*. In the long story of the Abrahamic pilgrimage we can trace the interlocking relationship between pilgrimage as a physical movement and transformation (from a migration) into faith's pilgrimage.[48] Pilgrimage as physical movement is not to be identified with faith's pilgrimage in which the promises or demands are bound up. Pilgrimage refers to the relationships from which promises and demands will flow. Since pilgrimage as physical movement is closely intertwined with God's way of transforming his people, namely, discipleship, pilgrimage as physical movement is to be understood not only as "a historical or geographical note, but a theological program."[49] The Abrahamic pilgrimage as a theological program can be traced in his physical journeys.

The Lord had said to Abram, "Leave your country, your people and your father's household and go to the land I will show you. I will make you into a great nation and I will bless you; I will make your name great, and you will be a blessing. I will bless those who bless you, and whoever curses you I will curse; and all people on earth will be blessed through you (Gen 12:1–3). Scripture tells us nothing about what motivated Terah to leave Ur of the Chaldeans (Gen 11:31). It is probable that God's call to Abraham, mentioned in the book of Acts 7:2–3, was the motivating factor. Cassuto maintains that Abram's journey from Ur was likely initiated under the providence of God. Abraham seldom had the chance to settle in a single place or situation. From the day that Abram left Ur he became a wanderer (a pilgrim). Abram lived for a while in Haran (Gen 11:31), but he had to leave Haran too (Gen 12:4). Thus the Abram account begins with God's command to Abram to forsake his own territory, God appearing to be the subject of the first verb at the beginning of the first

---

47. Brueggemann, *Genesis*, 121.

48. Pilgrimage as the life of faith is one that keeps Israel in pursuit of the promise of land. In fact, the relationship between them can be traced throughout the whole Bible.

49. Brueggemann, *Genesis*, 122. In fact, commentators tend to be more preoccupied with literary-critical or historical-critical matters for the Abrahamic account.

statement (Gen 12:1). Thus W. D. Davies sees that the pilgrim motif is primordial in the Jewish consciousness not a late, compulsory result of its history.[50] Although the narrator does not offer an explanation as to why God chose Abram from the descendants of Shem, God calls Abram and initiates a relationship with him. At the same time this "call" of God encompasses a wonderful promise to Abram. *I will bless those who bless you, and whoever curses you I will curse* (Gen 12:3). Those who act favorably toward Abram would win the blessing of God.[51] Those who are hostile and evil to Abram would come under the curse of God. This "cause-effect relationship" clearly indicates Abram's distinctive relationship with God.[52]

The journey from Haran to Canaan (Gen 12:4–5), featuring Abraham's obedience, was the initiation of Abrahamic pilgrimage. Yet Scripture says nothing about Abram's itinerary from Haran to the land of Canaan. As Cassuto points out, it is possible to suggest that such details were probably of no importance to its aim.[53] Given, however, are details of his journey in Canaan, namely, the journey through the land from north to south, from Shechem, where he builds an altar (12:6–7), to Ai where he builds another altar (12:8), and to the Negev (12:9). These stopping-places in Canaan are mentioned again in similar form in the account of Jacob's journey (Gen 33:18; 35:7) and in the account of Joshua's conquests (Josh 8:30). The intention behind the narrative becomes clearer as it draws the boundaries of the journeys with special references to Shechem, Ai, and Bethel. The author intended to present to us, through the symbolic conquest of Abram, how the token was first given to Abram and afterwards repeated to Jacob, with a kind of forecast of what would happen to his descendants later.[54] *So Abram left, as the Lord had told him* (Gen 12:4). As God told him to do so, Abram

---

50. W. D. Davies, *Gospel and the Land*, 406.

51. Noticing the singular "him who curses you" in contrast to the plural "those who bless you," von Rad concludes that the narrator does not yet consider what God begins here primarily as "a sign that is spoken against" (Luke 2:34) but as a source of universal blessing. See von Rad, *Genesis*, 160.

52. Stigers, *Commentary on Genesis*, 136.

53. Traces of them are still discernible in the reference to Damascus-Eliezer, the inheritor of Abram's house; apparently the saga told how the patriarch went journeying from place to place until he arrived at Damascus. See Cassuto, *Commentary on the Book of Genesis*, 2:322.

54. Ibid., 305–7.

left his established location. Only Sarai, his wife, and Lot, his nephew, accompanied him. Claus Westermann argues against the traditional interpretation, claiming that the patriarchs did not have the concept of "homeland" in the modern sense. It was, therefore, easy to leave the land and his family.[55] However, Westermann's argument does not substantiate the claim made, for there is nothing in the Scripture nor in the social background to support his argument. In the ancient Near East breaking with his family ties meant renouncing his inheritance and his right to family property.[56] If this cultural background is correct, leaving his father's household and emigrating was a risky decision to take. Abraham's commitment to Yahweh's calling involved an exodus from such a background. Thus Genesis presents the story of Abraham, in particular, as an exodus from Ur to the promised land: the phrasing of, "I am the Lord who brought you out of Ur of the Chaldeans to give you this land" (Gen 15:7), typologically foreshadows the nation's exodus to Canaan.[57] In both cases, a leaving was a prerequisite in order to obtain the promise given. This link between the two cases demonstrates journeying with God as a pattern of obedience to the promise.

At this stage no reason is given as to what brought Abram to that decision. It is, however, important to ask how Abram might have conceived of God when God told him to leave his father's household. God called Abram, when he dwelt in the city of Ur, a center for the worship of the moon god Sin (Gen 11:31; 15:7; Josh 24:2).[58] *Your fathers lived of old beyond the Euphrates, Terah the father of Abraham and of Nahor; and they served other gods* (Josh 24:2). It is clear from Joshua 24:2 and 14 that Abram came from a family that shared the commonly held polytheis-

---

55. Westermann, *Genesis 12–36*, 148.

56. A man was identified in the ancient world as a member of his father's household. When the head of the household died, his heir assumed that title and its responsibilities. It is also identified with ancestral lands and property. See Walton and Matthews, *IVP Bible Background*, 35.

57. See Sheriffs, "Moving on With God," 49–50.

58. Names such as Terah, Laban, Sarai, and Milcah appear to suggest some connection by the family with a lunar cult. If this reflects the probability that the Terah family stemmed from a center at which the moon was worshiped then this would be confirmatory of Abram's connection with Ur. This city had as patrons the moon god Sin and the moon goddess Ningal (a Sumerian equivalent of Sarah, with the meaning, "queen"), deities that were prominent also in the worship conducted at Haran until the end of its history. See Dumbrell, *Covenant and Creation*, 55–57.

tic beliefs of that time.[59] *They served other gods. Then I took your father Abraham from beyond the river* (Josh 24:2–3). James L. Kugel claims that "they" in Joshua 24:2 and 14 presumably refers to Abram's father, Terah, and his brother, Nahor. Kugel thinks that while the family served other gods, Abram became convinced that in truth there was only one true God.[60] It, however, seems unlikely that Abram had a monotheistic belief about a true God when he was called. Jean-Marc Heimerdinger claims that, unlike the great Canaanite gods of the area, the God who revealed himself to Abram was his personal God.[61] Since the gods were not a theoretical notion but a real power in the ancient Near East, it is not surprising that people in the massive polytheistic systems related to "personal gods," who were often then adopted as family gods and worshiped from generation to generation.[62]

People in the systems must have constantly confronted the forces that were active either as helping or as opposing people. The personal god, seen as a source of blessing and good fortune, was believed to be in every sphere of life.[63] Abram, in this type of system, might have perceived God as a personal God, not "the true God," when the Lord first spoke to him (Gen 12:1). Westermann and P. R. Williamson argue that there is no incontestable evidence within the Genesis material that patriarchal religion was in any sense polytheistic.[64] That later ancient Jewish texts (Jdt 5:6–9; *Jub.* 11:14–17, 12:12–24; Philo, *Abraham* 71; *L.A.B.* 23:5; Josephus, *Ant.* 1.154–157) also extensively developed the tradition of Abraham the monotheist and Abram's opposition to idolatry seems strongly to supports the claim that Abram was a monotheist.[65] Despite

---

59. Asking the reason why God singled out Abraham and suggesting a possibility that if God called Abraham alone, this is another way of saying that Abraham was quite unique within his family.

60. Kugel, *Bible As It Was*, 133–48.

61. Heimerdinger, "God of Abraham," 41–55.

62. Ibid., 43–46. See also Walton and Matthews, *IVP Bible Background*, 36–37.

63. It is generally accepted, though not always with conviction, that Abraham worshiped El, the Canaanite god. Some scholars, however, have pointed out that El, the God of Abraham, shared little of the complex personality of the Canaanite god El. See Heimerdinger, "God of Abraham," 41. Various proposals have been made by a number of scholars. See McKane, *Studies in the Patriarchal Narratives*, 195–224.

64. Nevertheless, Westermann admits that the designation "monotheism" is not appropriate. See Westermann, *Genesis 12–36*, 109. Williamson, "Abraham," 12–23.

65. See Kugel, *Bible As It Was*, 133–48; Lotowitz and Scherman, *Genesis*, 359–60.

this latter belief, however, there is no evidence in the text that Abram worshiped the true God. Indeed, a personal god was a familiar religious concept in the culture of the time. Therefore, it is likely that the step to belief in the one true God was via belief in a personal god.

When Yahweh appeared to Abram, he did not reveal himself to Abram as the only God (Gen 12:7). Throughout the Abrahamic narrative, we find no evidence of Yahweh trying to make or coerce Abraham into having a monotheistic belief. Instead, he promises Abram that he will be given the land (Gen 12:7) if he obeys. Although Yahweh, during the entire course of Abraham's pilgrimage, seems to remain as the personal God of Abraham, as the narrative proceeds, it becomes clear to us that the Genesis narrator tracks down the transformation that Abraham underwent from the stage of having a relationship with the personal god to that of having a relationship with the one true God. Moberly argues that though the move from alien territory to the promised land in obedience to God's call would be an obvious context to make a point about religious allegiance, the text of Genesis shows no interest whatever in this, apart from Genesis 35:2 and 4 where Jacob told his family and those with him, "Get rid of the foreign gods you have with you, and purify yourselves, and change your clothes" (Gen 35:2).[66] Although the Genesis text has no clear sense of reference on the point, it cannot be said that the Genesis text shows no interest in it. Thus Moberly might have missed the overarching picture of the Abraham narrative to track down the point.

A journey for Abraham begins with a new trial, a severe famine. Immediately after sojourning in the promised land, Abram was forced by a severe famine to leave the land and go down to Egypt. There, Sarai was in great danger (Gen 12:11–20). It is noticeable that it happened immediately after God appeared unto him (Gen 12:7) and the building of the altar in the promised land (Bethel) where Abram proclaimed the name of the Lord his God (Gen 12:8). Although God had "walked" and spoken with Adam, Enoch, and Noah, this is the first time in Scripture where we read of an actual appearance of God. After walking right through the promised land, Canaan, to which God had told him to go, and in which he had promised to bless him, Abram went down to Egypt to dwell גּוּר *gûr* (Gen 12:10). The verb גּוּר "to live as an alien" is derived from the noun גֵּר alien.[67] Various versions have different translations for

---

66. Moberly, *Old Testament*, 88.
67. Westermann, *Genesis 12–36*, 163.

גּוּר "to settle there (the traditional Masoretic Text)," "to sojourn there (KJV, RSV, ASV, DBY, YLT, LXE)," "to dwell there (NKJ, WEB, RWB)," "to reside there as an alien (NRS)," "to live for a while (NIV)." Although A. H. Konkel states that גּוּר lends itself as a metaphor for the pilgrimage of life, Diether Kellerman thinks that גּוּר suggests a potentially permanent resident in a foreign land.[68]

If Kellerman's suggestion is correct, then a long-term settlement comes as no surprise, despite having just been promised "this land, Canaan" (Gen 12:7). Abram had known where he was going in general, but not where he would settle in particular. Finally he was promised this land to settle (Gen 12:7). Now he chooses to live in Egypt. Although the New International Version inserts "(live) for a while" to dilute the intention of long-term settlement, the insertion does not properly serve in this text, whereas "(to settle, live, dwell or reside) as an immigrant, alien or foreigner" would be a more proper insertion.[69] Abram might not have had any other option, because the famine was "severe."[70]

On the way down to Egypt, he had feared that Sarai's appearance would catch the attention of the Egyptians and so he prepared to sacrifice his wife to save his own life (Gen 12:11–13).[71] No reason is given why he could feel secure in Canaan but not in Egypt. His prediction

---

68. Konkel, "גּוּר," 837; Kellerman, "גּוּר," 439–49.

69. Kellerman, "גּוּר," 439–49.

70. Famine is a frequent motif in the Old Testament (Gen 26:1; 43:1; 47:4; Ruth 1:1; 2 Sam. 21:1; 2 Kgs 4:38; 8:1). The famine is one of the basic, critical, human experiences, attested from the earliest records of man right down to the present day.

71. Abraham's trip down to Egypt results in the near-loss of Sarai into the harem of Pharaoh. Lot's choice of the portion like Egypt ends in his near-destruction in the overthrow of Sodom and Gomorrah. Choosing the fertility of Egypt over faithfulness to the promise leads to disastrous consequences. Hagar's son, Ishmael, is not just a continuing problem for Abraham and Sarah, but his descendants will be a thorn in Israel's flesh. The Egyptian option, while apparently attractive, always leads to disaster in the long run. See Dugid, "Allure of Egypt," 420–23. Egypt prefigures the ambiguity of future relationships—on the one hand as a place of shelter and succor in time of distress: on the other hand as a place of mortal danger. See Sarna, *Genesis*, 93. In Hebrew "to have faith" means "to make oneself secure in Yahweh" (hence the preposition בּ after וְהֶאֱמִן (וְהֶאֱמִן בַּיהוָה)). See von Rad, *Old Testament Theology*, 171. Or "fixing oneself on Yahweh." See von Rad, *Genesis*, 185. It is possible to assume that going into Canaan was a step making himself secure in Yahweh, whereas going down to Egypt was a step making himself secure in his own cleverness in himself. The departure from Canaan was already an act of unbelief in the sense of the narrative. In the sense of "faith defined" it is not surprising that Abram feared this time.

came true. Sarai was taken into Pharaoh's house (Gen 12:15). Abram's compromise had seemed to be working out very well, but it soon turned out to be a disaster (Gen 12:10–16). However, Yahweh does not allow his work to founder at the very beginning; he saves it and elevates it beyond all human deficiency.[72] *But the Lord inflicted serious diseases on Pharaoh and his household because of Abram's wife Sarai* (Gen 12:17). Through "this saving intervention by God with special interest,"[73] the narrative, which began so humanly, goes on to speak of "Yahweh's loyalty and help with a reprimand."[74] *What have you done? . . . Now then, here is your wife. Take her and go!* (Gen 12:18–19). Wenham argues that this echoes the garden of Eden story.[75] Pharaoh asks the same questions that God asked Adam in the garden, and Pharaoh expels Abram from his land just as God expelled Adam from his garden. This story certainly suggests typology based on the later bondage in Egypt and the Exodus.[76] *So Abram went up from Egypt to the Negev . . . he went from place to place until he came to Bethel . . . There he called on the name of the Lord* (Gen 13:1–4). As soon as Abram came to the very spot where he had built the altar when he went up from Haran (Gen 12:8), he proclaimed the name of Yahweh, his God. Cassuto sees that

> his return to Canaan is not just an ordinary migration on the part of a shepherd wandering from place to place; it is the return to the land appointed for his mission, and the mission of the offspring, of a man who had dedicated himself and his descendants to a new faith.[77]

The figure of Abram, who brought a rebuke upon himself (Gen 12:10–20), has undergone change (as a man showing self-effacing generosity in chapter 13 and as a warrior in chapter 14) in the narrative.

The Lord said to Abraham . . . Rise up, walk through the length and breadth of the land for I will give it to you (Gen 13:17). As Helfmeyer

---

72. Westermann, *Genesis 12–36*, 168.
73. Von Rad, *Genesis*, 170.
74. Westermann, *Genesis 12–36*, 167.
75. Wenham, *Genesis 1–15*, 291.
76. Abraham's exodus from Egypt is also compared with Babylonian exile (Isa 41:8–8, 18–19; 43:1–2, 14–16; 48:20–21; 49:8–12; 51:2–3, 9–11; 52:3–12), Jesus' return to Palestine from Egypt (Matt 2:15), and the Exodus to the church's experience in Christ (1 Cor 10:1–12).
77. Cassuto, *Commentary on the Book of Genesis*, 2:364.

offers a theological use of walking הָלַךְ in the Creation narrative (Gen 3:8) and the Exodus (Exod 13:21) as "God's going"[78] and "an expression of the intimate relationship between Yahweh and mankind,"[79] the frequent use of the Hebrew root הָלַךְ—to walk and go—in Genesis 12:1, 13:17, 17:1, 22:2, 24:40, and 48:15 demonstrates its significant implication in Abraham's life. It is noted that the Hebrew meaning might cause confusion, because in English "walk" and "go" are different verbs. Not only does Yahweh go himself, he also causes others to go (God led Israel through the desert [Isa 48:21; Jer 2:6; Hos 2:16; Amos 2:10; Ps 136:16]).[80] God caused Abraham to go. Abraham's journey was walking as the pattern of obedience. In this case, the metaphor of walking and the physical act of walking, the literal step (journey) and the life experience, meet closely. Although this walking did not actualize the promise yet, the literal journey as walking towards the promise was the prerequisite of bringing the promise into actualization.[81]

After this, the word of the Lord came to Abram in a vision . . . So shall your offspring be. Abram believed the Lord (Gen 15:1–6). Although we should not consider this the first exercise of saving faith (that probably occurred when God first called Abraham in Ur [cf. Heb 11:8–10]), we have to notice that after being given the covenant promise four times, being said three times, and Yahweh appearing once (Gen 12:1–3, 7; 13:14–17; 15:4–5), the narrative finally states that Abram believed the Lord, and that this was credited as righteousness. Without a doubt Wenham sees that the verbal form implies continued repeated acts of faith, and suggests that the reason to mention "he believed the Lord" is because of the staggering nature of the promise made to an old man.[82] The obedience that led Abram to leave his father's household was counted as an act of faith. However, as we come to the questions, "When Abraham first responded to Yahweh, what was his deciding factor?" and "Did he perceive him as a personal god or the true God, YHWH?" the question more clearly becomes, "Why did the Genesis narrator finally state that 'he believed the Lord' after being given the covenant promise three times, including being said twice, and having appeared once?" Considering that Abram

78. Helfmeyer, "הָלַךְ," 402.
79. Helfmeyer quotes von Rad and Driver. See ibid., 402.
80. Ibid., 403.
81. I am indebted to Sheriffs for this point. Sheriffs, "Moving on With God," 49–60.
82. Wenham, *Genesis 1–15*, 334.

came from a family that shared the polytheistic beliefs of that time (Josh 24:2,14), and that people in the polytheistic belief systems must have constantly been confronted with forces that were active in every sphere of life, either as helping or as opposing people, it is doubtful that Abram perceived the Lord who spoke to him (Gen 12:1) to be the true God. It was probable that the God who revealed himself to Abram was not the only God to Abram, for Abram might have first responded to the command by God on the basis of polytheistic belief. Sheriffs's comment reinforces this point.

> We tend to take monotheism for granted as the only rational faith alternative to no faith at all, to atheism, but covenant with God in the OT has the backdrop of polytheism. The opposite of faith in the Pentateuch is not unbelief but reliance on other deities and powers.[83]

Abraham's worship looks similar to pagan modes of worship such as setting up altars to commemorate sacred experiences, and using titles for God from the pagan mythologies.[84] God, however, meets Abraham at his level of understanding. Although the way of worship was expressed in the language and culture of the time, Abram's monotheism has been building up through the intervention of God in Egypt. And Abram finally comes to the stage where he begins to recognize the true God who is trustworthy. He believed (the Hebrew אמן is better translated "trusted") the Lord (Gen 15: 6). When Abraham believed the Lord, did he also cling to what had been promised? It might be true that the promise does not come first; rather, faith comes first. However, let us consider "the nature of that faith (not in the sense of an analysis of the act of believing but in the sense of an analysis of what is believed)."[85] There is, then, not such a dichotomy between "believing in God" and "believing God," between the God who had promised and what had been promised. As Bernhard Anderson states, it is the belief that is appropriate to a relationship, as

---

83. Sheriffs, "Faith," 283.

84. Cassuto argues that the fact that the offering of sacrifice is not mentioned tells that the altars constructed by Abram were not cultic altars but are tokens of the sanctification of the land of Yahweh and of the symbolic conquest of the country. See Cassuto, *Commentary on the Book of Genesis*, 2:328–29. However, this is not persuasive, considering the Mount Moriah episode (Gen 22). Heimerdinger traces the titles for God in relation to the personal God. See Heimerdinger, "God of Abraham," 43–51.

85. N. Wright, *Climax of the Covenant*, 3.

when one says: "I believe my friend," that is, put my trust in him or her.[86] This concept becomes clear as we come to the term "righteousness." *He credited it to him as righteousness* (Gen 15:6). Gerhard von Rad postulates that righteousness is not an ideal, an absolute norm, which is above men, but rather a term of relationship.[87] Although Ezekiel 18:5, "Suppose there is a righteous man who does what is just and right," supports the view that righteousness is defined in terms of moral conduct, here the faith Abram proved was "the right response to God's revelation."[88] Belief alone has brought Abram into a proper relationship to God.[89] Thus the terms "believed" and "righteousness" based on "the relationship between God and man" offer a pivotal clue to understand the goal of pilgrimage as well as the conclusion of the Abrahamic pilgrimage.[90] This is, however, not the end of faith's pilgrimage, but a beginning.

Chapter 16 might throw serious doubt on whether Abram came to a strong faith all at once after he had believed the Lord, and was credited as righteousness (Gen 15:7). Abram and Sarah waited for ten long years after the fourth promise had been given (Gen 15), but they still remained childless. Up to this time no specific promise has been made that the heir should come from Sarai. The suggestion that Abram seemed to assume that Sarah would be the mother of the countless descendants is possible. It is, however, noticeable that a surrogate heir through Hagar is made only after Yahweh's promise of a biological son in Genesis 15. At this stage Laurence Turner, thus, offers a possibility to solve a riddle that whether Abram would risk his life for Lot, when in Egypt he had been unwilling to risk his life for Sarai. Turner suggests that in Abram's eyes his nephew, a strongly possible surrogate heir, is of more value to him than his wife.[91] Williamson points out that this would certainly explain why Lot has such a prominent place in the Abraham narrative up until the birth of a physical son to Abraham (Gen 16).[92] Sarai's proposal in chapter 16 should have had Abram rethink "from whom." Human discretion,

---

86. B. Anderson, *Contours of Old Testament Theology*, 100.
87. Von Rad, *Genesis*, 170.
88. Wenham, *Genesis 1–15*, 330.
89. Von Rad, *Genesis*, 170.
90. Ibid. Von Rad states that verse 6 certainly has the effect of a conclusion.
91. L. Turner, "Announcements of Plot," 61–70.
92. Williamson, "Abraham," 12–33.

however, takes control of the matter.[93] Abram left it to the discretion of Sarai. Ishmael came into being by Hagar, Sarai's Egyptian maidservant, after eleven years had passed since the promise (Gen 15:4).

Thirteen years had passed since Ishmael was born. Twenty-three years had elapsed since God made a covenant with Abram (Gen 15:18). When Abram was ninety-nine years old, the Lord appeared to Abram and identified himself as God Almighty (Gen 17:1). And the revealed Lord orders Abram to walk before him and be blameless (Gen 17:1). Metaphorically walking הָלַךְ implies human life as a journey.[94] Helfmeyer makes a survey of walking הָלַךְ in the case of nomadic groups, especially those engaged in transmigration.

> For nomadic groups it is not surprising that *halakh* should represent the focus of activity. They live "on the move"; their life is mostly spent wandering. This experience may lead to an understanding of human life as a way or a pilgrimage. After his many "goings," a man finally "goes away": he dies. Beforehand, however, nomadic groups know by experience, and their settled neighbors know by memory, that their wanderings have a purpose, that they follow this or that leader, that the success of their journey depends on their conduct. Thus the word *halakh*—above and beyond its concrete spatial meaning—takes on the meanings "conform to a norm, follow someone, behave." Since it is impossible to think of a journey undertaken without a specific goal, *halakh* also means "plan, set about."[95]

For Helfmeyer "to walk before him" is also to live and move openly before him.[96] Westermann also elucidates the meaning of the phrase "walk before me": God orders Abraham (now representing Israel)[97] to live his life before himself in such a way that every single step is made

---

93. The solution that Sarai adopted was comprehensible at that time. A Nuzi text states that when a barren wife supplies a concubine to her husband, the child that is born belongs to the barren wife. Westermann quotes Speiser. See Westermann, *Genesis 12–36*, 239.

94. Helfmeyer, "הָלַךְ," 391.

95. Ibid., 389–90.

96. Helfmeyer quotes Driver. See Helfmeyer, "הָלַךְ," 392–93.

97. When we reach Deuteronomy, "walking before the LORD" will have gained specific content in terms of the stipulations of covenant, epitomized by the Ten Commandments, and will be presented to the whole nation Israel as a way of life in the promised land. See Sheriffs, *Friendship of the Lord*, 37.

with reference to God and every day experiences him close at hand.[98] Whereas, the word "be blameless תָּמִים" draws attention, the word "תָּמִים" simply means "whole," but is translated "perfect" or "blameless." However, this translation does not convey the accurate meaning of the word. Although Westermann is ambiguous in stating that the word is consciously secular, it is right to see that the word is neither a moral nor religious echo, but it aims at "total and unconditional dependence on God."[99] It is, thus, plausible to see the word not "in the sense of moral perfection but rather in relationship to God."[100]

Verse 22, "When he had finished speaking with Abraham, God went up from him," confirms that the appearance is actual and vivid, not a vision. This time the narrative states that Abram fell facedown (Gen 17:3). Abram's attitude when encountering the Lord has changed in comparison to the last four contacts with the Lord: three spoken and one theophany (Gen 12:1–3, 7; 13:14–17; 15:4–5). Such a silent gesture (prostration) indicates submission and adoration to the only and true Lord whom Abram has been appreciating. God responded to the reaction by changing Abram's name. Most scholars, however, interpret the changed name "Abraham" as a dialectal variant, nothing more than a lengthened form of Abram, which means, "exalted father." Charles Alders, however, relates the name to an Arabic word *rueham*, which means "a great number" and an ancient Hebrew word such as *raham* meaning "multitude."[101] "Abraham" could then mean "father of a multitude." Thus the changed name "Abraham" signifies a confirmation of what God promised. It draws attention to the fact that names had power in the ancient world; names are also important in the Bible because they are often, but not always, more than just a label and are seen to express the character of the person, or at least the hopes and sentiments associated with the name.[102] Other instances of a change in name signifying a change of direction and purpose in a person's life are Jacob who was

---

98. Westermann, *Genesis 12–36*, 259.

99. Ibid.

100. Von Rad, *Genesis*, 198.

101. Alders, *Genesis*, 306.

102. The giving of names in the ancient world was a significant act. A name was believed to affect a person's destiny; so the person giving the name was exercising some degree of control over the person's future. Often names expressed hopes or blessings. At other times they preserved some details of the occasion of the birth, especially if the occasion appeared significant. See Walton and Matthews, *IVP Bible Background*, 55.

called Israel (a prince with God), Simon who was called Peter (rock), and Saul who was called Paul.[103] The changed names have become symbols of a new reality, a changed status before God. If the names of Abraham and Sarah did not properly signify God's premeditated blessing for Abraham, God would have given them a totally different name. Furthermore, God introduces "circumcision" as a physical sign of the covenant and an act of confession.[104] If leaving Haran is a starting point in Abraham's pilgrimage, the changed name and circumcision are obviously a turning point in Abraham's pilgrimage. "My covenant," to which God refers nine times in chapter 17 (the term "covenant" occurs thirteen times in chapter 17), is signified by the external expressions (name changes and circumcision).[105] It is clear that God bestowed with the name Abraham the covenant as a unique, permanent, and binding relationship.

The whole land of Canaan, where you are now an alien, I will give as an everlasting possession to you and your descendants after you; and I will be their God (Gen 17:8).

It is noticeable that verse 8 encompasses present status (an alien) and future status (an everlasting possession).[106] As it occurs again in Genesis 28:4, 36:7, 37:1, 47:9, and Exodus 6:4, it becomes clear that present status (an alien) is a prerequisite for future status (an everlasting possession). This is the overarching blueprint of pilgrimage. Westermann points out:

> P's [priestly account] intention here is not merely to indicate the contrast between the period when Abraham wandered as an alien in Canaan and the period when Israel lived there as in the land promised and granted to her; P is speaking at the same time to his own contemporaries to remind them that it is always possible for Israel to be an alien.[107]

103. Williams, *Genesis*, 90.

104. Since Babylonians did not practice circumcision, the observance of this custom was a *status confessionis* for the exiles. See von Rad, *Genesis*, 201.

105. The Hebrew word of the term "covenant" is more appropriately translated "obligation" and "promise." See von Rad, *Genesis*, 199.

106. Abraham was called the Hebrew (Gen 14:13). "The Hebrew" is not a term used by Israelites by themselves, but only by non-Israelites of Israelites (Gen 39:14; 41:12). It seems to be more of a social categorization than an ethnic term. The Apiru are usually on the periphery of society—foreign slaves, mercenaries, or even marauders. Here Abram fits this description well: he is an outsider *vis à vis* Canaanite society. See Wenham, *Genesis 1–15*, 313.

107. Westermann, *Genesis 12–36*, 263.

[T]o you and your descendants after you (Gen 17:8). Israel, descended from Abraham, is also destined to be in a unique, permanent, and binding relationship with the true God. *I will be their God* (v. 8). This focal point of the covenant has become the basis of all saving interventions on the nation's behalf, and the initiation of all subsequent divine interventions to lead God's people into faith's pilgrimage, providing pilgrimage with a goal and history with a meaning.[108] This permanent relationship between God and Israel has continuously reminded Israel of God's promise of prosperity and land, and of her obligation to walk before God and be blameless. Westermann again makes a valuable point on this.

> Israel lives only from the action of her God; but God's action in history allows both for the gift of the land and expulsion from it. The promise of the land remains in force—even now; but it does not mean any claim to the land. The only thing that is of vital importance is that God stand by the people, even if it is a people expelled from the land: "I will be your God." This is the way P [priestly account] spoke to the people of his age while unfolding God's promise to Abraham.[109]

Soon after the marvelous theophany (Gen 18) and God's judgment on Sodom (Gen 19), the scene of Genesis 20 is set within a framework of journey. Abraham had left Mamre near Hebron and traveled southwest to the Negev. Then he settled down for a time in Gerar, northeast of Beer-sheba and east-southeast of Gaza in the western Negeb. The reason why Abraham left Mamre is unknown. It is hard to understand how Abraham and Sarah would once again agree that Sarah was his sister (Gen 20) after experiencing the mighty intervention of God and God's protecting care in Egypt (Gen 12), encountering the marvelous theophany (Gen 18), and witnessing Sodom's judgment by God (Gen 19).[110] We would expect to see this failure coming in Genesis 17:17–18 when Abraham completely doubted the promise, laughed at God, and appealed to the son already in hand. Thus Genesis 17:17–18, as a prelude to this

---

108. Von Rad argues that "I will be their God" does not belong originally to the ancient patriarchal promise, but is, rather, an antedating of the substance of the covenant at Sinai. See von Rad, *Genesis*, 200.

109. Westermann, *Genesis 12–36*, 262–63.

110. Genesis 12 leaves open all the possibilities for what might have happened to Sarah with the king. Whereas Genesis 20 excludes the possibility that Abimelech could have touched Sarah.

shameful experience (Gen 20), already showed that Abraham, the father of faith, was unable to trust, and willing to rely on an alternative to the promise. The righteous prophet who boldly pleaded for saving Sodom (Gen 18) again failed to trust in God (Gen 20). God again showed his faithfulness through his divine intervention (Gen 20:3–7).

Early the next morning Abimelech summoned all his officials, and when he told them all that had happened, they were very much afraid . . . (Gen 20:8). From the redactor's point of view, Westermann offers a possible background to the scene that the Abraham story wants to tell that generation that the fear of God can indeed exist even outside of Israel and warns them against a narrow-minded thought pattern of friend versus foe and an attitude inspired by uneasiness about the wickedness of others.[111] As Wenham points out, Abraham is after all not such a saint as we might have concluded from chapter 18, nor were all the inhabitants of Canaan so depraved as those who lived in Sodom.[112] Genesis 20, however, closes with a glimmer of hope that through this shameful experience Abraham seems to have finally learned the full lesson of faith. The final outcome of the event is rather positive, for we cannot trace him questioning God, ever again.[113]

Some time later God tested Abraham . . . Take your son, your only son . . . sacrifice him there as a burnt offering (Gen 22:1–2). God had not directly spoken to Abraham for many long years.[114] Chapter 22 begins

---

111. Traditional source critics ascribed this chapter to the Elohistic source (E). However, Westermann (*Genesis 12–36*, 319–20), Wenham (*Genesis 16–50*, 68–69), and Ronning ("Naming of Isaac," 1–27) have followed Van Seters (*Abraham in History*) in arguing that chapter 20 is not an independent version of the story 12:10–20. They regard chapter 20 as a supplement to the Yahwistic source (J) rather than part of its sources. However, Hoffmeier ("Wives Tales of Genesis," 81–99) suggests that all three wife-sister stories (Gen 12, 20, 26) are possibly separate events that, when viewed together, make sense in light of the ancient Near Eastern practice of diplomatic marriage. Westermann, *Genesis 12–36*, 329.

112. Wenham, *Genesis 16–50*, 75.

113. We find Abraham questioning God in Genesis 15:2, 17:17–18, and 18:23–33. For Abraham the birth of Isaac (Gen 21) and watching him grow might have become a concrete confirmation of the full lesson of faith in the true God, knowing that God had wonderfully kept his promise.

114. Some time has elapsed between chapters 21 and 22. Abraham's reference to Isaac as a "lad" (v. 5) suggests that Isaac is neither a toddler nor a man who is physically in the prime of life. Early Jewish tradition (Midr. *Genesis Rabbah* 56:8) suggested that Isaac was thirty-seven at the time of his binding by Abraham. This number is arrived at by subtracting the age at which Sarah gave birth to Isaac, ninety, from the age at which

with God's silence broken. At the last stage of his journey Abraham faced a test. When God first told Abram to leave his homeland, God did not mention "the land of Canaan," but "the land that I will show you," testing Abraham. In fact Abraham's whole life seems to be one long series of challenges and tests from the very start. However, the sentence "God tested Abraham" (Gen 22:1) refers to the significance of the story.[115] As such, the answer to the question "for what purpose?" is becoming clear as we consider Abraham's polytheistic background. As I argued earlier, that Abram's concept of God being monotheistic is difficult to accept is supported by two facts: there is no portrayal in the text as a God that Abram already worshiped and the personal god was a familiar religious concept in the culture of the time. When Yahweh appears to Abraham, he neither reveals to Abraham that he is the only God, nor forces Abraham to abandon his polytheistic belief (Gen 12:7). Although Yahweh, during the entire course of Abraham's pilgrimage, is to remain as the personal god of Abraham, as the narrative proceeds, it becomes clear to us that the Genesis narrator seems to track down the transformation that Abraham underwent from the stage of having a relationship with a personal god to that of having a relationship with the true God. The true God had patiently and diligently waited until Abraham came to a certain stage of appreciation of God. Thus the test for Abraham at the last stage of his pilgrimage was to discover what kind of God the true God has meant to Abraham.

The test begins with a rather positive response to God's call: "Abraham! Here I am" (Gen 22:1).[116] God had appeared three times (Gen 12:7; 17:1; 18:1) and talked to Abraham three times (Gen 12:1; 13:14; 15:1), before calling him (Gen 22:1). It is only in chapter 17 that the nar-

---

she died, one hundred twenty-seven, which was a sudden death caused by discovering that Abraham was about to slaughter Isaac. By putting Isaac in his late thirties, Jewish tradition gives a much larger role to Isaac than Christian tradition, which has highlighted the obedience of Abraham and the faithfulness of God. See Hamilton, *Genesis, Chapters 18–50*, 100.

115. The purpose of the test is obvious that in the wilderness wondering (Exod 15:25; 16:4; 20:20; Deut 8:2, 16) through false prophets (Deut 13:1–4) or through foreign oppression (Judg 2:22; 3:1, 14), God tested Israel's loyalty for a time of syncretism. Deuteronomy 8:2 and 16 clearly indicate that "testing" is to discover "what was in your heart" and to "humble you" at such a time, which faced syncretism most directly.

116. Hamilton argues against the traditional translation of הִנֵּה. The Hebrew is lit. "behold me." Hamilton translates it as "yes." This, however, appears to be a weak argument. See Hamilton, *Genesis, Chapters 18–50*, 97.

rative states that, of the six experiences, Abraham responded to God's call by falling facedown (v. 1). However, Abraham answered with the response of a servant (Here I am) twice in this story (Gen 22:1, 11).[117] The reply is certainly the last word in the relationship with God that has long been developed through the faith pilgrimage of Abraham. Although Wenham interprets the reply as "Abraham's attentiveness and potential obedience," it seems more than that.[118] As we trace the entire course of the Abrahamic pilgrimage, the articulation would be the conclusive response to the true God whom Abraham had fully appreciated through God's divine intervention (Gen 12, 20), the six encounters with the true God (Gen 12:1; 12:7; 13:14; 15:1; 17:1; 18:1), witnessing Sodom and Gomorrah destroyed (Gen 19), and finally the birth of Isaac (Gen 21). Having Isaac was certainly for Abraham the full confirmation of who God was. As the Abraham story moves towards its conclusion, a number of incidental details reinforce how important "an heir" was to Abraham.

Take your son, your only son, Isaac, whom you love, and go to the region of Moriah . . . I will tell you about (Gen 22:2). This requirement is reminiscent of the first call from God, "Leave your country, your home land, your father's household, go to the land I will show you" (Gen 12:1). This parallel intensifies in chapter 22 as the conclusion of the pilgrimage of faith for Abraham. Particularly in 2 Chronicles 3:1, "Moriah" is connected with Jerusalem, though it is related to David rather than to Abraham in the text.[119] Despite the omission of any reference to Abraham in 2 Chronicles 3:1, the connection demonstrates a typological relationship between them as the destination of pilgrimage.

The articulation of verse 2 "your only son, Isaac, whom you love" (Gen 22:2) stresses Abraham's affection for his son too. Thus the command to sacrifice him as a burnt offering must have been a startling blow to Abraham. The promise of God is that through Isaac his descendants will be reckoned (Gen 21:12). The command of God is, however, that Isaac must be killed. This means that there will be no descendants, no future. The entire pilgrimage from Genesis 11:30 has been for nothing. Isaac was a free gift from God, and God wanted to know if Abraham

---

117. Moses and Samuel had the same response when God called them by name (Exod 3:4; 1 Sam 3:4, 6, 8).

118. Wenham, *Genesis 16–50*, 104.

119. Hamilton explores the meaning of "Moriah." See Hamilton, *Genesis, Chapters 18–50*, 102–3.

could give up the free gift of the promise. In response to the call, Abraham obeyed without any outward reluctance. *Early next morning Abraham got up* (Gen 22:3). At this stage there is nothing said about the inner feelings Abraham experienced, but a demonstration of his great resolution. Three days' journey might be that of agony, which was the last stage of the entire course of Abrahamic pilgrimage.[120] It is, however, possible that Abraham would be quite confident that God would do something about it, considering all God had done and promised to Abraham.

He said to his servant, "stay here. . . . we will worship and then we will come back to you . . . " Father? . . . where is the lamb for the burnt offering? . . . God himself will provide the lamb for the burnt offering, my son (Gen 22:5, 8). Wenham suggests three possibilities for Abraham's enigmatic responses on the way to Moriah.[121] It probably was a mixture of all three possibilities (white lie, disobedience, and hope). Despite the ambiguity, verse 10 clearly indicates that Abraham stretched out the hand and took the knife to slay him. It is noticeable that the word "slay" is used. Although in his heart Abraham had already done the decisive act, the literal act was a sign of fearing God, a complete action of obedience coming from knowing God. It is not certain if Abraham took the decisive action, still believing in the promise "your descendants will be reckoned through Isaac" (Gen 21:12). The question should be left unanswered. Verse 12, however, confirms that Abraham took the literal action in the fear of God. *Do not do anything to him. Now I know that you fear God, because you have not withheld from me your son, your only son* (Gen 22:12).

Again, it is necessary to draw attention to the question, "Was the test necessary?" Did God not know Abraham's loyalty before the test? Th. C. Vriezen says that the communion between the holy one and man is the essential root-idea of the Old Testament message concerning God.[122] Moberly believes that the logic of God's "need to know" is that

---

120. "Three days" is a standard biblical Hebrew idiom for an indefinite short period of time (e.g., Josh 1:11; 2:16, 22; 2 Sam 20:4; John 1:17; 3:3), just as "forty days" (or forty years) is the idiom for an indefinite long period of time. See Moberly, *Bible, Theology and Faith*, 110.

121. First, it could be a white lie to disguise the true nature of the sacrifice. Second, it could be read as implying that he does not intend to sacrifice Isaac after all. Third, it may be read as an affirmation of faith, that although he has been told to sacrifice Isaac, yet somehow the promises made to him that "your descendants will be named through Isaac" would be fulfilled. See Wenham, *Genesis 16–50*, 107.

122. Vriezen, *Old Testament Theology*, 134.

of relationship and response.¹²³ Testing is thus a fundamental idea of the Old Testament message concerning the relationship between God and man. The fact that a relationship is essentially two sided, and begins with a mutual response, indicates how in Genesis 22 the dynamics of Abraham's relationship with God make sense of God's "need to know" in relation to Abraham's perception of the true God. Abraham has not been forced or asked to acknowledge God as God up until now, since he experienced God's divine intervention (Gen 12, 20), the six encounters with the true God (Gen 12:1; 12:7; 13:14; 15:1; 17:1; 18:1), witnessing Sodom and Gomorrah destroyed (Gen 19), and finally the birth of Isaac (Gen 21). Now the true God needs to know whether Abraham sees him as he is— *the very expression of the name and nature of God.*¹²⁴ It is, thus, natural to construe God's "knowing" in relation to his "testing." Moberly goes on to say,

> The concern of the texts is for a deepening of the encounter between God and people. Although the primary emphasis falls upon the appropriate human response, this response is relational at the same time as being moral, and this relationship is not conceived as one-sided but rather God is engaged within the encounter in such a way that the outcome is a genuine divine concern. When Abraham is depicted as "one who fears God," the divine pronouncement "now I know," rather than "now people will know," indicates that the deepened relationship is in some way an intrinsic concern of God even as it also constitutes the nature of mature humanity.¹²⁵

These dynamics of God's relationship with Abraham become even clearer in the light of the extraordinary title "friend of God" (Isa 41:8; 2 Chr 2:7; Jas 2:23). Although the two terms may in fact be close in meaning, Abraham's "fear" of God is not to be identified with his "friendship" with God.¹²⁶ Abraham's "fear" of God refers to the relationship from

---

123. Moberly, *Bible, Theology and Faith*, 79.

124. Ackroyd defines "to know that I am Yahweh" as the expression of the name and nature of God. See Ackroyd, *Exile and Restoration*, 234.

125. Moberly, *Bible, Theology and Faith*, 106–7.

126. Having defined the relationship with God as the most desirable kind—a real and mutual life-enhancing relationship—Moberly offers an explicit linkage between "friend of God" and the Hebrew verb *ahav*. The Hebrew verb used of Abraham in Isaiah 41:8 and 2 Chronicles 2:7 is "*'ahav*," a verb conventionally rendered "love," which can have a wide range of meaning (as can "love" in English). But rabbinic tradition is likely to

which his "friendship" with God will flow. Thus the test in chapter 22 refers to the existence of the relationship and the effect it would have. The test of God was to see whether Abraham feared God. Abraham as one who feared God chose to obey the true God. Von Rad notes that "the fear of God" must not be considered as a special emotional reaction to the reality of God that is experienced as *mysterium tremendum*, but rather as an inevitable consequence of knowing God, which then results in obedience (Gen 20:11; 42:18; 2 Kgs 4:1; Isa 11:2; Prov 1:7; Job 1:1, 8).[127] It would not be a problem to see *fear of God* in the Old Testament as an apt human response to God.

JACOB PILGRIMAGE

Jacob's pilgrimage was started by a family conflict over who should receive the patriarch's blessing. Isaac's plan to bless Esau (Gen 27:1-4) was thwarted by Rebekah's deceptive plan (27:5-17) and Jacob's ruse (27:18-26).[128] Isaac bestowed on Jacob his blessing that was meant for Esau (Gen 27:27-29). Esau intended to kill Jacob for cheating him and his inheritance. Having realized that, Rebekah and Isaac sent Jacob to Haran (Gen 27:41—28:5).[129] The framework of the journey again seems to play a major part in unfolding the plot of the Jacob narrative.

Jacob left Beersheba and set out for Haran (Gen 28:10). Jacob's journey from Beer-sheba to Haran is a distance of about six hundred miles

---

be near the mark when it links Abraham's *ahav* with the Shema, the summary proclamation of Israel's faith (Deut 6:4-5), where Israel's response to God, which is to be lived out through obedience to Torah, is depicted as "love" (*'ahav*). So one way of understanding "You shall love YHWH" in Deuteronomy 6:5 is "Be like Abraham." It is natural to suppose that the climactic episode in the story of Abraham's walk with God illuminates their relationship with particular clarity. See Moberly, *Bible, Theology and Faith*, 73.

127. Von Rad, *Genesis*, 241-42.

128. Isaac and Rebekah do not seem able to communicate honestly with one another on important matters. Bruce Waltke points out that the family members are paired in seven dialogues: Isaac and Esau (27:1-4), Rebekah and Jacob (27:5-17), Isaac and Jacob under the guise of Esau (27:18-29), Isaac and Esau (27:30-40), Rebekah and Jacob (27:41-45), Rebekah and Isaac (27:46), and Isaac and Jacob (28:1-5). Jacob and Esau never meet, and Rebekah and Isaac meet only briefly. Typically in Hebrew narrative only two characters dialogue at one time. Here, however, the number of separate meetings and their manner imply intentional exclusion and reflect deep division within the family. See Waltke, *Genesis*, 373.

129. Isaac did not know about Esau's intention. Rebekah told Isaac that she wanted Jacob to marry a woman from her family. Rebekah's deceit pleased Isaac for obvious reasons.

(more than a month's journey).[130] Some suggest that Jacob was forty years old, while others calculate his age at seventy-seven years old when he left his father's household to go to Haran. Jacob took a journey that made the focus of his life shift dramatically from Canaan to Mesopotamia. The Jacob narrative that up to now only records the deeds of a disgraced Jacob moves from the family conflict to a direct encounter with God in a dream. Thus the journey motif seems to provide a framework for a theophanic encounter. *When he reached a certain place, he stopped for the night because the sun had set* (Gen 28:11). Jacob would have traveled over the central ridge route from Beer-sheba through Hebron, through Bethlehem, past Jerusalem, and on through Gibeah, Mizpah, and Bethel (also called Luz).[131] It must have taken considerable time to reach Padan-aram (Gen 28:2; 29:1).[132] The Jacob narrative, however, focuses on only two days, singling out only one place, which gave new meaning to Jacob's journey. He had gone as far as he could in the daylight. It was not a prearranged resting place to pass the night. The setting of this scene is identified only as "a certain place." Given the randomness this text emphasizes, we can see no reason for supposing with Cassuto that the erection of an altar presents Jacob conquering the land "ideally in the name of the Lord."[133] The text does not imply that Jacob realized that this place had been important to his grandfather, Abraham. However, it is not tenable to say that it was just pure coincidence that Jacob sets up altars on the same location that Abraham had erected altars. It was near Bethel that Abraham built an altar (Gen 12:8; 13:3), and this was a place to which Jacob would later return (Gen 35:1). Thus the Jacob narrative seems to furnish us with these particular stopping places as a symbolic sign of the future conquest of Israel as described in the book of Joshua.

Taking one of the stones there, he put it under his head and lay down to sleep. He had a dream in which he saw a stairway resting on the earth . . . the angels of God were ascending and descending on it . . . (Gen 28:11–12). Jacob put one of the stones under his head. Jacob did not use the stone

---

130. Opinion over the distance of Jacob's journey varies. Some suggest that it would have taken over twenty days (about four hundred miles).

131. Rigsby, "Jacob," 463; Walton and Matthews, *IVP Bible Background*, 58.

132. This place only appears in Genesis. It is either a designation for the general area of northern Mesopotamia or perhaps another name for Haran. See Walton and Matthews, *IVP Bible Background*, 58.

133. Cassuto, *Genesis*, 2:304.

as a cushion for his head, but as a protection behind his head (various passages also support this [1 Sam 19:13, 16; 26:7, 11f, 16; 1 Kgs 19:6; Jer 13:18]).[134] Between the start of his journey at Beer-sheba and the end of his journey at Haran, the Jacob pilgrimage begins with God's choice to encounter Jacob in his dream. Jacob saw in his dream the stairway as the passageway between heaven and earth.[135] Having supported Rashi's suggestion that the ascending angels are those responsible for Jacob's homeland, and the descending ones are those responsible for the foreign land to which he is going, Wenham sees that this vision of the angels is an assurance of God's protection for Jacob, even though he is leaving home.[136] Faced with a formidable trip and an uncertain future ahead, as Brueggemann puts it, Jacob's dream was not "a morbid review of a shameful past, but rather the presentation of an alternative future with God."[137] It should be noted that God did not offer a single word of rebuke to Jacob, but only blessing and promise.

I am the Lord, the God of your father Abraham and the God of Isaac . . . I will give you and your descendants the land on which you are lying . . . I am with you and will watch over you wherever you go, and I will bring you back to this land. I will not leave you until I have done what I have promised you (Gen 28:13–15). Saying he is *the God of Abraham and the God of Isaac* indicates the reaffirmation of the promises and blessings given to the fathers, and their reapplication to Jacob. "I am with you," I am *really* with you, emphasizing the immediacy of the word הנה, Wenham inserts "really."[138] Yahweh choosing Jacob does not leave any possibility of Jacob choosing Yahweh as his God. This text demonstrates that the initiation of the divine companionship, *being with*, by Yahweh

---

134. Westermann points this out, referring to Gunkel, B. Jacob, and others. See Westermann, *Genesis 12–36*, 454.

135. The comparable word in Akkadian is used in Mesopotamian mythology to describe what the messenger of the gods uses when he wants to pass from one realm to another. It is this mythological stairway that the Babylonians sought to represent in the architecture of the ziggurats. These had been built to provide a way for the deity to descend to the temple and the town. Jacob's background would have given him familiarity with this concept, and thus he would conclude that he was in a sacred spot where there was a portal opened between worlds. See Walton and Matthews, *IVP Bible Background*, 59.

136. Wenham, *Genesis 16–50*, 222.

137. Brueggemann, *Genesis*, 243.

138. Wenham, *Genesis 16–50*, 218, 223.

himself is a major characteristic of Jacob's pilgrimage. The assurance "I am with you and watch over you" would come into effect on condition that a journey was taken. Thus, God bestowed Jacob's pilgrimage with a divine assurance of protection. "I will bring you back to this land," the promise of homecoming, is highlighted as a conclusion of God's promises, divine presence and protection. God promised to accompany Jacob to the promised land. W. L. Holladay lists twenty-five references where the Hiphil of *šûbs* means motion back to a point of departure with God as subject and human beings as object.[139] About half of these twenty-five references are to God bringing his people back from exile.[140] Jacob as a pilgrim will leave the land, but there is certainty that God will bring him back to the land at the end of pilgrimage. In the text Yahweh appears six times as the subject "I." This indicates that promise and blessing is a pure gift from God not gained through human deeds, and confirms that his protection of Jacob will continue in all his pilgrimage ("until I have done what I have promised you" [Gen 28:15]). The fact that the Jacob narrative singles out only this one event in the lengthy journey seems to suggest that this event gave a new meaning to the journey. Thus Bethel would become to him a lifelong monument of the relationship (covenant) God unconditionally made with him in his pilgrimage.

When Jacob awoke from his sleep, he thought, "Surely the Lord is in this place, and I was not aware of it." He was afraid and said, "How awesome is this place! This is none other than the house of God; this is the gate of heaven." Early the next morning Jacob took the stone he had placed under his head and set it up as a pillar and poured oil on top of it. He called that place Bethel, though the city used to be called Luz (Gen 28:16–18). Jacob came to a place called Bethel, which was later to become the major Canaanite city, Luz, and many pilgrims gathered after it became a center for pilgrimage at the reign of Jeroboam (1 Kgs 12:26–29).[141] What gives Bethel its significance is not the tradition, but God's encounter with Jacob on this particular occasion. Furthermore, the startling element of the Bethel incident is the relational God who bound himself to this ex-

139. See Hamilton, *Genesis, Chapters 18–50*, 243.

140. Ibid.

141. Place names change based on the appearance of new peoples or significant events. A place can quite well be called by the later name. Luz is probably the old name of the place. See Westermann, *Genesis 12–36*, 458. Von Rad says that Bethel must have been known as a cult center before the time of Israel because a god named Bethel was worshiped there. See von Rad, *Genesis*, 286.

iled one and initiated the relationship. Jacob was certainly overwhelmed by the encounter with God. However, his response to Yahweh's words reveals that he does not have much interest in the God encountered and the promise given there.

Then Jacob made a vow, saying, "If God will be with me and will watch over me on this journey I am taking and will give me food to eat and cloths to wear so that I may return safely to my father's house, then the Lord will be my God and this stone that I have set up as a pillar will be God's house, and of all that you give me I will give you a tenth" (Gen 28:19–22). *If God will be with me . . . then the Lord will be my God*. Here Jacob confirmed the divine promise, *I am with you*. However, the whole context suggests that the Lord will be his God if God is true to his self-interest. If God is not true to these, Jacob might raise the question of whether Yahweh will continue to be his God. Thus, some are cynical about his motives in making the vow, given the "conditional 'if' clauses," whereas others take Jacob's words as expressing the spirituality of a true vow.[142] It is, however, certain that the tone of his vow reveals that the Bethel incident has not changed Jacob in terms of knowing God. For Jacob the vow must have been an expression of gratitude and love in this solemn moment, in view of the uncertain future ahead. It is noted that Jacob still adds an "if" (v. 20). This God whom Jacob met in Bethel was the God whom his father, Isaac, and grandfather, Abraham, had met and told him about. "I am the God of Abraham and Isaac" (v. 13) indicates that the God who revealed himself to Jacob was the same God that Jacob knew from hearing about him. However, we might raise the question of whether Jacob perceived Yahweh at Bethel in the same way that Abraham had appreciated Yahweh at Mount Moriah. The conditional "if" clause might throw serious doubt on the question. In Bethel he actually saw and heard God in a special way. Jacob of course acknowledged the omnipresence of God ("Surely the Lord is in this place" [Gen 28:16]). However, Jacob's first perception regarding God would have been comparable to Abraham's acknowledgement of God at first. The conditional "if" (v. 20) clause would suggest that at this stage Jacob might have perceived the God of Bethel as a personal god, not the one true God. *Of all that you give me I will give you a tenth* (Gen 28:22). Despite his uncertainty regarding the

---

142. While it is true that some OT vows have conditional "if" clauses, not all do, and the reader who has seen the characterization of Jacob unfold so far is entitled to be cynical of his motives here. See G. Davies, "Vows," 792–93.

Pilgrims and Disciples, Mixed Metaphors? 35

way that he perceives God, the vow to give a tenth of what he receives as the only part of Jacob's promise indicates a seriousness about Jacob's relationship with God, as well as awareness of the source of his provision. Allen P. Ross notes that

> the structure of the speech changes to the second person in a personal address to God directly. His gratitude and submission to God would be expressed through the paying of a tithe. So Jacob did more than consecrate Bethel as a place of worship for the nation of Israel. He himself was moved to worship there, and his acts formed a pattern for later worshipers to follow in the offering of their devotion and their substance to God.[143]

Then Jacob continued on his journey (Gen 29:1). The journey initiated by family conflict was reoriented by the encounter with God. He headed towards the same place for much the same purpose (avoiding assassination and finding a wife), but now Jacob's journey ahead would become faith's pilgrimage with a theological content. As a stone had become a pillar, and Luz had been renamed *Bethel*, so too a fugitive was transformed into a pilgrim through an encounter with God.

The next two chapters (29–30) record Jacob's twenty long years away from his home. Spending the next twenty years as part of his uncle's household, Jacob managed to build up extensive holdings of his own, including two wives and two concubines, and twelve children (eleven sons and one daughter). Although he received unfair treatment from his uncle, on the whole this was a successful period of Jacob's life in Haran where his wives and concubines produced virtually all of the family of Israel. God took care of him, as he had promised.

Jacob noticed that Laban's attitude toward him was not what it had been. Then the Lord said to Jacob, "Go back to the land of your fathers and to your relatives, and I will be with you" (Gen 31:2–3). Jacob knew that he could not stay much longer in Haran. Was this a coincidence? Or was God's providence behind the events? God also told him to leave Laban and return to Canaan. This time Jacob acted promptly on God's command. He gathered his family and property and set out for Canaan (Gen 31:17). As a pattern of obedience the leaving became an obligatory prerequisite in order to receive what is promised. *Jacob, however, took fresh-cut branches from poplar, almond and plane trees and made white stripes on them by peeling the bark and exposing the white inner*

143. Ross, "Jacob's Vision," 234.

wood of the branches . . . (Gen 30:37). *The God of my father has been with me* (Gen 31:5). *If the God of my father, the God of Abraham and the Fear of Isaac, had not been with me, you would surely have sent me away empty-handed. But God has seen my hardship and the toil of my hands, and last night he rebuked you* (Gen 31:42). It is interesting to contrast chapter 30 with chapter 31. Jacob gave all the credit to the Lord in chapter 31, whereas chapter 30 indicates that he was cunning and adept at sympathetic magic. Source criticism seems to offer a feasible answer to the puzzle.[144] However, by appealing to the knowledge of biology and zoology Hamilton claims that Jacob in chapter 30 was not deceptive; his knowledge of zoology was far from primitive.[145] Regardless of the different arguments it is certain that God must have been the one who was behind the blessing. There is a clear indication in Genesis 31:12 that God's blessing was upon Jacob. Although he was still dependent on his own wisdom, Jacob's explanation in chapter 31 probably represents his sober reflections on the happenings of the past few years. *Jacob also went on his way, and the angels of God met him* (Gen 32:1). Jacob journeyed on until he saw the angels of God. He saw them and called the name of that place Mahanaim (i.e., two camps). Although it is not clear if Jacob perceived the presence of the angel as God's help, after this he sent a messenger to Esau to tell him of his return. The messenger returned announcing that Esau was coming to meet him with four hundred men. Again there is no explicit statement as to Esau's intention. However, the clear implication is that Jacob anticipated the possibility of a hostile encounter with Esau. Thus his heart was terrorized by the thought of Esau and the possibility that Esau would attack his group.

In great fear and distress Jacob divided the people who were with him into two groups . . . (Gen 32:9). It is clear that Jacob did not understand the presence of angels as God's help (Gen 32:1). There is no indication

---

144. Some exegetes believe that the account in 30:25-43 belongs to J (Jahwist) and that in 31:4-13 to E (Elohist). J portrays Jacob simply as a clever and fortunate adversary to Laban, whereas E justifies Jacob's actions as obedience to divine revelation. See Hamilton, *Genesis, Chapters 18–50*, 288.

145. The flock tended by Jacob had only monochrome animals in respect of phenotype. As regard genotype, however, a third were pure monochromes (homozygotes) and two-thirds were heterozygotes (who contained the gene of spottedness). By crossing the heterozygotes among themselves, Jacob would produce, according to the laws of heredity, 25 percent spotted sheep. See Hamilton, *Genesis, Chapters 18–50*, 284. Hamilton quotes from Feliks, "Biology," *EncJud*, 4:1024–27.

that he intended to depend on that help. *"Go back to your country . . . and I will make you prosper." "Save me, I pray, from the hand of my brother Esau . . . " I will pacify him with these gifts I am sending on ahead; later, when I see him, perhaps he will receive me . . .* (Gen 32:9–11, 20). At Bethel Jacob experienced the divine companionship, *I am with you*, and recalled the promise in distress. Although he prayed to God in distress, in terms of dependence on God for deliverance from the trouble, Jacob's next move indicates that the prayer did not change his basic approach to solving his problem. Jacob's intention of sending the gift was clear. This seems to be the same approach that he took to get the birthright. Therefore, Jacob's prayer reflects only his partial dependence on God. *After he had sent them across the stream, he sent over all his possessions. So Jacob was left alone, and a man wrestled with him till daybreak . . .* (Gen 32:23) Jacob's solitude serves the situation. For it was a kind of struggle in which a person can engage only in a place of solitude. The man might have waited until Jacob was alone, without possessions or protection. We are not told the identity of the man. Westermann along with Franz Delitzsch, Hermann Gunkel, and von Rad suggests that the man who attacked Jacob was a demon.[146] Westermann cites Exodus 4:24–26 to support this view.[147] It is noted that the struggle takes place while Jacob and Moses are on return journeys to Canaan and Egypt, respectively. Giving a few examples from Scripture, Hamilton, however, claims that it is not unusual or unheard of in the OT for supernatural beings to assume human form.[148] J. P. Fokkelman might be right in pointing out that "we can only learn this adversary's identity by judging him by his words and actions as Jacob does."[149] *But Jacob replied, "I will not let you go unless you*

---

146. To argue this point Westermann considers three features that suit the hostile demon: (1) It is essential for Jacob to be alone during this struggle; (2) the struggle must be an attack on one who is defenseless; (3) both robber and attacker must conceal their identity. See Westermann, *Genesis 12–36*, 516–18.

147. Westermann notes that Exodus 4:24–26 takes places on the way and at night in the same manner, and names the attacker as a demon, secondarily as Yahweh, as the textual variants show (Kittel's *Biblia Hebraica*). See Westermann, *Genesis 12–36*, 517.

148. Jacob will later identify the man as Elohim/God (Gen 31:11–13) and Hosea 12:4 identifies him as an angel. This idea is present in three other places: Genesis 18–19, which begins with three men standing in front of Abraham; Judges 6, where Yahweh's angel sat under oak tree and shortly engaged Gideon in conversation; and Judges 13, where Manoah and his wife take Yahweh's angel to be a man of God. See Hamilton, *Genesis 18–50*, 329–30.

149. Quoted in Curtis, "Structure, Style and Context," 134.

bless me" (Gen 32:27). Although it is still not certain as to the way Jacob perceived the opponent, von Rad is probably correct in suggesting,

> It is better not to explain this as an especially pious quality; it is more correct to consider this request as a primitive human reaction to an encounter with God. This clutching at God and his power of blessing is perhaps the most elemental reaction of man to the divine.[150]

The man asked him, "What is your name?"... Your name will no longer be Jacob, but Israel, because you have struggled with God and with men and have overcome... Why do you ask my name? Then he blessed him there (Gen 32:28). God had sent angels to meet Jacob. Here God himself came and made a relationship through wrestling with him, changing his name, and bestowing his blessing, although God did not reveal himself. It is noted that God is always the one who initiates a relationship and a blessing. Jacob whose name means "a cheat" was given a new name, Israel, which means, "El will rule" or "God contends," in which God will recognize him.[151] In such a way God is not the subject but the object of Jacob's struggle.[152] Kugel offers yet another explanation of Jacob's new name. This explanation sees in "Israel" four separate Hebrew words, *is ra a el*, "man who saw God" (or perhaps *yasur el*, "[he] sees God").[153] Considering the meaning of *Peniel* ("face of God"), where the event occurred, Kugel's understanding of the name fits exceptionally well within the context. However, the change of name from Jacob to Israel does not mean that from this point on Jacob is transformed. Many exegetes claim that what the narrative highlights here seems to be Jacob's assertiveness for blessing or his success in wrestling with God and with people. However, the focal point of the narrative is the fact that Jacob met God. The next reference (v. 30) to the visual act confirms this. So Jacob called the place Peniel, saying, "It is because I saw God face to face, and yet my life was spared" (Gen 32:30). The impact of the encounter was appalling

---

150. Von Rad, *Genesis*, 321.

151. What is the meaning of the name "Israel"? "El will rule" is the original linguistic meaning. Ross offers various suggestions for the etymology of "Israel." He claims that both Genesis 32:28 and Hosea 12:3 interpret the meaning of the name with a verb "to fight." Therefore, based on the context in Genesis, the verb should be understood in the sense of fighting. Ross, "Jacob at the Jabbok," 346–47.

152. Von Rad, *Genesis*, 322.

153. Kugel, *Bible As It Was*, 227.

for Jacob. After the struggle at Yabbok, a blessing pursued last night is not his main concern any longer but seeing God face to face.[154] He named the place Peniel, that is, "the face of El." Jacob's own interpretation of his encounter in verse 30 confirms that Jacob understood the man as God himself. Until now, the narrative has focused only on Jacob struggling with a man, not on him seeing divinity. Finally, the text concerns the God of Jacob. The emphasis here on seeing God would be the conclusive response to the true God whom Jacob had appreciated throughout his entire life. Seeing God face to face was certainly for Jacob the full confirmation of who God was. Jacob's Peniel experience, seeing God face to face, evokes the typical pilgrimage experience of the encounter with God. Thus Gunkel sees the pilgrimage motifs embedded within a whole stratum of patriarchal narratives in relation to the pilgrimage traditions of various cult sites.[155] As the Jacob story moves towards its conclusion, meeting Esau reinforces what "seeing God face to face" meant to Jacob.

He himself went on ahead and bowed down to the ground seven times as he approached his brother (Gen 33:3). The meeting with Esau occurred immediately following Jacob's encounter with the God of his fathers. Before the Peniel experience, Jacob had stayed behind his party. After the experience, he became the vanguard of his party. It is probably safe to say that, although Jacob's transformation was not complete, the change in Jacob had begun and included a moral dimension. Some exegetes try to trace the moral transformation of Jacob. However, what the narrative focuses on in the theme of the entire section is Jacob (the real nature of the transformation in Jacob), and his relation to knowing God, not the moral transformation. Therefore the main concern of the narrative is "nevertheless, God was with him and Jacob met God." *For to see your face is like seeing the face of God, now that you have received me favorably* (Gen 33:10). The statement, "to see your face is like seeing the face of God," seems to tie chapters 32 and 33 together and provides a significant clue for the interpretation of Jacob's entire pilgrimage as well as the incident at the Yabbok. Jacob's subsequent meeting with his brother Esau is to show how this face-to-face encounter at Peniel has a significant meaning for Jacob. No man survived after seeing God (Gen 48:16;

---

154. It described a "person to person" encounter, without help or hindrance of an intermediary. Hamilton quoted this from various sources. See Hamilton, *Genesis 18–50*, 336.

155. Gunkel, *Legends of Genesis*, 30–34.

Exod 19:21; 24:10; Judg 6:11, 22; 13). Jacob saw God, and yet his life was spared. This meant that he could look at Esau face to face, and his life would be spared. Brueggemann points out that the overall structure of the Jacob narrative moves from estrangement (conflict with Esau, with Laban, and with the mysterious man) to reconciliation.[156] As the pinnacle of the Jacob narrative, reconciliation with God is now concluded with reconciliation with Esau. Thus the encounter with God at Peniel was a decisive experience and a turning point in the life of Jacob.

Having wrestled with God (Gen 32:22–32) and been reunited with Esau, Jacob entered the promised land from the northeast for the first time in over twenty years. He came first to the city of Shechem that is in the land of Canaan (Gen 33:18), and he camped before the city. He traced the long and arduous route that Abraham traveled about one hundred twenty-five years earlier. *Then God said to Jacob, "Go up to Bethel and settle there, and build an altar there to God, who appeared to you when you were fleeing from your brother Esau"* (Gen 35:1). As Wenham points out, this chapter comes as an anticlimax after a series of dramatic episodes.[157] However, from a pilgrimage point of view this closing narrative certainly appears to be the climax of Jacob pilgrimage. It was the first time that God commanded Jacob to build an altar to the God who had appeared to him in Bethel. The verb "go up" in the Old Testament has overtones of pilgrimage, which often means "to go on a pilgrimage" (1 Sam 1:3; Ps 122:4; etc.), and this move by Jacob to Bethel actually does have all the characteristics of pilgrimage.[158] God's command to Jacob to "build an altar" is a reminder of God's command to Abraham "to offer a burnt offering." This time Jacob's test seems much easier than Abraham's.[159] Jacob was as prompt as Abraham (Gen 22:3), and he immediately instructs his household to prepare for the journey.

So Jacob said to his household and to all who were with him, "Get rid of the foreign gods you have with you, purify yourselves and change your cloths. Then come, let us go up to Bethel, where I will build an altar to God,

---

156. Brueggemann, *Genesis*, 208.

157. Wenham, *Genesis 16–50*, 328.

158. See Wenham, *Genesis 16–50*, 323; Westermann, *Genesis 12–36*, 550; von Rad, *Genesis*, 336.

159. Wenham, however, suggests that if he was scared to travel because of Canaanite hostility (cf. 34:30), it may have taken more courage than it seems. See Wenham, *Genesis 16–50*, 323.

who answered me in the day of my distress and who has been with me wherever I have gone . . . (Gen 35:1). The household purified themselves. When God directed Jacob to go back to the land (Gen 31:3), he did not practice this renunciation. Although God did not command the renunciation, this time Jacob instructed his household to cleanse themselves. Jacob must have seen going up to Bethel in terms of a pilgrimage with a cultic significance, considering the vow ("If God will be with me . . . so that I return safely to my father's house, then the Lord will be my God" [Gen 28:20–21]). Jacob made his journey to Haran and Bethel where it actually does have all the characteristics of pilgrimage.[160] The pilgrimage to Bethel sums up Jacob's entire life. The act of renunciation and purification was, therefore, a response to the God who gave protection and provision to Jacob, and the whole family. It is not certain whether or not they understood or accepted philosophical monotheism. However, it may be safe to suggest that they probably accepted Yahweh as the true God in terms of their family patron deity. The appreciation of who God was (knowledge of God) became a driving force for Jacob to make his household join the pilgrimage by freeing themselves from small images that belonged to the cult of heathen gods.

Jacob and all the people with him came to Luz (that is, Bethel) in the land of Canaan. There he built an altar, and he called the place El Bethel, because it was there that God revealed himself to him when he was fleeing from his brother (Gen 35:6–7). The journey from Shechem to Bethel was certainly a regular pilgrimage in ancient Israel.[161] Von Rad claims that Joshua 24:1, 23, 25, and Judges 20:26 confirm that Jacob was its initiator. Contra von Rad, the custom of this pilgrimage is traced back to Abraham himself. On his way from Haran (Paddan-aram), like his grandfather, Jacob also builds altars to the Lord in Succoth (Gen 33:16), Shechem (Gen 33:20), and Bethel (Gen 35:7). An altar in Shechem was

---

160. The history of the sanctuary at Bethel is well known to us. Its great period was certainly in the time after the reform of Jeroboam I, when it was a center for pilgrimage (926 BCE, 1 Kgs 12:26–29). In fact, after the Assyrian occupation in 722, Bethel still had significance as a sanctuary of Yahweh (2 Kgs 17:28). It was then destroyed by Josiah and appears never to have recovered from this blow (2 Kgs 23:15) But Bethel must have been a widely known cultic center in pre-Israelite times as well; a god with the name Bethel was worshiped here. The OT shows us that this god was still known to the Israelites because Bethel is not always used as a place name only, but is occasionally used as a divine name as well. See von Rad, *Genesis*, 286.

161. Ibid. 336–37.

called El-Elohe-Israel, which means "the God of Israel," and an altar in Bethel was called El-Bethel, which means "God of Bethel."[162] Cassuto claims that Jacob likewise passes through the land and conquers it, like Abraham, ideally in the name of the Lord (apart from the actual conquest of Shechem by his sons) and he, too, erects upon it altars as the tokens of this ideal conquest.[163] It is the stopping place and this division of the country that is mentioned again in a similar form in the account of Jacob's travel after his return from Paddan-aram. Cassuto indicates the obvious parallels between Abraham and Jacob's altar tokens. Both serve to divide the land into three regions, each south of the other. In a further parallel, Abraham bought for the full price a specific place in the land—the field of Machpelah near Hebron—while Jacob also acquired a given area in the vicinity of Shechem against full payment.[164] What is the editor's intention in furnishing us with these particular stopping places? Foreshadowing the future conquest of Israel in the book of Joshua, the Jacob narrative traces Jacob's journey in the manner that the Abraham narrative does in the Abrahamic journey. Thus, pilgrimage for Jacob is not only a physical movement.[165] It is also a pilgrimage of faith that encompasses "a theological program" in the whole context of the Jacob narrative.[166] The fact that the compilation of this story is dated to the post-exilic period also allows this theological element further to involve the shift from the Jacob narrative to the story of the sons of Jacob, Israel. Thus the Jacob narrative traces the Jacob cycle to encourage the exiles to see the return journey to Canaan in a positive light.[167] It also presents the

---

162. Rather than "El-Elohe-Israel," Westermann believes in an entirely different theological point of view, which has nothing to do with the patriarchal period land emerging from the appendage (v. 20), the name of the altar set up in Canaan: "El, the God of Israel." It is the result of the religious struggle after the settlement to sedentary life in Canaan; the worship of the God of Israel replaces the cult of the Canaanite El, "El" is now the God of Israel alone. See Westermamn, *Genesis 12–36*, 531.

163. Cassuto, *Commentary on the Book of Genesis*, 2:304–6.

164. Ibid.

165. Von Rad claims that the Jacob narrative is to be understood as Jacob's life as a wandering in the whole context of Jacob stories. See von Rad, *Genesis*, 337.

166. I am borrowing the term from Brueggemann, as a helpful way to understand the significance of the pilgrimage paradigm in the narrative. See Brueggemann, *Genesis*, 122.

167. The Jacob narrative takes an ambivalent approach to the journey. It is presented as being difficult, awkward, and dangerous. However, it also claims that former exiles would be made welcome and live prosperously.

Pilgrims and Disciples, Mixed Metaphors? 43

interlocking relationship between pilgrimage as physical movement and transformation into faith's pilgrimage, namely, knowing God through encounter with God on the way.[168]

So Israel set out with all that was his, and when he reached Beersheba, he offered sacrifices to the God of his father Isaac . . . I am the God, the God of your father . . . Do not be afraid to go down to Egypt, for I will make you into a great nation there. I will go down to Egypt with you, and I will surely bring you back again (Gen 46:1–4). As going up to Bethel (Gen 35:1) plays as the climax of Jacob's pilgrimage, going down to Egypt as the father of the nation bearing his changed name, Israel, plays as the conclusion and fulfillment of his entire life. God promised that he would make Jacob to be a great nation there. God specifically indicates *there* to emphasize the necessity of going down to Egypt. As Hamilton points out, God's first talk to Abraham (12:1–3) and Jacob (28:13–16), and final talk to Abraham (22:15, 18) and Jacob (46:2–4) are God's promises.[169] It is noted that most divine promises in the Abraham and Jacob narratives were given within journey frameworks. Journey as the main framework of pilgrimage played a significant role as God unfolded his promises to his chosen people. An invitation to Pilgrimage became a crucial necessity for God to fulfill his promises for his people. The journey that had begun with the command to Abraham to leave Haran concludes with Jacob's journey down into Egypt. There is, therefore, "a firm link between Jacob's journey down into Egypt, which concludes the patriarchal story, and the exodus from Egypt, which begins the history of the people."[170] *I will surely bring you back again* (Gen 46:4). In this promise God typified Israel's homecoming pilgrimage (the Exodus). Initiating that journey would be essential to fulfill the promise. *And Jacob said to Pharaoh, "The years of my pilgrimage are a hundred and thirty. My years have been few and difficult, and they do not equal the years of the pilgrimage of my fathers . . .* (Gen 47:9–10). Pilgrimage מְגוּרֵי חַלֵּי שְׁנֵי מְגוּרַי is the same root as the verb גּוּר (live awhile) in Genesis 47:4. Jacob summarized his life and his fathers' lives as a pilgrimage before the Pharaoh of Egypt. Jacob realized that he was chosen and given the divine promise by God, yet the prom-

---

168. This is the core of pilgrimage in the light of discipleship. Pilgrimage as the life of faith kept Israel in pursuit of the promise of land. In fact, the relationship between them can be traced throughout the whole Bible.

169. Hamilton, *Genesis 18–50*, 590.

170. Westermann, *Genesis 12–36*, 156.

ise had remained unfulfilled. Until the promised land is received, his life as a pilgrim is incomplete. Therefore, this summary of his life, "the years of my pilgrimage," could be the total appreciation of who he was before God, offering a crucial motif for the whole of the patriarchal narrative. This unique expression, "the years of my pilgrimage," is significant for the pilgrimage motif to stand on firm ground.[171]

Conclusion

In the formulation of the history of Israel, Creation, together with historical events (the Exodus, the times of exile), had decisive significance for the historical interpreter. In Israel's understanding Creation and history are inseparably related. Creation is the foundation of the history of Israel. Thus for Israel the concern of the historical drama is not really the original sin of Adam, the origin of evil, the consequence of the Fall, or bringing in death. It is, rather, the calling from God for Israelites to grasp the reality of God as the Creator and that of mankind as his creatures, and finally to live on his terms in the land given by him.[172] They are homeless on this earth. Life outside the garden is *life away from one's true home*. They are no more than exiles wandering and yearning for a return to the Edenic state, *being with God*, the final destination of pilgrimage. Expulsion, *the first journey mankind has ever taken*, was, therefore, the result of the rescue rather than that of judgment. This positive approach to Creation offers a starting point to the pilgrimage paradigm in discipleship perspective.

Abraham's obedience to God on Moriah as the prototype for Israel in Jerusalem emphasizes how the Abrahamic pilgrimage foreshadows the history of Israel. Abraham's journey to Moriah and offering Isaac on Moriah foreshadows pilgrims that come to sacrifice in the temple at Jerusalem, displaying obedience to God in their lives. The Abrahamic pilgrimage, which began with the divine command that has brought Abraham out of Ur, concludes with Abraham's total appreciation of the true God and submissive response to the true God on Moriah.[173] The

---

171. This phrase is found only here in Genesis. The phrase "land of sojourning" is found in Genesis 17:8, 28:4, 36:7, 37:1, and in Exodus 6:4.

172. The garden of Eden is the promised land that God's people were forced to leave, but to which they long to return.

173. Williamson concludes that there can be no question as to the identity of Abraham's God as far as the final editor of Genesis was concerned: Abraham was a follower of Yahweh, and thus his religion, however primitive, was a form of Yahwism.

overarching significance of Abraham's narrative, which is set within journey framework, embodies faith's pilgrimage with theological content.

It is also noted that journey as the main framework of pilgrimage played a significant role as Jacob narratives unfolded. An invitation to pilgrimage became a crucial necessity for God to fulfill his promises for his people. Abraham's journey to the promised land concludes with Jacob's journey down into Egypt in the patriarchal story. That was, however, the beginning of the history of the people. *The years of my pilgrimage*, Jacob's summary of his life and his fathers' lives, could be the total appreciation of whom he was before God and who God really was, offering a crucial motif for the whole of the patriarchal narrative. In fact, the pilgrimage motif encompassing the journey motif has not been said to be a distinctive feature of the patriarchal narrative as a whole. For it has not been classified as one of the main themes for grasping the idea behind the narrative. However, in the sense that motif is a recurring theme or idea in a literary, it is not surprising that the pilgrimage motif in the patriarchal narratives, where its occurrences are prominent, can be traced throughout the history of Israel.

See Williamson, "Abraham," 13.

2

Pilgrimage as a Paradigm for the People of God

THE EXODUS AND WILDERNESS

As Jacob's journey down into Egypt concludes the patriarchal story, the Exodus from Egypt establishes the change in Israel's identity as God's elect people. The Exodus was the beginning of Israel's corporate life as his people. This change in identity is established in God's first words, "my people" (Exod 3:7). Fulfilling the divine promise given to Abraham in Genesis 15:13–14, the migration of Abraham from Ur of the Chaldeans and the migration of Jacob and the Israelites to Egypt become part of a process that led to the Exodus and the initiation of God's people.[1] For example, presenting the Abrahamic journey as an exodus from Ur to the promised land, the phrasing of Genesis 15:7, "I am the Lord who brought you out of Ur of the Chaldeans," resonates with Israel's exodus to Canaan. Therefore, the paradigm of pilgrimage trailed in the whole life of the patriarchs also becomes (the larger paradigm underlying the plot of Exodus) one of dominant patterns—the journey in the wilderness toward the promised land—in Exodus, Numbers, and Joshua. The Exodus is one of several journeys that form a pattern linked by the text itself. The Exodus was not only seen as a historical event of the past, but also became a permanent symbol as a national event of religious significance in the memory of Israel. Nahum Sarna sums up the impact of the Exodus event upon Israel.

---

1. "Know well that your offspring shall be strangers in a land not theirs, and they shall be enslaved and oppressed . . . but 1 will execute judgment on the nation they shall serve, and in the end they shall go free with great wealth" (Gen 15:13–14).

> In periods of national crisis, the Exodus experience of the past serves to strengthen faith in God's redemptive powers, and provides comfort and hope for the future. The religious calendar of Israel and its rituals and practices are all reinterpreted in terms of the Exodus. The New Year is changed to the spring (Exod 12:2): the great agricultural festivals that relate to the rhythm of nature and the life of the soil are all reinterpreted and historicized in commemoration of the Exodus (Exod 23:14; Lev 23:42–43; Deut 16:9–12.)[2]

Thus, the Exodus has become a memorialization for Israelites that offers the basis for the pilgrim festivals as national liturgy.[3] *Moses! Moses! And Moses said, "Here I am"* (Exod 3:4). The voice calling to Moses in Horeb, the mountain of God, was the prelude of the central event in the Old Testament. Such a call in Scripture is a common feature in the Old Testament that often indicates a dialogue, which God is about to initiate. Abraham, Jacob, and Samuel were repeatedly called (Gen 22:11, 46:2; 1 Sam 3:10), when God spoke to them. Although to know the degree to which Moses knew about Israel's God before this time is not clear, the fact that Moses responded in exactly the same manner as both Abraham and Jacob indicates that his reply, "Here I am," suggests a possibility that at his first encounter with God Moses expected some sort of divine encounter at the burning bush.[4] Together with the fire, the voice, and the call, Moses's encounter with God at the burning bush foreshadowed Israel's Sinai encounter. Deryck Sheriffs suggests the relationship between the burning bush encounter and the Sinai covenant occasion.

> Like the sign of Passover blood, the call of Moses is a necessary preliminary to covenant-making with the nation. The burning bush encounter has a presence—address-commitment—relationship pattern similar to the Sinai covenant occasion in a way that invites comparison between Moses' individual experience and the experience of the nation.[5]

---

2. Sarna, *Exploring Exodus*, 2–3.

3. Pilgrimage was making trips to Jerusalem on the pilgrim festivals, which were Tabernacles, Passover, and Pentecost.

4. A translation of Moses's reply, the Hebrew הִנֵּנִי is lit. "behold me," or "it is I." No translation captures the essence of the original. As Hamilton and Enns see, it would be simple to think of it as a "yes" response. It, however, appears a weak argument to translate it as "yes." See Hamilton, *Genesis, Chapters 18–50*, 97; Enns, *Exodus*, 97.

5. Sheriffs, "Friendship of the Lord," 66.

The calling out of Moses's foreshadowing the bringing out of Israel (Exod 3:8, 10, 12) was a preliminary to leading God's people into the promised land (Exod 3:8, 17). Why then must he remove his sandals? *Take off your sandals, for the place where you are standing is holy ground* (Exod 3:4–5). This is a sign of reverence common in the ancient Near East.[6] It should be noted that normally sandals were not worn inside the home indicating that putting on of sandals (Exod 12:11; cf. Acts 12:8) meant readiness for a journey.[7] Note that the place did not become a place of pilgrimage. Apart from Bethel, which became a center for pilgrimage during the reign of Jeroboam (1 Kgs 12:26–29), in Israel what gave a place its holiness and significance for pilgrimage lay in the presence of God and a historic experience, not in a built up tradition or mythological justification. It was, therefore, no coincidence that as the center for pilgrimage, Jerusalem later became the holiest place in the history of Israel for the stationing of the Ark of the Covenant and the Temple Mount.

God who first announced his holiness identified himself as the God of Moses's own family and ancestors, reminding Moses of what he had forgotten during his long exile. *I am the God of your father, the God of Abraham, the God of Isaac and the God of Jacob* (Exod 3:6).[8] The divine self-identification shows that God who was bound together with Abraham, Isaac, and Jacob in the covenant relationship would initiate the same relationship with his people through Moses. *I have indeed seen the misery of my people in Egypt* (Exod 3:7). "My people" at the beginning and at the end of the speech indicates that God's divine election had already taken place with the fathers of Israel before the Exodus. Together with Moses, God will bring his redemptive deliverance for his people. As God commanded Abraham and Jacob to do, Moses was asked to leave his settlement to initiate a journey with his people. *So now, go* (Exod 3:10). This pattern of obedience, previously demonstrated by Abraham and Jacob, became a compulsory prerequisite for Moses in order to receive what was promised.

So I have come down to rescue them from the hand of Egyptians and to bring them up out of that land into a good and spacious land, a land flowing with milk and honey—the home of the Canaanites, Hittites, Amorites, Perizzites, Hivites, and Jebusites (Exod 3:8–9). God saw their

---

6. See Durham, *Exodus*, 31; Houtman, *Exodus*, 1:351–53; Sarna, *Exploring Exodus*, 15.
7. Houtman, *Exodus*, 1:347.
8. The Hebrew of verse 6 is singular, "God of your father," not "God of your fathers."

afflictions and God remembered his covenant with Abraham, Isaac, and Jacob (Exod 2:24). As the continuation of the relationship between God and Abraham, Isaac, and Jacob, God's deliverance in bringing the people out into the promised land is embedded as a paradigm in the people. As such a paradigm, for the people the emphasis on the land rooted in (from) the Creation is obvious in the Old Testament (Exod 3:8; Deut 12:9; Josh 22:19). In line with the view of Cornelis Houtman and Terence Fretheim, Peter Enns suggests that entrance into Canaan is, in a manner of speaking, a return to the garden.[9] In the series of expressions regarding the land, the land flowing with milk and honey (Exod 3:8), Israel's lasting resting place (Deut 12:9), and God's own land (Josh. 22:19), the garden of Eden became a prototype of the promised land for Israelites: "I am sending you to Pharaoh to bring my people the Israelites out of Egypt" (Exod 3:10). As in the Creation, "expulsion" from a judge's point of view could also be described as "a journey" from a rescuer's point of view, for God's bringing his people out (3:8, 10, 12) became a preliminary action to bringing them into covenant and the promised land (3:8, 17). The God who intervened in the historical drama of mankind as both judge and rescuer appeared as the rescuer in the Exodus. *When you have brought the people out of Egypt, you will worship God on this mountain* (Exod 3:12). The theophany to Moses at Horeb, the mountain of God, was read in the light of the subsequent events at Sinai. Worshiping God in the mountain of God offers a preview of the covenant relationship at Sinai as the destination of the Exodus. Worshiping God at Sinai also offers a reminder of the holy mountain or the Holy City, Jerusalem, as the destination of pilgrimage. Thus John Durham is correct to conclude that the experience of Moses in Exodus 3:1–12 is an exact foreshadowing of the experience of Israel, first in Egypt, then in the deprivation of the wilderness, and finally at Sinai.[10]

This is what the Lord says: "Israel is my first-born son, and I say to you, 'Let my son go, so he may worship me'; and if you refuse to let him go, behold I will slay your first-born son" (Exod 4:23). *This is what the Lord says: "Let my people go, so that they may hold a festival to me in the*

---

9. Houtman states that the reference to milk and honey is mythological language referring to divine sustenance, which evokes images of paradise. See Houtman, *Exodus*, 1:357. Fretheim sees a connection between paradise and the "new creation" theme. See Fretheim, *Exodus*, 58–59. See also Enns, *Exodus*, 99.

10. Durham, *Exodus*, 30.

desert" (Exod 5:1). Back in Egypt, Moses and Aaron asked Pharaoh to free the Israelites. The sonship of Israel is enunciated as a key motif in the Exodus struggle with Pharaoh. The statement, "Israel is my first-born son," as the main motive for liberating the Israelites gives a summary of God's love to his people. Thus Jeremiah (Jer 3:19; 31:9) and Hosea (Hos 11:1) also employed sonship language to express Israel's privileged relationship to God. The privileged relationship entails the responsibility to worship God. The concept of sonship is reinforced with the proclamation of his ownership. *I will take you as my own people. Therefore, say to the Israelites . . . I will take you as my own people, I will be your God. Then you will know that I am the Lord your God, who brought you out from under the yoke of Egyptians* (Exod 6:6–7). Durham and Brevard Childs suggest that the phrases, "I will take you as my own people" and "I will be your God," in the future tense point to the fact that Israel is not his people until the covenant of Mount Sinai.[11] However, this argument has already lost its ground, considering "my people" have already been identified in Exodus 3:7, 10 and Exodus 5:1. For the Israelites the Exodus was not mere rescue, but an experience of knowing God. This was seen first in the Lord's encounter with Abraham and Jacob, and now in Exodus as Moses experiences a theophany at the burning bush (Exod 3:1; 4:17), then for the Israelites in the pillar of cloud and fire (Exod 13:21), on the top of Sinai (Exod 19:16–19), and in the covenant inauguration ceremony (Exod 24:9–11). Finally the tabernacle was the conclusive pinnacle of the promise, "I will be their God" (Gen 17:8) that God made with Abraham and the continuous reminder to the people of God of his presence with them (Exod 25:8). *Then you will know that I am the Lord your God* (Exod 6:7). Thus, the *knowing God motif* as the key experience for the Israelites becomes one of the main themes of Exodus, as it was in the Abrahamic and Jacob narrative.

God brought down a series of plagues on Egypt, for Pharaoh refused to free the people (Exod 6–11). The time was ripe for the tenth plague that would make the Exodus possible. *Eat it with your cloak tucked into your belt, your sandals on your feet and your staff in your hand. Eat it in haste; it is the Lord's Passover . . . and I will bring judgment on all the gods of Egypt. I am the Lord. The blood will be a sign for you on the houses where you are; when I see the blood, I will pass over you* (Exod 12:11–13). In chapter 12 the narrative relating to a series of plagues disappears and

---

11. See Durham, *Exodus*, 79; Childs, *Book of Exodus*, 115.

Yahweh's Passover appears, theologizing the Exodus. The center of the narrative shifts from Pharaoh and plagues to the people of Israel and the commands given them by Moses and Aaron. It is quite probable that many elements of the Passover ritual suggest that it may be adapted from a nomadic ritual in the ancient Near East that sought to protect herdsmen from demonic attack and to ensure the fertility of the herd.[12] Having been given theological significance by the Israelites, its meaning was transformed and adopted into the heart of the Exodus event. Exodus 12:26–27, "And when your children ask you, 'What does this ceremony mean to you?' then tell them . . . " and 13:16, "And it will be like a sign on your hand and a symbol on your forehead that the Lord brought us out of Egypt with his mighty hand," clearly state the theological significance of Passover to the Israelites. Passover was not just a one-night event, but also a lasting reminder of what God had done for his people and what he has continued to do so for his people.[13] Regardless of the origin of Passover, Passover became one of the central rituals in the Israelite religion enabling them to know "who God is—the very expression of the name and nature of God," the name of Passover: I am the Lord, commemorating the day of redemption. After the tenth plague had befallen Egypt, Pharaoh at last relented. *Leave my people, you, and the Israelites! Go, worship the Lord as you have requested* (Exod 12:31). The Israelites started on their way out of the land of Egypt. It should be noted that the Feast of Passover marked the beginning of the journey. Sheriffs suggests the connection between the Passover meal and the journey.

> In this way, moving out of Egypt and moving on with God to an encounter symbolized by the covenant meal at Sinai associates a relationship with God with two simple human activities, eating and walking. Both the eating and the journeying take on symbolic significance. In the fullness of time, eating the New Covenant meal will reinforce the symbolism of communing in a rite which connects Passover and Sinai.[14]

When Pharaoh let the people go, God did not lead them on the road through the Philistine country, though that was shorter. For God said, "If

---

12. See De Vaux, *Ancient Israel*, 3–15; Walton and Matthews, *IVP Bible Background*, 94.

13. Rabban Gamaliel in the Mishnah Pesahim says, "In every generation a man must so regard himself as if he came forth himself out of Egypt." Enns quotes from the Mishnah Pesahim 10:5 (Danby, *The Mishnah*, 151). See Enns, *Exodus*, 249.

14. Sheriffs, "Moving on With God," 49–50.

they face war, they might change their minds and return to Egypt." So God led the people around by the desert road toward the Red Sea. The Israelites went up out of Egypt armed for battle (Exod 13:17–18). Although there is uncertainty about the locations of the places named for the exodus route, as Durham puts it, the route of Israel's exodus from Egypt might be focused not on its location, but on its purpose. The purpose as to why the Lord chose the route for his people is clearly stated in verse 18.[15] The chosen route to the promised land and the divine guidance of the pillar of cloud and fire indicate that the Exodus is more than just a leaving; rather, it is a purpose driven departure. *By day the Lord went ahead of them in a pillar of cloud to guide them on their way and by night in a pillar of fire to give them light . . . Neither the pillar of cloud by day nor the pillar of fire by night left its place in front of the people* (Exod 13:22). As they journeyed, God led them with a pillar of cloud during the day and a pillar of fire during the night. These were constantly with the Israelites throughout the wilderness wandering. Cloud and fire are presented as a sign of God's presence in the Old Testament (Exod 13:21; 19:18; 24:17; 1 Kgs 8:11; Isa 6:4–6). God's revelatory activity in the pillar of cloud and fire, and God's dwelling with the people (Exod 40:34–38) suggests that in the wilderness journey God's divine guidance and presence was a tangible assurance for the Israelites.[16] The pillar of fire and cloud shows that God played the central role as the guider and protector as the Israelites journeyed. This motif of the Lord's guiding presence, which played a part in the journey pattern in the Exodus narrative, is also expressed elsewhere in the Old Testament (Pss 77, 78; Isa 42:16; 52:12).

Soon after the Israelites had left, however, Pharaoh regretted his decision and dispatched his army. When the Israelites saw the Egyptians

---

15. Cassuto shows that three routes were possible. The first was the route known as "the way of the sea" along the Mediterranean seacoast; this was the military road of the Egyptians, which was used on their expeditions northward. The middle course lay in the direction of Beer-sheba and the Negeb, which leads to the heart of the land of Canaan via the territory of the Philistines—not the Philistines who settled in the southern Shephelah in the twelfth century BCE, but those tribes of related stock, who apparently preceded them and made their home in Gerar and the surrounding area. The southeast route, towards the peninsula of Sinai, would not bring the migrants nearer to the land of Canaan, but on the contrary would take them further away from it. Yet it was precisely this direction that was chosen out of the three. See Cassuto, *Commentary on the Book of Genesis*, 2:291–369.

16. We note that God went with the people, but not in their midst. The tent of meeting was placed outside the camp (Exod 33:7).

approaching, they panicked, but by God's divine intervention the Red Sea split in two and the Israelites crossed to the other side. Then God finished them off. *Thus the Lord saved Israel that day from the Egyptians; and Israel saw the Egyptians dead on the seashore. Israel saw the great work that the Lord did against the Egyptians. So the people feared the Lord and put their trust in him and in Moses his servant* (Exod 14:30–31). The Israelites feared the Lord through "seeing the divine work." Although the term "fear of the Lord" is often cited in biblical texts in relation to moral or ethical behavior (Gen 20:11; 42:18; Lev 19:14, 32; Deut 25:18; Job 1:1, 8), Abraham's testing (Gen 22:1–19) and the Israelites at the Red Sea (Exod 14) show that "fear of God" is woven from obedience, trust, and belief (particularly, in Exodus 14 belief is seen as a prerequisite of fear of God). "The fear of the Lord" provides the key to interpreting the journey that Abraham and the community traveled. At the last stage of Abraham's faith pilgrimage, God wanted to know that the community of the nation had experienced "the fear of the Lord." It is not certain what stages of faith the nation had reached. For in the narrative it is not possible to trace Israel's faith in the wilderness as a progression from an elementary faith to maturity. Although Israel's faith in the Exodus narrative is displayed as fluctuating, the overall picture of Israel's faith in the wilderness can be understood as a process of knowing who God was, namely a progressive development through the fluctuation in Israel's faith in history.[17]

Then Moses led Israel from the Red Sea and they went into the Desert of Shur (Exod 15:22). *The whole Israelite community set out from Elim and came to the Desert of Sin* (Exod 16:1). *The whole Israelite community set out from the Desert of Sin, traveling from place to place as the Lord commanded* (Exod 17:1). By providing places and landmarks, the Exodus narrative tries to make the route of Israel's journey in the wilderness clear to us (Numbers 33 lists more than forty places of encampment and setting forth). There has been difficulty in identifying the geography of some places in the wilderness, especially given the uncertainty about the locations of the names for the first stage of the Exodus route. Durham tries to offer a probable solution for the unanswered questions.

> . . . the varied and sometimes apparently conflicting information about Israel's wilderness travels must be understood as the result

17. Sheriffs categorizes Israel's faith in the books of Exodus and Numbers as high points and low points. See Sheriffs, "Moving on With God," 49–60.

of an attempt to combine into a single route the traditions of the separate travels of a number of tribal groups. The overlapping areas, the separate but synonymous designations of Exodus, Numbers, and Deuteronomy, may thus be seen to represent accurate memories that were never intended to be taken as a single route, and the major points of gathering for "the whole company of the sons of Israel" may be said to be at least four: the Red Sea, Kadesh-Barnea, Sinai/Horeb, and a ford of the Jordan River just north of the Dead Sea. Of these sites, only one can thus far be located with complete certainty: Kadesh-Barnea.[18]

Despite the fact that there is still uncertainty about some unknown places listed, recently Charles R. Krahmalkov notes that geographic lists from Egyptian temples—including two on the walls at Karnak— link remarkably well with the Exodus itinerary recorded in Numbers 33 and Joshua 15.[19] The purpose of the route of Israel's wilderness wandering is clearly stated in Exodus 13:17-18. God deliberately led them by a roundabout way rather than by way of "the land of the Philistines," which would have been nearer.

In the third month after the Israelites left Egypt—on the very day—they came to the Desert of Sinai . . . (Exod 19:1). Sinai is the place in the wilderness to which Moses asked Pharaoh to let his people go in order to worship God. In fact, it is not unreasonable to suggest that everything from the Abrahamic pilgrimage on has been leading up to the Sinai event. Immediately after the Israelites arrived at Sinai, as the culminating scene of the Exodus, God made the first divine speech to his people at Mount Sinai on this very matter of the relationship between God and Israel. *I carried you on eagles' wings and brought you to myself. Now if you obey me fully and keep my covenant, you shall be my own treasured possession . . . you will be for me a kingdom of priests and a holy nation* (Exod 19:4-6). Here the reason for the journey to Sinai offers the most profound theological interpretation of pilgrimage: "I brought you to myself." The mountain is not the destination of the Exodus. The destination of the journey was bringing the Israelites to God himself. God was the focus and the goal of the Exodus to which the whole physical journey, namely walking, was directed. Like the patriarchs' narratives, the whole exodus story was about journeying and what happened on the

---

18. Durham, *Exodus*, 218.
19. See Krahmalkov, "Exodus Itinerary Confirmed," 55–79.

way. The physical journey, therefore, was the outward visible procedure in which God brought about his providence. *When you have brought forth the people out of Egypt, you will worship God on this mountain* (Exod 3:12). The call of Moses was to bring the people to God. Now the experience of Moses at the burning bush became that of the whole community at Sinai. God's presence as a reality accompanied the Israelites from the beginning of the journey. The pillar of cloud and fire was a divine demonstration of God's presence. However, the Israelites had not entered into a full relationship with God until they had experienced the covenant-making occasion at Sinai.

Moses led the people out of the camp to meet with God, and they stood at the foot of the mountain. Mount Sinai was covered with smoke, because the Lord descended on it in fire (Exod 19:17–18). The imagery is even more explicit in Exodus 24:17 and in Deuteronomy 4:11–12. *Now the Presence of the Lord appeared in the sight of the Israelites as a consuming fire on the top of the mountain* (Exod 24:17). . . . *While it blazed with fire to the very heavens, with black clouds and deep darkness. Then the Lord spoke to you out of the fire. You heard the sound of words but saw no form: there was only a voice* (Deut 4:11–12). God's promise to Abraham in Genesis 12:2 to make him a great nation finally came into shape. As a treasured possession, a kingdom of priests and a holy nation (Exod 19:5–6), the Israelites underwent a great national theophany. God enabled the chosen nation to have knowledge of him. What is striking about this theophany is that it made knowing "who God is" a basic and conditioning element in the existence of Israel as a nation (the covenant between Israel and God was based on "knowing who God is"). Walther Eichrodt offers an expansion of this point.

> . . . it must be noted that the establishment of a covenant through the work of Moses especially emphasizes one basic element in the whole Israelite experience of God, namely *the factual nature of the divine revelation*. God's disclosure of himself is not grasped speculatively, not expounded in the form of a lesson; it is as he breaks in on the life of his people in his dealing with them and moulds them according to his will that he grants them knowledge of his being.[20]

As the pilgrimage that the fathers underwent became the chosen nations at the Exodus and in the wilderness, the theophany that the fa-

---

20. Eichrodt, *Theology of the Old Testament*, 37.

thers experienced became the chosen nations at Sinai but without an intermediary. On their journeys the fathers had knowledge of God by encountering him in various ways. God started the same process to the gathered community by a divine appearance. However, the Israelites trembled because thunder, lightening, the trumpet sound, and smoking of the mountain accompanied the divine presence. *Moses said to the people, "Do not be afraid. God has come to test you, so that the fear of God will be with you to keep you from sinning"* (Exod 20:20). This fear of the Lord is presented again in Exodus 20:20. The fear of the Lord provides the key to interpreting the journey that Abraham and the community traveled. For the fear of the Lord was the byproduct of the divine encounter with God as the main feature of the pilgrimage experience. One further essential feature of the pilgrimage experience was divine teaching. God came down in fire upon the mountain and spoke the Ten Commandments. In addition to the Ten Commandments, God gave the Israelites numerous other laws at Mount Sinai. It is noticeable that the Ten Commandments were received after the pilgrimage to the holy mountain of God. *Then Moses led the people out of the camp to meet with God, and they stood at the foot of the mountain* (Exod 19:17). The numerous other laws, the book of the covenant, are concerned with ordering a wide range of daily life, from sexual ethics (22:19), to care of the disadvantaged (22:21–27), to worship calendars (23:14–17), and to loyalty to Yahweh (20:23). As a whole, their function is woven into the Ten Commandments, drawing out the implications of the Ten Commandments.

According to Exodus 23:14–17, 34:22–23, Leviticus 23:10–36, and Deuteronomy 16:16, pilgrimage was to be made three times a year. *Three times a year you are to celebrate a festival to me . . . Three times a year all men are to appear before the Sovereign Lord* (Exod 23:14, 17). The three major festivals were associated with the agricultural harvest calendars: the Feast of Unleavened Bread in the spring took place at the time of the cereal (barley) harvest, the late spring/early summer Festival of Weeks occurred seven weeks later at the time of the wheat harvest, and the Festival of Booths in the early autumn happened at the time of the harvest of summer fruit. *No one is to appear before me empty-handed* (Exod 23:15). Each pilgrimage feast required tithes and sacrificial gifts, drawn from crops and livestock; this was the occasion of great joy (Isa 9:2; 16:9–10). Although most of the information regarding the three festivals derives from post-biblical sources, the Exodus narrative confirms that the three festival pilgrimages associating particular harvests with events celebrated from Israel's tradition, became religious at Mount Sinai.[21] As von Rad has commented: "The recognition of a close relationship between the Sinai narrative and a cultic ceremony carries us a great step forward."[22]

When the people saw that Moses was so long in coming down from the mountain they gathered around Aaron and said, "Come, make us gods who will go before us . . . He took what they handed him and made it into an idol cast in the shape of a calf . . ." (Exod 32:1–4). This golden calf incident casts a doubt about the Israelites' Yahwism. In fact, the sense of uniqueness concerning God amounts to a monotheistic faith, namely faith in the one true God, throughout. The Israelites, therefore, had a sense of uniqueness concerning God at an early stage of the Exodus. It was demonstrated in the Song Moses and the Israelites sang after the great power the Lord had displayed (Exod 15), expressing their fear of the Lord, after encountering the theophany at Mount Sinai (Exod 20). Their perception of the God they worshiped, however, was probably still on a primitive level. The golden calf incident clearly demonstrates that the Israelites failed to see the Lord as the one true God at this stage. They might have seen God as one who existed amongst many. Thus the Israelites' understanding of God at this stage might be defined as "incipient monotheism."[23] Although it is, as mentioned before, not possible to trace Israel's faith in the wilderness as a progression from an elementary faith to maturity, it might be correct to say that in terms of her perception concerning God it was gradual and progressive. He who had delivered Israel out of Egypt with mighty power, and who had revealed his character to Israel, was the one true God. H. H. Rowley rightly points out that Israel's monotheism came therefore through the progressive perception of the character and being of the God she worshiped.[24] Rowley also claims that the Israelites' monotheism was as truly personal as our own.[25] However, that point misses the fact that the Exodus was

---

21. See M. Smith, *Pilgrimage Pattern*, 52, on pilgrimage in ancient Israel.

22. Von Rad, *Problem of the Hexateuch*, 21.

23. Some have sought to coin a suitable expression by which to define the particular Israelite understanding of God, such as "incipient monotheism." See Clements, *Old Testament Theology*, 73.

24. Rowley, *Re-discovery of the Old Testament*, 93.

25. Ibid.

the beginning of Israel's corporate life as God's people (this change in identity is established in God's first speech, "my people," in the opening verse [Exod 3:7]) and the covenant was given to the nation, not to individual Israelites. Jeremiah 31 certainly individualized and internalized "a new covenant" (v. 31). *Everyone will die for his own sin* (v. 30) . . . *I will put my law in their minds and write it on their hearts* (v. 33). Ezekiel confirmed this new individualization of the relation of Israel to God, proclaiming individual moral responsibility, "The soul who sins is the one who will die" (Ezek 18:3). Here Oliver O'Donovan's concept of the role of the remnant and the faithful individual is helpful.

> The individualism that is often found in the literature that faces the fact of exile is not individualism in any of its modern senses, but rather focuses on the role of the faithful individuals in conserving the "memory and hope" (undergirding their society) that can "reach out towards the prospect of restructuring." This is the point of the new covenant.[26]

Throughout the whole period of the Old Testament, this covenant with the "corporate personality" of Israel, as H. W. Robinson points out, remains the all-inclusive fact and factor, whatever the increase in the consciousness of individuality.[27] Thus, "Israelite monotheism" is better understood as corporate, not as personal. The first command of the Ten Commandments teaches what the Israelites' monotheism was all about. As a new mode of social existence along with God, the Ten Commandments were received on making a pilgrimage to the holy mountain of God and presented the foundational layer for those who make pilgrimage with God.[28] Sheriffs points out that:

> In choosing this new God who is dangerously jealous and radically compassionate, the peasant community always found it had also chosen a new mode of social existence along with the new God. This God may not be chosen apart from a particular social existence.[29]

---

26. J. Gordon McConville cites O'Donovan. See McConville, *Deuteronomy*, 433.

27. H. W. Robinson, *Corporate Personality*, 51.

28. For use of the phrase, "social existence along with God," in depicting the Ten Commandments, see Sheriffs, *Friendship of the Lord*, 85.

29. Sheriffs cites key terms from Brueggemann. See Sheriffs, *Friendship of the Lord*, 85.

The foundational layer is woven into a theophany at Mount Sinai. *I am the LORD your God, who brought you out of the land of Egypt, out of the house of slavery; you shall have no other gods before me* (Exod 20:2). This command sums up so much that is central in the Old Testament. He proclaimed himself Israel's God, wanting to journey with Israel and expecting Israel's response to Yahweh's coming in past and present. His longing to be with his chosen nation was enhanced by instructing her to build the tabernacle. In the Exodus narrative Sinai was the destination of their journey from the Exodus point of view. The Israelites could not go further than Sinai. Mount Sinai became the most holy place called "the mountain of God." However, the tabernacle became the portable Mount Sinai as the powerful visual symbol of God's presence. Exactly nine months after the Israelites arrived at Mount Sinai, the tabernacle was constructed and took its place in the midst of the camp (Exod 33:7–23). The tabernacle was filled with the glory of Yahweh. The final chapter of the Exodus narrative mentions journey, focusing on the tabernacle with its powerful visual symbols of God's presence. *So the tabernacle was set up on the first day . . . Then the cloud covered the Tent of Meeting, and the glory of the Lord filled the tabernacle . . . In all the travels of the Israelites, whenever the cloud lifted from above the tabernacle, they would set out . . . So the cloud of the Lord was over the tabernacle by day, and fire was in the cloud by night, in the sight of all the house of Israel during all their travels* (Exod 40:34–38). Therefore, the end of the Exodus is not just the end of the story but the beginning of a new journey. It was God who made the promise to Abraham. It was God who brought the people to this mountain. With his presence before his people God was now in charge of their new journey. He was with them in their midst every step of the way, protecting and guiding them. God determined the journeys of the Israelites by oral communication. *The whole Israelite community set out from the Desert of Sin, traveling from place to place as the Lord commanded* (Exod 17:1). This is also the case in Leviticus 24:12 and in Numbers 3:16, 39, 51; 4:37, 41, 45, 49; 13:3; 33:2, 38; and 36:5. However, the journey of Israel was determined by the rising and setting of the cloud of the tabernacle in Exodus 40:34–38. Though its primary destination was still God himself (Exod 19:4), the promised land somehow eclipsed by Mount Sinai in the Exodus narrative, was set forth as the destination. Thus Israel's journey, which continued through the book of Numbers, was a movement towards the fulfillment of a promised goal, with all the problems faced along the way. Numbers traces the journey from Sinai (Num 1:1—10:10) through the wilderness (Num 10:11—21:35) to the plains of Moab east of the Jordan (Num 22–36). *Then the Israelites set out from the Desert of Sinai and traveled from place to place until the cloud came to rest in the Desert of Paran* (Num 10:12). *At the Lord's command Moses recorded the stages in their journey. This is their journey by stages* (Num 33:2). From the beginning of the Exodus the Israelites were not observers of the journey but participants in it. The journey initiated community continued as far as the wilderness of Paran. Providing more than forty places of encampment and setting forth, Numbers 33 describes the route of Israel's wilderness journey in great detail. Because of the difficulty of identifying the geography of some places in the wilderness, there has been a great deal of inconclusive debate among the commentators as to where most of these places are located. Among them, Martin Noth offers a suggestion that some of the places mentioned may have been an Israelites' "pilgrimage route" from Sinai to Canaan.[30]

Despite the fact that there is still uncertainty about some unknown places listed, recently, Krahmalkov noted that geographic lists from Egyptian temples—including two on the walls at Karnak—match remarkably well with the Exodus itinerary recorded in Numbers 33 and Joshua 15, concluding that the Israelites' invasion route described in Numbers 33:45b–50 was in fact an official, heavily trafficked Egyptian road through the Transjordan in the late Bronze Age.[31] Krahmalkov concludes that this archaeological discovery indicates that the places mentioned in the biblical accounts did in fact exist at the time, and if the biblical writers in these stories knew so well what they were talking about, the writers of other biblical accounts of the conquest also knew what they were talking about.[32] However this may be, the itinerary of the wilderness wanderings reminded generations of Israelites who God was and what he had done for his people, as they looked back at Israel's journey as a homeless people constantly on the march. However, the wilderness wanderings might have been, as Bruggemann pointed out, a surprise to Israel in terms of landlessness, for that was not the promise of Exodus.[33] Particularly when wilderness wandering lasted for years,

30. Noth, *Exodus*, 242–46.
31. See Krahmalkov, "Exodus Itinerary Confirmed," 55–79.
32. Ibid., 62.
33. Brueggemann, *Land*, 28.

the wilderness was no longer about a place but a state of mind. The Israelites grumbled. *Now the people complained about their hardship in their hearing of the Lord . . .* (Num 11:1). *How long will this wicked community grumble against me? I have heard the complaints of these grumbling Israelites* (Num 14:27). *Your children will be shepherds here for forty years, suffering for your unfaithfulness . . .* (Num 14:33). We note that although the wilderness narrative in Numbers (Num 10:11—25:18) is similar in form and content to that in Exodus 15-18, Numbers indicates that after Sinai the failure was punished. The golden calf apostasy might be an explanation for the reason. The golden calf incident (Exod 32:1-4) clearly demonstrates that the Israelites failed to see the Lord as the one true God at this stage. They might have seen God as one that existed amongst many. If this was the case, it was probable that God would have wanted to challenge their primitive-level perception of him. Trials and punishments Israel underwent in the wilderness wandering could be understood as part of the challenging process. Wilderness was not simply a desert that made the journey longer. It was a space that shaped their identity as the people of God. This identity did not come easily for Israel or for God. God trained Israel through trials and punishments.[34] Were the forty years' wandering in the wilderness a punishment for Israel? Von Rad sees the wandering in the wilderness as the time when the relationship was at its fairest, the time of the first love of Jahweh and Israel.[35] Bruggemann brings out the point that the wilderness and Yahweh belong to each other.

> As Yahweh's presence transforms wilderness, so wilderness suggests the peculiar mode and parameters of Yahweh's presence . . . it is also the place where Yahweh is present with and to his people. Israel characteristically "looked to the wilderness" and there discerns his inscrutable presence.[36]

It is no wonder that Deuteronomy draws the bold conclusion, "You lacked nothing."[37] *The Lord your God has blessed you in all the work of*

---

34. This perspective emerging from a view of the wilderness period as God's presence and discipline (testing and trial) is surely a perspective on pilgrimage experience the Lord Jesus Christ intended to teach his disciples on the way to Jerusalem.

35. Von Rad, *Old Testament Theology*, 281–82.

36. Brueggemann, *Land*, 43.

37. Ibid., 28–44. Brueggemann brings this out well in his chapter headed "You Lacked Nothing."

your hands. He has watched over your journey through this vast desert. These forty years the Lord your God has been with you, and you have not lacked anything (Deut 2:7). *During the forty years that I led you through the desert, your clothes did not wear out, nor did the sandals on your feet. You ate no bread and drank no wine or other fermented drink. I did this so that you might know that I am the Lord your God* (Deut 29:5–6). Deuteronomy also confirms the *knowing God motif* as the key experience for the Israelites as previously seen in the Abrahamic and Jacob narratives and in Exodus. At the bank of the Jordan, Deuteronomy reviews the wilderness wandering as a journey that made the Israelites come to the stage of acknowledgement that the Lord was God and that there was no one besides him. Deuteronomy affirms the oneness of God. *Hear, O Israel: The Lord our God, the Lord is one. Love the Lord your God with all your heart and with all your soul and with all your strength* (Deut 6:4–5). The discussion about whether Deuteronomy is monotheistic in the strict sense requires very careful attention. As Ronald Clements sees it, it affirms that there is only one Yahweh, but it does not make any categorical denial that other deities with other names exist (their existence is clearly assumed in Deuteronomy 32:9).[38] If the oneness of God here is not quite monotheistic in the strict sense, although it comes close to it, it might be better understood in the context of his relationship with Israel. As God's oneness is conceived in relational terms, the oneness of Yahweh the God of Israel could approximate to a concept of the one true God that has been fabricated from the Abrahamic narrative. The above suggestion is made convincing in the light of numerous translations of the six words of the Shema (v. 4).

> C. H. Gordon has suggested, "Yahweh is our God, Yahweh is 'One'" (*JNES* 29 [1970] 198). The late M. Dahood translated the whole verse as follows: "Obey, Israel, Yahweh. Yahweh our God is the Unique" (*RSP* I [1972] ~61), 5. D. McBride rendered it: "Our God is Yahweh, Yahweh alone!" (*Int* 27 [19731 274]).[39]

J. Gordon McConville also proposes four possible translations, suggesting that the oneness, which is part of God's nature, is better understood as unity or integrity.

---

38. Clements, *Deuteronomy*, 50.

39. Duane Christensen quotes from various sources. See Christensen, *Deuteronomy 1–11*, 143.

Pilgrimage as a Paradigm for the People of God 63

> 1. The Lord is our God, the Lord alone. 2. The Lord our God, the Lord is one. 3. The Lord is our God, the Lord is one. 4. The Lord our God is one Lord.[40]

Clements's conclusion is quite appropriate in relation to Israel.

> The entire context of the affirmation in Deut 6:5 makes it clear that Yahweh is superior to all other gods in his power and his love. It is made absolutely plain that there is no other god like him, even if it is not stated that there is no other God. In many respects it is this bold claim that marks the most important feature of monotheism so far as the Bible is concerned; hence it has often been described as a form of practical monotheism.[41]

When these people describe God as "our" God, such a call indicates that Israel's identity as a nation is inseparably linked to God himself. It is for this reason that the oneness of God is followed up with the relational prime point, "Love the Lord your God with all your heart and with all your soul and with all your strength" (Deut 6:5). There is also an emphasis on "walking in his ways" and keeping his commands. *See I set before you today life and prosperity, death and destruction. For I command you today to love the Lord your God, to walk in his ways, and to keep his commands, decrees and laws . . .* (Deut 30:15).

The Israelites, whose journey had begun in Egypt, passed through Kadesh and the wilderness to Moab, and about to move on to Canaan, were asked for a wholehearted commitment to God's will. The call of Deuteronomy to choose between life and death involves an inseparable covenant commitment by loving the Lord, walking in his ways, and keeping the commandments.[42] Walking in his ways means living obediently, keeping the commandments as a response of loving the Lord our God. Thus J. Gary Millar suggests that Deuteronomy builds on the concept of Israel's ethical journey.[43] In fact the term "ethical" requires discussion, for in terms of Israel's relationship with God and the knowing God motif, "being ethical" does not properly represent Israel's faith journey. From Deuteronomy's point of view, the journey, the physical act

---

40. McConville, *Deuteronomy*, 140–41.
41. Clements, *Deuteronomy*, 50.
42. This calling matches the call of Jesus for people to follow him.
43. Millar, *Now Choose Life*, 78.

of walking, is combined with its spiritual and metaphorical nuances.[44] This "journey" means more than a simple transition from bad behavior by keeping the commandments. In particular, Deuteronomy 30:15 closely links "life" to the walking metaphor, calling on Israel to choose life. Thus the "journey," as Millar sees it, becomes "a pregnant metaphor for life with Yahweh" and a necessary process to choose life with God.[45] Sheriffs comments that:

> The widespread distribution and adaptability of the "walking" metaphor within the Bible and outside it suggests that the whole complex of associated metaphors of life journey, path, and body-movement is a basic human way of interpreting our passage through time.[46]

We also note that the journey for Israel is inseparably linked to the land as a divine gift to the nation. At the bank of the Jordan the journey of Israel reaches its climax, facing the promised land, Canaan. *They are not just idle words for you—they are your life. By them you will live long in the land you are crossing the Jordan to possess* (Deut 32:47). For the Israelites as a nation on the move, "a life of obedience is life on the move towards the land."[47] Deuteronomy makes it very clear that it is a matter of life and death. As the destination of the journey was bringing the Israelites to God himself (Exod 19:4), God was life itself to the Israelites. *For the Lord is your life* (Deut 30:20). Life lies ahead of those who move forward to the promised land. Death lies ahead of those who return to Egypt. Life belongs to those taking a journey with God or walking in his ways. Deuteronomy clearly indicates that the journey for Israel was an important dynamic element in living as the people of God. Thus, journey as a core metaphor of life also becomes "a model for ongoing life in the land."[48]

---

44. It is noted that the "follow" and "walk" metaphor in the New Testament originated in the Old Testament. The NT develops a concept of discipleship in terms of a change of heart (lifestyle) and community, using phrases such as "follow me" (Mark 2:14), "walk by the spirit" (Gal 5:16, Rom 6:4, 8:4), and "walk in the light" (1 John 1:6–8).

45. Millar, *Now Choose Life*, 73.

46. Sheriffs, *Friendship of the Lord*, 111.

47. Millar, *Now Choose Life*, 73.

48. Ibid., 75.

Although the journey was not yet finished, the crossing of the Jordan was as momentous as the Exodus experience in terms of the promise about to be fulfilled. Finally, Israel came to the land. As Israel occupied it, the key places conquered were precisely the stopping places that are cited in the account of Abram and Jacob's travel. There is a parallel. *Then Joshua sent them off, and they went to the place of ambush and lay in wait between Bethel and Ai, to the west of Ai—but Joshua spent that night with the people* (Josh 8:9). *From there he went on toward the hills east of Bethel and pitched his tent, with Bethel on the west and Ai on the east. There he built an altar of the Lord* (Gen 12:8). When Abraham entered the land of Canaan, he journeyed at first as far as Shechem, and subsequently up to Ai-Bethel. Jacob followed the same route. *Jacob . . . arrived safely at the city of Shechem in Canaan . . . There he set up an altar and called it El Elohe Israel* (Gen 33:18–20). Immediately after the capture of Ai, Joshua also went up to Shechem and built an altar. *Then Joshua built an altar on Mount Ebal an altar to the Lord* (Josh 8:30). Joshua gained control over the line Ai-Bethel-Shechem. These key places mentioned are, as Cassuto sees it, not only coincidental, but also clearly have a specific motive.

> According to this tradition the token was first given to Abram and afterwards repeated to Jacob, and the significance of the duplication is to corroborate and ratify . . . the possession of the land gained in the days of Joshua was already implied, in essence, in the symbolic conquest that the first patriarchs had effected in their time, and that it was all predestined and foretold from the beginning in accordance with the Lord's will. It remains to add that the two places discussed were not only considered key points geographically, but also as religious centers of the Canaanite population. Hence the proclamation by Abram of the name of ה' YHWH at these places signifies the proclamation of the supremacy of ה' YHWH, the God of Abram, over the gods of Canaan.[49]

As such, in the context of a journey, Abrahamic pilgrimage, which had guaranteed the promised land, became the overarching structure in which the journey of Israel from the book of Exodus to Joshua was embraced.

---

49. Cassuto, *Commentary on the Book of Genesis*, 2:306.

EXILE, RESTORATION, AND JERUSALEM

Exile

The Israelites were a pilgrim people on their way to the land that God had promised (Deut 12:9; 25:19). They had not yet reached their destination. Since Israel's inception, the destination of her journey was God himself (Exod 19:4). This truth for Israel was not limited only to their journey from Egypt to Canaan. In the new land of promise and fulfillment the Israelites would discover that they did not inherit what God had promised. Until the Israelites realized the fact that God was the destination of their journey, their pilgrimage had to continue. Whenever Israel turned away from God, here enemies surrounded her. Israel felt the need for a king and centralized government. The people thought that in having a king like other nations (1 Sam 8:5) they had the solution to their problems. A monarchy in Israel meant that the nation had to pay a high price with taxes and forced service of the state (1 Sam 8:11–18). The emergence of a state required centralization and the building of the temple. For Israel the tabernacle had become the powerful visual symbol of God's presence in the wilderness period.

The tabernacle or tent, according to 1 Chronicles 21:29 and 2 Chronicles 1:3, found a home on the high place at Gibeon.[50] After the entry of the Israelites into Canaan, the ark appeared at Shiloh (1 Sam 3), was captured by the Philistines (1 Sam 4), and eventually arrived at Jerusalem (2 Sam 6). During the wilderness wanderings, the ark went before Israel on her journey (Num 10:33–34). Thus the ark became the Alpha and Omega of the journey for Israel. For Israel nothing was more intimately connected with the presence and power of God than the ark. Since Israel, as von Rad puts it, thought of the ark as the throne of Yahweh, for her "wherever the Ark is, Jahweh is always present."[51] Walter Kaiser, after considering six possibilities for what the ark signified, considers that the most plausible explanation is a pledge of God's presence, a presence not automatic, nor mechanical.[52] This thinking about the ark is traced in 1 Samuel 4:1—7:2.

---

50. Eichrodt claims that this information, in spite of it only occurring in a late source, possesses a high degree of intrinsic probability. See Eichrodt, *Theology of the Old Testament*, 111.

51. Von Rad, *Old Testament Theology*, 237.

52. Was the ark (1) a witness to that presence, (2) a guarantee of Yahweh's presence,

Let us bring the ark of the Lord's covenant from Shiloh, so that it may be with us and save us from the hand of our enemies . . . So the Philistines fought, and Israelites were defeated . . . The ark of God was captured (1 Sam 4:3, 10, 11). The circuitous journey of the ark to Jerusalem began when the Philistines defeated sinful Israel twice. The covenant people lost to the Philistines at the first clash. The elders responded by sending to Shiloh for the ark. Israel believed that as long as the ark, the emblem of divine presence, was with them, they were safe. In spite of having the ark, Israel lost again to the Philistines at the second clash. This time the ark was captured. The equation, the ark = God's presence = victory, no longer applied. Thus for Israel, defeat with the ark would be even more devastating than defeat without the ark. The devastating defeat was as Brueggemann understands the event, "a much more urgent theological crisis in Israel."[53] For defeat and capture of the ark by the Philistines suggested that the God of Israel had abandoned his people. The ark was the medium through which God led Israel in her wanderings and in war (Num 10:33, 35; 1 Sam 4:3; 2 Sam 11:11).

After the settlement in Canaan, this concept of God's guidance and presence in the midst of his people is inseparably connected with the holy places where the ark stayed. Von Rad considers that there are many allusions, which suggest that cultic location connected to every town at which the inhabitants offered sacrifice to Jahweh (1 Sam 9:11–14; 16:5).[54] A permanent temple building was erected in Shiloh (1 Sam 1).[55] The erection of the temple in Jerusalem followed and this location became inseparably connected with the ark. It seemed that most of Israel continued to make pilgrimages to regional and national shrines or the central sanctuary. Bethel (1 Sam 10:3) is also mentioned as a regional shrine for pilgrims in the pre-monarchic period. Based on his study of the Pentateuch, Noth includes Shechem and the site of Sinai as pre-monarchic pilgrimage sites.[56] What identifies these places for pilgrimage

---

(3) a pledge or earnest of his presence, (4) a domicile of the Deity, (5) identical with Yahweh, or (6) an extension and representation of his presence? See Kaiser, *Toward an Old Testament Theology*, 159.

53. Brueggemann, *First and Second Samuel*, 32.

54. Von Rad, *Old Testament Theology*, 21.

55. This was the place where a light burned continually (1 Sam 3:3) and where an oracle could always be obtained by incubation (1 Sam 3:2; 1 Kgs 3:5).

56. Noth, *Pentateuchal Traditions*, 80–81, 83, 85, 138, 199, 221.

was that they were places where God had revealed his will to his people. Therefore, Eichrodt points out the character of the sacred localities as places not where Yahweh dwells, but where he manifests himself.[57] However, von Rad denies any daily significance for the ark on the daily experiences of Israel. He claims that the Jahweh who sat enthroned upon the ark was at first only of limited significance for the everyday concerns of the Israelite farmer.[58] Nevertheless, von Rad acknowledges that the tent was the focal point of a group of worshipers.[59] However, von Rad contradicts himself, for the ark was the focal point of the tent and Israel was a worshiping community. Pilgrimages to regional and national shrines or the central sanctuary were for Israelites the time to confirm their identity as the people of God. The God who sat enthroned upon the ark was probably of limited significance for the everyday concerns of the Israelite farmer, but not for the everyday spiritual concern of the Israelites.[60]

Uriah said to David, "The ark and Israel and Judah are staying in tents, and my master Joab and my lord's men are camped in the open fields. How could I go to my house to eat and drink and lie with my wife?" (2 Sam 11:11). Uriah's response to David's ploy indicates well that his sense of priority was religiously based with the ark and it is particularly noted that he identified the ark with Israel and Judah. Eichrodt accepts the possibility that the veneration of the ark of God was the effect of the wave of Canaanite influence.[61] Yet, his argument is not that convincing. Since the ark of God was the milestone of Israel's journey into Canaan and the confirmation of the presence and power of God, it is not surprising that the veneration of the ark of God came into being after conquering Canaan. Canaanite influence might have offered a helpful environment, but it was not the cause of the practice.

They set the ark of God on a new cart and brought it from the house of Abinadab . . . David and the whole house of Israel were celebrating with all their might before the Lord, with songs and with harps, lyres, tam-

---

57. Eichrodt, *Theology of the Old Testament*, 103.
58. Von Rad, *Old Testament Theology*, 21.
59. Ibid.
60. For this claim von Rad assumes that partial and local obligations, such as the annual sacrifice, at which kinsmen met (1 Sam 20:6, 29; 2 Sam 15:7, 11f) had greater importance for Israel than Jahwism. See von Rad, *Old Testament Theology*, 21.
61. Eichrodt, *Theology of the Old Testament*, 105.

bourines, sistrums, and cymbals (2 Sam 6:3–5). Almost twenty years had passed since the ark was placed in Abinadab's house (1 Sam 7:1). It is quite probable that by "bringing the ark into Jerusalem," David achieved the beneficial presence of the ark, which could make Jerusalem the focal point of Israelite religion.[62] Since the ark had some religious significance for the northern tribes too, bringing the ark into Jerusalem made the whole of Israel look to David and the city. Birch describes a possible situation at that time.

> David was faced with the problem of locating his capital. He could not afford to show favouritism to either the Judean or the Israelite groups that had made him king. Jerusalem was located on the boundary between Judah and Benjamin and was now the literal city of David, belonging to none of the Israelite tribal groups. It has been suggested by many scholars that with Jerusalem David gained not only a politically neutral capital but an urban Canaanite (Jebusite) center with many of the scribes, tradesmen, architects, and managers necessary to establishing a full-scale monarchy and its attendant bureaucracy.[63]

Contra this idea, A. Anderson argues that if, as is very likely, the Perez-Uzzah etiology (2 Sam 6:3–8) was part of the original narrative, then the implication is that the choice of Jerusalem as the ark's resting place must have been part of Yahweh's plan and not simply a stroke of David's political genius.[64] The ark narrative as a whole shows the two sides of the coin, disaster and blessing, supporting Anderson's view. The ark brought with it disaster for Eli and his sons (1 Sam 4), the Israelites forces (1 Sam 4), the Philistines (1 Sam 5), and the people of Bethshemesh (1 Sam 6). Yet the ark also brought with it blessing for the house of Obed-edom (2 Sam 6: 11) and David. Because of the double-sided effect of the ark, David was not certain whether to bring the ark into Jerusalem following Uzziah's death. The ark stayed for three months at Obed-edom's house. The Lord showed his willingness to let the ark be moved by blessing Obed-edom's family (2 Sam 6:11–14). At last the ark reached its destination. This ark narrative strongly points out that God himself had chosen Jerusalem.

---

62. Eugene Merrill suggests that the Davidic procession provided impetus to the Psalms designated "song of Zion" (Pss 46, 48, 76, 84, 87, 122, 132). See Merrill, "Pilgrimage and Procession," 263–64.

63. Birch et al., *Theological Introduction*, 238.

64. A. Anderson, *2 Samuel*, 100.

They brought the ark of the Lord and set it in its place inside the tent that David had pitched for it, and David sacrificed burnt offerings . . . (2 Sam 6:17). The ark was set "in its place" inside the tent. The expression "in its place" has caused some debate. It is possible that there was already an existing Jebusite shrine or sanctuary.[65] If so, then "in its place" might, as some have suggested, allude to a Jebusite shrine or sanctuary. However, considering the whole context of the ark narrative, Anderson is possibly right in saying that "in its place רֶשׁ חֲלֻשְׁמִצְּרַצּ תִּסְעַמוֹ בִּמְקֹו" may refer to 1 Samuel 5:11 where the Philistines send the ark away that it might return "to its place לִמְקָ רֶשׁ חֲלֻשְׁמִצְּרַצּ תִּסְעַמוֹ." This was finally achieved with the transfer of the ark to the city of David.[66] With the ark, Jerusalem was beginning to be established as the focal point of Israelite religion and was becoming the only holy site for which the Israelites were to make pilgrimage.

After the king was settled in his place and the Lord had given him rest from all his enemies around him, he said to Nathan the prophet, "Here I am, living in a place of cedar, while the ark of God remains in a tent.". . . That night the word of the Lord came to Nathan, saying,". . . I have not dwelt in a house from the day I brought the Israelites up out of Egypt to this day. I have been moving from place to place with a tent as my dwelling. Wherever I have moved with all the Israelites, did I ever say to any of their rulers whom I commanded to shepherd my people Israel, "Why have you not built me a house of cedar?". . . I will raise up your offspring to succeed you . . . He is the one who will build a house for my name . . . (2 Sam 7:1–13).

David the king longed to build a house for God. Through Nathan the prophet, God responded that he had never needed such a house but had been content with a tent and a tabernacle. There are various approaches on this matter. H. G. May considers that the ark was a miniature temple.[67] Roland De Vaux suggests that Nathan's attitude may have perpetuated the tradition of "the tent of meeting" which represented a "manifestation theology."[68] Some scholars, including Birch, note that the text here reflects the tension in Israel between the freedom of God

---

65. For this point Anderson quotes Rowley's "Zadok and Nehushtan," and Rupprecht's *Der Tempel von Jerusalem*. See A. Anderson, *2 Samuel*, 106.

66. Ibid.

67. May, "Miniature Temple," 222–27.

68. De Vaux, "Jerusalem and the Prophets," 302.

expressed in the mobility of the ark and tent, and the fixity (even the possession) of God represented in a temple, which was associated with Canaanite religion.[69] Birch's note makes the most sense. *I have not dwelt in a house from the day I brought the Israelites up out of Egypt to this day. I have been moving from place to place with a tent as my dwelling* (2 Sam 7:5–7). God led his people in the context of a journey. God preferred to remain as the pilgrim God with his pilgrim people. That might explain why God did not desire a house (2 Sam 7:7). However, God promised David that the son who would reign after him would build a temple for the Lord (2 Sam 7:13). Nevertheless, it was David who not only made the Jebusite city the capital of the two kingdoms, Judah and Israel, but also at the same time made it the place of the invisible presence of God by having the ark brought to Jerusalem. *I have indeed built a magnificent temple for you, a place for you to dwell forever* (1 Kgs 8:13). Solomon built God's temple as a lasting habitation for the Lord. Jerusalem as a whole was "the city of God, which the Most High has made his dwelling" (Ps 46:4).[70] The Lord has chosen Jerusalem desiring it for his resting-place. *This is my resting-place forever* (Ps 132:13–14). Thus Israel began to view Jerusalem as God's holy habitation and the capital of God's kingdom. It is, as Anderson points out, very likely that the transfer of the ark to the city of David became an annual event.[71] No doubt, of all the pilgrimage sites such as Dan, Bethel, Gilgal, and Beer-sheba, with the ark and the central sanctuary built by Solomon, Jerusalem finally became the center of national pilgrimages.[72] Eugene Merrill offers a probable linkage with the ancient Near Eastern world:

> Just as the suzerain-vassal treaties of the ancient Near Eastern world stipulated that the vassal kings make regular journeys to the city of the great king to return their homage and reaffirm their loyalty, so the Mosaic Covenant texts spelled out the need for Israel's representatives to present themselves before YHWH

---

69. Birch et al., *Theological Introduction*, 238.

70. Richard Clifford notes that the symbol of Jerusalem as a mountain for the divine dwelling reflects a common ancient Near Eastern idea. See Clifford, *Cosmic Mountain in Canaan*, 131–60.

71. A. Anderson, *2 Samuel*, 108.

72. The national shrines in Dan and Bethel built in the Northern Kingdom by Jeroboam I were also national pilgrimages (1 Kgs 12:28–30). Bethel, Gilgal, and Beer-sheba are known to have been destinations of pilgrimage shrines in the time of Amos (Amos 5:4–6).

as an act of corporate or community affirmation that YHWH was the God of Israel and Israel was the people of YHWH.[73]

Those who trust in the Lord are like Mount Zion, which cannot be shaken but stands fast for ever (Ps 125:1). The Lord had founded Jerusalem, how could it be shaken? Due to the presence of the Lord, the Holy City was believed to be the eternal city. Israel could believe in the invincibility of Jerusalem. In 701, Sennacherihb, the Assyrian king, invaded Judah, but withdrew from the siege of Jerusalem (2 Kgs 18–19). Though it was not the origin of it, the deliverance of Jerusalem at the last moment perhaps strengthened the concept of the inviolability of the city. The security of Jerusalem even became an image for the security of those who believed in God. Thus in the course of time Jerusalem became more and more a "religious" center as well as being a political center as the capital of the kingdom. However, it is noted that the city could become dangerous, when God's protection and blessing were restricted to a particular place. Eichrodt points to the danger of sacred sites becoming religious:

> The more emphatically a religion becomes tied to the sacred sites, the more dangerous are their inevitable effects on the idea of God and on his worship. The holy place, especially when it is also thought of as the dwelling-place of the divinity, leads to the localization of the Godhead and the limitation of his sphere of influence. Indeed, where it is a question of a number of rival cultic sites, the result is sometimes the disintegration of the divine Being into minor deities. Moreover, the cultus itself, when too much importance is attached to the precise place at which sacrifice is to be offered, tends very easily to ascribe all value and efficacy to its own procedure and so to have a prejudicial effect on the personal element in worship.[74]

Eichrodt pointed out that the occasional loss of the ark provided a counterpoise to the materialistic conception of the divine presence and the false confidence than can arise from a belief in the secure possession of the national God.[75] The fall of Jerusalem threatened the doctrine of Yahweh's commitment to the temple. Thus Jeremiah warned the Israelites against false confidence concerning the temple in Jerusalem. *This is what*

---

73. Merrill, "Pilgrimage and Procession," 262–63.
74. Eichrodt, *Theology of the Old Testament*, 103.
75. Ibid., 111.

the Lord Almighty, the God of Israel says: Reform your ways and your actions, and I will let you live in this place. Do not trust in deceptive words and say, "This is the temple of the Lord, the temple of the Lord, the temple of the Lord!"* (Jer 7:3-4). *Then Jeremiah said to all the officials and all the people: The Lord sent me to prophesy against this house and this city all the things you have heard* (Jer 26:12). The Northern Kingdom, that had resisted the ministries of Hosea and Amos who called them back to God, had been taken into captivity. The Southern Kingdom maintained a precarious existence for almost a further century and a half, insisting that the heathen could never take Jerusalem because God dwelt in the temple, and false prophets cried, "Peace! Peace!" (Jer 8:11). Jeremiah, however, declared that there was no room for complacency or peace but stressed the impending judgment upon idolatrous Judah. False prophets, whose messages only proclaimed what their hearers wanted to hear, frequently opposed Ezekiel, like they had Jeremiah (Ezek 13:1–10). The false prophets made optimistic predictions of a quick return from exile and peace when there was no peace (Ezek 13:10). Following Judah's exile, the advice of Jeremiah to the exiles in Babylon was that this return was not imminent (Jer 29:1–9).[76]

Rain will come in torrents (Ezek 13:11). Ezekiel warned of God's impending judgment by the violent thunderstorm to sweep them away. Ezekiel clearly indicates that God gave the people an opportunity to turn from their idols and live because God did not wish to leave his people. *And he said to me, "Son of man, do you see what they are doing, the great abominations that the house of Israel are committing here to drive me far from my sanctuary"* (Ezek 8:5-6). He was being driven away. As long as the covenant God made with Abraham was ignored, when God was

---

76. J. Paterson's comments on this passage deserve quotation. "For the exiles, incited by their prophets, were refusing to settle down: their only thought was of speedy return to the homeland. Their hatred of Babylon led to riots which resulted in the summary 'taking-off' of two of their most prominent and rabid prophets (22). Here Jeremiah lays a cool hand on hot heads lest by their rashness they should all perish in a pogrom in Babylon. All this is easily understood. Deuteronomy had made it impossible for a good Jew to live in an alien land. If Jerusalem be the only place where worship of Yahweh is possible, and if all life's activities such as building, planting, marrying and begetting children be associated with the religious cult, how could they escape a feeling of total frustration. For the cult was impossible in Babylon: only in Jerusalem could Yahweh be worshipped. Here Jeremiah writes to say that the world is God's world and God is not limited to Jerusalem and its Temple." Davies quotes Paterson. See W. D. Davies, *Gospel and the Land*, 37.

driven away, they had to be driven away also. *"I will stop all her celebrations: her yearly festivals, her New Moons, her Sabbath days—all her appointed feasts . . . I will punish her for the days she burned incense to the Baals . . . and went after her lovers, but me she forgot,"* declares the LORD (Hos 2:11–13). Hosea indicates that God will cancel every event related to weekly, monthly, and annual religious celebrations. No hint is given as to what means are to be used for to cause the cessation of these activities. Though the cessation of annual festivals and pilgrimages implied that Jerusalem would be taken, this was never articulated until the prophets such as Jeremiah and Ezekiel spoke unthinkable thoughts that the kings and their subjects could never face. Hosea offers the cause, her idolatry and failure to remember God, as the unthinkable thought. God who was driven away should initiate another journey, exile, for his people in order to bring them back to himself. For God claimed that he was the initiation and destination of their journey throughout the Exodus event. Isaiah particularly reinforces the point. Isaiah proclaims that the one who is returning is God himself (Isa 46:10).

Behold, the Lord God comes with might, and his arm rules for him (Isa 46:10). God who was driven away (Ezek 8:5–6) returns to Jerusalem bringing Israel with him. Ezekiel saw the Israelites arriving at Jerusalem as God coming to the Holy City. When God was driven away, they had to be driven away too. When God returns to Jerusalem, God brings Israel with him. *"The glory of the Lord departed from the threshold of the temple . . . they stopped at the entrance of to the east gate of the Lord's house"* (Ezek 10:18–19). The glory left the Holy City. So should Israel. "Exile" is that moment when the glory is gone, when Israel must learn to live without God in the world.[77] The glory hovering over the Mount of Olives shows God's reluctance to depart. Thus Ezekiel saw a glimmer of the hope of a restored Jerusalem, with a restored temple in which sacrifices would again be offered. Through the affliction of captivity, Jeremiah also saw that Israel would be prepared for a brighter future. *There is hope for your future, says the Lord, and your children shall come back to their own country* (Jer 31:17). Hope, however, was conditional on a change of heart.

You will seek me and find me when you seek me with all your heart . . . and will bring you back from captivity (Jer 29:13–14). Ezekiel also stresses the importance of the new heart and new spirit. *I will give you a new heart and put a new spirit in you . . . and move you to follow my*

---

77. Brueggemann, *Ichabod Toward Home*, 12.

decrees . . . *you will be my people and I will be your God* (Ezek 36:26–28). Paul Joyce sees "a new heart" with two senses, the heart as the locus of the moral will and as the symbol of inner reality, as distinct from mere outward appearance.[78] He also describes "a new spirit" in the moral sense.[79] It seems to be more convincing that Ezekiel 36:27 stresses the aspect of moral response: "I will put my Spirit in you and move you to follow my decrees and be careful to keep my laws." However, Joyce's interpretation conveys only one of the consequences of having a new heart and a new spirit. The meaning of the two terms could be better understood in the whole context of exile rather than as a stated statement. Since the new heart and the new spirit refers to the gift of a renewed capacity to respond to Yahweh in obedience, the gift is to come back to God by knowing who God is.[80] The formula "you will be my people and I your God" as a renewal of the Sinai covenant indicates that the new heart and the spirit are understood in a relational sense. The meaning of the two terms is more than ethical. The whole context of the exile and the concept of *walk* and *way* reinforce this understanding. The main concern of Jeremiah was the past and future *way* of his people. *This is what the Lord says: "Stand at the crossroads and look; ask for the ancient paths, ask where the good way is, and walk in it, and you will find rest for your souls. But you said, "We will not walk in it"* (Jer 6:7). For Jeremiah, he who walks on the good way obtains the rest of salvation. God's eyes were upon all the movements (ways and walking) of his people. He was able to see the movements in the heart and mind. However, Israel had prepared a way by which she brought evil upon herself. Jeremiah, therefore, appeals to his people to return to God and renew their relationship with him by walking in his ways (Jer 7:23).

I will show the holiness of my great name, which has been profaned among the nations, the name you have profaned among them. Then the nation will know that I am the Lord, declares the Sovereign Lord (Ezek 36:23). In Ezekiel God concludes the divine activity, the exile, that Israel may know that he is the Lord. God longed to be recognized as he was by his people who did not know him properly. As God had guided Abraham and Jacob in their lives throughout their journey and had led Israel as a nation to the promised land, God reversed the process, and caused them

---

78. Joyce, *Divine Initiative*, 109.

79. Ibid., 111.

80. Ibid.

to be carried away to Babylon, sojourn in Babylon, and return to the promised land, in order for his idolatrous people to know and return to him. Thus the purpose of the new heart and the new spirit was to know who God is first, not to have the moral will that is the consequence of the appreciation of who God is, so that the covenant relationship may be restored. This understanding is supported by the fact that Ezekiel, like Jeremiah, expressly envisages the judgment as a purging (Ezek 20:37-44; 22:17-31; 26:11). *I will take note of you as you pass under my rod, and I will bring you into the bond of the covenant* (Ezek 20:37). Thus Babylon as the rod in God's hand brought the people to recognize what they were and come to the acknowledgement of who he was. The divine activity, the exile, which was to chasten and train the rebellious Israel is clearly closely related to discipline, offering a ground for the discipleship paradigm within the journey theme.

Restoration and Jerusalem

The hope of bringing Israel back to the place where they belonged (Jer 29:14) became a reality. After King Cyrus of Persia conquered Babylon, he issued a decree releasing the Jews to return to their homeland. *This is what Cyrus king of Persia says: . . . Anyone of his people among you—may his God be with him, and let him go up to Jerusalem in Judah and build the temple of the Lord, the God of Israel, the God who is in Jerusalem* (Ezra 1:3). It is believed that only a small remnant longed to return. Ezra indicates that there were 42,360 free citizens, 7,337 slaves, and 200 temple singers (Ezra 2:64-65). They were the pilgrims who journeyed back to Jerusalem, eagerly anticipating the fulfillment of the prophecies of Isaiah, Jeremiah, Ezekiel, etc. The pilgrims returning to Jerusalem were crucial for Israel's continuance.

You have punished us less than our sins have deserved and have given us a remnant like this . . . While Ezra was praying and confessing, weeping and throwing himself down before the house of God, a large crowd of Israelites—men, women and children—gathered around him. They too wept bitterly (Ezra 9:13—10:1). The exile had a great impact on the faith of the people. The books of Jeremiah, Ezekiel, and Isaiah entail and reflect the crucial events of the fall of Jerusalem and the destruction of its temple. As a result, the remnant was determined not to follow the idolatry of their fathers (Ezra 9-10). The Israelites saw idolatry as the nations' besetting sin. Israeli scholar Yehezkel Kaufmann has summarized the effect of the exile upon the appreciation of Israel's monotheistic faith:

> Vestiges of an ancient fetishistic idolatry reinforced by foreign influences, continued to exist among the people down to the fall of Judah. It was the catastrophe of the Fall that aroused in the people a spirit of remorse. The pious viewed the sin of idolatry as the crucial national sin . . . The Fall worked a revolution. The nation accepted the verdict that God's wrath had poured down upon them for the sin of idolatry. And they drew the ultimate conclusion from their monotheistic faith: all traces of idol-worship must be extirpated. It was thus in the realm of the cult that the final victory of monotheism in Israel took place.[81]

Thus a journey for Israel is not just a physical movement, but also a pilgrimage of faith that encompasses "knowing God" and "obedience to God as a consequence of knowing God." In the long story of Israel from the Abrahamic pilgrimage to the return to Jerusalem from Babylon we can trace the interlocking relationship between pilgrimage as a physical movement and transformation (from a migration) into faith's pilgrimage. Since pilgrimage as physical movement is closely intertwined with God's way of transforming his people, namely, discipleship, Israel's physical journeys, the exile, and the return, are to be understood not only as "a historical or geographical note, but a theological program."[82] Von Rad observes the history of Israel from the Exodus to the return to Jerusalem as that the nation is always on pilgrimage.

> In Egypt or Babylon the only possible salvation after any political or religious disturbance of which there were many—was that the nation should return to these primeval sacral orders which found expression in myth and the cycle of the festivals: but Israel emphasized the unique character of any events that had occurred. Consequently a survey of the great movements of her history gives us the impression of a lack of repose—the nation is always on pilgrimage—and the constant emergence of new religious ideas seems to leave her a stranger in time. The impression that she was travelling along a road which could not be retraced is undoubtedly strengthened by the self-portrait drawn in her surviving literature.[83]

---

81. Kaufmann, "Biblical Age," 79.
82. Brueggemann, *Genesis*, 122.
83. Von Rad, *Old Testament Theology*, 320.

Pilgrimage as the life of faith was one that kept Israel in pursuit of the promised land. During the exilic period, Jerusalem as the center of the promised land remained its religious center, despite the destruction of the temple and the disappearance of the ark. How could this be? It was known Jerusalem was God's dwelling place. *The Lord is there* (Ezek 48:35). For Ezekiel the heart of Jerusalem is the presence of Yahweh himself. However, the presence of God was not restricted to Jerusalem only. In Jeremiah 3:16–17, Jeremiah denies the equality (the Ark of the Covenant of the Lord [the temple] = his presence), envisaging Jerusalem as the throne of Yahweh. The message is clear that the ark and the temple might pass away, yet the presence of Yahweh is the heart of the city, so that trust in God is not the same as trust in a place. Thus the prophets proclaimed the hope of restoration: the rebuilding of Jerusalem and its walls (Jer 30:18–19; 31:38–39), the glory of Yahweh returning to the Jerusalem Temple (Ezek 5:5; 38:12), and the "new Jerusalem" as the center of the nation's hope (Isa 40:1–2; 52:1, 7–8; 60–62).

The memory of the exile and the return exerted great influence upon the faith of Israel, and became, as Brueggemamn describes, "a governing paradigm for all successive Jewish faith."[84] With a surge of theological reflection upon the exile and the return, theological literature, including the book of Lamentations and part of the Psalms, expresses the rage, sadness, grief, and deep sense of loss as well as joy, praise, and thanks that were experienced through the exile and the return. As a result, the exile, in addition to the Exodus, became a dominant paradigm for Israel's faith, namely the self-understanding of Judaism or Jewishness. Thus the pilgrimage framework well embraces the two decisive events in the history of Israel.

The story of the exile and restoration puts Jerusalem in perspective. The name Jerusalem occurs 49 times in Isaiah, 102 in Jeremiah, 26 in Ezekiel, and 8 in Micah.[85] The book of Psalms brings the major

---

84. Brueggemann, *Theology of Old Testament*, 184.

85. The name Jerusalem occurs more than 650 times in the OT, frequently in the historiographies (1–2 Sam, 1–2 Kgs, Ezra, Neh, and 1–2 Chr).

elements of pilgrimage and the sense of going up that is focused on Jerusalem.[86] Jerusalem occurs particularly in the fifteen Songs of Ascent (Pss 120–134) in relation to the pilgrimage theme. In fact Michael Goulder argues that tradition mainly supports the "ascent from exile" tradition, in one form or another, and has nothing for an ordinary pilgrimage based on one of the three annual feasts.[87] Thus the heading עֲלוֹת שִׁיר לַ֫רֶשׁ הַֽמַּעֲלוֹת of Psalms 120–134, the songs of the goings up, could mean "the ascent from the exile."[88] Cuthbert Keet notes that Psalms 122 and 134 presuppose that the temple and its services are fully operative.[89] Following Keet's point, Goulder considers that the songs are the product of the "goings up" of the fifth century, and dates them in Nehemiah's time.[90] There seems to be no difficulty in accepting his suggestion.[91]

---

86. See Merrill, "Pilgrimage and Procession," 271. Merrill shows the whole picture of Psalms in relation to pilgrimage.
  a. Goal of Pilgrimage
    1. Zion/Jerusalem (Pss 84:5, 7; 122:3, 6; 125:1; 126:1; 128:5; 129:5; 132:13; 133:3; 134:3)
    2. The Temple (Pss 84:2, 10; 122:1; 116:28–25; 132:5–7)
  b. Purpose of Pilgrimage: Payment of Offerings/Vows/Tribute (Pss 116:14, 18–19; 118:27; 126:6)
  c. Universal and Scattered Origins of Pilgrimage (Ps 120:5)
  d. Path of Pilgrimage
    1. Building of the Highway (Ps 84:5)
    2. Irrigation of the Desert (Pss 84:6; 114:8)
    3. Drying of the Rivers (Ps 126:4)
    4. As an Ascent (Ps 122:4)
  e. Mode of Pilgrimage
    1. As a Stream (Ps 126:4)
    2. With Divine Protection (Pss 84:11; 113:7–9; 115:9–11; 116:6, 8; 118:5–14; 121:3–8; 124:1–3, 6, 8; 125:1–2)
    3. With Song and Rejoicing (Pss 118:15, 24; 126:5–6; 132:9)

87. Goulder, *Psalms of the Return*, 20–21. Goulder's argument is plausible, considering the statement of Cyrus king of Persia: "The Lord, the God of heaven, has given me all the kingdom of the earth and he has appointed me to build a temple for him at Jerusalem in Judah. Anyone of his people among you—may the Lord his God be with him, and let him go up" (2 Chr 36:23).

88. The wording of Psalm 121 has the slight exception שִׁיר לַ֫רֶשׁ הַֽמַּעֲלוֹת (song of/for the goings up). The ascents whereby Israel will at some future time go up from the lands of the exile to the land of Israel. See Baker and Nicholson, *Commentary of Rabbi 22*, 2–3.

89. Keet, *Psalms of Ascents*, 12.

90. Goulder, *Psalms of the Return*, 20–33.

91. If the songs stemmed from Nehemiah's time, as Goulder suggests, we should

Although all the fifteen Songs of Ascent (Pss 120–134) are not in ordinary pilgrimage form having to do with one of the three annual feasts, it is certain that such going up is characteristic of the three major festivals in Israel.[92] Thus, the whole context of the songs is certainly interwoven with the pilgrimage framework.

There is no evidence in Psalm 120 that it was written for use by pilgrims on their journey to Jerusalem. However, Psalm 121 does have the feel of a journey. Although there is no conclusive evidence of pilgrimage to Jerusalem, the journey motif is widely noted and there is no obvious difficulty in understanding Psalm 121 in the light of the context of pilgrimage. *I lift up my eyes to the hills—where does my help come from? My help comes from the Lord, the Maker of heaven and earth. He will not let your foot slip—he who watches over Israel will neither slumber nor sleep . . . The Lord will keep you from all harm—he will watch over your life; the Lord will watch over your coming and going both now and forever* (Ps 121:1–3, 8). Psalm 121 praises God who is the help of the pilgrim making a journey to the Holy City. He guards pilgrims' way and watches over their lives. Most commentators observe that Psalm 121 has two speakers, the first speaker for verses 1–2 and the second speaker for verses 3–8.[93] Having almost understood verses 7–8 as a concluding blessing, it is quite probable that the second speaker is a priest, an elder, or a national leader giving a farewell benediction to the pilgrim making his journey to Jerusalem, or perhaps leaving the temple to return

---

expect them to display some triumph in having begun to reverse the exile, and considerable devotion to Jerusalem, the newly fortified capital. Goulder offers the evidences for his claim: "Our feet are standing within thy gates, o Jerusalem (122:2); Blessed be the LORD, Who hath not given us as a prey to their teeth. Our soul is escaped as a bird out of the snare of the fowlers: The snare is broken, and we are escaped (124:7–8); When the LORD turned the fortunes of Zion, We were like unto them that dream . . . Then said they among the nations, The LORD have done great things for them." See ibid.

92. The term עלה is apparently related to the pilgrim's ascent of Mount Zion to Jerusalem for worship. However, it may also reflect the processional ascents to the temple by the pilgrims themselves in the final stage of their pilgrimage, or by the processional choirs who led the gathered pilgrims in worship and celebration (cf. 2 Sam 6:12; 1 Kgs 13:33; 2 Kgs 23:2; Neh 12:37; Ps 42:4; Isa 26:2; 30:29; Jer 31:6; Mic 4:2). Also these songs are likely to have been among those sung by the returning exiles from Babylon as they ascended the mountains to Jerusalem and home (Ezra 2:1; 7:7). Most of the songs have Jerusalem as a central focus of celebration, and the themes of unity, brotherly love, family, and prosperity of life were natural expressions of a worshiping pilgrimage community.

93. See Kirkpatrick, *Book of Psalms*, 736; Westermann, *Living Psalms*, 290.

home.[94] The psalm says that God would keep the pilgrim's "life" from all harm. The pilgrim's "going out and coming in" are under the vigilant watch of God. It may be noted that Joshua used the key term *watch* six times in the Psalms in recounting the Exodus/wilderness journey (Josh 24:17).[95] For this reason Anthony Ceresko suggests that:

> In singing this psalm, the pilgrims on the way to Jerusalem and the "house" of Yahweh would have had little difficulty in imagining themselves as reliving the Exodus experience of their ancestors who also journeyed to God's "house," (i.e., the Promised Land).[96]

I rejoiced with those who said to me, "Let us go to the house of the Lord." Our feet are standing in your gates, O Jerusalem. Jerusalem is built like a city that is closely compacted together. That is where the tribes go up, the tribes of the Lord . . . (Ps 121:1). Psalm 122 begins with the joy of a pilgrim arriving at the temple for one of the major annual festivals.[97] Sigmund Mowinckel claims that the annual pilgrim feast was the autumn festival (Tabernacles), although there is no specific indication for such an interpretation in the psalm.[98] A pilgrim might have sung this psalm at the beginning of the pilgrimage when fellow travelers had gathered (Ps 122:1b) and after they entered Jerusalem (Pss 122:2; 84:3). Psalm 122 is the song of an individual singer who has entered the area of the sanctuary. It, however, presents the corporate aspect of pilgrimage. For traveling together with others could minimize the dangers an individual traveler could face on the way. He made a pilgrimage to Jerusalem with his tribe (v. 8). The tribes may best be viewed as a term denoting clans or some other subdivision within a tribe, such us "families."[99] Psalm 122

---

94. So Gunkel, Mowinckel, Weiser, Kraus, and A. Anderson do. However, Seybold sees a father and his son going up to Jerusalem for the pilgrim festival. Kirkpatrick and Jacquet suggest a group of pilgrims encouraging one another *en route*, whereas Eaton and M. Dahood believe that it might be a national leader. See Goulder, *Psalms of the Return*, 42.

95. Barker, "Lord Watches Over You," 172.

96. Ceresko, "Psalm 121," 508. Ceresko makes an interesting suggestion that the psalm was a prayer of a warrior (probably the king) who looked to God for help in his battles in the hills.

97. The pilgrim might be an individual or a choir. See Mowinckel, *Psalmenstudien V*, 35–36. Was the psalm on arrival at the city (Jacquet), or in a procession of worship (Allen), or on departure (Delitzsch)? See Goulder, *Psalms of the Return*, 47.

98. Mowinckel, *Psalmenstudien V*, 35–36.

99. Bratcher and Reyburn, *Psalms*, 1056.

sings the joy of being in Jerusalem whereas Psalm 84, as Artur Weiser points out, provides "a valuable testimony to the mood of the festival pilgrims" in an exodus context.[100] *Blessed are those whose strength is in you, Who have set their hearts on pilgrimage. As they pass through the Valley of Baca, they make it a place of springs* (Ps 84:5–6). Exodus 23:17 and 34:23 and Deuteronomy 16:16 show that pilgrim's were required to attend the holy site three times a year to worship in order to encounter God. Before Jerusalem became the only sanctuary for pilgrimage, Shilo had been a holy site. First Samuel 1:3, 21 and 2:19 indicate that one pilgrimage to Shilo a year met the requirement of the worship obligations. The distance might have been a great hindrance for ordinary male Israelites to make pilgrimage three times a year. Pilgrimage to Jerusalem was proven to be even harder because of the longer trip. Thus various psalms (Pss 42:5; 43:3; 63:3; 84:2–3, 5–6, 11; 87) express the difficulty of making pilgrimage on a regular basis that resulted in the Israelites having a deep sense of longing for the Holy City.

My soul yearns, even faints, for the courts of the Lord; my heart and my flesh cry out for the living God (Ps 84:2). This deep sense of desire to go to Zion is also traced in Isaiah 2:3, Micah 4:2, and Jeremiah 31:6.[101] *What does your God require of you?* (Deut 10:12). This requirement of God is asked again in the prophets. As the life of Abraham and of the Exodus generation was symbolized by walking towards a destination defined by God's promise, the life of Israel was to be answered by walking in his ways. McConville conceives this as the internalizing of the journey, the physical reality.[102] Sheriffs also envisages the walk as the internalizing of the Torah.[103] Isaiah sang of the *walk and way* metaphor. *And a highway will be there; it will be called the Way of Holiness. The unclean will not journey on it; it will be for those who walk in that Way; wicked fools will not go about on it* (Isa 35:8). Psalm 119:1 is a reflective response to the walk, journey of life metaphor.[104] *Blessed are they whose*

---

100. Weiser, *The Psalms*, 566.

101. "This is what Isaiah son of Amoz saw concerning Judah and Jerusalem . . . 'Come, let us go up to the mountain of the Lord, to the house of the God of Jacob. Let him teach us his ways, so that we may walk in his paths.' The law will go out from Zion and the word of the Lord from Jerusalem" (Isa 2:1–3; Mic 4:2). Come! Let us go up to Zion, to YHWH our God (Jer 31:6).

102. See McConville, "Pilgrimage and 'Place,'" 19–20.

103. See Sheriffs, *Friendship of the Lord*, 114–50.

104. Studies have suggested that Psalm 119 draws on Deuteronomy, Isaiah, Jeremiah, and Proverbs.

ways are blameless, who walk according to the law of the Lord (Ps 119:1). The Old Testament is not alone in underlining the concept of the walking metaphor. The teaching of the New Testament develops the walking metaphor in terms of a discipleship perspective, using phrases such as "following Jesus" and "walking in the light and in the Spirit."

Psalm 48 affirms that Jerusalem is the place of divine residence, and that God is there as the king. The notion of God as king was apparently central for the Jerusalem Temple. *Great is the Lord and greatly to be praised in the city of our God. His holy mountain, beautiful in elevation, is the joy of all the earth, Mount Zion, in the far north the city of the great King. Within its citadels God has shown himself a sure defence* (Ps 48:1–3). Mowinckel posits that in all probability the enthronement idea has been combined with "the feast of Yahweh" in Jerusalem.[105] Mowinckel's assertion of the message of the Jerusalem festival appears to be within the main framework of pilgrimage paradigm that has been traced from the very beginning of the Abrahamic pilgrimage.

> *The fundamental thought connected with the Jerusalem feast* is that Yahweh is coming (Pss 96:13; 98:9) and "revealing himself," "becoming revealed" and "making himself known" . . . In the festal experience it is first of all through his works, his "saving works" that Yahweh reveals himself, manifesting to all the world who and what he is.[106]

The Lord has made his salvation known and revealed his righteousness to the nations (Ps 98:2.). *God is within her citadels, hath made himself known as a defense* (Ps 48:4). *God hath made himself known in Judah, his name is great in Israel. In Salem is now his pavilion, In Zion his abode* (Ps 76:2). "Knowing God" paradigm in the pilgrimage framework was a vivid reality, not an abstract concept, through the history of Israel, particularly the Jerusalem festal experience. The reality reexperienced through the cult is no longer first and foremost the cyclical course and renewal of nature, but the historical "facts of salvation."[107] Jerusalem in the Old Testament is, therefore, more than a place where Yahweh dwells.

All men coming to Jerusalem is a picture of the universalizing of salvation vividly pictured in the pilgrimage context. *Praise awaits you,*

---

105. Mowinckel, *Psalms in Israel's Worship*, 1:140.
106. See ibid., 136–44; italics mine.
107. Ibid., 139.

O God, in Zion; to you our vows will be fulfilled. O you who hear prayer, to you all men will come (Ps 65:1–2). Jerusalem becomes a place of hope for the gathering together of the scattered nation (Isa 27:13; 35:10; 51:11; 2:11; Zech 6:15). Isaiah 40–66 features the eschatological pilgrimage of the nations to Jerusalem with the servant theme. Particularly, in Isaiah 56:6–8 God promises that the foreigner and stranger will be brought to the holy mountain, his house of prayer. The remnant of Israel will be a kind of offering to God, so that all mankind may come to him in a transformed Jerusalem, the new heavens and the new earth (66:20–23). The entire process of movement is clearly that of pilgrimage. Writing the name of non-Israelites is another expression of the universalizing of salvation. *I will record Rahab and Babylon among those who acknowledge me . . . The Lord will write in the register of the peoples. This one was born in Zion* (Ps 87:2–6). It is clear that the two psalms in relation to salvation are based on the pilgrimage framework. Jerusalem becomes the participation of the gentiles in the community. The eschatological image in Isaiah 25:6–10 confirms the point: "On this mountain the Lord Almighty will prepare a feast of rich food for all peoples, a banquet of aged wine—the best of meats and the finest of wines." Pilgrimage feast in Zion for all people is the primary metaphor in this vision. Prophecy took control of the pilgrimage feast in order to lend its proclamation for the salvation of the entire world a more vivid expression. Thus Jerusalem in the overall picture remains a focus of God's purpose for the future. Eichrodt points out the future importance of Jerusalem as the center of salvation:

> It is from Jerusalem that the knowledge of the true God is to spread; and in worshipping him at this place the unity of all peoples in submission to the God of Israel is to find its symbolic expression.[108]

Conclusion

The structural use of the journey framework and the larger context of the journey, which took the people out of bondage, through the wilderness, on their route "home" to the promised land, can be traced from Exodus to Joshua, as seen in the pilgrimages of Abraham and Jacob. Thus like the patriarchs' narratives the whole exodus story was about journeying

---

108. Eichrodt, *Theology of the Old Testament*, 107.

and what happened on the way. From Exodus to Joshua, Israel's wilderness wandering is pursued in terms of the several stages of a faith journey. *I brought you to myself* (Exod 19:5). Here the reason for the journey to Sinai gives the most profound theological interpretation of pilgrimage. The mountain or the promised land was not the destination of the Exodus. The destination of the journey was bringing the Israelites to God himself. God was the focus and the goal of the Exodus in which the whole physical journey, namely walking, was engaged. The physical journey was the outward visible procedure through which God brought about his revealed providence. Thus, the knowing God motif as the key experience for the Israelites becomes one of the main themes of Exodus as it was in the Abrahamic and Jacob narratives. In Deuteronomy, particularly, the metaphor of life as a journey is dealt with in greater depth. For the Israelites as a nation on the move, "a life of obedience is life on the move towards the land."[109] The Israelites should have known that a life of obedience is a life on the move towards not the land, but God himself. Thus they were still on their way. The perspective emerging from Israel's journey including the wilderness period and the allusion of the "walking in his ways" metaphor offers a fundamental image of the pilgrimage (journey) paradigm.

After the settlement in Canaan, the concept of God's guidance and presence in the midst of his people was inseparably connected with the holy places where the ark stayed. Since the ark had some religious significance for the northern tribes too, bringing the ark into Jerusalem bound the whole of Israel to David and the city. Jerusalem with the ark became the focal point of Israelite religion. In the course of history Jerusalem thus increasingly became the "religious" as well as the political center as the capital of the kingdom. It should, however, be noted that the understanding of the city could become dangerous when God's protection and blessing are restricted to a particular place. As Eichrodt points out, the occasional loss of the ark provided a counterpoise to the materialistic concept of the divine presence and the false confidence, which might arise from a belief in the secure possession of the national God in one's midst.[110] Consequently the fall of Jerusalem seemed to be in order to break up the unity of God and place, so that trust in God might be separated from trust in a place.

109. Millar, *Now Choose Life*, 73.
110. Eichrodt, *Theology of the Old Testament*, 111.

Thus through the divine activity of the exile, Israel was to know that he was the Lord. God longed to be recognized as he was by his people who did not know him properly. Through the journey framework God had guided Abraham and Jacob in their lives and led Israel as a nation to the promised land. Again, God brought the similar framework and process—being carried away to Babylon, sojourn in Babylon, and the return to the promised land—to enable his idolatrous people to know who he was and to come back to him. Thus the exile and restoration for Israel were not just a physical movement, but also a pilgrimage of faith and the rod in God's hand that brought the people to recognize what they were and who he was. In the long history of Israel, from the Abrahamic pilgrimage to the return to Jerusalem from Babylon, we can trace the interlocking relationship between pilgrimage as a physical movement and God's way of transforming his people, namely, discipleship. Israel's physical journeys, the exile and the return, are, therefore, to be understood not only as "a historical note, but a theological program."[111] With the theological reflection upon the exile and the return, the prophets and Psalms proclaim that the exile and the return were not merely a wandering through the wilderness toward the promised land, but a pilgrimage to the holy mountain, Jerusalem. The pilgrimage framework embraces the two decisive events in the history of Israel that became the dominant paradigm for Israel's faith, namely the self-understanding of Judaism or Jewishness.

---

111. Brueggemann, *Genesis*, 122.

3

Jesus and the First Two Passover Pilgrimages

IN THE PREVIOUS CHAPTERS the journeys of Adam, Abraham, and Jacob have been examined to discover what they came to know about who God is. This pattern of encounter is also prominent in the journey of Israel following the Exodus, the forty years in the wilderness, as well as the Babylonian exile and restoration. In her journeys Israel learned that God was the true destination of their journeys. It is noted that הָלַךְ *halak*, as Helfmeyer sees it, seems to be used to describe the visit to a sanctuary with added sacral overtones occasioned by the purpose and goal of the pilgrimage or journey (Gen 22:5; 25:22; Exod 3:19; Judg 19:18; 1 Sam 9:9; 1 Kgs 3:4; 1 Chr 21:30; Isa 2:3; 30:29; Jer 3:6; Mic 4:2; Pss 55:15; 122:1; Eccl 4:17; etc.).[1] In this context the meaning of הָלַךְ, physical journey, is much more than spatial. Considering journey as an act of traveling from one place to another, it becomes natural to connect physical journey with pilgrimage. So pilgrimage for Israelites was a journey that was made to the temple in Jerusalem in performance of a vow or for the sake of experiencing some form of divine blessing. Since pilgrimage to the temple in Jerusalem was to meet with God, pilgrimage became a vehicle through which God was encountered and revealed, because those who participated in a journey met God on their way.

Eventually under David and especially Rehoboam, worship was centralized in Jerusalem and this made the feasts and pilgrimage to Jerusalem more important (cf. 1 Kgs 12:26–33; 2 Kgs 10:28). As a result, pilgrimage to Jerusalem became a national occasion and the feasts became designated as pilgrim occasions (1 Kgs 8:65; 2 Chr 7:8–9; 8:13;

---

1. Helfmeyer, "הָלַךְ," 391.

30:5; 31:3; 35:18). Although the information regarding the three pilgrimage feasts in the OT is general and fragmented, it is noted that the Feast of Tabernacles was earmarked as that which would draw Israel to Jerusalem (Zech 14:14–16). When we examine the NT, the feasts have clearly become connected with pilgrimage occasions and each feast has a significant meaning for Jesus' pilgrimage to Jerusalem. Josephus informs us how deeply the three pilgrimage feasts became embedded in the life of Israel at his time (*J.W.* 2.42–43; 2.515; 5.199; 6.421–422; *Ant.* 4.203–204). Thus it is possible to say that the three pilgrimage feasts at the time of Jesus had become opportunities to come to God, to meet with and learn from him. It is noted from the information we have that Jesus made his journeys to Jerusalem only in relation to pilgrimage feasts. This fact draws our attention to the OT background. Thus treating each of the pilgrimage feasts in connection with Jesus' journeys to Jerusalem is in order in the following chapters.

In the previous chapters we have seen that journeys were the way the participants met with God, so what happened to them on their journeys was significant. In the light of this, Jesus' pilgrimages to Jerusalem become significant because they were purpose-driven journeys to make the people he encountered know who God was and who he was in the context of the pilgrimage feasts. In the journeys reported in the OT texts, those who participated in the journey, as well as the readers who travel vicariously, benefited. In contrast with the journeys in the OT, mostly, apart from the final Passover feast in which he died, the pilgrimages for Jesus were nothing to do with what happened to Jesus himself. However, one could think of Jesus' pilgrimages as modes of instruction for the people Jesus encountered as well as the readers of the Gospels.

In the journeys in the OT the people who participated in the journey grew in their understanding of who God is. Jesus' journeys to Jerusalem in relation to the feasts are not exactly the same pattern as that of the OT. Those who participated in the pilgrimage with Jesus are presented as blind and rebellious—it is only the conclusion of the journey. However, Jesus' pilgrimages to Jerusalem educated the disciples, the people Jesus encountered, and the readers of the Gospels, so achieved a gradual progression toward the full comprehension of who God and Jesus are. Since making himself known was Jesus' agenda from the very beginning of his pilgrimages, each pilgrimage to Jerusalem plays an important role in revealing the work of Israel's Savior.

SETTING THE SCENE—PASSOVER IN RETROSPECT

Unfortunately, the information regarding the Feast of Passover in the OT is general and fragmented. Because of this it is best treated in the beginning of Jesus' Passover pilgrimage, where the feast has clearly become connected with pilgrimage occasions and has a significant meaning for Jesus' ministry.

Taking Exodus 11–13 as a starting point, one notes that God announced to Moses the tenth plague that was to be the divine chastisement of the Egyptians. Moses warned Pharaoh of the impending slaughter of the Egyptian firstborn and firstlings. God prescribed the Passover regulations to Moses. *This month is to be for you the first month, the first month of your year. Tell the whole community of Israel that on the tenth day of this month each man is to take a lamb for his family, one for each household* (Exod 12:1). Exodus 12:1–20 presents God's command on the eve of the Exodus. A pascal lamb was slain and eaten at night in haste in each household. Its blood was sprinkled on the doorposts and lintel. God passed over the houses of Israelites but he struck the Egyptian firstborn. From this action the Hebrew noun *Pesah* rendered "Passover" in English usage took its name.[2] As Pharaoh and his people then begged the Israelites to leave quickly, the Israelites took unleavened bread in haste. It is not certain whether that was because they had bound up their kneading-troughs in expectation of the journey or because they did not have enough time to allow the dough to ferment. Exodus 12–13 concludes the account of the first Passover with various regulations concerning the future observance of the Passover, particularly with respect to the involvement of foreigners (Exod 12:42–51) and the way in which the Israelites are to remember the Passover and their deliverance from Egypt (Exod 13:1–16). Exodus 11–13 discloses three different ceremonies associated with the Passover feast: *the Passover sacrifice, the feast of Unleavened Bread, and the consecration of the firstborn.* Whatever one may think of the details of this history, the Passover sacrifice and the Feast of Unleavened Bread were certainly of a different character in terms of their origin.

It has, therefore, been debated as to the character of the feasts. Until recently, in order to establish the original character of Passover, many scholars focused on comparing descriptions of Passover from the four

---

2. The etymology of the Hebrew *Pesah* is uncertain.

generally recognized biblical sources and analyzing particular words used in those descriptions. The source hypothesis based on the use of special terminology, words and phrases peculiar to one or more sources, has not proved to be a reliable method for the task.[3] Many scholars have adopted an approach to the Passover texts within the framework of ancient Near Eastern history and religion, and with a modified source hypothesis.[4] Although the same tools are employed, the results of the work appear to be at variance, producing a growing number of explanations for Passover.[5] However, it seems inappropriate to establish our argument on a single piece of evidence, ignoring other evidence, for the paschal ritual contains each element of the explanations. Thus discovering the original character of Passover appears to depend on the appropriate method to interpret the Passover texts.

What is beyond any doubt is that the details of Passover indicate the features of a nomadic lifestyle.[6] There are good grounds for the proposition that the Passover sacrifice in particular can best be explained in the light of the features of a nomadic lifestyle such as eating the meal at night and at the beginning of a journey, the roasting of the animal whole, etc. By contrast, the characteristics of the Unleavened Bread feast indicate the features of an agricultural feast. At the beginning of the barley harvest in spring or April, the first fruits of the harvest without any ingredients from the previous harvests were eaten. The feast lasted for seven days, symbolizing and celebrating a new beginning. Thus it continued to represent the new beginning for the people as they took their first steps on their road to freedom.[7]

At the Exodus God killed the firstborn of Egypt and spared the firstborn of Israel. The blood of the lamb sprinkled on the doorpost

---

3. Beer, McNeile, Steuernagel, Arnold, Guthe, Gray, May, and R. Pfeiffer belong to this group.

4. Mowinckel, Nicolsky, Pedersen, and Engnell belong to this group.

5. De Vaux and Kraus give undue emphasis to apothropaic rite, Wellhausen to thanksgiving festival, Beer to harvest festival, Pedersen to sanctification ritual, Mowinckel to ritual drama, and Engnell to New Year's festival. See Prosic, "Passover in Biblical Narratives," 46; De Vaux, *Ancient Israel*, 489; Kraus, *Worship in Israel*, 46–49; Pedersen, *Israel*, 398; Wellhausen, *Prolegomena*, 83–94.

6. Van Seters and Wambacq emphasize Israel's capability of creating religious rituals. The arguments against the nomadic origins of this sacrifice are not convincing. See Engnell, *Critical Essays*.

7. Yee, *Jewish Feasts*, 51.

marked the firstborn sons and daughters of God, while the firstborn sons of the Egyptians were slaughtered. God, therefore, claimed that the firstborn belong to him (Exod 13:2, 12; Num 3:13). The blood of a lamb protected the firstborn of Israel, and the whole family was to eat of the lamb. The consecration of the firstborn replaced by the paschal lamb, according to some, is interpreted as a sacrifice to God. Although such interpretations find no basis in the text of Exodus, it is a fact that the death of the firstborn in Egypt became the reason for the consecration of the firstborn in Exodus 13.[8] The Passover event was thus put at the forefront of Israelite thought and theology.[9] The Passover sacrifice was a constant reminder that the firstborn belonged to the Lord. Houtman, in line with Julius Wellhausen, believes that the custom originally was an expression of gratitude, suggesting that the consecration of the firstborn was tantamount to recognizing the deity as owner of land and livestock, author of fertility, and entitled to all the crops and animals.[10]

In relation to the origin of Passover, many scholars have adopted different pictures based on different assumptions.[11] Was Passover originally a nomadic feast? Was Passover originally a New Year's festival of other nations in the ancient Near East? Was the Unleavened Bread originally a harvest festival? Was the firstborn son originally sacrificed and did the practice of redeeming him arise later? These are all technical questions worthy of study but not essential for our own enquiry. This is a matter of trees and forest. As long as we are interested in trees we will not be able to see the forest. What is clear from our own enquiry is that, whatever its origin, and whatever its precise ritual structure, its meaning and purpose should be investigated within the context of the Passover narratives. It is quite safe to say that these feasts had their own particular meaning before they were later associated and reinterpreted in light of

---

8. For lack of evidence in Exodus, Houtman rejects the sacrificial point of view. See Houtman, *Exodus*, 2:163. However, he recognizes the point that the death of the firstborn became the reason for the consecration of the firstborn in Exodus 13.

9. Having examined the use of this term in biblical literature, Tom Holland suggests the basis of understanding atonement through the sacrifice of the firstborn. See Holland, *Contours of Pauline Theology*, 237–73.

10. Houtman, *Exodus*, 2:164.

11. Segal, Childs, Sarna, and Houtman provide lucid summaries of the diverse explanations of the holidays' possible original significance and their historicization. See Segal, *Hebrew Passover*, 78–188; Childs, *Book of Exodus*, 184–95; Sarna, *Exploring Exodus*, 85–89; Houtman, *Exodus*, 2:146–66.

the historical event of the Exodus. It is evident from the framework of the Passover narratives that the descriptions of Passover vary from occasion to occasion, and that the celebration of each Passover narrative has a different purpose and meaning. Tamara Prosic notes that:

> ... even the prophets speak of riddles, allegories and parables as a means of wisdom. Exactly because the biblical text is also a symbolic text I believe that instead of accounting and classifying differences in the Passover ritual as they appear in various sources, it is more fruitful to start the investigation of its original character with an analysis of its symbolic connotation within the context of certain narratives where its celebration is mentioned.[12]

In the book of Exodus the Passover is mentioned in connection with the impending tenth plague and the journey that would follow. The consideration for safety on a journey that marked the nomadic feature of Passover now became a concern of the Israelites as they journeyed from Egypt.[13] Although the Passover meal was eaten in haste, the Israelites were to be already fully dressed and ready for the journey from Egypt, the Exodus.[14] *This is how you are to eat it: with your cloak tucked into your belt, your sandals on your feet and your staff in your hand. Eat it in haste: it is the Lord's Passover* (Exod 12:11). The Israelites as shepherds depended upon tending flocks and herds for their existence (Gen 46:31–34). During the settlement in Egypt, the Israelites were given Goshen to live as shepherds (Gen 46:31—47:5). Is it then reasonable to assume that shepherding was the only way for them to exist for 430 years? With the evidence that Isaac sowed crops (Gen 26:12) and that Joseph dreamed of the field in which his brother's sheaves stood bound and bowed down to Joseph's sheaf (Gen 37:7), it is clear that the Hebrew patriarchs must have already been acquainted with agriculture. They tended their flocks, but they also sowed seeds in the right season. Thus it is, as J. B. Segal suggests, quite probable that they were semi nomads.[15]

---

12. Prosic, "Passover in Biblical Narratives," 47.

13. Shepherds in a nomadic society observed a rite at the spring of the year when they would migrate to the highlands to pasture their flock. The sacrifice of a young animal was offered to ensure the fertility and safety of the flock as it made the journey to greener pastures.

14. This is reminiscent of the desert traveling dress of either nomads or their temporary counterparts, pilgrims. See Gerlach, *Antenicene Pascha*, 26.

15. See Segal, *Hebrew Passover*, 78–113.

This might mean that when the Israelites were given the instructions for the Passover, it was not something new for them. They could interpret the Passover feast with meaning, particularly the meaning of journey. J. Halbe claims that the eating of unleavened bread is typical for travelers and nomadic life.[16] Leonhard Rost argues that the original setting of Pesach was the migration to higher summer pasture signaled by the end of the winter rains.[17] Thus he goes on to suggest that Passover was originally connected to a semi-nomadic festival that took place during migration and was designed to protect the nomads and their flock throughout the annual spring migration from the desert to arable land.[18] Shepherds in a nomadic society might have observed a rite at springtime before migrating to the highlands to pasture their flocks. The possible details about the nomadic background, as Menahem Haran points out, could not be more than speculation.[19]

The Exodus narrative symbolized by the Passover involves two simple human activities, eating and journeying (walking). The Passover highlights the symbolic significance of the two activities. Both the eating and journeying have become a fundamental image of spirituality and in Exodus/the Passover they develop a symbolic significance. It is, therefore, probable that Jesus construed his pilgrimage to Jerusalem and the Last Supper with the twelve disciples as the fulfillment of God's plan within the Passover framework. Although eating the sacrificial meal (the Last Supper) as the prelude to the Exodus has been discussed in academic circles, journeying to the promised land, pilgrimage to Jerusalem, has received no attention. As part of the pilgrimage pattern, the journey motif is certainly written large into the Exodus narrative. It is noted that the Passover resets Israel's reckoning of time. God commanded Israel to count the beginning of her history as starting on the first month of the year, although the actual feast follows on the fourteenth of Nisan.[20] Thus

---

16. Houtman quotes Halbe. See Houtman, *Exodus*, 2:156.

17. Rost, "Weidewechsel," 205–16. Childs claims that Rost's theory retains a high level of historical and geographical specificity that differentiates it from the usual patterns of comparative religion, in which all festivals, whether spring or fall, begin to look alike. See Childs, *Exploring Exodus*, 189.

18. Rost, "Weidewechsel," 205–16.

19. Haran, *Temples*, 320–21.

20. By tradition, the Jewish people observe the fascal New Year in the seventh month of the Jewish calendar, in the fall, but the religious calendar begins in Nisan, the first month.

it continued to represent the new beginning for the people as they took their first steps on their road to freedom.[21]

After the Exodus, when the Israelites settled in Canaan and became farmers, the Passover acquired a new meaning. With the rise of agriculture, the Passover is considered by some to have faced an acculturation in the wake of the cultural change. The features of an emerging new farming community possibly influenced the meaning and purpose of the Passover feast. There were certainly changes in the regulations concerning the celebration of the Passover feast. After entering Canaan only those who were circumcised were allowed to participate in the festival. The Passover came to have a defining significance for the Israelites' identity. *In the days to come when your son asks you "what does this mean?" say to him "with a mighty hand the Lord brought us out of Egypt, out of the land of slavery. When Pharaoh stubbornly refused to let us go, the Lord killed every firstborn in Egypt, both man and animal. This is why I sacrifice to the Lord the first male offspring of every womb and redeem each of my firstborn sons." And it will be like a sign on your hand and a symbol on your forehead that the Lord brought us out of Egypt with his mighty hand* (Exod 13:14–16). Exodus 13 signifies the importance of the Passover for the whole nation through all generations, declaring the clear purpose of the Passover sacrifice. After the Exodus and journey to the promised land, the meaning of Passover went beyond the meaning of a commemoration festival. The Passover was seen to be one of the pivotal moments in the history of the Israelites and has subsequently been celebrated as such.

Within this framework the original Passover in Egypt marked the end of the period in which the Israelites were slaves; it brought in the era of freedom.[22] The Passover in Canaan, on the other hand, closes the nomadic life, the unsettled existence of life in the wilderness, and inaugurates an agricultural life, the sedentary conditions of life in the promised land

---

21. Yee, *Jewish Feasts*, 51.

22. I am indebted to Prosic for this framework. Prosic makes an antithetical correlation between the two stages in the history of the Israelites: slavery/freedom (exodus), wanting/abundance (Canaan), nonexistence of law/establishment of law (Sinai), temporary sanctuary/permanent sanctuary (Solomon), worship of many/worship of one (Hezekiah, Josiah), and exile/homeland (return from exile). See Prosic, "Passover in Biblical Narratives," 50–52. It must also be noted that the land of Egypt is called the house of slaves.

(Josh 5:10–15).²³ The next mention of the feast was Solomon's Passover. Having brought certain sacrifices three times a year—sacrifices that 2 Chronicles 8:12–13 defines as the three festivals— Solomon's Passover concludes the period of the Tabernacle, the temporary dwelling place of God, and begins the era in which the temple becomes the permanent sanctuary.²⁴ As a result of the Israelites having a national center, they would see Passover as a national celebration of thanksgiving. It is noted that in Solomon's Passover the king has a notable role in burning the offerings on the altar. Hundreds of years later the reforms of Hezekiah and Josiah (2 Chr 30 and 35) give a prominent place to keeping the Passover. Hezekiah called the whole nation to the proper worship of God in Jerusalem in order to reunite the nation, restoring the Passover and in a sense showing the fulfillment of the Lord's promise to Solomon in his response to the dedicatory prayer (2 Chr 30:1–12). Josiah performed his massive religious reformation program with the celebration of the Passover (2 Kgs 23:21–23; 2 Chr 35:1–18). Thus Hezekiah and Josiah's Passovers come as a sign that the dedication of the Israelites to God was reestablished, so ending the years of faithlessness. When the destruction of the first temple in Jerusalem disrupted the celebration of Passover at the official shrine, the exilic prophet Ezekiel envisioned a future time when the temple would be rebuilt and the Passover observed again (Ezek 45:21–24). In spite of much resistance by the Samaritans, Ezekiel's vision was realized (Ezra 1:2–11). The temple was rebuilt and the Passover was celebrated as the first feast by the returning exiles (Ezra 6:19–22). The Passover after the restoration of Israel reminisces on being a stranger in a foreign land and celebrates the new life in the promised land.

Whenever the Israelites had a national celebration, they would naturally turn to the Passover. The Passover offering and the eating of unleavened bread, whatever the original state of the feasts was, became "an intermediary element between the two stages in the history of the Israelites."²⁵ After analyzing the Passover texts it is possible to conclude that the meanings of Passover perceived by the participants were conditioned by a full and complete portrait of the feast as originally celebrated.²⁶

23. The Israelites were wholly nomadic for forty years in the wilderness.

24. In 1 Kings the three occasions on which Solomon burnt offerings are generally regarded as an allusion to the three annual feasts.

25. Prosic, "Passover in Biblical Narratives," 51.

26. We should, therefore, not attach much significance to the details of the Passover

The Passover was probably chosen to symbolize the crucial changes in the history of Israel due to the powerful symbolic representation that the Passover had for the Israelites. Thus Prosic claims:

> In the case of Passover, our task is to establish whether the Passover narratives as part of certain historical narratives have any symbolic function and whether that particular function can be seen as a projection of the original purpose and meaning of Passover.[27]

JESUS AND THE FIRST PASSOVER PILGRIMAGE (LUKE 2:41–52)

It was suggested in the preceding section that the feasts of Passover were historicized to commemorate and remember the Exodus, and to heighten and stimulate memories of the momentous events in the history of Israel. Passover associations provide one of the bases for the Jerusalem festivals, the three national festivals (Exod 23:14–17), referred to in the Gospels and the book of Acts. The birth narrative comes to a climax with an account of the temple incident (Luke 2:41–52). The temple narrative serves to illuminate the person of Jesus as he showed his interest in the temple as hinting at his relationship to God. As such, did the twelve-year-old Jesus on the threshold of adult life impose his own meaning and purpose on his Passover pilgrimage (journey) to Jerusalem?

When the time of their purification according to the Law of Moses had been completed, Joseph and Mary took him to Jerusalem to present him to the Lord, (as it is written in the Law of the Lord, "Every firstborn male is to be consecrated to the Lord . . . " (Luke 2:22–23). Many scholars have not explored the Passover—the heart of the Exodus, nor the death of the firstborn—the heart of the Passover, although recognition of the Exodus motif is growing. In Exodus we are introduced for the first time to the concept of the firstborn of Israel. Every firstborn male of the mother was to be set apart or consecrated to God (Exod 8:2, 12; Num 3:13).[28] God affirmed that the firstborn sons of Israel belonged to him because he spared them in Egypt when he destroyed the firstborn of the Egyptians (Exod 13:1–2).

---

rite as described in the Passover texts.

27. Prosic, "Passover in Biblical Narratives, 47–48.

28. In this verse it is the Piel imperative form, so it is a command to put something into action.

The original idea was that the firstborn consecrated to God was supposed to serve the Lord in his life, but the Levites took over the special service of the Lord and replaced the firstborn. Since the consecration of the tribe of Levi redeemed the firstborn of the generation of the Exodus (Num 3:40–41), paying five shekels (twenty denarii) to the sanctuary (the temple) redeemed every firstborn at one month of age (Num 18:16). We note, however, that it is not certain that there was any custom of bringing the child to the sanctuary for the presentation and redemption. Joseph Fitzmyer, therefore, denies that anything is said about a presentation of the child in the Jerusalem Temple either in the OT or in the Mishnah.[29] In the light of Nehemiah 10:35–36, "We obligate ourselves . . . to bring to the house of our God, the firstborn of our sons . . . as it is written in the law," and the possible allusions of 1 Samuel 1 and 2 we could suggest that Fitzmyer overlooked a possibility that this practice might be observed in the Judaism of OT times. As J. Nolland argues, Nehemiah 10:35–36 and 1 Samuel 1 and 2 could reflect popular practice in the Judaism of NT times.

Raymond Brown has brought to our attention a claim that Luke followed the model of the Samuel story that had the child presented in the sanctuary at Shiloh, although he knew something about the custom of presentation as described in the Law.[30] This parallelism between the Samuel story and the account of the presentation of Jesus in the temple does not fit completely, for Samuel was presented and left at the sanctuary at Shiloh, whereas Jesus was consecrated to God, neither redeemed for a price, nor left in the Lord's service. The law of presentation had the child redeemed for a price and not left in the Lord's service. This is probably the reason for Nolland to maintain that the allusion of 1 Samuel 1:28 remains secondary to our interest in the observance of the law.[31]

Is it, then, right to say that Luke's inaccurate knowledge of the exact customs and the conflict between two customs, purification and presentation, have been a cause of the confusion?[32] Since most scholars have

---

29. Fitzmyer, *Luke I–IX*, 425.
30. Brown, *Birth of the Messiah*, 450–51.
31. Nolland, *Luke 1–9:20*, 117.
32. Women were supposed to purify themselves, not men. Luke seems to think that the reason for going to the temple was the consecration or presentation of Jesus (v. 27), when only the law concerning the purification of the mother mentions the custom of going to the sanctuary. (It is doubtful if a journey to the temple was still practiced to any great extent in the Judaism of NT times.) Luke mentions nothing of the price (five

focused on *what they did* on the basis of the exact law and custom, not *why they did it* on the basis of the result of the action, Luke's purpose has not been properly appreciated. When the days for their purification were completed, Joseph and Mary brought Jesus up to Jerusalem to present him to the Lord and to offer a sacrifice according to the commands in Exodus (Luke 2:22–24). Thus Jesus, Mary's firstborn son, was set apart or consecrated. In fact, they could have just made a payment to a scribe to redeem the firstborn child. That would be enough to meet the requirement of the law. However, in Luke's presentation of the child in the temple there is no mention of paying the prescribed ransom for the firstborn. What Jesus' parents did was what the law instructed for a firstborn. So the absence of a ransom has led many, including Darrell Bock, to see Jesus' dedication as a reflection of Exodus rather than Numbers.[33] In an effort to solve this conundrum, Tom Holland argues:

> What is not mentioned, and this is incredible considering it would be the most important thing that every Jewish couple had to do on the birth of their firstborn, is that they never redeemed the child. The child was no longer Joseph and Mary's, for he was the Lord's firstborn, for they failed to redeem him. This makes sense of Mary singing Hannah's song (1 Sam 2:1–10; Luke 1:46–55), for she too gave her son to the Lord. It also explains why Jesus was surprised that Joseph and Mary had not expected him to be in the temple when he was found to be missing from the returning pilgrim party (Luke 2:49). The reply, "Did you not know that I must be about my Father's business?" and his presence in the temple was part of his preparation, and suggests that Jesus was conscious of a priestly calling from his youth. Again, it explains why he should say that Mary was not his mother (Luke 8:19–21). The natural ties had been severed because they had not redeemed him.[34]

Having identified the role of firstborn as a family representative in the Passover and as becoming the redeemer, Holland rejects the traditional ontological interpretation by presenting the term πρωτότοκος in

---

shekels) required for redeeming the firstborn child from the service of the Lord; rather he connects with that event the sacrifice of the two doves or pigeons which was really related to the purification of the mother. See Brown, *Birth of the Messiah*, 448.

33. See Bock, *Luke*, 1:237; Marshall, *Gospel*, 117; Reicke and Bertram, "παρίστημί," 841.

34. Holland, *Contours of Pauline Theology*, 271.

the context of redemptive history.³⁵ Thus Luke reveals that Jesus would operate from within God's purpose.³⁶ Holland's understanding nicely fits Luke's purpose to call attention in the calling of Jesus. Luke's focus remains clear that no redemption price was paid, for the child was not redeemed but rather consecrated to the service of God.³⁷ He truly belongs to the Lord.

Every year his parents went to Jerusalem for the Feast of the Passover. When he was twelve years old, they went up to the Feast, according to the custom. After the feast was over, while his parents were returning home, the boy Jesus stayed behind in Jerusalem . . . (Luke 2:41-43). From this passage, pilgrimages to Jerusalem to celebrate Passover seem to have been annual (v. 41) and customary (v. 42). Thus we can see that the feasts clearly became connected with pilgrimage occasions and the pilgrimage practice, as we have already noticed in the writings of Jewish literatures including Philo, Josephus, and rabbinic works, exerted a great impact on the lives and expectations of Jews in Second Temple Judaism. One, however, should not too readily infer from these statements that during the feasts the whole of the population streamed to the temple in Jerusalem. It is unlikely that every male went up to the temple three times a year in the Second Temple period as was the instruction. *For I will drive out nations before you . . . and no one will covet your land, when you go up three times each year to appear before the Lord your God* (Exod 34:24). Rabbinic literature does not mention such an obligation, but categorizes the commandment as a command that has no limit (*m. Pesah* 1:1; *b. Pesah.* 70b; Midr. *Tanhuma* on Exod 29:1).³⁸ It tells that the formal obligation was, as S. Safrai puts it, regarded as "a positive action to be encouraged but not demanded."³⁹ It is, therefore, safe to suggest that people might have gone up to Jerusalem every year or once every few years, or even, in the case of the Diaspora, only once in their lifetime. This reality is reflected in Luke 2:41-42, where it is stated that Jesus' parents went to Jerusalem once every year, and that they were pious Jews who were

---

35. Ibid., 237-73.

36. Green, *Gospel of Luke*, 141.

37. Marshall, Reicke, and Caird have the same view. See Marshall, *Gospel*, 117; Reicke and Bertram, "παρίστημι," 840; Caird, *Gospel of St. Luke*, 64.

38. Safrai and Stern, *Jewish People*, 899.

39. Ibid., 900. *b. Pesahim* 70b, Midrash *Tanhuma* on Exodus 29:1 and *m. Pesah* 1:1 categorize the commandment to make a pilgrimage as a command that has no limit.

faithful both to the general rule and the traditional faith. Haran points out that pilgrimages to the temple were mostly regarded as praiseworthy manifestations of piety and fear of God.[40]

Did the boy Jesus go on pilgrimage to Jerusalem with his parents each year? The details of the pilgrimage commandment in three places of the Exodus (Exod 5:1; 10:9; 32:5) prove that the entire family joined in the pilgrimage, though in principle only the males were obliged to appear before the Lord. Luke also clearly indicates that the pilgrimage to Jerusalem was in reality an event not only for the whole family but also for the whole town. Although Luke says that Jesus went up to Jerusalem with his parents at the age of twelve, the narrative does not imply that this was Jesus' first visit to Jerusalem. It is quite possible that Jesus celebrated the Passover pilgrimage with his parents year after year.

From Luke we see that Joseph and Mary chose the Feast of Passover to go up to Jerusalem. There were three annual festivals that Jewish men were required to celebrate by making a pilgrimage to Jerusalem. I. Howard Marshall claims that, in practice, only the Passover was strictly observed among the three annual festivals.[41] This is probably because of the place of Passover in the history of Israel. In a similar vein most commentators seem to follow this view. It is, however, questionable because the Feast of Tabernacles (Booths) was the most important and the most crowded of the three annual pilgrimages to the temple.[42] In recognition of its importance, Leviticus calls it *the feast of Yahweh* (Lev 23:39) and Josephus *the holiest and the greatest of Hebrew feasts* (*Ant.* 8.4. 1). It was also simply called *the feast* in Ezekiel 45:25 and 1 Kings 8:2, 65.

We should note that the Feast of Tabernacles (Booths) was a farmers' feast, the Feast of Ingathering. The Passover came at the full moon of the first month of a vernal new year. It was, therefore, celebrated on the fifteenth of the first month (Nisan), the month corresponding to April that marked the end of the rainy season. Regarding the date of Pentecost, two views are taken. According to the Dead Sea sect and the book of Jubilees (*Jub.* 15:1; 16:13; 44:1–4), the Feast of Pentecost (Weeks) fell on the morrow of the Sabbath (Saturday) following the end of Passover. From the book of Joshua (Josh 5:11) the morrow of the Sabbath was, however, the morrow of the first day of Passover, and this is supported

40. Haran, *Temples*, 294.
41. Marshall, *Gospel*, 126.
42. See De Vaux, *Ancient Israel*, 495; Wise, "Feasts," 237.

by the Septuagint (Lev 23:15f) and by statements in Philo (*Spec. Law* 2.175) and Josephus (*Ant.* 3.250–52).[43] Thus Pentecost came fifty days after the first day of the Passover (seven weeks after the cutting of the first barley and cereal grains). The Feast of Tabernacles (Booths) came in the autumn. It was on the first full moon after the autumnal equinox (September 21), which marked the beginning of autumnal and winter rains in the land. Considering the dates of each feast, Haran's suggestion that the Feast of Booths was the most crowded of all the three festivals seems to be convincing.

> The farmer is very busy and would certainly not take time off to make a pilgrimage to the temple, except for a very brief stay—at the beginning of the season and at its end. But after the ingathering, when the rainy season starts, and the crops have been brought in, he can well reward himself for his exertions, celebrating for seven consecutive days.[44]

The calendar of the three feasts leaves us in no doubt that the Feast of Tabernacles was at least for farmers a convenient time for lengthy celebrations. Josephus confirms that agriculture was the main source of livelihood for the intertestamental Jews. *As for ourselves, therefore, we neither inhabit a maritime country, nor do we delight in merchandise, nor in such a mixture with other men as arises from it; but the cities we dwell in are remote from the sea, and having a fruitful country for our habitation, we take pains in cultivating that only* (*Ag. Ap.* 1.12). Although Judea had a relatively flat area just north of Jerusalem that offered favorable conditions for both farming and cattle raising, Galilee had the advantage of agriculture as well as the fishing industries around the sea of Galilee.[45] The soil and climate of Galilee made it the most fertile and productive region of the country.[46] Galilee was, therefore, generally better suited to agriculture than was Judea.

What then was the driving force for Joseph and Mary to pick the Passover feast to come to Jerusalem? As a carpenter, Joseph, assisted by Jesus, would make his livelihood by making agricultural tools and furniture, and by working on building projects. This means that he was not

---

43. Safrai and Stern, *Jewish People*, 858.
44. Haran, *Temples*, 298.
45. See Jeremias, *Jerusalem*, 3–57; Freyne, *Galilee*, 1–19, 155–200.
46. Freyne, *Galilee*, 15.

bound by the farming season. It would be easy for Joseph as a carpenter to take time off for his preferred pilgrimage feast. Although Marshall's claim that in practice only the Passover was strictly observed among the three annual festivals is unconvincing, the place of Passover in the history of Israel probably made it the feast preferred by Joseph and Mary, and most of the Nazareth traveling-party.[47] The feasts of Passover and of Unleavened Bread marked the beginning of Israel's history as God's chosen people. For there was no feast that could compete with the Passover in commemoration of this historic moment.

What then would be the reason for Luke to depict Jesus' Passover pilgrimage particularly at the age of twelve? Since Jewish boys assumed adult responsibilities at the age of thirteen (*Pirqe Rabbi Eliezer ʿAbot* 5:21), the age of twelve was seen as a significant age in religious development. Josephus also indicates that Samuel began to prophesy when he was twelve years old (*Ant.* 5.10, 4). That Josephus dates the beginning of Samuel's ministry as a prophet to his twelfth year supports Luke's portrayal of a child who was beginning to make his transition from childhood to adulthood. Therefore, Jesus' visit to the temple at the age of twelve may have served the purpose of preparing Jesus for the responsibilities that lay ahead—particularly in Luke's eyes, for what the unfolding redemptive events of his ministry to follow will bring. From the age of thirteen on, he would have been obliged to take part in the pilgrimage to Jerusalem. Thus what Luke saw was that something quite different happened in his pilgrimage at the age of twelve, namely something relating to his future ministry. What happened in the temple provides us with a key that enables us to grasp a significant element of the pilgrimage paradigm.

After the feast was over, while his parents were returning home, the boy Jesus stayed behind in Jerusalem . . . After three days they found him in the temple courts, sitting among the teachers, listening to them and asking them questions . . . His mother said to him, "Son why have you treated us like this? Your father and I have been anxiously searching for you." "Why were you searching for me?" he asked. "Did you not know that I had to be in my Father's house?" But they did not understand what he was saying

---

47. "Caravan/traveling-party" is not used elsewhere in the NT but is found in Josephus (*J.W.* 2.587; *Ant.* 6.243). The reason for a traveling-party of pilgrims going from Galilee to Jerusalem (or vice versa) was the need to pass through inhospitable Samaritan territory (See Luke 9:53; cf. Josephus, *Life* 52 §269) or to avoid attacks by highway robbers (see Luke 10:30).

to them . . . *But his mother treasured all these things in her heart* (Luke 2:43–51). After three days Mary and Joseph found the twelve-year-old Jesus sitting among the temple teachers and the crowd who were amazed at his understanding and his answers.[48] The text is not clear whether Jesus is in the house of instruction or in the outer court within the temple. The location could be the portico of Solomon (Acts 3:11; 5:12, 21, 25). For the first time in the Gospel narrative, Jesus is seen to take an active interest in the affairs of the Jerusalem Temple. In telling the story of Jesus, Luke also unfolds the story of Jerusalem in relation to the temple.

The Greek phrase ἐν τοῖς τοῦ πατρός μου is literally translated "in the . . . of my Father." The phrase has been understood in three ways: (involved) "about my Father's business" (KJV and NKJV), "among those people belonging to my Father," or "in my Father's house."[49] Although it is still not easy to say which is the best sense in the Lukan context, the most widely held view today is that the phrase translates, "in my Father's house." Bock supports the view due to the construction of ἐν and the neuter plural definite article), τοῦ (genitive), and the frequency of the idiom for being in one's house in Genesis 41:51; Esther 7:9; Job 18:19; Josephus, *Against Apion* 1.18 §118; *Antiquities* 16.10.1 §302; POxy vol. 3 #523 line 3.[50] This rendering is, however, less than satisfying in the context of Luke chapter 2.

Jesus at the temple in Luke 2:41–49 should be, as Holland sees, understood in the light of Jesus being presented in the temple in Luke 2:21–40. Mary and Joseph never redeemed the child, though every Jewish couple had to redeem on the birth of their firstborn. The child was not redeemed. Then he was no longer Joseph and Mary's, for he was the Lord's firstborn. Luke's focus remains clear that the child was not redeemed but rather consecrated to the service of God, for he truly belonged to the Lord.[51] The reply, "Did you know that I had to be in my Father's house?" could mean, "Didn't you forget that you consecrated me to God? So I ought to be here." For Luke it explains the strong sense

---

48. Most regard the phrase "after three days" as referring to the first day out by caravan, the second day back from the caravan, and the third day in Jerusalem. See Hendriksen, *Exposition of the Gospel*, 184; Marshall, *Gospel*, 127; Brown, *Birth of the Messiah*, 474.

49. "Among those people belonging to my Father" can be translated if τοῖς is understood as masculine plural.

50. Bock, *Luke*, 1:270.

51. See also Marshall, Reicke, Caird.

of identity that Jesus felt he belonged to the Lord as well as that he recognized himself as sent by the Father to reveal and to do his will. Thus Luke's explicit concern in chapter 2 is the juxtaposition of these two events: Jesus in the temple being presented to the Lord (Luke 2:21–40) and Jesus in the temple serving his Father's purpose (Luke 2:41–49), first his consecration and then the logical outworking of this. Jesus' strong sense of identity suggests that the feast had a significant meaning. Since Jesus was the revelation of God the Father, this Passover pilgrimage was not an occasion for Jesus to experience or meet God and transform, but a vehicle through which he made himself known to Mary and Joseph as the Son of God. Mowinckel notes:

> The fundamental thought in the festal experience is that Yahweh is coming (Pss 96:13; 98:9) and "revealing himself," "becoming revealed," and "making himself known" (Ps 98:2; Pss 48:3; 76:1–2; Ps 50:2), appearing as the one he really is, manifesting his works and his will.[52]

In his first Passover pilgrimage experience Jesus revealed himself, manifesting to all the world (this time to Mary and Joseph) who he was. This was "the message of the festival."[53] Thus Jesus' pilgrimages to Jerusalem became modes of teaching or instruction for the people he encountered and the readers of the Gospels, as the journeys reported in the OT texts are to benefit the readers, who without journeying, travel vicariously and learn from them.

In this act of revelation Mary and Joseph, however, did not understand fully what was being made known. Even though they seem to play a supporting role in the scene, Mary was very much part of the scene in Luke's perspective evidenced by the relation of the incident to the pilgrimage paradigm. For Luke, Mary represents those who are unable to see who Jesus really is. Although she received the revelation about the nature of the child (Luke 1:26–56), she still failed to comprehend who he was and what he was saying to her. Despite her misunderstanding, Luke notes that she treasured all these things within her heart. It suggests that Luke decided to include this scene in order to pinpoint the *gradually dawning awareness* of Mary about her son.[54] Mary's response to this

---

52. Mowinckel, *Psalms in Israel's Worship*, 1:142.

53. Ibid.

54. Fitzmyer sees Mary's comprehension about her son in a gradual progression. See Fitzmyer, *Luke The Theologian*, 57–85; *Luke I–IX*, 443–47.

temple event—*his mother treasured all these things in her heart*—indicates that there's more going on here than first meets the eye. For the plural phrase πάντα τὰ ῥήματα (Luke 2:51) indicates that Mary did not immediately come to a full understanding of who Jesus was, but only gradually, as he chose to reveal himself to her. Thus Mary in the Lukan picture was beginning to know who he was in the context of her own pilgrimage.

Luke's portrayal of Mary in the temple scenes puts Mary on an equal footing with the disciples in their confession regarding the person of Jesus. Through the difficulty that Jesus' contemporaries, even his own family, faced in trying to understand who he really was, Luke might have suggested that the comprehension of who Jesus was would be a complex problem for his readers too. He would have drawn our attention to the transition that Mary underwent from the stage of knowing Jesus with a personal attachment to that of having a relationship with him as the Son of God. By showing how even Mary did not understand the first revelation of the Son of God, Luke reveals to the reader that faith is not to preserve, but to grow and develop. Thus the leader is reminded that just as Jesus must "progress" in wisdom, so must those who follow Jesus' story, who, like Mary, "keep these words in their hearts."[55]

That Luke depicts Mary from the beginning as a believer (Luke 1:45) and portrays her as a disciple in "the upper room" in the company of the eleven disciples (Acts 1:13) supports the hypothesis of a gradual transformation in her understanding. Thus Mary in the Lukan story was presented as the model disciple who listens to the Word of God. *My mother and my brothers, they are the ones who listen to the word of God and act on it* (Luke 8:21). It is noted that the present participles, ἀκούοντες καὶ ποιοῦντες, are used. In this way Luke pictures Mary's Passover pilgrimage as that which brought her to recognition of who he was. In the festal experience Mary's Passover pilgrimage was a fresh opportunity to come to God and learn from him. Thus *God's coming and making himself known* (the Son of God in this case) became reality experienced and expressed through the Passover feast in Jerusalem. The Lukan gospel traces the first Passover pilgrimage, presenting the interlocking relationship between the festal experience and transformation into faith's pilgrimage, namely, knowing God through the encounter with Jesus. This is the core of pilgrimage in the light of discipleship and is a framework that we will see throughout the pilgrimages of Jesus and his disciples.

55. Johnson, *Gospel of Luke*, 61.

JESUS AND THE SECOND PASSOVER PILGRIMAGE
(JOHN 2:13—3:21)

The Word became flesh and made his dwelling among us (John 1:14). The Fourth Gospel reveals to the reader its distinctive equation of the journeys in the OT with the journey (incarnation) of Jesus as the Word of God in the prologue of the gospel. From the very beginning of the Gospel the narrative reveals Jesus' identity and vocation as the Word of God and his vocation. The Word was in the beginning with God and was God (John 1:1). The opening statement goes one step further, as the narrator affirms that "the Word was made flesh" (John 1:14), stating that the Word now has been born as a human being. The only one who has seen the Father made a cosmic journey from the world of God to the world of human beings and revealed the Father. Andreas Köstenburger notes that the phrase "come into the world" (John 1:9) with its corollary "return to the Father" is used to depict Jesus as the one who enters the world from the outside and returns to his place of departure, that is, the presence of God the Father (cf. 13:1, 3; 14:12, 28; 16:28; 18:37).[56]

Fernando Segovia particularly notes that the narrative of Jesus' public life or career (John 1:19—17:26) is to characterize the Word of God's journey into the world.[57] Arguing for the dominant role of the journey motif in the plot of the Fourth Gospel, Segovia explores the cosmic journey of the word of God from the world of God to the world of human beings, becoming flesh in Jesus of Nazareth, which provides a further overall framework for the plot.[58] He also provides a critical analysis of the broader theoretical discussion regarding the concept of plot itself through a series of repeated geographical journeys in the course of the public life of Jesus as the Word of God.[59]

Segovia makes a good contribution in advancing a literary-rhetorical reading of the plot of the Fourth Gospel in terms of the journey motif. Segovia explains the motif on the basis of the common literary technique of patterns of repetition and recurrence in ancient narrative, claiming that the Fourth Gospel has recourse to a very common liter-

---

56. Köstenburger, *John*, 35.
57. Segovia, "The Journey(s) of the Word," 37–46.
58. Ibid., 23–49.
59. Ibid.

ary motif of ancient narrative, namely, the journey or travel account.[60] Segovia also refers to a very specific kind of traveling, which gives rise in turn to a very particular narrative situation in the ministry of Jesus—a journey to Jerusalem encompassing a rather large amount of narrative material and leading to a final and fatal confrontation with the ruling authorities in Jerusalem itself. What Segovia overlooks here, however, are Jesus' pilgrimages to Jerusalem and their relevance to each feast. Though Segovia argues that in the Fourth Gospel the repeated journeys of Jesus to Jerusalem can function as a major key to the plot of the Gospel, he does not extend the journey motif to the pilgrimage paradigm due to a failure to recognize the importance of Jesus' pilgrimage to Jerusalem in the context of pilgrimage festivals.[61]

Throughout the Old Testament and the intertestamental period literature God has revealed himself to men within a journey framework. It is no wonder that the pilgrimage paradigm, which is the progress of the journey framework, was deeply embedded in Judaism. In the Fourth Gospel this journey motif is also carefully shaped into the Passover and Tabernacle pilgrimage paradigm, including "a feast of the Jews" (John 5:1) and "the Feast of Dedication" (Hanukkah; John 10:22) in relation to Jerusalem, particularly with the temple. In the Fourth Gospel the temple and Jerusalem festivals are closely woven into the plot of the narrative. Gale Yee and Raymond Brown point this out and underline the theme of Jesus' replacement of Jewish feasts like the Sabbath, Passover, Tabernacles, and Dedication, and Jewish institutions like the temple and worship in Jerusalem.[62] Both of them find the reason to reinterpret Jewish feasts and institutions in the need for distinguishing between the synagogue and the Christian community.[63] The need to reinforce Christian self-assertion against "exclusion from the synagogue," became apparent since the Johannine community no longer felt solidarity with the Jewish people.[64]

---

60. Ibid.
61. Ibid., 33; Segovia, "Journey(s) of Jesus," 539–41.
62. Yee, *Jewish Feasts*, 27; Brown, *John I-XII*, 1xx.
63. Brown, *John I-XII*, 1xx–1xxv. Depending upon the assumption that the Jerusalem feasts were still of crucial importance for Diaspora Jews, Brown argues that John is directed at Diaspora Jewish Christians still loyal to the synagogue.
64. Yee, *Jewish Feasts*, 26–27.

The Word of God had to make a journey into the world to make the Father and himself known. So the (cosmic) journey became the means of God's mission to redeem. As the knowing-God-through-journey motif is the main framework of pilgrimage (journey) paradigm in the Old Testament, John makes it clear that the Word of God should carry on Jesus' journey for the completion of his mission. John notes Jesus' mission as making the Father and himself known, regardless of outright rejection and open hospitality (the world rejected the light [John 1:10–11]) experienced along the way. His followers saw the light of the world (John 1:9) and the glory of God (John 1:14) in Jesus and in the midst of his people through the Word made flesh. In the OT, God's glory was said to dwell first in the tabernacle, and later in the temple. Moses met God and heard his word in the "tent of meeting" (Exod 33:9). Now people may meet God and hear him in the flesh of Jesus.[65] Considering the Greek verb ἐσκήνωσεν (John 1:14) now commonly translated "dwelt" more literally means "to pitch one's tent."[66] Jesus' "pitching his tent among us" is, as Köstenburger indicates, even more intimate through the incarnation of the Word than God's residence in the midst of Israel in the tabernacle (Exod 40:34–35).[67] The incarnate Word, according to John, was the true temple.

John thus follows immediately with his explanatory teaching in the narrative of the temple cleansing. Unlike the Synoptic Gospels, in the Fourth Gospel the temple cleansing incident occurs at the beginning of Jesus' ministry during the Feast of Passover after the first sign at Cana (John 2:13–25), and Jesus also made the regular pilgrimage to Jerusalem at the Feast of Passover as well as Tabernacles and Dedication. *When it was almost time for the Jewish Passover, Jesus went up to Jerusalem* (John 2:13). The text opens with a number of key terms "Passover," "Jerusalem," and "going up," which immediately create an atmosphere of pilgrimage for the entire scene. In the light of Jesus' reference to the temple as "his Father's house" in his first Passover pilgrimage (Luke 2:49), the reference to the temple in his second Passover pilgrimage, the first Passover pil-

---

65. Mowvley, "John 1:14–18," 136.

66. Köstenburger notes that this rare term is used only in the book of Revelation. See Köstenburger, *John*, 41.

67. There are many scholars who take John 1:9 as a preliminary reference to the incarnation. See Borchert, *John 1–11*, 112–13; Schnackenburg, *John*, 1:255; Laney, *John*, 41; Moloney, *Gospel of John*, 37; Köstenburger, *John*, 34–35; Ridderbos, *Gospel of John*, 43; Carson, *John*, 122.

grimage in John's Gospel (John 2:13-22) comes as a dramatic surprise. The entire scene was disturbed by the situation in the temple. Jesus found people selling cattle, sheep, and doves, and the moneychangers sitting at the tables (John 2:14). Jesus drove them out with a whip, accusing them of making "my Father's house a house of trade" (2:16). The animal vendors offered an essential service to the many pilgrims who wished to buy an unblemished animal for the Passover sacrifice in Jerusalem itself rather than bring them along on pilgrimage. The moneychangers also provided a service for the pilgrims to pay the annual temple tax in Tyrian coinage.[68] Since it has no basis in the text of John's Gospel, the claim that such business transactions were exploiting people by profiteering is not supported by modern scholarship, though, as Charles Barrett suggests, it does not mean that the trading itself was honestly conducted.[69] If so, business transactions at that time were customary and economically necessary for the temple to function. However, Jesus' response was swift and striking (John 2:15-16). To understand his temple action, we must ask the question, "What was intended by this temple action?" Interpretations of the incident can be classified into one of four categories.

First, there are those who claim that it was *an expression of the messianic consciousness of Jesus.*[70] Secondly, there are those who posit that Jesus made a prophetic statement against the temple.[71] Having suggested that Jesus symbolically and prophetically enacted judgment upon it—a judgment that, both before and after, he announced verbally as well as in action—Nicholas Wright concludes that Jesus' action in the temple was intended as a dramatic symbol of its imminent destruction.[72] However, there is a third approach that asserts that, from the writer's point of view, the old system, the Passover feast, was abrogated by the new order, the new Passover, inaugurated by Jesus Christ who would become a new

---

68. David Carson and Rudolf Schnackenburg believe that Tyrian coinage was chosen due to its high silver content. See *m. Bekerot* 8.7; Carson, *John*, 178; Schnackenburg, *John*, 1:346.

69. Though, "the house of robbers" (Mark 11:17) implies impropriety. See also Barrett, *Gospel According to St. John*, 198.

70. Gartner, *Temple and the Community*, 107. This view is also generally supported by the traditions.

71. Barrett, Gartner, Horsely, Casey, N. Wright, and E. P. Sanders read the event as a symbolic prophetic action.

72. N. Wright, *Jesus and the Victory*, 413-28.

Passover victim.[73] Köstenburger as well as Barrett and Christopher Evans note another possibility; that Jesus saw evidence that religious arrogance was disrupting Gentile worship in the only place that was open to them—the so-called Court of the Gentiles.[74] It should be noted for the purpose of this debate that Jesus spiritualized the temple, proclaiming himself to be the temple as that place of God's indwelling presence. The Fourth Gospel shares this spiritualization of the temple with the Qumran sect. However, there are two main differences between the Qumran sect and the Fourth Gospel.

In the Qumran community the Teacher of Righteousness is presented as a revealer of secrets, yet he was no more than that. In contrast, Jesus the Messiah not only revealed the mystery of God's character and purpose, but also revealed himself to be one with God. As the incarnate Son of God, he was the true Temple that the earthly temple prefigured. Another difference is that, whereas the sect was concerned with ritual purity, John's concern was with spiritual worship.[75] Despite differences between them, the Fourth Gospel, as Barrett indicates, shares Qumran's opposition to the Jerusalem Temple.[76]

Debates to find a reason for such action have established the different placings of the various pericopae in this passage. With the synoptic accounts, it is not clear what the authors saw as Jesus' motivation for this action, although John emphasizes elsewhere the destruction of the temple to make room for a new type of worship. *Take these things away . . . the hour is coming, and now is, when the true worshippers will worship the Father in spirit and truth, for such the Father seeks to worship him* (John 2:16; 4:23).

The temple-cleansing incident occurs at the first of several Passovers in the beginning of his ministry in John 2, whereas the synoptic tradition places it at the end of his ministry (Mark 11:15–18, [the only Passover Mark records]; Matt 21:12–17; Luke 19:45). Scholars have discussed this discrepancy in chronology. Barrett, Rudolf Schnackenburg, Herman Ridderbos, George Beasley-Murray, C. H. Dodd, Barnabas Lindars, and Maurice Casey argue that John used Marcan material and insist that it is improbable that there were two cleansings, one at the

---

73. Lightfoot, *St. John's Gospel*, 114.
74. See Evans, *St. John's Gospel*, and Köstenburger, *John*, for comments on John 2:14.
75. Barrett quotes Braun for the point. See Barrett, *Gospel According to St. John*, 201.
76. Ibid.

beginning and one at the end of the ministry, particularly considering the considerable hostility Jesus must have faced after challenging the temple system.[77] Contra to this view, Leon Morris, David Carson, William Hendriksen, P. W. Comfort, W. C. Hawley, and Köstenburger contend that because of the language of the two different incidents and Jesus' pattern of withdrawal (John 3:22; 6:15; 7:9–10; 8:59; 10:40), which made his ministry for two or three more years plausible, John and the Synoptics were talking about two different temple cleansings.[78] Brown has proposed another possibility that Jesus made his remarks about the temple on his first visit, yet the temple cleansing occurred at the end of his ministry (John 2:13–17).[79] Wright also maintains that Jesus seems to say this sort of thing more than once.[80]

Whatever tradition this narrative originally followed, the author of the Fourth Gospel has shaped his unique version of the tradition at the beginning with a clear theological agenda. The narrator provides an obvious introduction (John 2:13) and a conclusion that serves to lead into the story of Nicodemus (John 2:23–25). However, the narrative of the temple cleansing, together with that of the wedding at Cana, should be viewed as the continuous confirmation of the prologue of the gospel, "the Word became flesh and made his dwelling among us" (John 1:14). In both stories Jesus Christ who, in the gospel's prologue, was introduced as the Word of God, becomes the visible sign of the presence of God in his coming to the world as well as in what he does as a sign.

John states that, "the temple he had spoken of was his body" (John 2:21), adding that the disciples understood the deeper meaning only after the resurrection. John's own purpose is clearly to show what this incident reveals about Jesus' identity.[81] The interest, which the evangelist takes, confirms that John was interested in showing the meaning of the temple cleansing in the context of the pilgrimage framework. For the cleansing of the temple in Jesus' Passover pilgrimage (the presentation

---

77. See Barrett, *Gospel According to St. John*, 195; Schnackenburg, *John*, 1:344; Ridderbos, *Gospel of John*, 115; Beasley-Murray, *John*, 38–39; Dodd, *Historical Tradition*, 162; Lindars, *Gospel of John*, 135–37; Casey, *Is John's Gospel True?* 4–13.

78. Morris, *Gospel According to John*, 167; Carson, *John*, 177; Hendriksen, *Gospel of John*, 120–21; Comfort and Hawley, *Opening the Gospel*, 38; Köstenburger, *John*, 76–78.

79. Brown, *John I–XII*, 118.

80. N. Wright, *Jesus and the Victory*, 493.

81. Walker, *Jesus and the Holy City*, 163.

as it stands) is at the heart of the pilgrimage paradigm, *the destination of pilgrimage* and *knowing God through the encounter with Jesus*. Barrett finds John's thought quite distinctive.

> Since it rests not upon general observations or speculations about the relation of the human soul to God but upon the unique mutual indwelling of the Father and the Son (John 14:10 and often); the human body of Jesus was the place where a unique manifestation of God took place and consequently became the only true Temple.[82]

The evangelist proclaims to his community that the glory of God that was present in the tabernacle and is in the temple of Jerusalem dwells in Jesus Christ, whose human body is the new Temple (John 2:21). While Jesus challenged Israel's abuse of the temple, Jesus told Israel that its temple belonged to him, for he as the Son of God was the true place of worship, the Temple itself. *Destroy this temple, and I will raise it again in three days* (John 2:19). Jesus' prophetic speech of doom over the temple led to his confrontation with the Jewish leaders. His pronouncement was a prophetic protest against the corrupt religion that the Jewish leaders represented. In that temple, and in the presentation of the Passover feast, Jesus announced a new way of worship that God would establish in him. His message of the festal experience was that the expectations and promises of the feasts would not come to reality for Israel due to the sin of the people. Andrew Lincoln refines the point, making it the very core of pilgrimage.

> The goal of pilgrimage, temple worship, has been transformed christologically. Jesus is the true place of worship and so to go on pilgrimage is to come to Jesus.[83]

As God carried the Israelites out of Egypt to bring them to himself (Exod 19:4–6), Jesus proclaims that he is the goal of pilgrimage. Here the reason for pilgrimage to the temple in Jerusalem gives the most profound theological interpretation of pilgrimage: "I brought you to myself" (v. 4). As the mountain is not the destination of the Exodus, the temple is not the destination of pilgrimage, but Jesus, the Word of God made flesh. The destination of pilgrimage was bringing the Israelites to Jesus himself. Jesus became the focus and the goal of pilgrimage towards

---

82. Barrett, *Gospel According to St. John*, 201.
83. Lincoln, "Pilgrimage," 39.

which the whole of the physical journey pointed. The physical journey to Jerusalem for Jesus Christ, therefore, became the outward visible procedure by which God brought about his providence. From that time on, a journey with Jesus and to Jesus must have displaced the pilgrimage to Jerusalem. The goal of pilgrimage was not the temple in Jerusalem as the place where God was encountered, but Jesus himself as the fulfillment of the Temple where God was to be met. The purpose of Jesus' own Passover pilgrimage was thus to transform pilgrimage. It means that Jesus' Passover pilgrimage in the Fourth Gospel was for the benefit of others as well as for himself. For the disciples who journeyed with Jesus "the festal epiphany of Yahweh" was visibly expressed through Jesus, the true dwelling place of God.[84] The knowledge of Jesus was opened up, so that all may know Jesus as the Temple, the destination of pilgrimage.

However, the last words of the temple cleansing narrative say that the disciples did not understand what Jesus had said in the temple. *But the temple he had spoken of was his body. After he was raised from the dead, his disciples recalled what he had said. Then they believed the Scripture and the words that Jesus had spoken* (John 2:22). Though he revealed himself more clearly in his words than in his acts, the disciples did not understand that what Jesus meant was his own body, first destroyed and then raised from the dead, and that his body was the true Temple. Although the disciples experienced these revelations concerning Jesus, they still failed to comprehend who he was and what he was saying to them. Luke presents Mary's progressive awareness in her Passover pilgrimage with Jesus (Luke 2:41–51), whereas John does not seem to have staged this scene so as to pinpoint the *gradually growing awareness* of the disciples about his identity.

It is probable that the disciples gradually recognized him through various signs. However, in the Fourth Gospel misunderstandings of various sorts (about thirty misunderstandings) are, as Carson indicates, an important literary device.[85] The evangelist wishes his community to come to grips with the fact that the resurrection of Jesus was the turning point of salvation history. Although this point is not clearly expressed here, probably John is linking the resurrection of Jesus with the Holy Spirit

---

84. Mowinckel, *Psalms in Israel's Worship*, 1:142. Also, we are not actually told that his disciples accompanied Jesus, although they are naturally thought of as witnesses. Bultmann, *John*, 123.

85. Carson, *John*, 183.

(John 14–16). Thus part of John's purpose in telling the story is that the disciples came to the stage of a full comprehension only later on as they were aided by the Holy Spirit.[86] Ridderbos makes this point explicit.

> It was the resurrection, the witness of the Spirit (14:26; 15:26), and the Scriptures that "brought to their remembrance," that gave them the correct understanding of what Jesus had said and done. Thus they became aware of who he was and what he had said and meant. Neither the resurrection, nor the Spirit, nor the Scriptures, nor their faith was primary. What was and remained primary was the glory of the indwelling of God in Jesus.[87]

Presenting the interlocking relationship between the temple in Jerusalem as the indwelling place of God and Jesus, the new Temple, in the glory of the indwelling of God, the Fourth Gospel traces the temple cleansing in his second Passover pilgrimage and tells us that *God's presence, previously focused in the Jerusalem temple, is now to be found in the crucified and risen body of Christ.*[88] So we can see John's purpose in describing the temple cleansing in Jesus' first Passover pilgrimage at the very beginning of his ministry. We note that the plot of the Fourth Gospel is carefully shaped into the three Passover and Tabernacle pilgrimages including "a feast of the Jews" (John 5:1) and "the Feast of Dedication" (Hanukkah; John 10:22). For John the temple and Jerusalem festivals are closely woven into the plot of the narrative. Therefore, from the very beginning of Jesus' ministry, Jesus' replacement of the temple and Jewish feasts had to be signified as the foundation of his pilgrimages and the need of distinguishing between his own way of pilgrimage and the traditional way of pilgrimage.

Conclusion

The meanings of Passover mediated by participants were probably conditioned. The reasons as to why Passover was chosen to symbolize the crucial changes in the history of Israelites was probably due to the great symbolic representation of the Passover to which the Israelites could give their own meaning for the Exodus experience that had become a central part of the history of Israel. Whenever the Israelites had a national memorial, they would naturally see the Passover as the prime feast/

---

86. Carson, *John*, 183; Barrett, *Gospel According to St. John*, 201; Morris, *Gospel According to John*, 180, Köstenburger, *John*, 110.

87. Ridderbos, *Gospel of John*, 121.

88. Lincoln, "Pilgrimage," 38.

ceremony for national celebration. The feasts of Passover were historicized to commemorate and remember the Exodus, and to heighten and stimulate memory of the momentous events in the history of Israel.

As such, did the twelve-year-old Jesus on the threshold of adult life imprint his own meaning and purpose on his Passover pilgrimage to Jerusalem? Jesus' visit to the temple at the age of twelve may have had the purpose of preparing Jesus, particularly in Luke's eyes, for what the unfolding redemptive events of his ministry to follow will bring. What Luke saw was that something quite different happened in his pilgrimage at the age of twelve, namely something for his future ministry. Since Jewish boys assumed adult responsibilities on entry into the religious community of Judaism at the age of thirteen (*Pirqe Rabbi Eliezer ‹Abot* 5:21) the age of twelve was seen as a significant age in religious development. So Jesus at the temple in Luke 2:41–49 should be understood, as Holland sees it, in the light of Jesus being presented in the temple in Luke 2:21–40. Mary and Joseph never redeemed the child. The child was no longer Joseph and Mary's, for he was the Lord's firstborn. Luke's focus remains clear that the child was not redeemed but rather consecrated to the service of God. For, Jesus truly belonged to the Lord. The reply, "Didn't you know that I had to be in my Father's house?" could mean, "Did you forget that you consecrated me to God? So I ought to be here." For Luke it explains Jesus' strong sense of identity and why it was that Jesus felt he belonged to the Lord as well as recognizing himself as sent by the Father to reveal and to do his Father's will.

In the light of Jesus' reference to the temple as "his Father's house" in his first Passover pilgrimage (Luke 2:49), the reference to the temple in his second Passover pilgrimage (John 2:13–22) comes as a dramatic surprise. John's own purpose is clear in terms of what this incident reveals about Jesus' identity. John thus follows immediately with his explanation in the narrative of the temple cleansing. John states that, "He spoke of the temple of his body" (John 2:21). The interest, which the evangelist takes, confirms that John was interested in showing the meaning of the temple cleansing in a pilgrimage occasion. For the cleansing of the temple in Jesus' Passover pilgrimage is at the heart of the pilgrimage paradigm, *the destination of pilgrimage* and *knowing God through the encounter with Jesus*.

From the very beginning of the Gospel the narrative reveals Jesus' identity as the Word of God. The opening statement goes one step further, as the narrator affirms that "the Word was made flesh" (John 1:14), stating that the Word now has been born as a human being. The Word of God had to make a journey into the world to make the Father and himself known. As the knowing God motif experienced through pilgrimage is one of the main frameworks of the journey paradigm in the Old Testament, John makes it clear that the Word of God should carry on his journey for completing his mission of making the Father and himself known, regardless of what might be encountered along the way.

The evangelist proclaims to his community that the glory of God, which was present in the tabernacle and is in the temple of Jerusalem, dwells in Jesus Christ, whose human body is the new Temple (John 2:21). While Jesus challenged Israel's abuse of the temple, Jesus told Israel that its temple belonged to him, for he as the Son of God was the true place of worship, the Temple itself. So to go on pilgrimage is to come to Jesus.[89] The goal of pilgrimage has been transformed christologically.[90] The pilgrimages for Jesus can be viewed as being for the benefit of his people. It was through the medium of the pilgrimage that he revealed himself. In the festal experience, Jesus' first and second Passover pilgrimages were fresh opportunities for Mary and the disciples to come to know God, to meet with and learn from him. For them *God's coming and making himself known* became reality experienced and expressed through the Passover feast in Jerusalem.

Throughout the Old Testament and the intertestamental period literature God has made himself known to men within a journey framework. In Luke and the Fourth Gospel this journey motif is also carefully shaped into the Passover pilgrimage paradigm in relation to Jerusalem, particularly the temple. Thus the temple and Jerusalem festivals are closely woven into the plot of the narrative in the gospels of Luke and John, presenting the interlocking relationship between the festal experience and transformation into faith's pilgrimage, namely, knowing God through the encounter with Jesus.

---

89. Ibid., 39.
90. Ibid.

4

Jesus and the Tabernacles Pilgrimage

It is noted that the Feast of Tabernacles was earmarked as that which would draw Israel to Jerusalem (Zech 14:14–16). This appears to be the beginning of the subsequent pattern of pilgrimage feasts. However, OT information regarding the Feast of Tabernacles is general and fragmented, so it is best to be treated in the beginning of the Tabernacles pilgrimage in the NT, where the feast has clearly become connected with pilgrimage occasions and has a significant meaning for Jesus' journey to Jerusalem.

SETTING THE SCENE—THE TABERNACLES IN RETROSPECT

The cycle of the three major Jewish festivals is completed with the Feast of Tabernacles (Lev 23:33–43; Num 29:12–39; Neh 8:13–18; Hos 12:9; Zech 14:16–19), held in autumn, either September or October.[1] The calendar in Leviticus (Lev 23:33, 39) specifies an exact date "from the 15th to the 21st of Tishri." At the early stage, the Feast of Tabernacles is referred to as the Feast of Ingathering, being "at the end of the year" (Exod 23:16). However, a number of scholars point out that the phrase, "at the end of the year," rather indicates the beginning of the year. In particular, Exodus 34:22 signifies the phrase, "the turn of the year" (NIV) or "the return of the year" (RSV), not the end of the year, and suggests that the year was originally considered to begin in the autumn. In addition to Exodus 23 and 34, the harvest festival is at the turn of the year in Numbers 29:12–38, and appears to be the most important

---

1. See also *m. Sukkah* 5:2–4.

festival of the year, judging from the great number of sacrifices offered.[2] Deuteronomy 31 connects the feast with a public reading of the Torah at the end of every seven years, in the years of canceling debts, during the Feast of Tabernacles, stressing its significance. If this were the case, the reason for the claim would be that the Feast of Tabernacles in the autumn celebrated the beginning of the autumnal and winter rains, on which the life of the land depended for a new agricultural season and a fruitful harvest.[3]

This reckoning of the year from autumn to autumn reflects the ancient Jewish calendar, which was lunisolar. However, the calendar was eleven days shorter than the solar year. This meant that consistent observance of the calendar caused the three festivals to move out of their original season. In order to keep the festivals in line with the agricultural seasons, the traditional biblical and Jewish festal calendar developed a chronological system with New Year in spring and Tishri as the seventh month. Considering the result of external influences, mainly from Babylon, Hakan Ulfgard claims that the change in biblical chronology from an autumnal New Year to a spring New Year was a most significant expression of Babylonian political and cultural influence in the eastern Mediterranean region towards the end of the seventh century.[4] In the same vein he also expounds this ideological preference from which the Passover festival in spring emerges as the most important festival of the year in connection with the increased eastern (Babylonian) influence, instead of the ancient harvest and New Year festival in the autumn.[5]

Like the Passover feast Tabernacles was to last for seven days. Thirteen bullocks were offered for sacrifice on the first day diminished by one bullock each day. On the seventh day seven bullocks were offered

---

2. Although the festival is not explicitly mentioned by the name "festival to the Lord" (Num 29:12), most of the general details of its celebration correspond to the Tabernacles feast.

3. Pilgrimage festivals celebrated the seasons of the land, the sun's movement around the earth.

4. The transfer of New Year to spring must be regarded as resulting from the increased political and cultural influence during the formative biblical period from the succession of mighty empires in the northeast: Assyrians, Babylonians, Persians. Having followed E. Auerbach's outline for the change, George MacRae also claims that the year beginning in the spring was a Babylonian innovation, adopted by the Hebrews under the influence of Babylonia. See MacRae, "Evolution of the Feast," 253. See also Ulfgard, *Story of Sukkot*, 36–55.

5. Ulfgard, *Story of Sukkot*, 36–55.

(Num 29:12–34). An eighth day of the feast is added in Leviticus 23:36. On the eighth day an assembly was held and one bullock, one ram, and seven lambs were offered (Num 29:35–38). It is impossible to provide the exact function of the day, because of the obscurity of the origin of the eighth day. The eighth day has, however, been regarded as a solemn conclusion to the succession of the great feasts,[6] as an independent feast rather than as part of Tabernacles,[7] or as a conclusion for the feast designed to help the people make the transition back to normal life.[8] This might be "the last and greatest day of the Feast" alluded to in John 7:37.

The festival statement, "three times a year all your males shall appear before the Lord Yahweh" (Exod 23:17; 34:23) may simply have implied worship at the sanctuaries of Gibeon, Bethel, Gilgal, Dan, Beer-sheba, etc. and not necessarily at the tent of the ark itself at Shiloh. Thus Auerbach suggests that the pilgrimages enjoined in Exodus 23:17 were originally not connected with the three feasts, but were private obligations to be fulfilled at one's convenience at any time during the year.[9] However, the Deuteronomic festival statements provide a most developed version of the three pilgrimage feasts (Deut 16:1–17). Deuteronomy indicates that all males are to be present "at the place he will choose" (Deut 16:5, 11, 15). This Deutronomic principle connects the pilgrimages with the three feasts (Deut 16:16) and the sanctuary. All are to participate in the feast. All indicates, "you, your sons and daughters, your menservants and maidservants, the Levites, and the aliens, the fatherless and the widows" (Deut 16:11, 14). When all men were present at the sanctuary, the rest of the family must have celebrated the feast at home. The feast as a time of rejoicing was also emphasized, particularly for the successful harvest. *Be joyful at your Feast . . . For the Lord of your God will bless you in all your harvest and in all the work of your hands, and your joy will be complete* (Deut 16:14–15).

Leviticus 23 provides a much more detailed account of the Feast of Tabernacles. *On the first day you are to take choice fruit from the trees, and palm fronds, leafy branches and poplars, and rejoice before the Lord your God for seven days* (Lev 23:40). Although the role and function of this fruit is not explained, the various branches were used to build the

6. MacRae, "Evolution of the Feast," 258.
7. MacRae quotes H. Lesetre. See ibid.
8. Yee, *Jewish Feasts*, 72.
9. MacRae quotes Auerbach. See MacRae, "Evolution of the Feast," 254.

booths. All native-born Israelites were required to live in booths made of the various branches for the seven days of the feast. The designation "feast of booths" comes from this requirement. *Live in booths for seven days: All native-born Israelites are to live in booths so your descendants will know that I had the Israelites live in booths when I brought them out of Egypt. I am the Lord of your God* (Lev 23:42–43).

Psalms 43, 76, 81, 118, 132 are connected with the Feast of Tabernacles. Psalm 43:3–4 pictures a crowd in procession approaching the house of God with shouts of joy, observing a festival. So the modern Jewish synagogue ritual assigns Psalm 43 to Tabernacles. The Mishnaic description of Tabernacles confirms that this picture is most appropriate to the feast. Having drawn attention to the similarity between the word *sukko*, "in Salem is His abode" and *sukka*, "booth," H. St. J. Thackeray assigns Psalm 76 to Tabernacles. It is quite probable that the Hebrews who sang the psalm may have seen in it the idea that Yahweh too has his booth in Jerusalem.[10] Psalm 81 is also commonly thought to have been originally composed for Tabernacles. Verses 1 to 3 express the joy of the occasion with the playing of instruments, in particular blowing the trumpet at the new moon. Psalms 118 and 132 are also thought to be Tabernacles psalms. Psalm 118 contains explicit mention of the light theme (v. 27). Psalm 132 celebrates David's bringing the ark to Jerusalem, alluding to the feast. It is noted that the branches of a tree were carried during the festal procession (2 Macc 10:6–8). This festal procession might be alluded to in Jesus' triumphal entry (Matt 21:6–11; Mark 11:1–11; John 12:12–15).

Second Chronicles records that the feast was also observed in the time of Solomon (2 Chr 8:13) and Hezekiah (2 Chr 31:3). First Kings 8:2 in particular suggests that the feast associated with the period in the wilderness also has crucial connection with Solomon's temple dedication. Although 1 Kings' mention of the feast is not as clear as 2 Chronicles, the temple dedication seems to take place in the month of the Tabernacles celebration. A few chapters later 1 Kings presents Jeroboam's temple festival with a precise dating, the fifteenth day of the eighth month (1 Kgs 12:32). Ulfgard maintains that this might be attributable to the tension between a lunar-oriented calendar influenced by Babylon and a solar-oriented calendar.

---

10 MacRae quotes Thackeray. See ibid., 264.

The precise dating of Jeroboam's "anti-festival" (from the author's point of view) might then indicate the use in the northern kingdom of Israel of a lunar oriented calendar, influenced by Babylonia, in which the fifteenth day of the month (i.e., the day of the full moon) was an important festival day. On the other hand, the silence about the day on which Solomon's temple was dedicated might reflect the predominance in pre-exilic Judah of an agrarian, solar oriented calendar, in which the fifteenth of the month had no similar significance.[11]

In Ezra (Ezra 3:4) and Nehemiah (Neh 8:13–18) the feast was celebrated by the returning exiles from the Babylonian captivity, being associated with the temple cult and the Torah. The people who had forgotten the feast responded with fervency to Ezra, as he read Moses's words (Neh 8:14–15). In particular, Ezra 3:4 is another sign of the feast associated with temple dedication in biblical tradition. According to Nehemiah, the people built the booths on their roofs, in their courtyards, in the courts of the house of God, and in the squares by the Water Gate and the Gate of Ephraim (Neh 8:16). It is clear from the statement that the feast was associated with the wilderness wandering after the Exodus, and historicized to commemorate the wilderness period. The exilic experience appears to be of fundamental significance for those who belong to the community of the returned exiles. For them the Tabernacles celebration made clear their legitimacy as God's true Israel. Having noticed the tension between the remaining local population and the returning exiles in Ezra and Nehemiah, Ulfgard thus posits that legitimization is sought for the Torah brought from Babylon by Ezra and for the ideological self-understanding as constituting God's true Israel.[12] Giving the festival a historicizing meaning and connecting it with the central biblical ideological/theological concepts of "the Exodus" and "the temple" descriptions of its celebration (*halakic* rulings, cult concentration, pilgrimage to Jerusalem), Ulfgard claims, serve to strengthen ethnic and religious cohesion and ideological unity within emerging early Judaism marked by its exilic Babylonian background in its controversies with other claimants to the old traditions of Israel.[13] As we discussed in chapter 4, the Feast of Passover was highlighted with timely contextualized meanings

---

11. Ulfgard, *Story of Sukkot*, 102–3.
12. Ibid., 107–40.
13. Ibid., 47, 75.

for the momentous events in the history of Israel, so also the Feast of Tabernacles has developed its own character and meaning in the context of the history of Israel.

After the exile the prophet Zechariah saw the eschatological significance of the feast. He envisioned that the surviving nations would go up to the temple in Jerusalem to worship God during the Feast of Tabernacles (Zech 14:16). Since Tabernacles was the last and greatest festival of the Hebrew calendar, the festival was chosen by the prophet to speak of the ingathering of the various Gentile nations as well as of the final restoration of Israel. The prophet stressed the importance of making pilgrimage for the feast, warning that there will be no rain, if they do not go to the temple in Jerusalem to worship the King, the Lord Almighty (Zech 14:17). Earlier in Zechariah 14, the rain theme and the light motif were presented in both literal and symbolic ways (Zech 14:6–9).

In relation to the origin of Tabernacles, many scholars have adopted the picture that the Feast of Tabernacles had a sedentary origin, namely the Canaanite harvest festival, when the Israelites became permanent dwellers in Canaan.[14] Contrary to Mowinckel and to S. H. Hooke's *Myth and Ritual-school*, Hans-Joachim Kraus proposes a different origin for the feast.[15] Having not denied that there is some connection between the Canaanite sedentary harvest festival and the Feast of Tabernacles, Kraus seeks the real origin of the feast in a "Tent of Meeting" festival among the nomadic tribes of Israel.[16] Kraus points out that the Israelites en route from Egypt did not dwell in booths but in tents, and attempts to find a cultic basis for an early tent feast that later developed into the Feast of Tabernacles, as we know it.[17] Although his work has been criticized for lack of clear supporting textual evidence for a tent feast among the nomadic tribes, he certainly deals with some important aspects of the Feast of Tabernacles that the traditional argument has failed to explain adequately.[18] Thus George MacRae claims that scholars should not disregard the capability of Israel in shaping its own cult and theology, because

---

14. Mowinckel and successive scholars who have adopted this view are Hooke, Engnell, A. R. Johnson, and Eaton.

15. His theory has had no general support.

16. MacRae quotes Kraus to argue a quite different proposal for the origin of the feast. See MacRae, "Evolution of the Feast," 259–63.

17. Ibid., 260.

18. Ibid.

not all parallels between biblical Israel and its neighbors have to be due to direct influence.[19]

The Israelites as shepherds depended on tending flocks and herds for their livelihood (Gen 46:31–34). With the evidence that Isaac sowed crops (Gen 26:12) and that Joseph dreamed of the field in which his brothers' sheaves stood bound and bowed down to Joseph's sheaf (Gen 37:7), the Hebrew patriarchs might have already been acquainted with agriculture. They tended their flocks, but they also grew crops. Thus it is, as J. B. Segal suggests, quite probable to suggest that they were semi-nomads.[20] If this was the case, the Israelites, having a stronger nomadic lifestyle, might have been accustomed to living in tents or the tent might have been widespread enough for the Israelites to have developed a tent feast. Therefore, Kraus and MacRae's argument still allows much room for debate and consideration.

Although the relationship between nomadic and sedentary customs in the history of the feast is not clear, it is certain that it is impossible to separate them in Israel's history apart from the forty-year nomadic period in the wilderness. As the Passover celebration was suggested to be made up of a nomadic shepherd feast and a sedentary agricultural feast, we may postulate this embracing solution that the Israelites might have developed and combined both forms of the feast, having encountered and adopted both nomadic and sedentary lifestyles. It is, however, noted that the possible details about the sedentary and nomadic background cannot be more than speculation. What is clear is that, whatever its origin, and whatever its precise ritual structure, its meaning and purpose has remained an occasion for thanksgiving and rejoicing in the harvest. It is thus quite safe to say that the feast had its own particular meaning before it was later associated and reinterpreted in the light of the wilderness period of the whole exodus experience.

While the Feast of Passover was historicized in remembrance of the Exodus event, the Feast of Tabernacles was associated with the wilderness wandering of Israel. Mowinckel, however, maintains that it was the Feast of Tabernacles, not the Passover, that was originally associated with the story of the Exodus, combining the feast with the Creation.[21]

19. Ibid., 264–67.

20. See Segal, *Hebrew Passover*, 78–113.

21. Here is the essence of Segal's quote of Mowinckel: Mowinckel holds that in post-Exilic Israel the festival of Tabernacles, which was the occasion for the formal enthrone-

> Tabernacles was the New Year festival on which the king formally ascended his throne or renewed annually his royal dignity. It was the season of Creation; and Creation myths, widespread throughout the Near East, are echoed in the history of Israel. Just as the world was created from water, so the nation of Israel had been created from the sea through which they passed on their release from Egypt.[22]

For him the Creation represents the creation of Israel as the Lord's chosen people, which is an historical foundation for the kingdom of God, manifested in the Exodus from Egypt. Creation and the rise of Israel should become one: Creation reaches its climax in the rise of Israel.[23] Mowinckel also finds in Psalms 47, 93, and 95–100 that the enthronement of God as King stands as the dominant theme, particularly in relation to the Feast of Tabernacles that was the New Year celebration. A chief characteristic of the Psalms can be found in the phrase "Yahweh has become King" (Pss 47:8; 93:1; 96:10; 97:1). This celebration also proclaims the kingship of God as his reign or rule (Pss 46:10; 47:3; 95:3; 96:7; 97:6, 8, 10–12; 98:9; 99:4). God "comes" (Ps 98:9), "makes himself known" (48:4; 76:2f; 98:2), and "goes up" (47:6) to the temple to seat himself on his throne (Pss 93:2; 97:2; 99:1). This is the pinnacle of the enthronement psalm that Mowinckel finds.

> For Yahweh's enthronement day is the day when he comes (96:13; 98:9) and "makes himself known" (98:2), reveals himself and his "salvation" and his will (93:5; 99:7), when he repeats the theophany of Mount Sinai (97:3ff.; 99:7f.) and renews the election (47:5) of Israel, and the covenant with his people (95:6ff.; 99:6ff.).[24]

The feast in which Yahweh became King is bound up with God's works of salvation in the life of the people through which he manifests to the entire world who he is. For Israelites God's *coming* and *making himself known* becomes reality expressed through the symbols and rites of the feast and reexperienced by the pilgrims who join the feast every

---

ment of the king, had little meaning. This is reflected in the Passover documents. In the early narratives of J and E2 the Pesah had been the festival of the tenth plague. With Deuteronomy it gained greater importance; the Pesah, instead of Tabernacles, was regarded now as the commemoration of the Exodus, although it was still not the principal festival of Israel. See Segal, *Hebrew Passover*, 85–86.

22. Ibid.

23. Mowinckel, *Psalms in Israel's Worship*, 1:154.

24. Ibid., 1:118.

year. Thus Mowinckel considers the festal experience as the *message* of the feast.[25] Although Mowinckel does not directly refer to the idea of the pilgrimage paradigm, his understanding of the enthronement psalms combined with the Feast of Tabernacles highlights the knowing God motif, one of the main pilgrimage paradigms, and offers the underlying dynamic of the feast.

Since his coming as King was the main idea of the feast, it is no wonder that the Feast of Tabernacles was known as "the day of Yahweh."[26] God "remembers his creation" and comes to bring renewal to the natural world.[27] In the light of the repeated creation and renewal of life and nature, the Feast of Tabernacles that was a New Year festival had a special connection with the rainy season, which closed the agricultural year and opened the new one. Zechariah 14 recognizes rain for a fruitful harvest as a gift from God in response to the pilgrimage the Israelites made (Zech 14:17). The rain motif was also connected with the theme of light (Ps 118:27; Zech 14:6–9). In the feast God comes and brings along with him rain to defeat drought and light to vanquish the evil powers including the enemies of Israel.

The Mishnah shows how pilgrims traveled to the temple for the Feast of Tabernacles (*m. Bikkurim* 3:2–5), with a vivid picture for procession—that pilgrims would be met by the music of the flute until they reached the Temple Mount (*m. Bikkurim* 3:3–5).[28] The Mishnah also describes the water (*m. Sukkah* 4:9) and light (*m. Sukkah* 5:2–4) ceremony of the temple during the festival.

From the biblical tradition to the intertestamental literature the Feast of Tabernacles, like the Feast of Passover, underwent a development from whatever was its original celebration to a "historicized" one. Although some of the original ideas have remained right down to the Second Temple period, all these symbols and rites of the feast were gradually reinterpreted in the context of the history of the Israelites.

25. Ibid., 1:142.

26. Ibid., 1:119. The Feast of Tabernacles was also simply considered "the feast."

27. Mowinckel quotes Fiebig. See ibid., 1:122.

28. Some of the intertestamental literature refers to the feast. The book of Jubilees mentions that the feast originated with Abraham (*Jub.* 16:20–31) and Jacob (*Jub.* 32:1–9). Josephus describes it in *Ant.* 3.10.4. The only addition to our picture is that the booths were made in homes for protection from the cold at the change of season. Philo deals with it in *Special Law* 2.204–213 where he offers mystical interpretation of the feast.

Generally speaking, the feast that was identified with the wilderness period was a time of joy and thanksgiving as well as that of petition to God for rain. In the water drawing ceremony, the pilgrims looked to a future time, the eschatological hope of salvation, expecting that life-giving waters would one day flow from the temple and fill the land for his people, as water flowed from the rock in the wilderness. In John 7 and 8 all that we have found out about the Feast of Tabernacles is thrown into sharp relief. In Jesus' Tabernacles pilgrimage the feast is given new meaning and significance.

JESUS AND THE TABERNACLES PILGRIMAGE (JOHN 7:1—10:21)

Considering the quantity and value of sacrifices offered to the Lord, it is not surprising that the Feast of Tabernacles was called the great feast of the Jewish year, exerting a great impact on the lives and expectations of the Jews. Thus Josephus called it "a most holy and most eminent feast of the Hebrews" (*Ant.* 8.4.1§ 100). The festival also became the most joyous occasion of the Jewish year, because it came at the completion of harvest.

As such, a question is raised: When we consider how popular and important the Feast of Tabernacles was in Jesus' time, why is it that such a significant feast has been neglected in the Synoptic Gospels? The Synoptic Gospels do not offer any record of the Jesus' Tabernacles pilgrimage; it is found only in John's Gospel. If Jesus thought about popularity and effective revealing of his identity, he would have chosen Tabernacles, which was the most crowded among the three feasts. Although the Feast of Tabernacles was the most joyous and crowded pilgrimage festival among the three pilgrimage feasts, most of the time Jesus chose the Feast of Passover to go to Jerusalem. This confirms the strong probability that Jesus thought about the meaning of the feast and the meaning of his pilgrimage when he planned or arranged his journey to Jerusalem. His pilgrimage to Jerusalem was very much purpose and intention driven. This is supported by Robert Lightfoot's comment that Jesus went to Jerusalem only "in connection with a festival."[29] This becomes clearer in terms of the way Jesus used the feasts to proclaim his message and to reveal who he was. The riddle of John 7:8–10 presents the intention of Jesus' journey to the Feast of Tabernacles.

---

29. Lightfoot, *St John's Gospel*, 148.

But when the Jewish Feast of Tabernacles was near, Jesus' brothers said to him, "You ought to leave here and go to Judea, so that your disciples may see the miracles you do. . . . " Jesus told them, "The right time for me has not yet come; for you any time is right. . . . You go to the Feast, I am not yet going up to the Feast. . . . " However, after his brothers had left for the Feast, he went also, not publicly, but in secret (John 7:2-10).

The manuscript tradition of verse 8 has preserved two readings in the Greek: ἐγὼ οὐκ ἀναβαίνω (I am not going up) and ἐγὼ οὔπω ἀναβαίνω (I am not yet going up). Instead of ἐγὼ οὐκ ἀναβαίνω reading ἐγὼ οὔπω ἀναβαίνω has been generally rejected, because this reading is regarded as an attempt by early scribes to avoid the difficulty created by Jesus' going to Jerusalem in verse 10.[30] Chrys Caragounis, however, argues contra the explanations that οὔπω is a later correction for the originality of οὐκ.[31] Since the reading οὐκ is currently and dominantly accepted, what was felt to be a textual problem has, nevertheless, become an interpretation issue. Many attempts have been made to provide a possible solution for the problem.

When Jesus told his brothers that he would not go up to Jerusalem, he probably meant that he did not follow what his brothers asked him to do in Jerusalem. Thus for Morris and Carson verse 8 merely implies that he is not going up now, until the Father signals him to go to Jerusalem.[32] Although verse 8 strongly implies that he would not go to Jerusalem this time, the fact that later he went to Jerusalem in secret has provoked debates. For the solution of this difficulty John Bernard simply suggests that Jesus "altered his plans afterwards (v. 10)."[33] Barrett assumes that when Jesus spoke with his brothers, his time to go to Jerusalem had not yet come, but the proper time would come soon.[34] Jesus might have meant attending later festivals, not this one. For Francis Moloney a moment of revelation for Jesus would be associated with another feast.[35] These explanations, however, do not solve the contradiction.

We have to note that Jesus emphasizes twice, in verses 6 and 8, that his time has not yet come. *The right time for me has not yet come; for you*

30. Moloney, *Gospel of John*, 239.
31. See Caragounis, "Jesus, his Brothers," 177-87.
32. Morris, *Gospel According to John*, 354-55; Carson, *John*, 309.
33. Bernard, *Exegetical Commentary*, 270.
34. Barrett, *Gospel According to St. John*, 313.
35. Moloney, *Gospel of John*, 238.

any time is right. The Greek word καιρός used here is different from ὥρα in John 2:4. However, verse 30, "his time has not yet come," employs ὥρα, like Jesus responded to his mother in 2:4, "My time has not yet come." On this view, καιρός and ὥρα mean the same thing. Through the term καιρός we see clearly that Jesus' times were determined by his Father's providence.

Having noticed the significance of the meaning of "his time," Brown tackles the problem by positing "two levels of meaning." When Jesus speaks of his time, he means "his hour" not to come at the Festival of Tabernacles but to go up to the Father.[36] Although Jesus' continual reference to the relationship with the One who sent him (John 3:17, 34; 4:34; 5:23, 24, 30, 36–38; 6:29, 38–39, 44, 57; particularly 7:33, "I go to the one who sent me") indicates that the Father is the destination of his journey, Brown's interpretation is flawed because of the fact that Jesus is going up, not to the Father, but to this particular feast.

Considering a comparison with John 2:4 where Jesus refused his mother's demand and later did exactly what she had required, it is quite probable that Jesus' "I am not going up" is, as Barrett, C. Giblin, Ridderbos, and Schnackenburg point out, simply a rejection of his brother's inadequate expectation and understanding (John 7:3–5),[37] not an absolute denial of his intention to visit the feast at the proper time.[38] Although Jesus' plain answer is "no" to the question, we have to notice that his answer is conditioned by his brother's inadequate expectation, it is obvious to use this feast as a vehicle for his message. So the debate whether we take "not" or "not yet" as the original reading would not be a matter to consider after all.

The reasons as to why Jesus decided to go to Jerusalem for the Feast of Tabernacles was probably due to the great symbolic representation of the feast, through which Jesus had to reveal and claim himself to be the fulfillment of the feast. Jesus did go up to Jerusalem in secret in the middle of the festival and began to teach in the temple court (John 7:14), yet "He never participated in the feast."[39] The discretion of his journey was exactly the opposite of what his brothers asked him to do. There

---

36. Brown, *John I–XII*, 308.

37. See Schnackenburg, *John*, 1:142; Ridderbos, *Gospel of John*, 260; Giblin, "St. John's Portrayal of Jesus," 197–211.

38. Barrett, *Gospel According to St. John*, 312–13.

39. Stephen Motyer pinpoints this aspect. See Motyer, *Your Father the Devil?* 127.

is no evidence that his disciples accompanied Jesus on his Tabernacles pilgrimage. Although they are naturally thought of as witnesses, it is not certain that they were present with Jesus when he revealed himself. However, the incomprehension of Jesus' brothers serves a broader function as the modes of instruction for the readers. The Fourth Gospel shows the readers how even the closest of the people did not understand him. Thus the brothers' misconception about Jesus' journey had to be signified in the need of distinguishing between his own way of pilgrimage and the traditional way of pilgrimage. In his own way of pilgrimage, Jesus "went up" to Jerusalem for the feast and finally, on the cross, goes to the Father. Helfmeyer points out that whenever "going" is mentioned in Israel, the Hebrew mind can conceive of spatial going only as determined by specific places, persons, or actions.⁴⁰ Thus in this context, "going up" for Jesus meant setting forth with a destination. Stephen Motyer thus posits:

> His apparent vacillation is a vivid means both of distancing himself from the Jerusalem celebration, and of remaining in contact with it in order to proclaim its fulfillment.⁴¹

Jesus' teachings provoked different reactions to him. During the feast, the authorities searched for him, asking, "Where is that man?" There was a great deal of debate regarding Jesus' identity among the crowds (John 7:12). They could not express their opinion about him because of fear of the Jews (v. 13). The Jews here refer to the authorities that searched for Jesus in verse 11. Some believed in him as the Messiah, whereas some reacted to their perception of Jesus' blasphemy by trying to arrest him. *No one knows where the true Messiah will come from, but everyone knows that Jesus is from Galilee* (John 7:25–27). This misconception arose because of the misleading notion that the Messiah's origins were to be hidden by God when he appears. Therefore, Jesus' origin should not have been known to anyone, if he was indeed the Messiah. For the Jerusalemites Jesus could not be the Messiah, for they knew where Jesus came from. Such knowledge about the Messiah does reflect popular messianism at that time.⁴² Although many pilgrims still believed him on the basis of

---

40. Helfmeyer, "הָלַךְ," 390–91.

41. Ibid.

42. See 1 Enoch 46, 48:2–6; 2 Esdras 7:28, 13:32; 2 Baruch 29:3. On this see Bernard, *Exegetical Commentary*, 273–74.

the miraculous signs (John 7:31), Jesus' response to the misconception opens with a proclamation by crying out. *Then Jesus, still teaching in the temple courts, cried out, "Yes, you know me, and you know where I am from. I am not here on my own, but he who sent me is true. You do not know him, but I know him because I am from him and he sent me"* (John 7:28–29). The verb κράζω appears four times in John (John 1:15; 7:28, 37; 12:44). Morris argues that it denotes a loud shout.[43] For Barrett and Carson it was to introduce a public and solemn pronouncement.[44] Jesus pronounced that only those who recognize who he is, the incarnate word, know God the Father. In sending his Son, God was in fact revealing himself to them and making himself known as he really was.[45] Since Jesus is the revelation of the Father (John 14:6–9), without Jesus and his word there is no possibility of knowing God. Since knowing Jesus is *knowing God* the Father, not recognizing Jesus is *not knowing God*. Ridderbos argues that "knowing" is not just intellectual but refers to total relatedness. It is rooted in a choice that embraces not only the intellect and not only the heart, but also the human will."[46] One who rejects the revelation through Jesus Christ cannot possibly know God, since knowing God is provided only through Jesus and his words. Therefore, Jesus' presence serves as a test of antecedent pretensions about knowing God.[47] One cannot help but note the irony. For those who joined the celebration rejoiced in their knowledge and allegiance to the one true God and each day of the festival they were supposed to confirm it, but they disregarded and rejected Jesus, the sent One of the one true God.

It is against this background that Jesus stood up and cried out on the last and greatest day of the festival. *On the last and greatest day of the feast, Jesus stood and said in a loud voice, "If anyone is thirsty, let him come to me and drink. Whoever believes in me, as the Scripture has said, streams of living water will flow from within him." By this he meant the Spirit, whom those who believed in him were later to receive. Up to that time the Spirit had not been given, since Jesus had not yet been glorified* (John 7:37–39). He spoke his words with great emphasis and authority in his mind. The Feast of Tabernacles forms the background for his

---

43. Morris, *Gospel According to John*, 366.
44. Barrett, *Gospel according to St. John*, 322; Carson, *John*, 318.
45. Ridderbos, *Gospel of John*, 269.
46. Ibid., 44.
47. Carson, *John*, 318.

revelation, his self-disclosure. In the feast, Jesus' self-disclosure is bound up with God's works of salvation in the life of the people through which Jesus manifests to the entire world who he is. Since for Israelites God's *coming* and *making himself known* becomes reality expressed through the symbols and rites of the feast, Jesus offers the underlying dynamic of the feast, making himself known as the living water.

In order to properly understand Jesus' self-revelation, we need to know the significance of the ritual of that feast. The Mishnah provides a vivid picture of the procession of the water-libation ceremony (*m. Sukkah* 4:9) and light (*m. Sukkah* 5:2–4) during the seven days of Tabernacles. On each of the seven days people with their palms and their willows made their way in procession down to Siloam and a priest filled a golden flagon with water. When the priest reached the Water Gate, the people returned to the temple reciting Isaiah 12:3: "With joy shall ye draw water out of the wells of salvation." Then they blew a trumpet blast, while the priest with the golden flagon went to the ramp to the altar and poured the water into one of the two silver bowls and the wine into the other bowl as an offering to God. At the same time as the priest poured the water into the basin, the people surrounding the altar would shout to the priest, "Raise thy hand!" to show that he really poured water into the basin.[48] Through a hole the water and wine flowed out onto the altar. While this was being done, Hallel (Pss 113–118) was sung to the accompaniment of flutes. When the choir came to the words, "O give thanks to the Lord" (Ps 118:1), "O work now then salvation" (Ps 118:25), and "O give thanks unto the Lord" (Ps 118:29), the worshipers waved their palms and willows at the altar. But on the seventh day the priests marched round the altar seven times to commemorate the victory at Jericho and the water was poured out to the base of the altar of burnt offering in the temple.

If Jesus' words were, as some commentators believe, given on the seventh day, it was probably at the most dramatic moment that Jesus stood and cried out, saying, "If any man is thirsty, let him come to me

---

48. By shouting the crowd made sure the priest had indeed poured the water and poured it properly. This tradition goes back to approximately 95 BCE when Alexander Jannaeus, one of the Maccabean priest kings, had shown his contempt for the Pharisees by pouring the water at this feast upon the ground, on which the people pelted him with their ethrogs, and would have murdered him, if his foreign bodyguard had not interfered, on which occasion no less than six thousand Jews were killed in the temple (*Sukkah* 9). See Edersheim, *The Temple*, 278–79.

and drink" (John 7:37).⁴⁹ Although it is still not certain whether the ceremony of the water drawing was held on the seventh day or eighth day, on the basis of the fact that many Jews in the first century consider the feast as an eight-day event,⁵⁰ many commentators favor a time following cessation of ceremonies on the eighth day.⁵¹ Regardless of the debates over the seventh-day setting with water drawing and torch-lighting ceremony and the eighth-day setting with joyful assembly and celebration, the whole dramatic ceremony of the feast, along with living in booths, would have given the feast its special character, leaving an impressive image or impact on the pilgrims during the celebration.

If Jesus' proclamation happened on the eighth day, which lacked the water libation and dancing, what Jesus indicated in declaring, "If any man is thirsty, let him come unto me and drink," was what was sought and celebrated during the seven days of the feast. This time Jesus invited the whole of Israel to come and drink of the living water he provides, just as the women at the well had previously been invited (John 4:13). It is quite probable that the idea of "living water" was not foreign to Jesus' listeners due to the water drawing ceremony, which also symbolized the hope and prayer for rain and fruitfulness as a harvest ritual, and a reminiscence of the water that sprang from the rock in the wilderness, as well as the two prophecies in Ezekiel 47:1–11 and Zechariah 14:16–19. The two prophecies recognize the temple and Jerusalem as the source of living water, expressing the eschatological hope of salvation. *Ever-deepening waters flow out from the Temple* (Ezek 47:3–6). *Everything will live where the river goes* (Ezek 47:9). *On that day living waters shall flow out from Jerusalem, half of them to the eastern sea and half of them to the western sea; it shall continue in summer as in winter* (Zech 14:8). Jesus declared himself as the present source of living water to those present at the feast who expected a future time when life-giving waters would flow from the temple. The allusion is unmistakable that through his proclamation Jesus completes his mission to bring life into the world (John 1:4; 3:15; 17:2). Leonard Goppelt indicates that "life," although the word is

---

49. Brown, *John I–XII*, 320; Bultmann, *John*, 302; Burge, *Interpreting the Gospel*, 227; Schnackenburg, *John*, 2:152; Ridderbos, *Gospel of John*, 272.

50. Josephus, *Antiquities* 11.5.5§157; *b. Sukkah* 48b; *m. Sukkah* 5:6; 2 Maccabees 10:6.

51. Barrett, *Gospel According to St. John*, 326; Carson, *John*, 321; Moloney, *Gospel of John*, 256; Morris, *Gospel According to John*, 373; Schlatter, *Der Evangelist Johannes*, 199.

fully compatible with Hellenistic concepts, conveys the idea of the new creation in this context.[52] This is why the life-giving water would flow, not from the Jerusalem Temple, but from Jesus who is the new Temple, perfecting all that has been promised by the water ceremonies of the Feast of Tabernacles.

Whoever believes in me, streams of living water will flow from within his heart (John 7:38). All who believe in Jesus will have life-giving water. The phrase, "within his heart," can be translated differently according to putting punctuation after "drink" (v. 37) or after "me." Putting a full stop after "me," some commentators take the phrase "his heart" as a christological reference.[53] Barrett claims that John used the word "heart" as a means to transfer the prophecy from the city to a person.[54] However, it is also probable that in this particular context the phrase must refer to the believer who is the source of life-giving water.[55] Those who come to Jesus to drink the living water can become the source of life-giving water for others. This reading seems to be more natural in this context. For the word *his* must refer to the preceding *he*, the believer. However, the important thing for us to appreciate is that Christ is the source and provider of the living water. This idea is clearly indicated in Jesus' invitation. His invitation to the woman at the well (John 4) also provides a key to understanding the text. As the source of living water Jesus becomes the new Temple from which the waters of life will be outpoured and the new Rock that provides water to satisfy the people's thirst as with Moses in the wilderness.

From the rich Jewish background for the Feast of Tabernacles John also draws this living water into the Spirit, which the water symbolizes (John 7:39). The picturesque presentation of the Creation scene in Genesis 1:2, "the Spirit of God was hovering over the waters," sets a precedent for the dual imagery of water and the Spirit. This Creation typology might be behind Jesus' demand for the new birth by water and the Spirit (John 3:5). Sukkah 5:55a: Rabbi Jehoshua ben Levi (c. 250) said, "Why did they call it (the court of women) the place of drawing water?

---

52. Goppelt, *Typos*, 184.

53. Barrett, *Gospel According to St. John*, 326–27; Carson, *John*, 323–25; Moloney, *Gospel of John*, 87; Ridderbos, *Gospel of John*, 273–74.

54. Barrett, *Gospel According to St. John*, 328.

55. Newman and Nida, *Translator's Handbook*, 246; Dodd, *Interpretation of the Fourth Gospel*, 349; Brown, *John I–XII*, 321–23.

Because it was from there that they drew the Holy Spirit, according to the word." Living waters that would flow from Jerusalem (Zech 14:8–9) would be naturally connected with a number of other texts about the spirit of God being poured out as water, such as Isaiah 44:3 and Joel 2:28. Thus the Mishna reflects the traditional expectation of the Spirit with the greatest delight, as the pilgrims entered into the procedures of the water drawing ceremony. *He that never has seen the joy of the Beth ha-She'ubah* (the water-drawing) *has never in his life seen joy* (m. Sukkah 5:1). As noted in the text, "Out of his heart shall flow rivers of living water" (John 7:38), Jesus proclaimed himself as the source of life-giving water with the Greek verb flow ῥεύσουσιν in the future tense. Therefore, the Fourth Gospel informs us that the gift of living water is the future gift of the Spirit (John 7:39). This futuristic interpretation of the water as the Holy Spirit is so significant for the link between the messianic symbol of the water (Ezek 11:19; 36:26–27; 39:29; Isa 44:3; Joel 2:28; 3:1), the Holy Spirit, and Jesus' glorification. It took Jesus' glorification through his life and his death to pave the way to Pentecost, and to open the floodgates for the Spirit to become the living water to all men. And so this link emerges for the Pentecost pilgrimage in the light of the gift of the Holy Spirit that the glorification of Jesus will bring.

Another distinctive ceremony of the Feast of Tabernacles was the nocturnal illumination of the women's courtyard in the temple with which Jesus' proclamation is introduced. *I am the light of the world; whoever follows me will not walk in darkness but will have the light of life* (John 18:12). As Jesus proclaimed himself a spring of living water on the last day of the Feast of Tabernacles, he now reveals himself as the light of the world. Jesus makes use of the light imagery within the context of the festival as background for the dialogue. Mishnah Sukkah 5:2–4 spoke of the light ceremony performed during the feast.

Four golden candlesticks were set up in the court of the women in the evening of the first day of the feast. The four tall golden candlesticks had four ladders to reach the candles and four golden bowls holding oil. Wicks were made from the drawers and girdles of the priest. When these wicks were lit, there was not a courtyard in Jerusalem that did not reflect the light of the *Beth haSheubah*. With the burning torches the worshipers danced to singing and to the playing of many instruments. When the two priests reached the court of the women in the ceremony procession, the priests turned towards the temple and proclaimed: Our fathers when they were in this place turned, "with their backs toward the Temple of the Lord and their faces toward the east, and they worshiped the sun toward the east" (Ezek 8:16); but as for us, our eyes are turned toward the Lord.

The light ceremony is certainly linked with "the OT faith in the Lord as the Light of his people (Ps 27:1)"[56] and expressed with a confirmation "Light is Yahweh in action."[57] The link between the light ceremony of Tabernacles and the use of the pillar of fire leading the wandering Israelites through the desert (Exod 13:21; 14:24; 40:38) indicates its association with recollection of "the nation's experience at the Exodus and the hope for a second Exodus."[58] Each day at the feast the priests proclaimed their allegiance to the one true God. And Jesus proclaimed himself as the light of the world (John 8:12) who is the one sent by the one true God (John 8:16, 18, 26, 29). The priests, however, turned their backs on the light of the world, knowing neither Jesus nor his Father. *They did not understand that he was telling them about his Father* (John 8:27). *Then they asked him, "Where is your father?"* (John 8:19). *Who are you?" they asked* (John 8:25). So they were the questions that Jesus had been answering throughout these encounters with the Jews at the Feast of Tabernacles. The questions in the narrative create a crucial point within the knowing God motif for the Tabernacles pilgrimage. During the celebration of Tabernacles Jesus revealed himself as the light of the world and the living water, responding to their ignorance of who Jesus is and who his Father is. Passages from the Old Testament show that God himself dwells in light (Dan 2:22), that he covers himself with light "as with a garment" (Ps 104:2), and his brightness is like the light (Hab 3:4). Thus Psalm 43:3 suggests that to come to the light is in reality to come to God who is the light and salvation (Ps 27:1). Hans Conzelmann points out:

> The Fourth gospel does not call God light, but God's manifestation in Jesus, for the relation of God and revelation is not described as an emanation of revelation from light but as sending.[59]

Thus *knowing Jesus sent by God* was *knowing God*, and vice versa. It is noticed that the verb *to know* in John 8:19 (οἴδατε) and in verse 55 (οἶδα)

56. Beasley-Murray, *John*, 128.
57. Conzelmann, "φῶς," 320.
58. Beasley-Murray, *John*, 127.
59. Conzelmann, "φῶς," 350.

is used six times to highlight the importance of the true knowledge of God and of the true recognition of Jesus. They were, however, not able to comprehend his revelation beyond what they saw. The incomprehension of the Jews *not knowing God* intensifies in verse 55 to make Jesus claim, "I do know Him." Thus Jesus' affirmation made it clear that the question, "who are you?" can be understood only in terms of the Father. But they did not grasp that Jesus was speaking to them of God the Father (v. 27). George Beasley-Murray said:

> To say, with Bultmann, that Jesus' knowledge of God is "no more nor less than his knowledge of his own mission" (301) is surely insufficient. Blank points out (as Schlatter did before him, Der Glaube, 219) that the Fourth Gospel never speaks of Jesus believing in God, but always of his knowing him, and he cites Thomas Aquinas, that Jesus knows God "as God knows himself" (Krisis, 245 and n. 48). The strong asseveration to the Jews, that to say he did not know God would make him "a liar like you," implies that they are not merely mistaken about their supposed knowledge of God but lying. That is manifest in their rejection of the revelation of God through Jesus and their hatred of the messenger.[60]

Jesus' "I AM" sayings, including, "I am the living water" (John 7:37–38 paraphrase) and "I am the light of the world," (John 8:12) speak on behalf of the Father in order to make God known. Jesus' Tabernacles pilgrimage was a journey to reveal to others something about God and as a vehicle to reveal who he was, so that others may come to know him and the Father. The evangelist presented Jesus' journey to Jerusalem for the Feast of Tabernacles as having two important elements: the revealing of Jesus' identity and the opportunity for the reader to be taught through his Tabernacle pilgrimage. This revelation that discloses God as the Father of Jesus would be known, when they lift up the Son of man in crucifixion (John 8:28). His crucifixion was the consequence of *not knowing God*, of the Jews not recognizing Jesus as the Son of God. John 15:21 also states that *not knowing God* is a reason for the persecution of Jesus' disciples. To the disciples who were also described as men who do not know, full knowledge is promised when Jesus is glorified after the crucifixion and sends to them the Holy Spirit (John 14:15–21; 16:7–15). This link thus emerges for the Pentecost pilgrimage in the light of the

---

60. Beasley-Murray, *John*, 138.

Holy Spirit that the glorification of Jesus will bring. Schnackenburg sums up the meaning of *knowing God* in relation to obedience to his will.

> In the name of Jesus Johannine Christianity denied Judaism's relationship with God, not belief in God (cf. 8:54) but obedience to his will, living union with God, for that is what this "knowing God" means. All supposed "knowledge" about God and salvation becomes shattering ignorance where there is no faith in him who possesses the true knowledge of God and reveals the way to salvation.[61]

It appears that the Feast of Tabernacles offers an appropriate setting for all the symbols and various aspects of Jewish messianic expectations through which Jesus manifests himself as Messiah. In their deeper meaning Jesus canvassed *knowing God*, which means obedience to his will, his living union with God (John 8:28–29). His living union with God is constantly referred to in terms of the "I and He" formula in the Fourth Gospel (John 7:28–29; 8:12–30, 48–59; 10:29–30; 14:6–7, etc). Jesus, the revealer of the Father, expressed the nature of God in the Feast of Tabernacles, claiming himself to be "the living water" and "the light of the world." So the feast became "the backdrop for Jesus' self-revelation as the one who brings salvation, drawing on the festival images of outpoured water and light."[62]

Jesus also went to Jerusalem to celebrate the Feast of Dedication, giving the Sanhedrin and the Jewish leaders another chance to see the light (John 10:22–23; 2 Macc 10:5–8).[63] The distinguishing features of the feast were the illumination of houses and synagogues, a custom probably taken over from the Feast of Tabernacles. He here reminded them of that great discourse that he had delivered at the Feast of Tabernacles two months before, adding solemnly, "I and my father are one" (John 10:30). On this occasion he was claiming not only to be Messiah, but also to be divine. And he as the light of the world appealed to his life and to his works, as undeniable proofs of his unity with the Father (John 10:34–38).

The Fourth Gospel that begins with the words "in the beginning" indicates that the original creation without light was the dark chaos in

61. Schnackenburg, *John*, 2:195.

62. Wise, "Feasts," 240.

63. It is also known as the festival of Lights. It was observed for eight days from the twenty-fifth of Kislev (i.e., about December 12) in commemoration of the reconstruction (165 BCE) of the Jewish Temple in Jerusalem, particularly the altar of burnt offering.

which man did not know God. However, the light of man that gives life came into the dark sinful world (John 1:1–13). As the Word of God, life, and light reveals the Father to man, those who love darkness reject the very life of God provided through Jesus Christ to the believer (John 5:25–26). Thus light is eternal life (John 1:4) by which man knows God. There is a strong probability that the light imagery, the reference to Jesus, also has a link with an Exodus typology theme, together with the rivers of living water (John 7). The Israelites in the wilderness were normally camped at night. However, on occasions, the people traveled by night as well as by day (Exod 13:21; 14:24; 40:38). What they had to do was to follow the pillar of fire when it lifted and went before the people as their guide. Although there is a distinction between the Angel of the Lord and the pillar (Exod 14:19), we read that it was the Lord himself who looked down from the pillar (Exod 14:24) and led his people in the pillar (Exod 13:21–22). As the pillar of fire was light for those on the way to the promised land, Jesus became the guiding light for his followers. As the prophet Isaiah invited the Israelites to walk according to God's word, "to come, let us walk in the light of the Lord" (Isa 2:5), so those who follow him will therefore never "walk in darkness."

Whoever follows me will never walk in darkness, but will have the light of life (John 8:12). *You are going to have the light just a little while longer. Walk while you have the light, before darkness overtakes you. The man who walks in the dark does not know where he is going* (John 12:35). In the Fourth Gospel[64] the term "light and darkness" occurs in conjunction with the Greek "walk περιπατέω,"[65] and Jesus' confrontation with his opponents is continually referred to as a battle between light and darkness (John 1:5; 3:19–21; cf. 9:4–5; 12:35–36, 46). In many passages of the Old Testament the call to walk according to God's word is proclaimed in the antithesis of good and evil that is expressed by the figures of light and darkness (Isa 5:20; 59:9–10; Job 24:13–17; 30:26). This is also true in the Fourth Gospel as well as 2 Corinthians 6:14 and 1 John 1:5–7.[66] Clearly the healing of the blind is conceived of as a "sign" of the

---

64. Luke 1:6 in the Synoptic Gospels is the only reference to a religious walk (πορεύομαι) instead, which echoes OT formulations. See Hauck and Schulz, "πορεύομαι," 575.

65. This is common in 1 and 2 John and in Romans (6:4; 8:4; 13:13).

66. The Bible never sees "light and darkness or good and evil" in equality, since darkness is never compatible in power with God's light. Thus the contrast between "light and darkness or good and evil" in the Bible can be understood as a realistic ap-

triumph of light over darkness, confirming his identity as the light of the world (John 9:1–7). In view of this, it should be noted that it was night when Judas went out from the last supper to betray the Lord (John 13:30), and that it is twice repeated and stressed that Nicodemus, before his new birth, visited Jesus at night (John 3:2; 19:39). Thus the notion of "walking in the light/darkness" indicates two ways in which people may choose to walk.

There is a dynamic equivalent of this parallel in the Dead Sea Scrolls (negative expressions: 1QS I 25, 1QS II 12, 1QS IV 12, 1QS V 11, 1QS V 5, 1QS VII 19, 1QS IX 10, 1QS XI 10). This *walk* metaphor is found everywhere in the Dead Sea Scrolls, in one form or another, shaping the way they saw themselves and the future. The community, therefore, appealed to its people to walk in his ways in order to have a relationship with him, stressing that, for the community, the mainspring of the ethical ideal derived from a sense of the inner spiritual qualities rather than external qualities. Drawing a parallel between "walking in the light" and "walking in the darkness," the Fourth Gospel also urges its community to walk in the light, and not in the darkness. "Walk in the light," as Heinrich Seesemann sees, refers not merely to practical conduct but to the whole stance of the believer or of faith itself.[67] In this regard, the Fourth Gospel might differ from the Dead Sea Scrolls, for it defines "light" as faith and perception, and the Dead Sea Scrolls as the sphere of the blessed.[68]

It is particularly noticeable that the thanksgiving hymns in the Dead Sea Scrolls clearly point out that the Holy Spirit is the medium to make it possible for humanity to walk in the perfect way that leads to salvation. *The way of man is not established except by the spirit which God created for him to make perfect a way for the children of men* (IQH XII 32). In the same way, to the disciples who were disheartened by Jesus' prediction of his death, Jesus promised his everlasting presence with them through the Holy Spirit (John 14:15–21). Through the Holy Spirit the light becomes the vivid manifestation in those in whom Jesus, the light of the world, dwells. Rudolf Bultmann makes it clear that

---

proach to the present problem, not as a cosmic dualism.

67. Seesemann, "πατέω," 945.
68. Conzelmann, "φῶς," 350.

> The light that the believer has is always the light that is Jesus . . .
> He gives light and He also is light: He gives it as He is it, and He
> is it as He gives it.[69]

Jesus' Tabernacles pilgrimage proves the organic connection between the festal experience and the goal of his pilgrimages. With all the rich experiences contained in the feast Jesus revealed his saving works through manifesting who he is as the light of the world and the living water. As Mowinckel finds that the enthronement of God as king stands as the dominant theme in relation to the Feast of Tabernacles (Pss 47, 93 and 95–100), so Jesus as the Messiah "comes" (Ps 98:9), "makes himself known" (Pss 48:4; 76:2f; 98:2), and "goes up" (Ps 47:6) to the temple to seat himself on his throne (Pss 93:2; 97:2; 99:1). For Jesus' Tabernacles pilgrimage was a revelation of who he really is. For Israelites God's *coming* and *making himself known* became reality through the revelation of Jesus expressed through and within the symbols and rites of the feast. Thus the Feast of Tabernacles combined with the enthronement psalms offers the underlying dynamic of the feast, the knowing God motif. This is what the Fourth Gospel intends and the readers should note.

In terms of beneficiary, Jesus' Tabernacles pilgrimage does not show the same pattern as the journeys recorded in the OT. In the journeys of the OT the people who participated in them gradually came to fully know who God the Father was. It was a lifelong journey. However, Jesus' revelation of himself is the main agenda from the first Passover pilgrimage and throughout all his subsequent visits to Jerusalem.

Conclusion

As we discussed with regard to the Feast of Passover in chapter 4, the Feast of Tabernacles has developed its own character with timely contextualized meanings for the momentous events in the history of Israel. While the Feast of Passover was historicized in remembrance of the Exodus event, the Feast of Tabernacles was associated with the wilderness wandering of Israel. Like the Passover celebration, the Israelites might have developed the Feast of Tabernacles, having encountered and adopted both a nomadic and sedentary lifestyle. It is, however, noted that the possible details about the sedentary and nomadic background cannot be more than speculation. It is clear that whatever its origin, and whatever its precise ritual structure, its meaning and purpose has remained an occasion

---

69. Bultmann, *John*, 261.

for thanksgiving and rejoicing in the harvest. In the light of the repeated creation and renewal of life and nature, the Feast of Tabernacles that was a New Year festival had a special connection with the rainy season, which closed the agricultural year and opened the new one. Zechariah 14 recognizes rain for a fruitful harvest as a gift from God in response to the pilgrimage the Israelites made (Zech 14:17). The water motif was also connected with the theme of light (Ps 118:27; Zech 14: 6–9).

Although some of the original ideas have remained right down to the Second Temple period, all these symbols and rites of the feast were gradually reinterpreted in the context of the evolving history of the Israelites. In Jesus' Tabernacles pilgrimage the feast was imbued with new meaning and further significance. Thus Jesus empties Tabernacles of its ritual significance and then leaves the ceremony behind, offering the light and water once offered there.[70] This confirms a strong probability that Jesus thought about the meaning of the feast and meaning of his pilgrimage when he planned or arranged his journey to Jerusalem. His pilgrimage to Jerusalem was very much purpose and intention driven. The discretion of his journey (John 7:14), however, indicates that his brothers' misconception about his journey had to be signified in the need of distinguishing between Jesus' own way of pilgrimage and the traditional way of pilgrimage. The reasons as to why Jesus decided to go to Jerusalem for the Feast of Tabernacles was probably due to the great symbolic representation of the feast, through which Jesus had to reveal who he was and claim himself to be the completion of the feast.

His teachings in the temple provoked different reactions. In response to the debate Jesus pronounced that only those who recognize who he is, the incarnate word, know God the Father. In sending his Son, God was in fact revealing himself to them and making himself known as he really was.[71] Since Jesus is the revelation of the Father (John 14:6–9), without Jesus and his word there is no possibility of knowing God. Since knowing Jesus is *knowing God* the Father, not recognizing Jesus is *not knowing God*. One who rejects the revelation through Jesus Christ cannot possibly know God, since knowing God is provided only through Jesus and his words. Therefore, Jesus' presence serves as a test of antecedent pretensions about *knowing God*.[72] For the pilgrims who

70. Burge, "Territorial Religion," 394.
71. Ridderbos, *Gospel of John*, 269.
72. Carson, *John*, 318.

joined the feast, God's *coming* and *making himself known* became reality expressed and reexperienced by the revelation of Jesus through the symbols and rites of the feast. For the feast in which Yahweh became King is bound up with God's works of salvation in the life of the people through which he manifests to the entire world who he is. With all the rich experiences contained in the feast the revelation of Jesus became the message of his Tabernacles pilgrimage. Thus his Tabernacles pilgrimage offers the underlying dynamic of the feast, the knowing God motif. This is what the Fourth Gospel intends and the readers should note. As in the journeys recorded in the OT the people who participate in pilgrimage with Jesus come gradually to fully know who God the Father was in their lifelong journey, so Jesus' pilgrimages to Jerusalem appear to be a gradual progression towards the full comprehension of God the Father and Jesus the Son for the disciples, the people Jesus encountered, and the readers of the Gospels. Thus Jesus' Tabernacles pilgrimage is a key element of Jesus' self-consciousness.

It is noted that the "knowing and not knowing God" motif runs through from the very beginning of the Gospel to the whole of the Tabernacles discourse and plays a significant role in the Johannine presentation of Jesus at the Feast of Tabernacles. The emphasis on the light and water themes in the Tabernacles rituals will be a clear indication of the messianic aspect of the feast with the knowing God motif. Becoming the living water and the light of the world and replacing the water and light of the Tabernacles rituals, Jesus in the Fourth Gospel spiritualizes the light and water themes that Jesus shows us to be fulfilled in his own person and in anticipation of eschatological blessings.[73] In particular, the futuristic interpretation of the water as the Holy Spirit (John 7:39) is so significant for the link between the messianic symbol of the water, the Holy Spirit, and Jesus' glorification. This link thus offers a prerequisite for the Pentecost pilgrimage in the light of the Holy Spirit that the glorification of Jesus will bring.

---

73. For Wai-Yee Ng the symbol of water in John is "anticipation" rather than "replacement" of what the symbol stands for. See Ng, *Water Symbolism*, 91.

5

Jesus and the Final Passover Pilgrimage (John 12–19; Luke 9–19)

JESUS THE PILGRIM AND THE WAY (LUKE 9:51—19:48)

IN CONTRAST TO MATTHEW and Mark, for Luke Galilee, though it is of course mentioned, has no fundamental significance as a locality.[1] It is Jerusalem (Judea) as the place of the temple that is highlighted in Luke. That the narrative in Luke 9:51—19:48 comprises almost 37 percent of the Gospel (424 of 1,151 verses) indicates that Luke, in line with the Fourth Gospel, emphasizes Jerusalem as the place for Jesus' main activity.[2] In contrast to Matthew and Mark, Luke shortens the Galilean ministry and builds up his pilgrimage to Jerusalem in the narrative. Thus most scholars refer to the section as "travel narrative," some as "journey to

---

1. In saying *Luke*, the intention is to exclude the book of Acts. The universalism within the Gospel of Luke is foreshadowed in Luke 1–2. Luke 2 shifts the attention from Herod, Judea, and Galilee, to Emperor Augustus and all the world (Luke 2:1). The angelic choir sees in the birth of Jesus a source of peace for all with whom God is pleased (Luke 2:14). In the Song of Simeon the servant's mission was both to his own people and to all nations (Luke 2:29–32). The universalism of Luke is also highlighted in the Nazareth scene of Luke 4:16–30 (Elijah and Sidon; Elisha and Naaman the Syrian, only in Luke at 4:26–27); and in several other places in the course of the Gospel (e.g., the good Samaritan parable, the incident of the ten lepers, the reference to the Samaritan villages, all exclusive to Luke, at 10:30–37, 17:11–19, and 9:51–55, respectively). The cleansing of the temple (Luke 19:45–46) is hinted to Isaiah 56:6–7, in which the foreigners are given a privileged place in the temple.

2. Bock offers these statistics. See Bock, *Luke*, 2:957.

Jerusalem"[3] or "central section."[4] According to Kenneth Bailey, the title "travel journey" is a misnomer and he prefers to call it the "Jerusalem document."[5]

In the same way that Craig Blomberg finds that this section is one of the most difficult to outline, Marshall also notes that the general themes of the section are hard to define and it is even more difficult to find any kind of thread running through it.[6] As such, the designations above could miss the intention of Luke's Gospel. Although the narrative builds up within the journey framework as the main form of Jesus' ministry,[7] the goal of the journey is no doubt totally focused on Jerusalem, "the place where Jesus' journey ends."[8] For Jesus' journey to Jerusalem was always purpose driven in terms of the meaning of each pilgrimage feast. Therefore, the temple as the true goal of Jesus' pilgrimage in Luke is more than the place where Jesus' journey ends.[9] Just as Jerusalem developed into the locus of the land, so the temple became the heart of Jerusalem.[10] The point of the journey was, as Luke unfolds the narrative, the temple in Jerusalem in relation to the Feast of Passover. The whole narrative is better understood from the perspective of what happened on the way to the temple in Jerusalem for the Passover feast, rather than of what happened during the journey itself. In a similar view E. Earle Ellis observes that it is not the journey as such which is of interest to Luke.[11] Many,

---

3. See Fitzmyer, *Luke I–IX*, 823.

4. See Evans, Ellis, and Bock.

5. Bailey, *Poet and Peasant*, 82–83.

6. Blomberg, "Luke's Central Section," 217; Marshall, *Gospel*, 401. Drury has a similar skepticism. See Drury, *Tradition and Design*, 138.

7. There has been a debate about the formation of the narrative. Currently, most scholars sustain the view that Luke arranged this section for theological intention, so this is the narrative of multiple journeys. However, Hendriksen claims one general journey without exact chronological sequence. He rejects three sequential Jerusalem journeys and the connection between John's Gospel and Luke's journey. See Hendriksen, *Exposition of the Gospel*.

8. Dawsey, "Jesus' Pilgrimage to Jerusalem," 226.

9. Ibid., 226.

10. In the view of most scholars, Luke wrote the Third Gospel at a time when the temple was no longer a functioning institution because it had been destroyed. Thus it is assumed that Luke reinterpreted Jerusalem and the temple in the light of the events of 70 CE. See Dodd, "Fall of Jerusalem," 47–54; Bruce, *Acts of the Apostles*, 16; J. Robinson, *Redating the New Testament*, 86–117.

11. Ellis, *Gospel of Luke*, 148–50.

Jesus and the Final Passover Pilgrimage (John 12–19; Luke 9–19)

including Marshall, add that from 9:51 onwards Jerusalem is continually in sight as the goal of Jesus' journeying.[12] However, they have overlooked the significance of the Feast of Passover for which the journey was intended as a pilgrimage to Jerusalem. The whole picture becomes clear when the characteristics of the narrative are assessed on the basis not of a genre study but of the plot of the narrative. In the very beginning of the Gospel, it was the custom of Jesus' family to make the pilgrimage to Jerusalem for the Feast of Passover (Luke 2:41–51). Jesus' final pilgrimage to fulfill the Father's will was also imprinted upon the whole narrative of Luke 9–19 as the pilgrimage to the Feast of Passover. The linking of the journey and the Passover (pilgrimage) makes the narrative more specific and so it can be called *the Passover pilgrimage narrative*.

As the time approached for him to be taken up to heaven, Jesus resolutely set out for Jerusalem (Luke 9:51). The whole narrative (Luke 9:51—19:48), which begins with Jesus' determination to go to Jerusalem for the Feast of Passover, closes with the cleansing of the temple (Luke 19:28–48). Conzelmann sees the temple cleansing as the goal of Jesus' journey to Jerusalem.[13] Although the temple theme does not frame the whole story, with the goal of his pilgrimage being the temple in Jerusalem, it marks the inner consistency and meaning of Jesus' pilgrimage. For Luke his Passover pilgrimage to Jerusalem was a way to show what kind of Messiah he was. The stress on Jerusalem, the place where he must suffer, is heightened by his awareness as the Suffering Messiah. Therefore, Jerusalem became the shadow of his destiny hanging over his ministry. Jesus' determination to go to Jerusalem at the very beginning of the whole section stresses that, "Jerusalem is from now onwards the goal of Jesus."[14] However, such an emphasis on the theological link between journeying and Jerusalem has overlooked the journey to Jerusalem in relation to a feast of pilgrimage. Therefore, his ultimate goal, Jerusalem, should be understood in the context of the pilgrimage paradigm. Conzelmann's claim that "Jesus' awareness that he must suffer is expressed in terms of

---

12. Marshall, *Luke*, 151.

13. For Conzelmann it was not Luke who created the journey motif. Luke found it in Mark and developed it into a scheme. See Conzelmann, *Theology of St. Luke*, 61–62, 75–76, 199.

14. Marshall, *Gospel*, 401.

the journey," could be expressed more specifically in terms of his final Passover pilgrimage to Jerusalem.[15]

There are three passion references (Luke 12:50; 13:33; 18:31–33) in the final Passover pilgrimage section and five predictions overall including Luke 9:22, 43–44. Although the Suffering Messiah theme is not consistently maintained throughout the entire section, Luke 13:33 ("I must keep going today and tomorrow and the next day—for surely no prophet can die outside Jerusalem") together with 9:51 ("setting his face to go to Jerusalem") clearly implies that Jesus understood his mission in terms of his pilgrimage to Jerusalem in relation to death. We note the two questions (Luke 9:7, 20) preceding the Passover pilgrimage narrative. Herod asked, "Who are you?" and Jesus reiterated the same question, "Who do you say that I am?" and marked the crucial turning point in the plot of the Gospel of Luke, revealing himself as the Suffering Messiah: "The Son of Man must suffer . . . and he must be killed" (Luke 9:22). Jesus' words about his suffering, rejection, and death were his response to the final Passover pilgrimage he would take. Thus the word δει must indicate Jesus' steadfast determination to go to Jerusalem in view of his impending death. Adrian Hasting stresses that Luke emphasizes only one; the last journey that took the Messiah to the cross.

> [F]or Luke there is one journey, one visitation, one supreme and decisive encounter culminating in Jesus' martyrdom and Jerusalem's destruction.[16]

It should, however, be noted that the Suffering Messiah theme is not the overriding theme of the entire section. Fitzmyer argues that it cannot be limited to the passion, since in 9:51 itself Luke is clearly thinking of the ascension of Jesus, and points out that the departure has to be understood as the complex of events that forms Jesus' transit to the Father: passion, death, burial, resurrection, and ascension/exaltation.[17] Luke's emphasis on Jesus' resurrection and ascension also suggests that Jesus prepared his "taking up ἀναλήμψεως (ascension)" in Jerusalem (Luke 9:51). Considering that the imagery of Passover had fused into Israel's self-consciousness, it is, nevertheless, not surprising that the passion lies at the heart of Luke's understanding of his Passover pilgrimage

---

15. Conzelmann, *Theology of St. Luke*, 65.
16. Hasting, *Prophet and Witness*, 120.
17. Fitzmyer, *Luke I–IX*, 167.

to Jerusalem and of Jesus' understanding of the purpose of his death as a Passover victim. Ezekiel tells of sacrifices for the sins of the people offered during the Passover (Ezek 45:18–25). Having portrayed Jesus who resolutely set out for Jerusalem (Luke 9:51), Luke, like Matthew and Mark, thus places the last meal at Passover, the great salvific event of the Exodus (Luke 22:14–23).

Luke's christological presentation remarkably parallels many Isaianic portraits.[18] This parallel is apparent in Luke's Suffering Messiah concept. In the vision of Isaiah 53 we see the inner meaning of the Passover lamb in relation to the Suffering Servant. The Lukan gospel brought the Passover setting into the center of his pilgrimage to Jerusalem. Although Luke's Gospel does not directly use the terms, "the Passover lamb" and "the servant of God," it is clear that the suffering role (Luke 2:34) of the Christ becomes a prominent theme for Luke's Gospel.[19] By linking exodus imagery to the wider context of his salvation ministry, Luke demonstrates Jesus' Jerusalem fate that was reflected in the final Passover pilgrimage as the death-driven journey. John and Luke particularly emphasize the innocence of Jesus (John 18:38; 19:4, 6; Luke 23:4) in keeping with the innocence of the Passover lamb.

The final Passover pilgrimage in Luke reflects Jesus' own consciousness that he had to fulfill the role of the Suffering Messiah (Servant) experiencing rejection, suffering, and death. This model enabled his disciples to come to terms with his death not as defeat but as achievement, and to see the whole "way" of Jesus from his public appearance through to his exaltation-enthronement at God's right hand. The citation from Isaiah 52 and 53 in Luke (Luke 2:35; 22:37; 23:32) demonstrates his mission as the Suffering Servant of God. That he must proceed to Jerusalem where he will suffer and die was the blueprint of Jesus' mission.

It is, therefore, not surprising that the public ministry of Jesus is presented in terms of a way: "I must keep going" (πορεύεσθαι)today and tomorrow (Luke 13: 33) and "The Son of man will go" (πορεύεται; Luke 22:22). There are two possible influences on Luke's use of the metaphor of the way. Although the terms for the pilgrimage or journey metaphor

---

18. The new exodus announcement of Isaiah 40:3–5 = Luke 3:4–6; the herald of Isaiah 61:1–2 = Luke 4:18–21; the suffering servant of Isaiah 53 = Luke 22:37 and Acts 8:32–33.

19. It is noted that it was the same Luke who records the actual title "servant of God" (Acts 3:13, 26) and refers to the Passover lamb (Acts 8:32–33).

are not found in Luke, as we already mentioned in chapter 3, the walk and way metaphor was important to the authors of the Qumran manuscripts.[20] As many NT scholars consider the Qumran community's use of "the way" as a major influence on Luke's use, particularly in the book of Acts, its theological significance for Luke begins to surface. There is, however, a certain tendency to consider that Hellenistic components could have influenced the Third Gospel. Baban claims that the Hellenistic imagery includes external references, such as the way as a solemn procession, a hero's journey, and the path to truth, wisdom, and light, or one's course of life.[21] Øivind Andersen and Vernon Robbins note that the way in which the NT writers engage in paradigmatic argumentation has amazing similarities with the way in which paradigmatic argumentation was employed throughout the ancient Mediterranean culture, and claim that with rich connotations and wide circulation, such metaphors encouraged Luke and other Christians to use Hellenistic journey paradigms.[22] Although the similarities make it possible, much evidence in the OT and the popularity of the journey motif in many cultures leave the claim in doubt. As we have already discussed from chapters 1 to 3, the structural use of the journey framework can be traced from Exodus to Joshua. It is also seen in the pilgrimages of Adam, Abraham, and Jacob. With the theological reflection upon the Exodus, the exile, and the return, the pilgrimage framework embraces the three decisive events in Israel's history that became a dominant paradigm for Israel's faith, namely the self-understanding of Judaism. Therefore, the *way* metaphor more likely emerged from Israel's journey including the wilderness period, the destruction of Jerusalem, the cessation of the sacrificial cult and of the monarchy, and the experience of the exile, which supplied the contours of the larger Judaic framework. In a very real sense the *way* metaphor was already embedded in the life of Israel before the proclamation of Jesus Christ.

"The Way" began when Jesus made the decisive choice to head toward Jerusalem (Luke 9:51). There is a clear affinity with the Fourth Gospel. Thomas asks: "Lord, we don't know where you are going, so how can we know the way?" (John 14:5). Jesus answers by saying that he is the

---

20. The term for journey is mentioned only once in the sense of travel of any distance being forbidden on holy days of rest (CD X 20).
21. Baban, "Luke's on the Road," 39–44.
22. Andersen and Robbins, "Paradigms in Homer," 29.

Way for them. *I am the way and the truth and the life* (John 14:6). In this fashion Jesus identifies himself and speaks of the way the disciples must go. The Fourth Gospel could not be clearer in proclaiming that Jesus alone is the Way to God. He is the one true vine in God's vineyard, so Israel must be grafted into him (John 15). It is certain that "the Way" is not presented in the Gospels in terms of territory, but it is understood spiritually.[23]

As they were walking along the road, a man said to him, "I will follow you wherever you go." Jesus replied, "Foxes have holes and birds of the air have nests, but the Son of Man has no place to lay his head." He said to another man, "Follow me" (Luke 9:58-9). A passage on the demands of discipleship appropriately follows his resolute determination to go to Jerusalem. Jesus, whose way is the cross, calls the disciples to follow him. He is thus the way for the disciples. In the Old Testament "walking in His way," namely following God (Deut 4:1-4, 6:14,10:12; 1 Sam 12:14; Judg 2:10-13; Isa 65:2; 1 Kgs 18:21) is used to express single-hearted devotion to God. Following God is metaphorically expressed as walking in the ways of God.[24] Elijah provided a sharp contrast of the choice faced when he called to the people of Israel who worshiped God in a syncretistic way. *How long will you waver between two options? If the Lord is God, follow him; but if Baal is God, follow him* (1 Kgs 18:21). Elijah's graphic statement was to challenge Israel to eliminate her religious ambivalence and to single-heartedly follow the Lord. The leaders of Israel were judged by the criteria of whether or not they were following God.[25] In particular, David was the supreme example of the king whose life was characterized by following God. The kings in Israel and Judah were portrayed either as good or bad in terms of whether they walked in the way David had followed (2 Chr 17:3) or in the ways the kings of Israel had followed (2 Chr 28:2).

In Luke this way is understood in terms of God's purpose. The word δει strongly implies that Jesus' Passover pilgrimage to Jerusalem was part of the divine purpose to proclaim the kingdom of God, which his whole way including his ministry, death, resurrection, and ascension

---

23. Gary Burge points out the same understanding. See Burge, "Territorial Religion," 394.

24. Helfmeyer, "הָלַךְ," 388–403.

25. Leaders include Joshua and Caleb (Num 32:12; Josh 14:8, 9, 14), the high priest (Zech 3:7), David (1 Kgs 14:8), Solomon (1 Kgs 9:6-7), Hezekiah (1 Kgs 18:6), and Josiah (2 Kgs 23:3).

will bring. Thus Luke shows that the way of salvation is found through faith (Luke 7:50; 8:48; 13:22–30; 17:19; Acts 10:43; 13:38–39; 16:31).[26] For those who long to enter into the way to salvation, the way of discipleship, are introduced to a pattern of life of following Jesus. Jesus revealed the pattern of life and salvation itself became the Way. Thus "follow me" means "follow me who is the only way to God and salvation." This idea of salvation as the way is emphasized in Luke's geographical perspective by Jesus' journey to Jerusalem. No wonder that an early designation of the first community of disciples in the book of Acts was also "people of the Way" (Acts 9:2; 19:9, 23; 22:4; 24:14, 22).

Having traced the root of "way" typology in John the Baptist's message in which he quoted Isaiah 40:3, "Prepare the way for the Lord" (Luke 3:4, 7:27; Mark 1:3), in the Greek Fitzmyer and S. H. Ringe make a clear linguistic connection between the Exodus and "way" for Luke as a special designation for Jesus' *salvific* mission in relation to *way into Jerusalem* and *way out from Jerusalem*.[27]

> This "way" is not simply expressive of his physical arrival in Jerusalem or of his progress toward the passion. It describes something greater, which begins with an *eisodos*, "entrance" (a compound of *eis*, "into," and *hodos*), that takes place only once John's "course" (*dromos*) has been run; and it ends with an *exodos*, "departure" (a compound of *ex*, "out of," and *hodos*), about which Jesus conversed with Moses and Elijah in the transfiguration scene.[28]

Having compared Luke 9:51—18:14 with Deuteronomy, Evans noted the agreement of order and concludes that Luke deliberately cast Jesus in the role of a prophet like Moses, who journeys through the central section of the Gospel to the borders of the promised land.[29] Thus the whole section of the Gospel was, for Evans, to present a new Exodus.[30] As Moses delivered Israel out of Egypt through the Exodus, the message of Jesus' Passover pilgrimage is certainly his salvation ministry in which

---

26. See Fitzmyer, *Luke I–IX*, 235–37, *Luke the Theologian*, 130–31; Marshall, *Luke*, 188–215.

27. See Fitzmyer, *Luke I–IX*, 169, 794; Ringe, "Luke 9:28–36," 96.

28. Ibid.

29. Evans, "Central Section," 42–50.

30. John Drury and Floyd Filson share the same view with Evans. See Drury, *Tradition and Design*, 138–63; Filson, "Journey Motif," 68.

Jesus sets the captives free and releases the oppressed (Luke 4:18–19). In the very beginning of the Gospel, Jesus' family made the pilgrimage to Jerusalem for the Feast of Passover (Luke 2:41–51). Jesus' final pilgrimage was also to keep the Feast of Passover. Jesus' discussion of his departure, the Exodus, with Moses and Elijah (Luke 9:31) suggests that Israel's exodus previewed Jesus' journey to Jerusalem in terms of the Feast of Passover, though there is a difference in the first Passover in Egypt that marked the beginning of the journey and Jesus' Passover, which was the conclusion of his earthly journey. In the same way Jesus' final Passover pilgrimage previews and serves as a prototype for the pilgrimage of his followers. W. C. Robinson endorses this understanding by describing Christ "as being on a pilgrimage toward suffering and glorification, because such pilgrimage is the lot of his messengers on this earth."[31] Considering the setting of the religious pilgrimage to the Passover feast for the whole section, it is certain that the memory of Israel's exodus to the promised land is woven into the narrative.[32] It is, therefore, natural for Luke to continue this typology in the book of Acts with an exodus theme.[33] This in fact is the view of David Moessner, that Jesus is the one like Moses, who suffers for a stiff-necked, stubborn generation while leading it to the promised land of salvation.[34]

Moessner's recapitulation of Moses in Jesus' Passover pilgrimage to Jerusalem is appealing, but raises some questions. Though one can detect the influence of the "prophet like Moses" on Jesus' final Passover pilgrimage to Jerusalem, Moses's death as being atoning is less convincing. Moessner claims that Moses as a suffering mediator leads the faithless and crooked generation of children to the promised salvation by dying outside the land.[35] More appealing is the possibility that the term "exodus" can also be used with reference to one's "departure" as in one's "death."[36] However, Moses in the Exodus narrative is better portrayed not as an atoning figure, but as one who liberates. The fact that the term

31. W. Robinson, "Theological Context," 27.

32. The Exodus theme is well established in Mark's central section. See Watts, *Influence of the Isaianic New Exodus*.

33. See Pao, *Acts and the Isaianic New Exodus*.

34. Moessner, "Luke 9:1–50," 575–605.

35. Ibid., 587.

36. Luke uses the Greek term ἔξοδος as a pun both for Jesus' death and his departure to heaven. See M. Strauss, *Davidic Messiah*, 271.

"exodus" also meant "the exodus from bondage in Egypt, particularly in the LXX and Hellenistic literature, supports this point."[37] Moses's death was certainly a consequence of the disobedience of a faithless generation. Nevertheless, Moses's death as atoning for the sin of Israel has no scriptural support. The story of the Exodus evokes notions of liberation more strongly than those of atonement.

One can also ask whether it is still possible to identify Jerusalem with the promised land? Conzelmann, for instance, indicates that the temple, not the city itself, was the real object of Jesus' journey and claimed that the temple was the true goal of the entire travel narrative.[38] Marshall, however, points out that Luke's interest was primarily in people, so Conzelmann's dissociation of the temple from Jerusalem was misleading.[39] For Marshall the significance of Jerusalem as the place of the crucifixion is that it is this place where the rulers of the Jews are to be found.[40] For Luke Jesus' journey to Jerusalem was a purpose-driven pilgrimage. Thus for Luke the temple, as the most important place in Jerusalem, symbolizes Jerusalem itself. Jerusalem was neither the promised land nor a cursed city. For Jesus Jerusalem was the place for his death and the temple was the place to reveal who he was and what God the Father's will was. Thus Jesus' pilgrimage to Jerusalem was a journey towards his death, not towards the city of Jerusalem itself. Jerusalem became the destination of his journey to complete the mission given by God the Father. In the book of Acts, Jerusalem as the destination of his journey is replaced by all Judea, Samaria, and the ends of the earth (Acts 1:8) to which the disciples should go for him. Luke emphasizes Jerusalem as a symbolical setting for the future as well as the final destination of Jesus' ministry.

James Dawsey notes two verbs in the Greek, το γο πορεύομαι (Luke 2:41) and to go up ἀναβαίνω (Luke 2:42), which often appear for describing the journey.[41] David Gill has claimed that in the central

---

37. Susan Garrett argues that Luke regarded the death, resurrection, and ascension as an "exodus" because in these events Jesus, "the one who is stronger," led the people out of bondage from Satan. See Garrett, "Exodus from Bondage," 656–80.

38. Conzelmann, *Theology of St. Luke*, 27; Davis, "Purpose of the Central Section," 164–69; Flender, *St. Luke*, 75.

39. Marshall, *Luke*, 154.

40. Ibid., 155.

41. Dawsey, "Jesus' Pilgrimage to Jerusalem," 217–32.

section πορεύομαι takes on "the function of a *terminum technicus* for Jesus' progress toward Jerusalem."[42] Along similar lines, Bo Reicke has suggested that another significant term of this section, ἀνάλημψις (Luke 9:51), connotes the idea of "pilgrimage."[43] His designation as the Pilgrim also rather neatly follows his resolute determination to go to Jerusalem. *Jesus replied, "Foxes have holes and birds of the air have nests, but the Son of Man has no place to lay his head"* (Luke 9:57–58). The discussion *how Jesus viewed himself* encounters difficulties because there are no clear-cut paradigms for understanding him. However, some Scriptures relating to what it meant to follow Jesus suggest that the set of relationships Jesus had with his followers reflected how Jesus viewed himself. Thus the fact that he bound disciples to himself needs to be given due weight in an evaluation of what Jesus was like and how he viewed himself. In particular, *the Son of Man* sayings in Luke 9:58 (cf. Matt 8:20–23) can be evaluated in that context. In fact, *the Son of Man* expression is one of the most debated and most enigmatic terms in the New Testament.[44] It is still inadequate to speak of one particular type of answer for the expression, despite tendencies in more recent research.[45] It is thus reasonable to suppose that the individual *Son of Man* sayings depend on their context. When we examine *the Son of Man* sayings in Luke 9:58, this investigation will attempt to explore the possibility that Jesus saw himself as a *Pilgrim*.

The homelessness of "the Son of Man" (Luke 9:58 = Matt 8:20) fits well with the pilgrimage paradigm. In Genesis 47:9–10 Jacob summarized his life and his fathers' lives as a pilgrimage before the pharaoh of Egypt. *And Jacob said to Pharaoh, "The years of my pilgrimage are a hundred and thirty. My years have been few and difficult, and they do not equal the years of the pilgrimage of my fathers"* (Gen 47:9–10). Jacob realized that he was chosen and given a divine promise by God, yet the promise had remained unfulfilled. Until the promised land is reached, his life as a homeless pilgrim is incomplete. Therefore, this summary

---

42. Gill, "Lukan Travel Narrative," 201.

43. Reicke, "Instruction and Discussion," 206–16.

44. The literature on the "Son of Man" is vast, and I make no attempt at covering it.

45. Three possible idiomatic senses of the expression: the circumlocutional sense (this man = I), the generic sense (man in general), and the indefinite sense (a man, someone). Three possible contexts of the sayings: those referring to the earthly life and circumstances, those referring to his passion, and those referring to the Parousia.

of his life, *the years of my pilgrimage*, could be the total appreciation of who he was before God, offering a crucial motif for the whole of the patriarchal narrative.

Jesus used this homelessness with special reference to himself, declaring that he had nowhere to go. Although Bultmann argues that the Son of Man reference is generic and applies to people in general, Marshall and Walter Liefeld claim that most people have homes, so the reference must be to Jesus.[46] For Martin Hengel "homelessness" has been Jesus' fate from his birth.[47] This homelessness fits well into the context of his itinerant ministry. Being in the position of not being able to make any satisfactory provision Jesus implied that whoever follows the way he would go must also share in his homelessness to become like the one who has sacrificed family and home for the sake of the kingdom (Luke 8:19–21; 9:58). To proclaim the kingdom of God, Jesus demanded the same renunciation that he had already made from those who wanted to follow him. Luke appears to stress this element even more emphatically (Luke 9:7–62; 11:41; 12:33; 14:33). Having believed that Jesus set a living example for those who wanted to follow him literally, Eduard Schweizer makes this point clearly:

> Jesus leads the way in practising a childlike life that renounces self-assurance and is focused entirely on God. Thus Jesus also makes this life possible for others.[48]

This requirement was for all who call themselves followers of Jesus. It is, however, noted that there were two different kinds of disciples: the itinerant disciples and the sedentary disciples.[49] The itinerant type of disciples in Luke literally renounced everything including family and possessions, and accompanied Jesus literally in his earthly ministry. The Twelve responded to Jesus' call and followed him literally, leaving everything behind. It is, however, not certain whether the seventy followed Jesus in his whole ministry including the journeys to Jerusalem in the same way the twelve disciples did.

---

46. Bultmann, *John*, 28 n. 3; Liefeld, *Luke*, 935; Marshall, *Gospel*, 410.

47. Hengel, "φάτνη," 55.

48. Schweizer, *Good News*, 286 (cf. 287).

49. We will use the terms, itinerant and sedentary, which Brian Beck employs in his book, although he does not appear to explore this point. See Beck, *Christian Character*, 95. Kyoung-Jin Kim has thoroughly examined the two types of disciples in Luke. See Kim, *Stewardship and Almsgiving*, 100–110.

Some responded to Jesus' call, still living at home with their family and work. Levi (Luke 5:27–29), the Galilean women (Luke 8:2–3), Martha and Mary (Luke 10:38–42), Zacchaeus (Luke 19:1–10), and Joseph of Arimathea (Luke 23:50–54) can be classified in the category of sedentary disciples.[50] Although they responded differently from the way that the itinerant disciples reacted, it is clear that Jesus accepted the sedentary disciples who responded to Jesus' demand in some other way. Luke records how the needs of Jesus the Pilgrim and his disciples were met during their journey to Jerusalem by the sedentary disciples. At the same time he presents Jesus' call for the renunciation of possessions more decisively than either Mark or Matthew.

Thus these two apparently different types of disciples could indicate that the point of the "homelessness of the Son of Man" and "following him" was the principle implied, not the particular prerequisite that Jesus required.[51] *Homelessness of the Son of Man* and *follow him* (Luke 9:58–59) was a reply to the would-be-disciple in Luke 9:57. Joel Green notes that Luke does not specify whether this would-be-disciple is male or female (in Luke-Acts, the Greek αὐτός does not necessarily designate a man) and claims that someone who showed willingness to follow Jesus in Luke 9:57 gives this scene a certain timeless quality.[52] Through this would-be-disciple and the picture of *homelessness of Jesus* and *follow Him*, Luke probably intended to tell the members of his community that they were called to be the disciples of Jesus according to the pattern of the two types of disciple and to be homeless as the pilgrims of Jesus who would journey with him (Luke 9:21–23).

It is noted that Luke gives careful attention to Jesus' audience during his Passover pilgrimage to Jerusalem. Three distinguished audiences emerged—the disciples, the crowds, and the enemies. To each group Jesus gave his teaching and claims. So the Passover journey and its climax became a work of instruction for those around him as well as the Lukan community.

---

50. Levi in 5:27–29 is not a member of the twelve disciples according to the list of the apostles in Luke 6:13–16.

51. Having examined the two types of disciples, Kim concludes in the same way that Luke is more preoccupied with the right use of possession than with literal renunciation of them. See Kim, *Stewardship and Almsgiving*, 100–110.

52. Green, *Gospel of Luke*, 407.

Luke mentions "Passover" six times (Luke 22:1, 7, 8, 11, 13, 15). This stresses that Jesus wanted to celebrate the Passover with his disciples. The celebration of the Passover meal was not to be disturbed. Clearly Luke realized that this meal had new significance. As the first Passover meal was eaten before the Exodus, Jesus had a Passover meal with his disciples before his death. It is highly suggestive for most scholars that the Passover meal recalled the Exodus. Passover for first-century Jews was not just to celebrate the deliverance from Egyptian bondage as a "memorial" but also to anticipate "an eschatological, even messianic, deliverance."[53] Since the Passover came to have a defining significance for the Israelites' identity, Jesus filled the Passover meal with his own meaning, anticipating final redemption through his death. *"This is my body given for you; do this in remembrance of me." In the same way, after the supper he took the cup, saying, "This cup is the new covenant in my blood, which is poured out for you"* (Luke 22:19–20). Jesus reinterpreted the symbols of the Passover and gave them new meanings, identifying the bread with the body of Jesus and relating the cup to the new covenant in his blood. Jesus revealed his coming death, his own suffering, and gave bread and wine "as a mode of re-presenting to themselves their experience of him (especially at this last supper)" for the sake of Jesus' followers and "as a new mode of celebrating Israel's feast of deliverance."[54]

By especially noting that "it was the day when it was required to sacrifice the paschal lamb" (Luke 22:7), Luke begins, L. T. Johnson claims, to invite the reader into the understanding of Jesus' death not as a meaningless accident of human greed or as the triumph of evil in the world, but as the fulfillment of God's plan for the Messiah.[55] So the Feast of Passover was the setting for Jesus' death. The meals in the last supper have a pivotal role to play in the Passover context. Thus Nolland claims that the Gospels use their narrative techniques not only to report historical events but also to interpret the significance of Jesus and his ministry.[56] So his body and blood replaced the Passover lamb, which was the center of the Passover sacrifice. The meaning of Passover has been transformed christologically. As the Passover lamb of the Exodus meal was to save the firstborn of Israel, Jesus as the Passover lamb of-

---

53. Fitzmyer, *Luke X–XXIV*, 1390.
54. Ibid., 1391–92.
55. Johnson, *Gospel of Luke*, 335.
56. Nolland, *Luke 18:35—24:53*, 1055.

fered himself to save the universe. The connection of this reinterpreted Passover with the reference to Jesus' death could not be clearer in the context of his action on the cross. Thus the memorial pattern of the Passover is now to be exploited in a new way in connection with the salvation achievement of Jesus.[57]

In Jesus' Passover pilgrimage the feast was imbued with new meaning and further significance. Jesus transformed the rituals of the Passover, proclaiming himself to be the Savior of the world. This confirms a strong probability that Jesus intended the meaning of the feast and his pilgrimage to illuminate his person and work. He acknowledged the great symbolic representation of the feast, through which he revealed who he was and so he claimed himself to be the completion of the feast. Like the Tabernacles pilgrimage, the revelation of Jesus became the message of his Passover pilgrimage with all the rich experiences contained in the feast. Thus his Passover pilgrimage offers the underlying dynamic of the feast, the knowing God motif. Nolland confirms that Jesus who is no longer present in his historical ministry will make himself known and confer ever afresh to the disciple community the benefits of his passion.[58] This is what the Lukan gospel intends and the readers who journey with Jesus should learn from his Passover pilgrimage.

KNOWING GOD MOTIF (JOHN 14)

The opening verse, "just before the Passover Feast," of chapter 13 sets the scene for the entire farewell discourse (John 13:31—16:33), building up Jesus' final Passover pilgrimage.

Charles Talbert has presented the Way of Jesus in Luke in five stages: dedication to God as an infant; confirmation of parental decisions as a responsible youth; empowering for service; rejection and suffering as the perfection of obedience; and glorification.[59] We note that the first two stages and the fourth stage happened on a Passover pilgrimage. In the first two stages the knowing process of Mary was dealt with in relation to the Passover feast.[60] Luke 9:44–45 and 18:34 in his final Passover pilgrimage twice emphasizes the fact that the disciples did not expect

---

57. Ibid., 1057.
58. Ibid., 1056.
59. Talbert, "Way of the Lukan Jesus," 237–49.
60. Chapter 4 deals with this.

Jesus' death. The lamb dies to make the world live. Why did Luke twice stress their failure to comprehend his death? It is probable that Luke wanted to show that the disciples could not understand the meaning of suffering in relation to God's purpose and wanted to show how their understanding gradually evolved.

The Passover feast plays a vital role in the Fourth Gospel too (John 2:13; 6:4; 12:1; 13:1; 18:14; 18:28). We see this at the beginning of the Gospel. John the Baptist possibly used the actual Passover lamb motif for Jesus. John the Baptist depicts Christ as, "the Lamb of God who takes away the sin of the world" (John 1:29). In the Fourth Gospel the meal also took place on the evening before Passover, so that in his account he has Jesus the Lamb of God crucified on the same day the Passover lambs were killed. In the Gospel "the Lamb of God" would take away sins through suffering and death, *the expiatory sacrifice of the Lamb*. It is thus not surprising that John records Jesus' death as taking place at the very time when the Passover lambs were being slaughtered at the temple. There was, as Holland concludes, a widespread appreciation of the significance of Ezekiel's description as a key to understanding the death of Christ.[61] J. K. Howard and James Dunn claim that the sin offerings mentioned during the Passover of Ezekiel 45:25 are acknowledged as the background of Jesus being the Lamb of God in John 1:29, and are seen as grounds for an atoning significance of the Passover in the New Testament.[62] Thus the Lamb became the Suffering Messiah who was crucified at the time of the Passover (John 18:28; 19:14, 31). Although this image is highly complex, of the many explanations that have been offered, a reference to the paschal lamb fits well with the whole context. By showing the death of Christ coincided with Passover (John 18:14, 28) the association of the Lamb of God with Passover identifies the lamb as a paschal sacrifice (John 19:36).[63] This Suffering Messiah is also identified with the Servant of God (John 12:38) who bears sin (Isa 53:11).

Jesus repeatedly spoke of being lifted up, of being betrayed, and of dying. Thus the disciples of Jesus had to come to terms with the fact that he was going to the Father via the cross. The way of Jesus was the cross.

---

61. Holland, *Contours of Pauline Theology*, 162.

62. Howard, "Passover and Eucharist," 331–32; Dunn, "Paul's Understanding," 132–33.

63. See Howard, "Passover and Eucharist," 331–32; Dunn, "Paul's Understanding," 132–33; Holland, *Contours of Pauline Theology*, 161–64.

Jesus and the Final Passover Pilgrimage (John 12–19; Luke 9–19)

He was despised and died a shameful death. His statement "I am the way" (John 14:6) declares that he becomes the destination of the way as well as the Way itself.[64] The way of the disciples was Jesus. That was the Way they should know.

In the Fourth Gospel the way of Jesus is more clearly related to the knowing God motif. *If you really knew me, you would have known my Father as well. From now on, you do know him and have seen him* (John 14:7). The Fourth Gospel uses the two words γινώσκω and οἶδα for "to know" in the Greek much more extensively than the other Gospels. The following table demonstrates this fact:[65]

	Matthew	Mark	Luke	John	1 John
γινώσκω	20	13	28	56	25
οἶδα	25	23	26	85	15

We must therefore ask the question, "What is the meaning of knowing God in the Fourth Gospel?" Dodd sums up what knowing God meant for a Jew.

> Accordingly, for the Greek, to know God means to contemplate the ultimate reality, τὸ ὄντως ὄν, in its changeless essence. For the Hebrew, to know God is to acknowledge Him in His works and to respond to His claims. While for the Greek knowledge of God is the most highly abstract form of pure contemplation, for the Hebrew it is essentially intercourse with God; it is to experience His dealings with men in time, and to hear and obey His commands.[66]

John's use of the two verbs γινώσκω and οἶδα indicates that the Fourth Gospel uses the two meanings distinctively, but on other occasions quite synonymously and without discrimination. The first verb γινώσκω denotes in ordinary Greek the intelligent comprehension of an object or matter (to come to know, to experience, or to perceive).[67] The second verb οἶδα means to know in an absolute sense without any emphasis

---

64. Bultmann states that "his case is different from that of the disciples; he does not need a 'way' for himself, as the disciples do, rather he is the way for them." Bultmann, *John*, 605.
65. Vanderlip, *Christianity According to John*, 105.
66. Dodd, *Interpretation of the Fourth Gospel*, 152.
67. Bultmann, "γινώσκω," 689.

upon having learned it.[68] It is also noted that the verb γινώσκω found side by side with verbs for *seeing* (John 14:7, 16–17) tells us that knowing is closely related to seeing.[69] This might indicate that the verb shares the Greek idea of knowing. However, the verb closely connected with *believing* stresses knowing through mutual fellowship. *Don't you believe that I am in the Father, and the Father is in me?* (John 14:10). The mutual relationship of the Father and the Son is expressed in terms of knowing (John 14:7). *And we have believed, and have come to know, that you are the Holy One of God* (John 6:69). Dodd provides the three points of God's knowledge of his people that LXX translators have given.[70] This is a summary of them: (1) God "knows" those who are his; (2) he has chosen them; and (3) he leads them to himself.[71] God knows his people in the sense of calling and electing them for his purpose, giving to them his revelation.[72] These three concepts not only represent the Hebraic understanding of the term "know," but also enforce the close association of the knowing God motif and God as the destination of pilgrimage (the pilgrimage paradigm), "I brought you to myself" (Exod 19:4). These three points clearly emerge in the teaching of the Fourth Gospel (John 10:14; 13:18; 6:44; 7:32).[73]

The primary reason for the journey of Abraham and Jacob was to know God as it was to be for the Israelites in the wilderness. Those who take a journey and labor to go through with the journey will be given

---

68. E. Lee, *Religious Thought*, 233–34.

69. Bultmann, "γινώσκω," 692.

70. The frequency of the references to knowledge gives to this theme an unusual prominence. D. George Vanderlip's four aspects of the knowledge of Qumran stand out: (1) The knowledge which they possess is held to be revealed to them by God; (2) it is an esoteric knowledge that is not to be shared with those outside the fellowship; (3) the knowledge that they possess involves a proper understanding of the law of Moses and an ardent desire and effort on their part to conform their lives to their unique interpretation of the law; and (4) there are also passages which indicate that the Qumran community thought of itself as the faithful in Israel who were preparing in the desert a highway for the messianic age and the knowledge they possessed involved special information concerning events that would take place at this "end time" before the new age dawned. These conclusions are discussed at greater length in his dissertation "A Comparative Study of Certain Alleged Similarities between the Literature of Qumran and the Fourth Gospel." See Vanderlip, *Christianity According to John*, 114.

71. Dodd, *Interpretation of the Fourth Gospel*, 162.

72. Ibid., 160.

73. Ibid., 162.

Jesus and the Final Passover Pilgrimage (John 12-19; Luke 9-19)

the prize of victory, *a proper consideration of God = knowing who God is*. Philo expresses this understanding in *On the Virtues* 20.102-104.[74] Thus the knowing God motif was not an abstract concept, but a vital reality throughout the history of Israel, particularly the Jerusalem festal experience. This reality was reexperienced through the pilgrim feasts in the temple of Jerusalem, which became more than a place where God dwells.

The disciples must see that their knowledge of Jesus is nothing less than knowledge of God. His identity was revealed as the one who made God manifest. *No one has ever seen God, but God the One and Only, who is at the Father's side, has made him known* (John 1:18). *From now on, you do know him and have seen him* (14:7). It means that knowledge of Jesus is knowledge of God.[75] This is a framework that we will see throughout the pilgrimages of Jesus and his disciples. However, when Jesus' teaching did not conform to their expectations, many disciples left him (John 6:66). In fact, the teaching apparently was designed to elicit this very reaction, because it revealed those who were true believers and those who were not. These individuals journeyed with Jesus as "disciples," but they were not truly in line with the purpose of Jesus' pilgrimage. They followed him, because he was an exciting new miracle performer (John 2:23-25). Once the disciples left, Jesus asked the Twelve a question. *"You do not want to leave too, do you?"* Simon Peter answered, *"Lord, to whom shall we go? You have the words of eternal life. We believe and know that you are the Holy One of God"* (John 6:67-69). Peter established a definition of what it meant to be his disciple: eternal life depended on Jesus being *the Holy One of God*. Discipleship for Peter was a matter of eternal life. Thus for the Fourth Gospel eternal life is described as "knowing" God and "knowing" Jesus Christ who alone reveals the Father and who is the one mediator between God and man (John 17:3). As knower and known Jesus reconstituted the relation for men by his own relation to the

---

74. "Moreover, after the lawgiver has established commandments respecting one's fellow countrymen, he proceeds to show that he looks upon strangers also as worthy of having their interests attended to by his laws, since they have forsaken their native land and their national customs, and the sacred temples of their gods, and the worship and honor which they had been wont to pay to them, and have migrated with a holy migration, changing their abode of fabulous inventions for that of the certainty and clearness of truth, and of the worship of the one true and living God. Accordingly, he commands the men of his nation to love the strangers, not only as they love their friends and relations, but even as they love themselves . . . " (*Virtues* 20.102-4).

75. For Philo God is known in his Logos.

Father.⁷⁶ The true followers of Jesus are people who make a faith commitment to him by knowing him and who know the way to the place where Jesus is going (John 14:4). The irony is, however, that they do not perceive what they have come to know. They knew Jesus, but failed to grasp who he really was. They neither knew him nor recognized that to know him is to know God. Thus we find that the number of those around him decreased as Jesus' destiny of the cross drew nearer. This was the result of failure by the disciples to conceive knowing God in their experience of Jesus and in relation to him. This decrease in number corresponds to the increasing clarification he gave in his earthly ministry—the reality of the intimate relationship between his followers and God. Dodd states that

> for John this experience is made possible through the recognition of Christ as the revelation of God, of Christ as inseparably one with God; and it finds its completion in an experience of our unity with Christ in God.⁷⁷

Keeping in mind Dodd's point, the meaning of the two verbs,⁷⁸ and the knowing God motif, we can clearly see that Jesus revealed himself and taught about God to the disciples and Israelites in a Hebraic mindset.

Despite the clarity of Jesus' claim, there was a fundamental divide in the understanding of the disciples between Jesus and the Father. It was Thomas who asked the question, "Lord, we don't know where you are going, so how can we know the way?" (John 14:5). Jesus replied that the way the disciples must travel, not his own way to the Father, was the way of the cross. Thomas claimed that he did not know where Jesus was going, nor did he know the way (John 14:5). Thomas had failed to distinguish between the way Jesus must take to return to his Father via the

---

76. Schnackenburg noted four ways in which Johannine knowledge of God differs from that of Gnosticism: (1) In John knowledge is not concerned with "self-knowledge" but with a genuine knowledge of God that leads to communion with God; (2) this knowledge of God is dependent upon a divine revelation and is essentially different from any Gnostic "revelation"; (3) Jesus is the mediator of salvation. His coming is anchored in history and not in a mythical, non historical revelation, as it is in Gnosticism; (4) whoever would know God must keep his commandments. This concern of John is not found in Gnosticism. Vanderlip quotes Schnackenburg. See Vanderlip, *Christianity According to John*, 195.

77. Dodd, *Interpretation of the Fourth Gospel*, 169.

78. Dodd claims that whatever difference of meaning the two words may originally have had would seem to have almost disappeared by our period, pointing out that there are places in the LXX where γινώσκω and οἶδα are variant readings, having no difference of meaning. See ibid., 152–53.

cross, and the way the disciples must take to join him. This is the same sort of error Philip made. *Philip asked, "Lord, show us the Father and that will be enough for us"* (John 14:8). *Jesus answered, "Don't you know me, Philip, even after I have been among you such a long time? Anyone who has seen me has . . . seen the Father. How can you say, 'Show us the Father'?"* (John 14:9). Philip's question appears to miss the point Jesus kept teaching, for the Father has made himself known in the Word who has become flesh. Therefore whoever has seen the incarnate Word has seen the Father. Like the people who participated their lifelong journey in the OT, the people who participated in a pilgrimage with Jesus came gradually to a stage to fully know God the Father through Jesus the Son of God. Thus the Fourth Gospel tells the readers that Jesus' pilgrimages to Jerusalem is the context of the gradual progression towards the full comprehension of both the disciples and the people who Jesus encountered regarding God the Father and Jesus the Son. So each journey to Jerusalem for Jesus became a vehicle to fulfill his earthly ministry and for those around him to know him.

It is no wonder that Jesus was ready for the misunderstanding (reaction) of Thomas and Philip. His focus was on the disciples' need to have faith in him. Thus Jesus asked the Father to give the Spirit to the disciples. *He will give you another Counselor . . . whom the world cannot receive, because it neither sees him nor knows him* (John 14:16–17). The Spirit is the means whereby the Father and the Son are present with and in believers. Thus the purpose of Jesus' request to his Father, that the Father might send the Spirit, is that this counselor might be with the disciples of Jesus forever (John 14:16). Jesus assures his followers, "for he lives with you and will be in you" (John 14:17). The entire section of chapter 14 envisions the giving of the Spirit subsequent to the glorification of Jesus (John 7:39) and knowing God the Father and the Son by means of the Spirit until his return. Jesus clearly indicates that asking for the Holy Spirit is conditioned by his departure. *It is for your good that I am going away. Unless I go away, the Counselor will not come to you; but if I go, I will send him to you* (John 16:7). Although the Father and the Son are involved in sending the Holy Spirit (John 15:26), the Holy Spirit will be given only as a result of Christ's death, resurrection, and exaltation. Thus the conclusion of Jesus' teaching on knowing God in the farewell discourse is the introduction of the Holy Spirit. The introduction, made just before the Passover feast (on Jesus' final Passover pilgrimage), made the Pentecost pilgrimage indispensable. Appearing as the one who he really was, Jesus made God the Father and the Holy Spirit known. This is reality visibly expressed through his saving works, manifesting to the world who he is.

Conclusion

Since the Fourth Gospel does not favor either Judea or Galilee, this could be an indication that localism or provincialism was no longer an important factor when the Gospel was written. The Fourth Gospel develops the presence of pilgrimage to Jerusalem in the context of the relation between Jerusalem and Galilee, and shifts the content of the festivals, including the holy place and the religious rituals, to Jesus Christ supplanting the major location of Judaism. In the conversation with a Samaritan woman Jesus declares that God will be worshiped neither on Gerizim nor in Jerusalem, but in Spirit and truth (John 4:21–24). Thus the place of worship is no longer relevant, because true worship must be in keeping with Christ, not with a place (John 14:6, 16, 25–26). As in the Feast of Tabernacles Jesus replaces two ritual symbols; water (John 7:37) and light (John 8:58), at Passover he becomes the sacrifice of the feast (John 19:31–37), dismissing the importance of holy places including the holy sites of Judea, Samaria, or Galilee. Jerusalem and the pilgrimage feasts had an important place in his ministry. However, this is not because of the significance of the feasts or Jerusalem, but because the feast typified Jesus Christ, who is the Holy Place, the true destination of people's pilgrimage and the completion of the pilgrimage feasts. Christology could not be clearer in answering the Jewish yearning for place.

In contrast to Matthew and Mark, for Luke it is Jerusalem (Judea) as the place of the temple that is highlighted. Therefore, the temple as the true goal of Jesus' pilgrimage in Luke is more than the place where Jesus' journey ends.[79] For Jesus' journey to Jerusalem was always purpose driven in terms of the meaning of each pilgrimage feast. Just as Jerusalem developed into the locus of the land, the temple became the heart of Jerusalem. Although the temple theme does not frame the whole story, as the goal of his pilgrimage, the temple in Jerusalem marks the inner consistency and meaning of his pilgrimage. For Luke his pilgrimage to Jerusalem was a way to show what kind of messiah he was. The stress on Jerusalem, the place where Jesus must suffer, is heightened by his aware-

---

79. Dawsey, "Jesus' Pilgrimage to Jerusalem," 226.

ness as the Suffering Messiah. Therefore, the final Passover pilgrimage in Luke reflects Jesus' own consciousness that he had to fulfill the role of the Suffering Messiah (Servant) in suffering and death. This model enabled his disciples to come to terms with his death not as defeat but as achievement, and to see the whole "way" of Jesus. "The Way" began when Jesus made the decisive choice to head towards Jerusalem (Luke 9:51). This is similar to the Fourth Gospel, which could not be clearer in proclaiming that Jesus alone is the way to God (John 15).

In Luke this way is understood in terms of God's purpose. The word δει (Luke 9:58–59) strongly implies that Jesus' Passover pilgrimage to Jerusalem was under the divine imperative to proclaim the kingdom of God, which his whole way of death, resurrection, and ascension would bring. A passage on the demands of discipleship appropriately follows his resolute determination to go to Jerusalem (Luke 9:58–59). Jesus, whose way is the cross on Calvary, asks the disciples to follow him. He is the way of the disciples. The homelessness of "the Son of Man" (Luke 9:58 = Matt 8:20) fits well into the context of his itinerant ministry. Jesus implied that whoever follows the way he would go must also share in his homelessness to become like the one who has sacrificed family and home for the sake of the kingdom (Luke 8:19–21; 9:58). This requirement was for all who call themselves followers of Jesus. However, two different kinds of disciples, the itinerant disciples and the sedentary disciples, could indicate that the point of the "homelessness of the Son of Man" and "following him" was the principle implied, not the particular prerequisite that Jesus required.

Luke 9:44–45 and 18:34 in his final Passover pilgrimage twice emphasize the fact that the disciples did not expect his death. Through stressing their failure to comprehend his death Luke wanted to show how their understanding of the meaning of suffering in relation to God's purpose gradually evolved. We see this in the Fourth Gospel too. By showing that the death of Christ coincided with Passover (John 18:14, 28) the association of the Lamb of God with Passover identifies the lamb as a paschal sacrifice (John 19:36). Jesus repeatedly spoke of being lifted up, of being betrayed, and of dying. Thus the disciples of Jesus had to come to terms with the fact that he was going to the Father via the cross. The way of Jesus was the cross. He was despised and died a shameful death. His statement "I am the way" (John 14:6) declares that he becomes the destination of the way as well as the Way itself. The way of the disciples was Jesus. That was the Way the disciples and the readers should know. This was reality expressed through the symbols and rites of the Feast of Passover and the responses of the disciples to its experiences later.

The disciples must see that their knowledge of Jesus is nothing less than knowledge of God. The mutual relationship of the Father and the Son is expressed in terms of knowing (John 14:7). However, when Jesus' teaching did not conform to their expectations, many disciples left him (John 6:66). They neither really knew him nor recognized that to know him is to know God. Thus we find that the number of those around him decreased as Jesus' journey to the cross drew nearer. This was because of the failure of the disciples to understand that they were encountering God himself in their experience of Jesus and in relation to him. The Fourth Gospel tells the readers that Jesus' pilgrimages to Jerusalem were a gradual progression towards the full comprehension for the disciples and the people Jesus encountered regarding God the Father and Jesus the Son. Thus Jesus asked the Father to give the Spirit to the disciples (John 14:16–17). It is the Holy Spirit whereby the Father and the Son are present with and in the believers. Although the Father and the Son are involved in sending the Holy Spirit (John 15:26), the Holy Spirit will be given only as a result of Christ's death, resurrection, and exaltation. Thus each of Jesus' pilgrimages plays an important role that culminates in the fulfillment of his earthly ministry in his pilgrimages. The entire section of John 14 envisions that the giving of the Spirit is conditioned by his departure (John 7:39; 16:7). Thus the conclusion of Jesus' teaching on knowing God in the farewell discourse is the introduction of the Holy Spirit. This means that Jesus' final Passover pilgrimage made the Pentecost pilgrimage indispensable.

6

Jesus and the Pentecost Pilgrimage

ASCENSION AS THE FULFILLMENT FOR HIS LAST PILGRIMAGE

As John and Luke (Luke 9:51) suggest, a time has been set for Jesus to fulfill the Father's plan of salvation. For Jesus his way was towards the passion, resurrection, and ascension. Thus the ascension, the journey to heaven, should not be isolated from what preceded and followed. The ascension of Christ is not only intimately connected with Pentecost, but is also related to the resurrection, which lies at the heart of the Christian faith. Within the complex of events surrounding Jesus' ascension to the Father and the descent of the Holy Spirit, the ascension of Christ, the empty tomb, the post-resurrection appearances, and Pentecost itself all testify to the resurrection of Christ.

Enoch (Gen 5:24) and Elijah (2 Kgs 2:1–12) also experienced this journey to heaven (ascension).[1] Moses, Aaron, and the elders of Israel (Exod 24:9–11), Micaiah (1 Kgs 22:19–23), Isaiah (Isa 6:1–13), and Ezekiel (Ezek 1, 10) beheld the throne (heavenly court) of God. The motif of the journey to heaven is a vitally important phenomenon in the apocalypses of the Pseudepigrapha. The Jewish apocalyptic movement is frequently associated with famous figures drawn from the past, like of Enoch, Abraham, and Levi, and presented in the context of the motif of the heavenly journey, which functions as a foretaste of a final ascent to

---

1. The Bible records five people who have ascended to heaven: Enoch (Gen 5:24); Elijah (2 Kgs 2:1–12); Jesus (Luke 24:51; Acts 1:9); Paul (2 Cor 12:2–4); and John (Rev 4:1).

heavenly life.² James Tabor categorizes the motif of the heavenly journey into four types in terms of the purpose of the ascent:

> 1. Ascent as an Invasion of Heaven 2. Ascent to Receive Revelation 3. Ascent to Immortal Heavenly Life 4. Ascent as a Foretaste of the Heavenly World.³

The first two categories are more characteristic of the ANE or archaic period, which would include most texts of the Old Testament, whereas the latter two categories are more typical of the Hellenistic period, which reflects the perspective of the New Testament.⁴ In the New Testament Jesus was raised from the dead, made immortal, and ascended to the Father.⁵ This action left a hope that his followers will experience the same at his return (John 14:1–3; 1 Cor 15:20–28; Rom 8:29–30). Having become the paradigm for his mortal followers, the ascent of Jesus to heaven is a step ahead of our ascension that is the ultimate experience of Christian living.

The actual account of the ascent of Jesus appears only in Luke-Acts (Luke 24:51; Acts 1:9), and is spoken of in the Fourth Gospel (John 20:17).⁶ However, the fact that Jesus foretold his ascension nine times in the Fourth Gospel (John 6:62; 7:33; 14:12, 28; 16:5, 10, 17, 28; 20:17) indicates the Gospel writers' emphasis on the event. According to this Gospel, resurrection, the post resurrection appearances and the giving

---

2. According to Hebrews 11, the righteous of the OT, such as Abraham, Moses, and the prophets, are included in the promised resurrection to immortal heavenly life. In 1 Enoch (first century BCE), the book of the Watchers (chaps. 1–36), Enoch is taken through the heavenly realms and shown cosmic secrets, even appearing before God's lofty throne. In the Similitudes of Enoch (*1 En.* 37–71), particularly chapter 39, Enoch relates how he was taken to heaven and how the experience transformed him. He is told that he will later ascend to heaven permanently and receive glory and immortal heavenly life (chaps. 70–71). Second Enoch (Slavonic) also reflects a similar pattern. Enoch's journey through the seven heavens, which lasts sixty days (chaps. 1–20), is followed by a return to earth. For the Greek version of the *Testament of Levi* (second century BCE), the Latin *Life of Adam and Eve* (first century CE) and the *Apocalypse of Abraham* the ascent to heaven functions as a vehicle of revelation. These Jewish writings from the Second Temple period share the notion of ascent in the Old Testament and elaborated this understanding of ascent.

3. Tabor, "Heaven, Ascent to," 91.

4. Ibid.

5. A similar resurrection from the dead followed by bodily ascension to heaven is prophesied for the "two witnesses" in the book of Revelation (Rev 11:7–12).

6. It is assumed in Matthew and Mark and spoken of in Paul (Rom 8:34).

of the Spirit happened in one single day, and there is no separate record of the ascension. The risen Christ appeared to Mary Magdalene, leaving the message to his disciples. *I am ascending to my Father and your Father, to my God and your God* (John 20:17). On the evening of that same day, he came to the eleven and gave them the Holy Spirit (John 20:19–23). Jesus already confirmed that the outpouring of the Spirit would follow as a result of the glorification of Christ. *It is for your good that I am going away. Unless I go away, the Advocate will not come to you; but if I go, I will send him to you* (John 16:7). The glorification of Christ followed his crucifixion, resurrection, and ascension. In the conversation with Nicodemus the Johannine Jesus says: "As Moses lifted up the snake in the wilderness, so the Son of Man must be lifted up, that everyone who believes may have eternal life in him" (John 3:14). When he is lifted up on the cross, then the people will know who he is (John 8:28). Although there is ambiguity whether lifting up meant lifting up on the cross or lifting up to glory, a future aspect of his glory is well presented in the texts. Since Jesus' way includes the passion, resurrection, and ascension, Jesus being lifted on high could be seen as "one continuous action of ascent."[7] Thus Veselin Kesich states:

> His death on the cross and the revelation that accompanied it, together with the resurrection and the Ascension, is the fulfillment of the incarnation.[8]

Barrett also concludes that the ascension was for John an essential act, completing what was done in the passion.[9] The lifting up high in 3:14 and in 12:32, 34 seems to be alluding to Jesus Christ having been lifted on high in crucifixion and glorified, and in him God is glorified. *If God is glorified in him, God will glorify the Son in himself* (John 13:32). In the high priestly prayer, Jesus looked back on his incarnate ministry and entrusted his immediate future to his Father. *Father, glorify me in your presence with the glory I had with you before the world began* (John 17:5). Only by entering into glory would his pilgrimage be completed and the Spirit bestowed upon his disciples (John 15:26).

---

7. Brown, *John I-XII*, 146; Lindars, *Gospel of John*, 157; Schnackenburg, *Gospel According to St. John*, 1:396. Some commentators would restrict the "lifting up high" in 3:14 and in 12:32, 34 to the crucifixion of Jesus, as in 8:28. See Bernard, *Exegetical Commentary*, 114.

8. Kesich, "Resurrection, Ascension," 258.

9. Barrett, *Gospel According to St. John*, 470.

Luke is in agreement with the Fourth Gospel that the Spirit is given only after his return to the Father. In the writings of Luke we find two accounts of the ascension on the Mount of Olives (Luke 24:50–53; Acts 1:9–11). The appearance of the risen Christ to the two disciples on the road to Emmaus (Luke 24:13–35) and the appearance to the eleven (24:36–49) are followed by the ascension. Luke ends with a description of Jesus being taken up to heaven from Bethany on the evening of the day of the resurrection that was the first Easter Sunday evening. All these events are presented in the form of *way* setting. The Mount of Olives is the highest range of hills east of Jerusalem, overlooking the city. This was the last stopping place for pilgrims on the way from Jericho to Jerusalem. In all likelihood Jesus traversed this mountain many times traveling to and from the feasts in Jerusalem. Although this route could have been avoided by taking the direct northern route through Samaria, according to Jewish custom, the eastern route was taken to avoid stepping on Samaritan soil. At the very end of the Gospel, the risen Christ led the disciples to Bethany, a village on the Mount of Olives.[10] There he lifted up his hands and blessed them like a priest, while he was taken up to heaven (Luke 24:50–53).[11] Among the numerous trips using this

10. The cursing of the fig tree, occurring the day after the triumphal entry, took place on Jesus' evening return to Bethany (Matt 21:17–19; Mark 11:11–14, 19–20) and probably occurred on this mountain. It is also likely that the Mount of Olives was in view when Jesus taught that the person of faith could say to the mountain, "'Go throw yourself into the sea,' and it will be done" (Matt 21:21). Also during his passion week, Jesus gave his disciples an eschatological outline (Matt 24; Mark 13) from "the Mount of Olives opposite the temple" (Mark 13:3; cf. Matt 24:3). Luke informs us that during the evenings of the passion week, Jesus tarried on Mount Olivet (Luke 21:37). The seclusion of the groves was probably heartily welcomed after the rigor of teaching in the temple all day. It is probably from this mountain that Jesus sent his disciples into Jerusalem (Matt 26:18; Luke 22:8) to prepare the Passover. After celebrating this feast in the city, they sang a hymn and went to the Mount of Olives (Matt 26:30; Mark 14:26; Luke 22:39; cf. John 18:1). Jesus' destination on the Mount of Olives was the garden of Gethsemane (Matt 26:36). This garden was probably located on the west side of Olivet, and here Jesus agonized before his Father in prayer (Matt 26:30, 36–46; Mark 14:26, 32–42; Luke 22:39–46; John 17). It was also in this place that Jesus was betrayed by Judas and seized by the soldiers (John 18:12; cf. Matt 26:47–57; Mark 14:43–50; Luke 22:47–54).

11. Jacob (Gen 49) and Moses (Deut 33) pronounced blessings just before their deaths. In the same way, Jesus pronounces a blessing at his final departure from the disciples. From Genesis 49–50, Deuteronomy 33–34, and Joshua 24, one can see common elements in such scenes. These include a farewell address or blessing (Luke 24:50–51), the departure of the one giving the blessing, the response of the witnesses, and an act of obedience or piety. Members of Luke's audience familiar with such farewell scenes

circuitous route, it may be noted that this last journey of Jesus' final week of ministry clearly mentions the Mount of Olives. *Jesus went out as usual to the Mount of Olives, and his disciples followed him* (Luke 22:39). Luke alone records that the place to which Jesus retreated was the Mount of Olives, whereas in the Fourth Gospel the place was a garden near the Kidron valley and for Matthew (Matt 26:36) and Mark (Mark 14:32) the garden of Gethsemane. It is probable that the Gospel informs the reader that the Mount of Olives was a place of prayer familiar to Jesus.[12] Thus Mikeal Parsons comments:

> [T]he narrator has reminded the reader not of the Triumphal Entry so much as the prayer scene on the mountain.[13]

As the last stopping place for pilgrims on the way to Jerusalem the Mount of Olives must have had a special significance for Jesus. During his final week Jesus did not lodge in Jerusalem, but probably in Bethany at the home of Mary and Martha or perhaps with Simon the leper (Mark 11:11; 14:3; Luke 21:37). For his ascension Jesus again took his disciples to that favorite place. This time Jesus stopped on the Mount of Olives not to head for Jerusalem, but to go to the Father above, his final destination, to be with him forever. Thus the ascension became Jesus' final pilgrimage to God.

When Jesus set his face to go to Jerusalem for the Feast of Passover, the narrative clearly indicates that the time was approaching for his being taken up (Luke 9:51). The ascension has been "the goal toward which the Gospel account has been heading since 9:51."[14] While the ascension is the last stage of his pilgrimage to God, it is also his departure in terms of the end of Jesus' earthly ministry. Thus, it is also the arrival in terms of the beginning of his heavenly reign as well as the decent of the Holy Spirit. By presenting the promise of the Holy Spirit (Luke 24:49) that is immediately followed by the ascension narrative Luke provided his readers with the framework to see that God's plan goes on through the descent of the Holy Spirit. It is noted that at the transfiguration Jesus

---

would expect Jesus' departure. Luke's description of Jesus lifting his hands in 24:50 may also be echoing Moses's action of lifting his hands in Exodus 17. See Litwak, *Echoes of Scripture*, 149.

12. Fitzmyer comments concerning the Lukan motif of Jesus' prayer on a mountain. See Fitzmyer, *Luke I–IX*, 616, 798–99.

13. Parsons, *Departure of Jesus*, 195.

14. Nolland, *Luke 18:35—24:53*, 1228.

talked with Moses and Elijah concerning his departure, the Exodus, which he was about to bring to fulfillment at Jerusalem (Luke 9:31). Joshua and Elisha inherited the spirit of Moses and Elijah at their departure (Deut 34:9; 2 Kgs 2:9). Likewise the sprit of God was transmitted to his disciples as Jesus departed from them and went to heaven to be with God the Father. He had come from the Father, and it was to the Father that he returned. Thus the ascension, Jesus' pilgrimage to God, in Luke and John is presented as the climax and fulfillment of his whole pilgrimage, namely his earthly ministry, for his death and resurrection would not be completed until he had ascended to his Father and sent the Holy Spirit. Edward Schillebeeckx provides a rationale for the whole of this Trinitarian relationship with regard to the ascension.

> Through His obedient life of love on earth, Christ "merited" the Holy Spirit for us: the Spirit of sanctification and completion. Pentecost is the great harvest festival of the redemption. So too, the whole incarnation is at the same time the revelation of the saving mystery of the Trinity: the revelation of the living God, Father, Son, and Spirit.[15]

It is clear that for the disciples that Jesus' pilgrimage to God resulted in fully knowing who God as the Trinity is. Thus Schillebeeckx is right in claiming that "the ascension, as Christ's being with the Father, is the principle of Pentecost."[16] Mediating relations between Pentecost and Jesus' Way including the passion and resurrection, the ascension completed what was done in the passion. However, in terms of the knowledge of God, what was done in the passion cannot be fully completed until the Holy Spirit descends upon the disciples, as he promised. For the full comprehension of the disciples regarding the saving ministry of the Trinity Jesus' Pentecost pilgrimage as imagery has to come in order to fulfill his earthly ministry and to begin his church.

PENTECOST AS THE BEGINNING OF THE CHURCH

Luke is the only writer to pass on to us the descent of the Holy Spirit during the Feast of Pentecost. In later Judaism, Pentecost was less important than Passover and Tabernacles in terms of the participation of pilgrims. Although a substantial number of Jews (Josephus, *Ant.* 14.337; 17.254)

---

15. Schillebeeckx, "Ascension and Pentecost," 353.
16. Ibid.

and the Diaspora Jews (Acts 2:5) participated in the feast, the number attending this feast was still the smallest of the three pilgrimage feasts. For Luke the Feast of Pentecost was, however, the occasion when the Holy Spirit came upon those in the Upper Room, and for the first time Peter and the eleven, empowered by the Spirit, confronted the Jews and the Diaspora Jews in Jerusalem and proclaimed the crucified and risen Christ as the Messiah and Savior (Acts 2:14–47). With the background of the Feast of Pentecost Luke dramatized the whole scene in detail. Thus the nature and celebration of this feast would answer the question as to why Pentecost would have been the occasion. Unfortunately, the information regarding the Feast of Pentecost in the OT is general and fragmented. Because of this we are limited to the NT texts for information about the Pentecost pilgrimage. Here the feast is clearly connected with pilgrimage occasions and has a significant meaning for Jesus' pilgrimage to God the Father. It also symbolizes the descent (journey) of the Holy Sprit to the disciples in Jerusalem with its Trinitarian implication.

Pentecost in Retrospect

In the Old Testament the Feast of Pentecost is variously called "the Festival of Harvest" (Exod 23:16), "the Festival of Weeks" (Deut 16:10), and "the day of the firstfruits" (Num 28:26). Israel was told to: "Celebrate the Festival of Harvest with the firstfruits of the crops you sow in your field" (Exod 23:16). It is, however, given no specific date to be observed. The issue of dating is probably due to its role in the developing meaning of the feast in later times. From the clue that the feast comes between the time of Unleavened Bread (Exod 23:15) and the Festival of Ingathering at the end of the year (Exod 23:16), it is very likely to have fallen between the two feasts. Deuteronomy 16:9–12 explains why it was named Weeks, though it still offers no date. *Count off seven weeks from the time you begin to put the sickle to the standing grain. Then celebrate the Festival of Weeks to the Lord your God by giving a freewill offering in proportion to the blessings the Lord your God has given you . . . Remember that you were slaves in Egypt* (Deut 16:9–12). The feast was for the people to rejoice before the Lord in view of his blessing and in remembrance of Israel's bondage in Egypt.

Leviticus 23:15–22 provides a formula for dating the festival and the details concerning the presentation of the sacrifices. *From the day after the Sabbath, the day you brought the sheaf of the wave offering, count off seven full weeks. Count off fifty days up to the day after the seventh Sabbath, and then present an offering of new grain to the Lord* (Lev 23:15–16). Leviticus still gives no exact date for it. It is, however, certain that it was celebrated on the fiftieth day after the sheaf of the wave offering was presented (Lev 23:15–16). Although the ambiguity of the phrase "from the day after the Sabbath" leaves room for debate about the correct times for presenting the sheaf of the wave offering, from all the details about the feast in the Pentateuch the beginning of the fifty days seems to be the day following Passover (Lev 23:9–11, 15), and the Festival of Weeks appears to fall in the third month of the year. James VanderKam suggests two possible dates on the basis of the two meanings of Sabbath, the weekly Sabbath and Sabbath in the sense of festival.

> *The weekly Sabbath.* If the words were read in this sense, the festival of weeks would always fall on a Sunday. The problem with this reading was that the text did not say which Sabbath day after Passover was the one intended. A second exegetical possibility was to read *Sabbath in the sense of festival.* This is not the first meaning of the term that comes to mind, but it is attested in the Bible. A clear example occurs in the legislation for the day of Atonement, which the biblical calendars date to the tenth day of the seventh month, whatever day of the week that maybe. Leviticus calls it "the Sabbath of complete rest" (Lev 23:32; see also v. 33). If we understand the Law about the Festival of Weeks in this sense, the word Sabbath could refer to first day of the festival of unleavened bread (the first holiday after Passover [see Josh 5:11]) or the last day of the same festival (the two most sacred days of the seven-day celebration are marked by special assemblies [Lev 23:7–8]). The fifty-day period would then begin from either 1/16 (the rabbinic option) or 1/23.[17]

Outside the Pentateuch only 2 Chronicles 8:13 (2 Chr 15:10–15 implied) mentions the festival in a list of the three annual feasts. Unlike the other two pilgrimage feasts, the Feast of Weeks is given no specific date and its name is mentioned only by name in lists of cultic festivals (Exod 23:16; 34:22; Lev 23:15–21; Num 28:26–31; Deut 16:9–12; 2 Chr 8:13). In addition, it is still an open question as to why Ezekiel failed to include the feast in his calendar for the restored community (Ezek 45:18—46:7).

---

17. VanderKam, "Covenant and Pentecost," 240; italics mine.

Pentecost was a harvest festival, as in the Old Testament and Judaism. In Numbers 28:26 and Deuteronomy 26:10 the feast is identified with "the day of the firstfruits," whereas in Exodus 34:22 it came to be known as the feast at the end of the wheat harvest. *He brought us to this place and gave us this land, a land flowing with milk and honey; and now I bring the firstfruits of the soil that you, O Lord, have given me. Place the basket before the Lord your God and bow down before him* (Deut 26:9-10). With the words of Deuteronomy 26:3-10, Eduard Lohse visualizes the whole scene of the feast.

> When the environs of the holy city were reached, the priests and Levites came to meet the crowds of pilgrims and conducted them into the temple. As religious songs were sung, they entered with baskets on their shoulders. The Levites struck up the song of praise and then the first-fruits were handed to the priests and a confession of thanksgiving was made to the God of Israel.[18]

Based on Leviticus 23 and Numbers 28, as the firstfruits of the new wheat harvest, Pentecost bread, the two loaves (Lev 23:17), baked from unleavened wheat meal were offered to God; and as burnt offerings, 3 calves, 2 rams, and 14 lambs; and as sin offerings, 2 goats (Philo, *Decalogue* 160; Josephus, *Ant.* 3.252f).

In later Judaism the Festival of Weeks became important to many groups. Having been related to the events of Mount Sinai and the patriarchs, the feast was given a historical meaning. Having recounted Exodus 19-24, Jubilees in the second century BCE shows that the Feast of Pentecost is closely related to the renewal of the covenant and the Torah. *"In the first year of the Exodus of the children of Israel from Egypt, in the third month on the sixteenth day of that month, the LORD spoke to Moses, saying, "Come up to me on the mountain, and I shall give you two stone tablets of the Law and the commandment, which I have written, so that you may teach them"* (*Jub.* 1:1). This beginning of Jubilees implies that the covenant with Moses (*Jub.* 1:1-26) on Mount Sinai (Exod 19) was made on the very day of the Israelites' exodus from Egypt. This suggests that the Feast of Pentecost was celebrated on 3/15, the fifteenth day of the third month. Together with 1:1, Jubilees 44:1-5 also implies that 3/15 is the date for the harvest festival.[19] The covenant with an oath that

---

18. Lohse, "πεντηκοστή," 47.

19. Jacob offered a sacrifice on 3/7, waited seven more days, then observed the harvest festival, and received a theophany on 3/16.

Moses as the mediator made with the Israelites on Mount Sinai occurred in the same month (*Jub.* 6:11).

Jubilees 6:18 shows that the Festival of Weeks had been celebrated in heaven from the day of creation onwards and that Noah and his family were the first to observe it on earth. The covenant with Abraham, his circumcision (*Jub.* 15:1; cf. 14:20), and Abraham's death all occurred on this festival (22:1). Isaac was born "in the third month; in the middle of the month (= 3/15), on the day that the Lord had told Abraham—on the festival of the firstfruits of the harvest (*Jub.* 16:13).[20] Jacob's son Judah was also born on it (28:15), and Jacob and Laban completed their settlement on 3/15 (29:7). Thus the Feast of Weeks is embedded in the whole story of Jubilees and becomes a main paradigm for the context. The message of the angel to Moses on Mount Sinai well sums up the fact that the Feast of Weeks was a festival for covenant making and covenant renewal.

Therefore, it is ordained and written in the heavenly tablets that they should observe the feast of Shebuot in this month—once per year—in order to renew the covenant in all (respects), year by year. And all of this feast was celebrated in heaven from the day of creation until the day of Noah, twenty-six jubilees and five weeks of years. And Noah and his children kept it…until Noah's death. And from the day of the death of Noah, his sons corrupted it until the days of Abraham, and they ate blood. But Abraham alone kept it. And Isaac and Jacob and his sons kept it until your days, but in your days the children of Israel forgot it until you renewed it for them on this mountain (Jub. 6:17–19). The rule of community refers to an annual ceremony at which candidates for admission entered the group and those who were already members apparently renewed their commitment (1QS I 16—III 12). Regardless of that, nothing in 1QS I 16—II 18 indicates that the annual ceremony was observed on the Festival of Weeks. It is very likely that for the Qumran community the feast was the annual occasion on which they acknowledged new members and renewed the Sinai covenant. No wonder that the community called it "the feast of covenant renewal." The text adds: "Thus shall they do, year by year, for as long as the dominion of Belial endures" (1QS II 19). In the ceremony, the Levites curse those who belong to Belial, and the priest proclaims the blessings that God has given to Israel. Those who enter into the covenant respond by saying, "amen, amen."

---

20. VanderKam, "Temple Scroll," 220.

Dating the feast becomes clear according to the Dead Sea Scrolls and the book of Jubilees (*Jub.* 15:1; 16:13; 44:1–4).[21] The Feast of Pentecost (Weeks) fell on the morrow of the Sabbath, that is, the morrow of the first Sabbath (Saturday) following the end of Passover. From the book of Joshua (Josh 5:11) the morrow of the Sabbath was, however, the morrow of the first day of Passover, and this is supported by the Septuagint (Lev 23:15f) and by the descriptions of Philo (*Spec. Law* 2.175) and Josephus (*Ant.* 3.250–252).[22] Thus Pentecost came fifty days after the first day of the Passover or on its last day (seven weeks after the cutting of the first barley and cereal grains). This means that the date of the feast came to be fixed in later Judaism and the feast was beginning to be called Pentecost, πεντηκοστή in the Greek texts of apocryphal books (Tob 2:1; 2 Macc 12:32), the writings of Josephus (*Ant.* 3.10.6; 13.8.4; 14.13.4; 17.10.2; *J.W.* 1.13.3; 2.3.1; 6.5.3), and the works of Philo (*Decalogue* 160; *Spec. Law* 2.176). Pentecost, which means "fiftieth," was chosen because it was celebrated on the fiftieth day after the "sheaf of the wave offering" was presented (Lev 23:15–16). Calculating the date of the festival, the fiftieth day after the "sheaf of the wave offering," may suggest that the feast was regarded "as the final day of the harvest season which began at the time of the wave offering."[23]

The book of Jubilees shows the association of the feast with the history of Israel, but ignores its close connection with Passover. In the Mishnah and Talmud the Feast of Pentecost celebrated the gift of the Law. For the rabbis including R. Jose bChalaphta and R. Elazar bPedath, the theophany of Sinai was important, for it emphasized the gift of the Law itself (Exod 19–20).[24] Linking the feast with the giving of the Law at Mount Sinai might be the result of the destruction of Jerusalem in 70 CE. Thus Lohse claims that it was the disaster of 70 CE that first forced the Jewish world to give new content to Pentecost, despite the evidence of Philo and Josephus who say nothing about this understanding of the festival.[25] Considering the rich overtones of the feast, it would not be

---

21. The Sadducees counted the fifty days from "the morrow after the Sabbath" and celebrated the feast on 6 Siwan (the third month), reckoning from the day after Passover. The Pharisees counted from the Sabbath after Passover, whenever that would come.

22. Safrai and Stern, *Jewish People*, 858.

23. VanderKam, "Weeks, Festival of," 895.

24. See Lohse, "πεντηκοστή," 49.

25. Ibid.

surprising to find that in some Jewish circles the festival was reflected as the renewal of the Sinaitic covenant and commemoration of the lawgiving at Sinai.

Pentecost in Prospect

Luke ends the Gospel with an explicit reference to the ascension of Jesus and begins the book of Acts with the same scene of ascension on the Mount of Olives (Luke 24:50–53; Acts 1:9–11).[26] Thus the ascension binds the two writings together. Robert Maddox puts it:

> The ascension is the major bridge from volume one to volume two: it is the necessary climax of the one and starting-point of the other.[27]

"The promise of my Father" in Luke 24:49 is explained as a baptism with the Holy Spirit in the book of Acts 1:5. In the Lukan story the story of "the promise of the Father" is bestowed on the first community of the disciples in Jerusalem on the Day of Pentecost. The "Pentecost" of the book of Acts 2:1, then, has theological significance and connotations

---

26. Parsons uses three categories to summarize the numerous attempts that have been made to explain the similarities and differences between these two accounts. *Interpolation Theories:* Conzelmann, Kusopp, Lake, Menoud, Wilder, and others, have proposed theories which, though they differ in details, assume that the ascension narrative was interpolated into the text when Luke and the book of Acts were divided upon acceptance into the canon. *Source Theories:* Moule suggested that after completing the Gospel, Luke received new traditions about the ascension that he incorporated into the book of Acts. Others have surmised that Luke knew both traditions and preserved them both without making a value judgment between them. *Theological Concerns:* Fitzmyer wrote that no small reason for referring to the ascension in both Luke and the book of Acts was "the emphasis that the double reference gives to the Ascension as the line of demarcation for two periods of Lucan salvation-history." J. G. Davies, on the other hand, suggested Luke may have shaped his stories around a Raphael typology in Luke 24 and an Elijah typology in the book of Acts. For P. A. van Stempvoort the narrative in Luke, with its blessings and Jesus' priestly gesticulation, gave what Stempvoort called a "doxological interpretation of the Ascension." The Acts account, on the other hand, with its emphasis on the activity of the Holy Spirit in the church, van Stempvoort dubbed an ecclesiastical-historical interpretation. S. G. Wilson slightly modified van Stempvoort's views, suggesting that the Acts account is Luke's pastoral interpretation of the ascension: it is the author's way of dealing with the problem of the delayed *Parousia*. J. H. Flender, using van Stempvoort's interpretation as a springboard, argued that the ascension in Luke is told from an earthly viewpoint, while the Acts narrative is from a heavenly viewpoint. See Parsons, *Departure of Jesus*, 189–199; and "Text of Acts 1:2 Reconsidered," 58–71.

27. Maddox, *Purpose of Luke-Acts*, 10.

that are not to be missed. The event appears to be the final stage of salvation history as a result of Jesus' final pilgrimage, but at the same time it denotes the beginning of the church as well as the initiation of the new pilgrimage for his people. We should then ask why the descent of the Holy Spirit should have occurred on that particular day. Some of the following reasons could be considered.

Having depicted the ascension of the risen Christ, Luke informs us that the following event is closely related to Jerusalem. *Then the apostles returned to Jerusalem from the hill called the Mount of Olives* (Acts 1:12). The most obvious reason to return to Jerusalem would be for the next pilgrimage festival, Pentecost.[28] Considering the eschatological significance of the city, the disciples may have anticipated the eschatological intervention of God, this time the descent of the Holy Spirit that was the promise of the Father. As the closing event of the Passover season, the Day of Pentecost ended the last day of the Passover that had been marked by the death and resurrection of Jesus.[29] It also began the hopes of the last age beginning to be fulfilled in the outpouring of the Spirit.[30] According to Acts 2, the Christian Feast of Pentecost had a particular meaning marked by the gift of the Holy Spirit and by the calling of all nations into the new church. Although the story in the book of Acts contains neither direct reference to the covenant at Sinai nor to Christ or the Holy Spirit as the new covenant, the nature and celebration of the old system of this feast are firmly embedded into the new system of the Christian Pentecost.

The book of Jubilees and the Dead Sea Scrolls give evidence that the Feast of Pentecost for many Jews in the middle of the second century BCE was associated with the renewal of the covenant and commemoration of the lawgiving at Sinai as well as its celebration of the offering of the firstfruits of the wheat harvest (*Jub.* 1:5: 6:11, 17; 15:1–24; 1QS I 7—II 19). E. Haenchen claims, "Insofar as he adopts the feast of Pentecost as the date of his episode, Luke is beholden to the Jewish heritage."[31] It is, thus, not surprising to claim that the descent of the Spirit at Pentecost contained

---

28. Luke depicts Paul hurrying to be in Jerusalem for the Day of Pentecost (Acts 20:16). In 1 Corinthians 16:8 Paul speaks of staying in Ephesus for a Feast of Pentecost according to the Jewish calendar.

29. Lohse, "πεντηκοστή," 45–48.

30. Dunn, *Jesus and the Spirit*, 142.

31. Dunn quotes E. Haenchen. See ibid., 140.

the overtones of an eschatological covenant renewal. Acts 2:39 and 3:25 indicate that the Holy Spirit was given for the fulfillment of covenant promise. As Dunn points out, it is, however, true that there is no evidence in Acts 2 (beyond the date itself, the issue in dispute) that Luke was aware of or conditioned by "the Jewish heritage."[32] Nevertheless, there are the rich overtones of the Jewish heritage to be reflected upon.

Jewish tradition relating to the offering of the firstfruits of the wheat harvest has some striking resemblances to the event of Pentecost in Acts 2. *When the day of Pentecost came, they were all together in one place . . . All of them were filled with the Holy Spirit and began to speak in other tongues as the Spirit enabled them* (Acts 2:1–4). It is clear that the Church was initiated when Jesus called the disciples, particularly the Twelve. Nevertheless, in terms of his pilgrimage perspective and sending the Holy Spirit to fulfill his salvation ministry, the gathered disciples might become symbolically the offering of the firstfruits as the beginning of the Church and the conclusion of his earthly ministry. Who are the "they" gathered in one place then? Were they the Twelve or the one hundred twenty disciples mentioned in Acts 1:15? The election of Matthias (Acts 1:23–26) to complete the number twelve before the descent of the Holy Spirit might suggest that the twelve disciples were those who received the gifts of the Spirit as highlighted by Luke. If that were the case, the "they" in Acts 2:1 would indicate the twelve disciples.

Luke's earlier indication of "a group numbering about a hundred and twenty" (Acts 1:15) strongly supports "they" in the place as being one hundred twenty disciples, including the twelve apostles. On the basis of the fact that in Jewish law a minimum of one hundred twenty Jewish men was required to establish a community with its own council, Marshall claims that the reason why the number is mentioned is that in Jewish terms the disciples were a body of sufficient size to form a new community.[33]

> Others have detected symbolism in the number, since the twelve tribes and the twelve apostles make twelve an obvious symbol of the church, and 120 is 12 x 10, as the 144,000 of the Book of Revelation is 12 x 12 x 1000. If the twelve represent the twelve tribes of Israel assembled at Sinai, the 120 are necessary to show the immediate expansion into a larger multitude. Yet others sug-

---

32. Ibid.
33. Marshall, *Acts*, 64.

gest that the 120 must have been only a percentage of the total Believing community.[34]

According to 1 Corinthians 15:6, there was one occasion when the risen Christ appeared to more than five hundred of his followers, probably in Galilee. E. von Dobschutz claims that the appearance to more than five hundred and the account of Pentecost are variant traditions of one and the same event, so the appearance of the Lord to five hundred was the birthday of the Christian mission.[35] As Dunn argues, it is very probable that 1 Corinthians 15:6 and Acts 2 are dealing with two different episodes, so the appearance to more than five hundred likely took place after Pentecost.[36] It is noted that the particles ὡσεί or ὡς are regularly used in Luke for numerical data. This appearance to more than five hundred indicates that the number of about (ὡσεί) one hundred twenty (Acts 1:15) could be a genuine estimate of the numbers present on the Day of Pentecost, which also connotes an obvious symbol for the church.

Completing the cycle of the typical fulfillment of the feasts, fifty days after the first Sunday following Passover, the Feast of Pentecost was celebrated (Lev 23:15–44). Following the pattern of Leviticus 23, another offering of firstfruits was made (Lev 23:20). At Pentecost, the ascended Christ as the "firstfruits of those who have fallen asleep" (1 Cor 15:20) sent the Holy Spirit and those gathered on that day became the firstfruits of his earthly ministry and of the full harvest of believers to come (cf. 2 Cor 5:5; Eph 1:13–14). Jesus' earthly ministry is completed by the descent of the Spirit, for the disciples finally became his proper followers on Pentecost. It is the moment when the disciples became pneumatic and from this moment on they would be under the guidance of the Holy Spirit. It is the Holy Spirit who empowered the disciples to first confront Israel and to make the first proclamation of the risen Christ to the Jews of Jerusalem. It was, indeed, the first time the disciples proclaimed Jesus Christ as the Savior.

Peter replied, "Repent and be baptized, every one of you, in the name of Jesus Christ for the forgiveness of your sins. And you will receive the gift of the Holy Spirit. The promise is for you and your children and for all who are far off—for all whom the Lord our God will call." . . . Those

---

34. Cited in Stott, *Message of Acts*, 52.
35. See Dunn, *Jesus and the Spirit*, 144–46.
36. Ibid.

who accepted his message were baptized, and about three thousand were added to their number that day (Acts 2:38–41). Three thousand came to the Lord that day so becoming the firstfruits of the first Christian community. Pentecost became the beginning (the firstfruits) of the Christian mission, the harvest. This might be what Luke emphasized in relation to the offering of the firstfruits on the Pentecost.

The Feast of Pentecost, then, provides the symbols with which Luke depicted the descent of the Spirit on the disciples. The three Pentecosts of the Qumran community could be further evidence of its relevance. Fifty days from the morrow of the Sabbath of the Passover octave occurred *the Pentecost of New Grain*; fifty days from the morrow of the Pentecost of New Grain, *the Pentecost of New Wine*; and fifty days from the morrow of the Pentecost of New Wine, *the Pentecost of New Oil*.[37] The Temple Scroll shows the association of "new wine" with Pentecost. Thus it is probable that the mockery expressed in Acts 2:13, "They have had too much wine," could be based on the Pentecost of New Wine. This means that Luke might have been aware of the association of Pentecost with the Pentecost of New Wine among such multiple Pentecosts.

As already noted, the main issue is whether Luke's theological presuppositions have been determined by Jewish traditions, which include the Feast of Pentecost. Although no clear evidence in Acts 2 indicates that the Feast of Pentecost influenced Luke, there are several reasons why the Holy Spirit should have fallen during Pentecost. Since Pentecost seems already to have been regarded as the feast of covenant renewal, it is also likely that the Feast of Pentecost, even in the time of Jesus, was coming to be regarded as the feast commemorating the lawgiving at Mount Sinai.

THE PENTECOST PILGRIMAGE AS THE FULFILLMENT OF THE YEAR OF JUBILEE

As the first significant event in the narrative of the book of Acts, Pentecost in Acts 2 plays a most important part of Luke's presentation. In particular, the missionary element of the event is highlighted through the gift of the Spirit who equipped the disciples for witness, and Peter's proclamation of the gospel that resulted in the conversion of some three

---

37. Fitzmyer quotes the Temple Scroll from Cave 11. See Fitzmyer, *Acts of the Apostles*, 234–35.

thousand hearers of the message. Thus Goppelt regards Acts 2 as programmatic for the book of Acts, in the same way that Luke 4:16–30 is for the Gospel of Luke.[38]

It is, however, worth noting that the Feast of Pentecost plays a role in the developing meaning in the Second Temple period (*Jub.* 1:1; 6:17–19; 14:20; 22:1–16; 1QS I 8—II 25). The strong probability that the Feast of Pentecost was coming to be regarded as the feast commemorating the lawgiving at Mount Sinai in the time of Jesus implies that Moses's ascent of Mount Sinai before the covenant and the Torah was given could be the prototype of Jesus' ascension in Acts 1 before Pentecost. Moses's ascent to God to receive the Torah with theophanic accompaniment (Exod 19) provides some plausibility that it was not new for Jews to hear that a Moses-like messiah ascended to God in order to give the gift of the Spirit to all Israel.[39] The fact that the story in the book of Acts contains no direct allusion to the Sinaitic lawgiving nor to the new covenant of which Christ is the mediator, means that we cannot with certainty link Pentecost with the giving of the Law on Mount Sinai.[40]

Nevertheless, the fact that Luke is certainly familiar with the idea of the covenant made with Israel (Luke 1:72; Acts 3:25; 7:8), with the concept of the new covenant (Luke 22:20), and the possible reference to Psalm 68 in Acts 2:33, suggests that there may have been some connection in his mind between the Pentecost event in Acts 2 and the Sinaitic covenant.[41] In Jewish thought of the Second Temple period, Jewish celebration of Pentecost was linked with the renewal of the covenant and the Law given at Sinai. Philo's exegesis that drew a parallel between the theophany at Sinai and the visible manifestation of the Spirit (*Decalogue* 9.33; 11.46–47) also strengthens this view. This strong plausibility makes it possible for us to associate Pentecost in Acts 2 with the giving of the Law. Max Turner in line with Odette Mainville cautiously considers the lawgiving at Mount Sinai as "a part of the explanation of the Pentecost event."[42]

---

38. Goppelt, *Apostolic and Post-Apostolic Times*, 20–24.

39. We can also think of Moses who was involved in the distribution of the Spirit upon the seventy elders (Num 11) and the Spirit on Elijah passing to Elisha (2 Kgs 2).

40. Marshall and Wilson are in the same line with this view. See Marshall, "Significance of Pentecost," 364; Wilson, *Gentiles and the Gentile Mission*, 126–29.

41. Dunn, Dupont, Knox, and Kirby claim that this is implicit. See Knox, *Acts of the Apostles*, 85; Dupont, "Ascension du Christ," 219–28.

42. M. Turner, *Power from on High*, 289.

The parallels are not of the kind that suggest the Moses/Sinai episode has become something like an allegory for Pentecost, such that the gift of the Spirit must necessarily be seen as a direct equivalent to the Law, and so either as the power to keep the Law or a superior substitute for the Law. The correspondence is looser than that. But the parallels do suggest Pentecost is viewed as part of the fulfillment and renewal of Israel's covenant, and so ensure that the gift of the Spirit will have a vital role in Israel's restoration.[43]

If Luke intends a parallel between Moses's giving the law and Jesus' giving the Spirit, the law—Pentecost connection can be found in the quotation of Isaiah 61:1–2 in Luke 4:18–19. *"The Spirit of the Lord is on me, because he has anointed me to proclaim good news to the poor. He has sent me to proclaim freedom for the prisoners and recovery of sight for the blind, to set the oppressed free, to proclaim the year of the Lord's favor." Then he rolled up the scroll, gave it back to the attendant . . . "Today this scripture is fulfilled in your hearing"* (Luke 4:18–21). Jesus' quotation from Isaiah 61:1–2 evokes echoes of the Year of Jubilee.[44] The use made of Isaiah 61 in Luke 4 is consistent with the Isaianic context. The mission of the Servant of Yahweh in Isaiah has strong elements of calling for liberation of the weak and the oppressed with these explicitly jubilary reasons for release (Isa 42:1–7; 58: 6–7; 61). If Pentecost is viewed as part of the fulfillment and renewal of Israel's covenant, the direct allusion to the Year of Jubilee in Luke 4:18–19 as the renewal of the old covenant will have a vital role in Israel's restoration. In what manner did Jesus intend the quotation from Isaiah to be understood? Is Luke 4:18–19 consonant with the meaning of the original context of the Year of Jubilee, or is it only an allusive use of the Isaiah material?

Scholars have highlighted the connections between Jesus' proclamation in Luke 4 and the Year of Jubilee.[45] Some claim that Jesus called for a literal enactment of the Year of Jubilee in Leviticus 25.[46] Sloan notes that Jesus used jubilary language and imageries both for the sense of spiritual forgiveness of sin and literal remission of actual debts.[47] For

---

43. Ibid.

44. Bock claims that this quotation is an amalgamation of Isaiah 61:1–2 and 58:6. See Bock, *Prophecy and Pattern*, 105–11.

45. See Sloan, *Favorable Year of the Lord*.

46. See Trocmé, *Nonviolent Revolution*; Yoder, *Politics of Jesus*.

47. See Sloan, *Favorable Year of the Lord*. Ringe thinks that major jubilee images

Marshall the year of the Lord's favor (Luke 4: 19) contains an allusion to the Year of Jubilee that was "symbolic of his own saving acts."[48] Fitzmyer only observes the Isaiah quote's connection with Leviticus 25:10–13 and Deuteronomy 15:2–10 and no conclusions are drawn.[49] Johnson claims possible Jubilee resonances, but points out that the Gospel does not offer further support for this being Luke's intention. For him Luke portrays Jesus' liberating work in terms of personal exorcisms, healings, and the teaching of the people.[50]

The active work of the Holy Spirit is highlighted in the first part of the Gospel (Luke 1:15, 35, 41, 67; 2:25–27; 3:16, 22; 4:18). Significantly, after Luke 4:18 that quotes Isaiah 61:1, "The Spirit of the Sovereign Lord is on me," the work of the Holy Spirit is hardly emphasized until the beginning of the narrative in the book of Acts. The work of the Holy Spirit does not seem to be a primary concern of Luke. In this regard, William Shepherd notes:

> Luke has now established the basic plot-function of the Holy Spirit in the narrative ... Luke omits further mention of the Spirit during most of the rest of the Gospel, for there is little need to remind the reader of the relationship between Jesus and Spirit.[51]

Thus David Pao claims that Luke 4 should be understood together with the narrative of Acts.[52] This reading is affirmed by the continuity of the narrative of the Spirit in the book of Acts and the wider pilgrimage program concerning the ministry of Jesus that is central to the Lukan narrative. Thus the relation of Luke 4:18–19 to the Pentecost event in Acts 2 and 4 need to be clarified in terms of how the Lukan community understood this narrative. We shall first need to clarify what part the Year of Jubilee (Lev 25) plays in Jesus' own proclamation (Luke 4:18–21) and in the Pentecost event (Acts 2–4). Between the Year of Jubilee in Leviticus

---

have been woven into various parts of the gospel narratives and the teaching of Jesus (e.g., the beatitudes, the response to John the Baptist [Matt 11:2–6], the parable of the banquet [Luke 14:12–24], various episodes of forgiveness, teaching on debts [Matt 18:21–35]). See Ringe, *Jesus, Liberation*.

48. Marshall, *Gospel*, 184.
49. Fitzmyer, *Luke I–IX*, 532.
50. Johnson, *Gospel of Luke*, 81.
51. Shepherd, *Narrative Function of the Holy Spirit*, 137.
52. Pao, *Acts and the Isaianic New Exodus*, 83.

and our present time stand Jesus' own proclamation (Luke 4:18–21) and the Pentecost event (Acts 2–4).

The Year of Jubilee is to be *yobel*, which, translated from Hebrew to English means jubilant. In the context of the LXX it means "release" and also carries the meaning of "forgiveness." Deuteronomy 15:1–18 provides an explicit statement regarding the terminology of release: the cancellation of debt (vv. 1–6), lending (vv. 7–11), and procedures for liberating Hebrew slaves (vv. 12–18). The Year of Jubilee is the logical extension of the Sabbath and the Sabbatical Year. Thus the Jubilee regulation is grounded in the concept of the Sabbath and the Sabbatical Year. According to Leviticus 25, the principle of Sabbath rest is applied to a seven-year period in which the final year is to be observed as a Sabbath to the Lord. The land could not be cultivated until the Sabbatical Year ended. During the Sabbatical Year, there must be no systematic harvesting of self-seeding crops or fruits. People were required to live simple lives, because there was no sowing or reaping of the land. The food that had been stored in preparation for the event could be consumed, along with anything that grew spontaneously from the land. No one claimed anything that the land then produced. All was common, to the rich, to the poor, to the Hebrew, and to the stranger. It was a token of the full restoration of equality. By this means the Sabbatical Year demonstrates that God is the supreme provider and man's chief duty is not to concentrate upon the accumulation of material possessions, but to glorify God by observing regular Sabbaths of worship and the principle of the Sabbatical Year.

Then have the trumpet sounded everywhere on the tenth day of the seventh month; on the Day of Atonement sound the trumpet throughout your land. Consecrate the fiftieth year and proclaim liberty throughout the land to all its inhabitants. It shall be a jubilee for you; each of you is to return to your family property and to your own clan. The fiftieth year shall be a jubilee for you; do not sow and do not reap what grows of itself or harvest the untended vines. For it is a jubilee and is to be holy for you; eat only what is taken directly from the fields. In this Year of Jubilee everyone is to return to their own property (Lev 25: 9–13). Under the Jubilee Year regulation, the same principle of the Sabbatical Year was applied. Furthermore, land had to be returned to its original owners, Israelite slaves had to be freed, and debts were canceled. By this means God is clearly reasserting his ownership of the land and his people. This theme of land, which has been one of the central pillars of the Israelites' faith, has developed its meaning in Israel's theology on the basis of the dual tradition of the land—God's divine ownership and God's gift to Israel. The land had been promised and was then given to Israel. This underlying principle is an affirmation of the Lordship of the Creator. This is clearly the prime motif for the return to the land, not the economic motif of an anticapitalist, because the theological principle originated in the redemptive act of the Lord who brought his people out of Egypt and sustained them in their journey to the promised land.

The land must not be sold permanently, because the land is mine and you reside in my land as foreigners and strangers (Lev 25:23). *Even if someone is not redeemed in any of these ways, they and their children are to be released in the Year of Jubilee, for the Israelites belong to me as servants. They are my servants, whom I brought out of Egypt. I am the Lord your God* (Lev 25:54-55). Every fifty years the Year of Jubilee gave the whole nation an opportunity to reflect upon the Lordship of the Creator, reminding his people of the fact that they had once been liberated from captivity in Egypt by the divine power of God, and they were now living in their own land as free citizens who belonged to God. For the Israelite this overriding principle of belonging—God's ownership of the land and the people—provided a kinship so that they may live as his family on his land.[53] It was the focus of identity, status, responsibility, and security for the individual Israelite.[54] If no kinsman came forward to release them, the Lord himself redeemed them, as He had done from the servitude of Egypt. By this means of Jubilee legislation, Israel's relationship with God was preserved in maintaining and restoring the broken relationship of such households or clans. *The land must not be sold permanently, because the land is mine and you are aliens and my tenants* (Lev 25:23). *Do not oppress an alien; you know the heart of an alien; you yourselves know how it feels to be aliens, because you were aliens in Egypt* (Exod 23:9). In particular, Leviticus 25:23 with Exodus 23:9 provides a rationale for the whole of this legislation. As Jacob defined his life as "the years of my pilgrimage" (Gen 47:9) before Pharaoh, God defined the Israelites in terms of being aliens in the world, tenants of God and pilgrims. Israel's experience as aliens and tenants in Egypt was the motivating force for the whole of Israel to respond to God's grace. Thus the Year of Jubilee

---

53. Israel had a three-tier pattern of kinship (the tribe, the clan, and the household).

54. C. Wright, "Jubilee, Year of," 1029.

was Israel's response to God confirming their sense of belonging to Him, providing a time for faith in his ability to provide food and for debtors and slaves to make a new beginning in life.

Although it is not clear that a Jubilee Year had ever been celebrated in the Old Testament, we can see some traces that reflect the enactment of the legislation. In 2 Chronicles 15:10–12 the assembly of Jews in Jerusalem in the fiftieth year of King Asa may reflect this celebration. There is evidence that kinship redemption was practiced (Jer 32; Ruth 4) and in the face of the Babylonian threat Hebrew slaves were released by the king, Zedekiah, after the insistence of Jeremiah (Jer 34:8–10). The act of Nehemiah (Neh 5), set in the framework of "release," informs the manumission of sons and daughters who had sold themselves due to debt (Neh 5:2), the return of fields and vineyards that were mortgaged to pay the king's tax (Neh 5:4, 12) and the remission of debts of grain and silver (Neh 5:10). Moshe Weinfeld notes that the act of Nehemiah bears closer resemblance to the reform of Solon than to the Mesopotamian proclamations of liberty, for Nehemiah did not intend that the remission of debts should be of a temporary nature as was the case in Mesopotamia, but rather, as an abiding principle.[55] Weinfeld also notes its relation to the nomadic society.

> [T]he institution is undoubtedly rooted in an ancient patriarchal tendency to preserve the ancestral holding and the familial sphere of ancestry, a tendency which is most characteristic of the nomadic society.[56]

Having suggested two possible periods for the emergence of a bold and original legislative concept such as the Jubilee, Robert North asserts the Mosaic origin of the Jubilee legislation for one obvious reason.[57] Margaret Rodgers summaries:

> That is that the legislation is intended to impose restrictions on the community, to curb the actions of some to ensure freedom and

---

55. Weinfeld takes a look at Mesopotamian and Solon's reform. In Mesopotamia the king proclaimed the liberty at the time of his ascension to the throne. See Weinfeld, "Sabbatical Year and Jubilee," 53–62.

56. Ibid., 59.

57. Following North, Rodgers notes that one was before and during the occupation of Canaan, when the Israelites were moving from a semi-nomadic to an agrarian way of life. The second was in the first years after the return of the exiles from Babylon. See Rodgers, "Luke 4:16–30," 76.

justice for all. That might be seen as appropriate to the Israelites entering Canaan under Joshua's leadership, for they were united, in good heart, keyed up by success and in full forward career. In contrast, the returning exiles are in his view dispirited, needing to be persuaded to return. They needed a spur and encouragement, not restrictive legislation of this kind.[58]

The question as to whether or not the Year of Jubilee was observed in continuity or intermittently, would provide us with clues as to whether Jesus called for the literal implementation of the Jubilee legislations or if he expected his followers to live by the Jubilee principle. Since the practicing of this legislation does not need individual determination but national determination, the silence about the enactment of a national Jubilee in the extant historical document of Israel might imply that it did not occur properly because of the scale of social disruption—in spite of the legislation. The enactment of Jubilee presupposes a situation where a man could still technically be restored to full ownership of the land. After a few generations many were, however, uprooted and pushed off their ancestral land altogether.[59] The situation made it impossible for them to be restored to full ownership of the land in any practicable sense whatsoever (Mic 2:2, 9; Isa 5:8). Thus eighth-century prophets such as Isaiah and Amos pronounced that Israel's neglect of the Jubilee was reckoned to be one of the causes of their being carried away to Babylon.

Despite the lack of clear evidence for the enactment of Jubilee in the history of Israel, the evidence from other ANE civilizations,[60] which came from centuries earlier than the origins of Old Testament, and all trace of the legislation in the Old Testament might still provide a

---

58. Ibid.

59. As some of Jesus' own parables indicate (Luke 7:41–42; Matt 18:23–35), debt was quite a major problem in first-century Palestine too. It is supported by Josephus's record that at the start of the Jewish War in 66 CE the first thing the rebels did was to burn the treasury where the records of debt were kept (*J.W.* 2.426–427). See N. Wright, *Jesus and the Victory*, 294.

60. C. Wright summarizes two views on the timing of the law. Some scholars see the law as a late, idealistic, formulation from the same period as the Holiness Code within the Priestly compilation to which this part of Leviticus is usually assigned. Others regard the jubilee as part of Israel's earliest, premonarchic laws, which fell into disuse. Scholars who have done the most research into the ANE parallels and the sociological background more commonly hold this latter position. Gottwald regards the redemption provisions, but not the jubilee, as reflecting "old conditions." See C. Wright, "Jubilee, Year of," 1028.

probability that the Jubilee regulations were not utopian ideals, but real practical regulations.[61] This does not mean that Jesus at the synagogue of Nazareth could have proposed a literal implementation of the Year of Jubilee, an actual national jubilee. The two facts that we do not find such an agenda[62] in the rest of Jesus' ministry, and that Jesus quoted from Isaiah, the prophetic texts, rather than from Leviticus, the Levitical law, may suggest that Jesus was using Jubilee imagery as a way of showing principles involved or the kind of response required by the arrival of the kingdom of God.[63] In Luke 4:16–30 what infuriated the congregation was not the claim "today this scripture has been fulfilled," but the different view of the foreigner: Elijah being sent to a foreign widow and Elisha healing Naaman the foreign general. That God's grace is for all without distinction of nationality and race was too much for the people in the synagogue at Nazareth. Thus J. A. Sanders broadens the focus of Jesus' original citation of Isaiah 61.

> By this enriching juxtaposition of the acts of Elijah and Elisha and Isaiah 61, Jesus clearly shows that the words meaning poor, captive, blind and oppressed do not apply exclusively to any in-group but, on the contrary, apply to those to whom God wishes them to apply.[64]

Luke 4:6–30 is indeed the significant beginning, presenting us with a pivotal point in Jesus' public ministry and outlining his whole ministry. If Jesus intended to summon Israel as a whole to celebrate the Year of Jubilee, he would have meant it in both a spiritual way and a practical way. Then the good news to the poor, the freedom for the prisoners, the recovery of sight for the blind, and the release of the oppressed (Luke 4:18–19) as the external work of the Holy Spirit could be actual implementations of his salvation ministry as well as metaphors for the salvation that comes through forgiveness in the crucified Christ Jesus. Having questioned whether the Jubilee-language in Luke 4 is metaphorical or

---

61. The existing Mishnaic legislation has the appearance of an ideal rather than a reality (e.g., *m. Roš Haššanah* 1:1; 3.5; *m. Arakin* 7:1–5). See N. Wright, *Jesus and the Victory*, 294.

62. There are two sides of the coin. In fact, we find agendas which actually go further, beyond even the most radical social or cultural reform. It is also noted that Jesus stresses more general elements that are more readily observable within his ministry.

63. See C. Wright, "Jubilee, Year of," 1028.

64. J. Sanders, *Isaiah 61 to Luke 4*, 97.

spiritual, N. Wright points out the possibility of understanding the Year of Jubilee in both ways.

> There is a danger here of being trapped into a spurious either/or: either Jesus wanted all Israel to celebrate the Jubilee, or he meant it all in a purely "spiritual" sense. Jesus intended his people, those who were loyal to him in the villages and towns, to form cells, groups or gatherings, much as the non-Qumran Essenes, or John's disciples, seem to have done-and, mutatis mutandis, much as the Haberim, the groups of Pharisees, must have done.[65]

Wright's understanding strengthens the close affinity between Luke 4 and Pentecost in relation to the Year of Jubilee.

> Although Jesus did not envisage that he would persuade Israel as a whole to keep the Jubilee year, he expected his followers to live by the Jubilee principle among themselves. He expected, and taught, that they should forgive one another not only "sins" but also debts. This may help to explain the remarkable practice within the early church whereby resources were pooled, in a fashion not unlike the Essene community of goods. Luke's description of this in Acts 4.34 echoes the description of the sabbatical year in Deuteronomy 15.4. I suggest, therefore—it is only a suggestion, but I think it reasonably likely historically—that Jesus intended his cells of followers to live "as if" the Jubilee were being enacted.[66]

Although Wright connects Pentecost (Acts 4:34) only with the Sabbatical Year, we can see that the meaning of the Year of Jubilee is clearly reflected in the ideal Christian fellowship of Acts 2:42–47. The same principle of the Year of Jubilee underlies the work of the Holy Spirit upon the first community of believers. In particular, the issue of dating is worth noting because it plays an important role in the developing meaning of the feast in later times, particularly in relation to the Year of Jubilee and the Pentecost. The fact that the Year of Jubilee was still used to calculate years shows its impact on Israel (The case can be found in the Qumran community [4Q390 17b–10]. Israel arrived at Mount Sinai in the third month after leaving Egypt, namely the fiftieth day after Passover (Exod 19:1). This provided the time to celebrate the giving of the Sinaitic covenant, the gift of the Torah. The fiftieth year after seven cycles of seven years was

---

65. N. Wright, *Jesus and the Victory*, 295.
66. Ibid.

called the Year of Jubilee.⁶⁷ It was proclaimed on the Day of Atonement by means of trumpet blasts throughout the land.

The meaning of Pentecost is fifty, the fiftieth day after Passover. The agreement of the number fifty between the two should not be overlooked as merely coincidental. The affinity of the two in content highlights "the fiftieth day" and the connotations that it carried. The connection between the Year of Jubilee in Luke 4 and the Pentecost event in Acts 2 and 4 could be justifiable in the light of their mutuality of number, and the role of the Holy Spirit. The Holy Spirit came at Pentecost. The believers of the community were filled with the Holy Spirit, drawing a picture of the extraordinary unity of the early Christian community. *And the community of believers was one in heart and mind. No one claimed that anything he possessed belonged to him; rather they had all things in common* (Acts 4:32–36). Emphatically Luke reports that no one in the Spirit-filled community claimed ownership of their possessions, sharing everything they had. As a result of the Pentecost event, Luke introduces the early Christian community in terms of its common ownership of material goods and unified community life (Luke 2:42-47; 4:32-35; 5:12-16). Unlike Matthew, who is more interested in the spiritual conditions of the individual, Luke equates spiritual conditions with physical conditions. Thus for Luke the gift of the Sprit involves not only a spiritual dimension but also a physical outworking. Luke was trying to emphasize that the Spirit-filled community lived "as if" the Year of Jubilee were being enacted.⁶⁸ Joint possession (Acts 2:44-45; 4:32) was a distinctive feature of the first Christian community. It refers jubilary practice and was the result of the work of the Holy Spirit.

In trying to apply the principle of the Year of Jubilee (Lev 25) that was given during the year that Israel camped at Mount Sinai, the church of Acts 2–4 seems to embody those ideal features in its structure, as the Qumran community had done (1QS I 11f, 5.2, 6; Josephus, *J.W.* 2.122).

---

67. Philo states the meaning of the number. However the number ninety-nine has been set forth and adorned not only by its affinity to the number one hundred, but it has also received a particular participation in a wonderful nature, since it consists of the number fifty, and of seven times seven. For the fiftieth year, as the year Pentecost and of the Jubilee, is called remission in the giving forth of the law, as then all things are given their liberty, whether living or inanimate. And the mystery of the seventh year is one of quiet and profound peace to both body and soul (Philo, *Questions and Answers on Genesis* 3.853–854).

68. N. Wright, *Jesus and the Victory*, 295.

Having had all things in common, the first church of the book of Acts lived a life of perfect union and was characterized by prayer, just as Israel had been unified and receptive to the Torah at Mount Sinai. VanderKam states that the ideal Christian fellowship in Acts 2:42–47 seems to be modeled on the notion that Israel at Sinai was a harmonious nation that unanimously accepted the Torah.[69] Having pictured Israel encamped at Mount Sinai after receiving the Torah, Luke would have idealized the Spirit-filled church of the book of Acts.[70] This church serves to provide a bridge between the past (Lev 25) and the present world transformed in Christ. Thus the question as to whether the Year of Jubilee was ever nationally enacted becomes irrelevant in view of this. The Year of Jubilee is to be interpreted on the basis of how its imagery can be read within a community, becoming a guideline for His community to put into daily practice. Luke himself points the way forward by not dwelling upon Jubilee imagery but by allowing it to be redefined by the content of Jesus' own ministry.[71] It is true that the Jubilee principle of freedom and release also strongly implies eschatological ideals that will be fully achieved and demonstrated in the Messianic age to come. Donald Blosser points out the close relation of the present aspect and the future aspect of the Year of Jubilee.

> These Jubilee acts are not simply to be expected in the future, they are to be given concrete expression among the people of God in the present. . . what had been expected in the future can now be experienced in the present because we are now living in the new age. . . characterized by Jubilee activity among the believers.[72]

The most important emphasis of this Jubilee legislation is the attitude of complete trust that is practiced in the present, looking forward to the Age to come. The future becomes the driving force to practice the principle of the Year of Jubilee in the present. Thus through the ascension to God and the sending of the Holy Spirit in his Pentecost pilgrimage Jesus Christ opens the door to the time of the true and actual Jubilee, which is about

---

69. VanderKam, "Covenant and Pentecost," 253.

70. There is no evidence that such sharing of property as Luke seems to describe was ever widely practiced in primitive Christianity. See Barrett, *Acts of the Apostles*, 169.

71. Willoughby, "Concept of Jubilee," 55.

72. Yoder, *Politics of Jesus*, 74. Yoder cites Blosser, "Jesus and the Jubilee: The Year of Jubilee and its Significance in the Gospel of Luke (PhD diss., University of Saint Andrews, 1979) 297.

returning to our owner. The enactment of the Year of Jubilee in the present is to be a preparation for the true and actual Jubilee. Stephen saw the glory of God and Jesus at the right hand of God before being stoned (Acts 7:55). For Barrett, Jesus is indeed standing because "he is about to come," but Luke believed that "the death of each Christian would be marked by what we may term a private and personal *parousia* of the Son of man."[73] The jubilary concept of eschatological restoration in relation to God's final restoration of Israel and all things is also found in Acts 1:6 and 3:21. The time of the true and actual Jubilee, when we return to our owner, is not yet come. The time of fulfillment of the Jubilee is to be the time of the Lord's glorious appearing. The ideal Christian fellowship in Acts 2:42–47 and 4:34 responded to this hope at the level of sharing all things in common,[74] fulfilling the hope of the Year of Jubilee in Leviticus 25. C. Wright summarizes the Jubilee model in the present and future sense.

> To apply the jubilee model, then, requires that people face the sovereignty of God, trust his providence, know his redemptive action, experience his atonement, practice his justice, and hope in his promise. The wholeness of the model embraces the Church's evangelistic mission, its personal and social ethics, and its future hope.[75]

The message of Pentecost is one of hope, speaking of the internal work of the Holy Spirit, an eschatological aspect of the Jubilee legislation, which rests on the principles of freedom; the freedom that his second coming will eventually bring about. The Pentecost experience should, therefore, be regarded as an essential part of the divine plan of salvation that his Pentecost pilgrimage brought with the descent of the Holy Spirit. Thus Jesus' Pentecost pilgrimage is not only the completion of his earthly ministry, but also becomes the beginning of his final pilgrimage (his glorious *Parousia*), providing the new pilgrimage model. Jesus' previous pilgrimages were focused on the temple in Jerusalem whereas Jesus' Pentecost pilgrimage, including his pilgrimage to God and the descent of the Holy Spirit, opens for those who will follow the Way of Jesus, the new dimension of pilgrimage, the pilgrimage to God in

---

73. Bruce, *Book of Acts*, 156. Bruce cites Barrett, "Stephen and the Son of Man," in *Apophoreta: Festschrift für Ernst Haenchen*, BZNW 30 (Berlin, 1964) 32–38.

74. Barrett points out that that "friends share all things" is one of the most widely quoted maxims in ancient literature. See Barrett, *Acts of the Apostles*, 168.

75. See C. Wright, "Jubilee, Year of," 1029.

Heaven. Since making the Father and himself known is the main agenda of Jesus' ministry from the very beginning of his pilgrimages in relation to the feast, each journey to Jerusalem plays a part to that end. This time in Pentecost in the case of his pilgrimage to Jerusalem with the Holy Spirit, the Father's promise (Luke 24:49; Acts 1:4), the disciples came to a stage to fully know who God is as the Father, Son, and Holy Spirit. The gradual progression of the disciples in the knowledge of God has been completed with the descent of the Holy Spirit.

It is noted that Jesus' Pentecost pilgrimage does not show the same pattern as that of Jesus' Passover and Tabernacles pilgrimages. Unlike Jesus' Passover and Tabernacles pilgrimages, in Jesus' Pentecost pilgrimage nobody seems to make a pilgrimage journey. Nevertheless, the Pentecost pilgrimage, like the other two, was for the purpose of self-revelation. In the OT God came to Jerusalem (Pss 96:13; 98:9) and made himself known (Pss 48:3; 50:2; 76:1–2; 98:2). Thus for the disciples at Pentecost the symbols and rites of the feast were experienced through the descent of the Holy Spirit in his saving works and expressed through the internal work of the Holy Spirit in relation to the Year of Jubilee. This was the message of Jesus' Pentecost pilgrimage for the Lukan community and the readers who will take a pilgrimage to God in the guidance of the Holy Spirit.

Conclusion

The previous chapters show that the feasts of Passover and Tabernacles have developed their own character and meaning for the momentous events in the history of Israel. As the Feast of Passover and the Feast of Tabernacles were historicized in remembrance of the Exodus event, including the wilderness wandering of Israel, in later Judaism the Feast of Pentecost was associated with the events of Mount Sinai and the patriarchs, and given a further historical meaning. The book of Jubilees and the Dead Sea Scrolls strongly imply that, in the middle of the second century BCE, the Feast of Pentecost was for many Jews associated with the renewal of the covenant and commemoration of the lawgiving at Sinai, as well as celebration of the offering of the firstfruits of the wheat harvest (*Jub.* 1:5; 6:11, 17; 15:1–24; 1QS I 7–2:19). In particular, the feast for the Qumran community was their annual occasion for acknowledging new members and renewing the Sinai covenant (1QS I 16–2.18).

The main issue is whether the Feast of Pentecost has determined Luke's theological presuppositions.

Luke is the only writer to pass on to us the descent of the Holy Spirit connected with the Feast of Pentecost. The descent of the Holy Spirit is closely connected with what preceded. Thus Jesus' Pentecost pilgrimage includes Jesus' ascension to the Father as well as the descent of the Holy Spirit. The ascension of Christ is not only intimately connected with Pentecost, but is also related to the resurrection, the heart of Christian faith. Since Jesus' way includes the passion, resurrection, and ascension, the ascension, Jesus' pilgrimage to God, was an essential act, completing what was done in the passion. Only by entering into glory was his pilgrimage completed and the Spirit bestowed upon his disciples (John 15:26). Thus the ascension, Jesus' ascent to God, is a departure in terms of the end of Jesus' earthly ministry. However, it is also an arrival in terms of the beginning of his heavenly reign and the decent of the Holy Spirit. By presenting the promise of the Holy Spirit (Luke 24:49), which is immediately followed by the ascension narrative, Luke provided his readers with the framework to see that God's plan went on through the descent of the Holy Spirit. Luke is in agreement with the Fourth Gospel that the Spirit is given only after his return to the Father. The ascension, Jesus' pilgrimage to God, is presented in Luke and John as the climax and fulfillment of his whole pilgrimage—namely his earthly ministry. Schillebeeckx defines the ascension—Christ's being with the Father, as the principle of Pentecost, and Pentecost as the great harvest festival of the redemption.[76]

For Luke the Feast of Pentecost was the occasion when the Holy Spirit came. With the background of the Feast of Pentecost Luke dramatically describes the whole scene in detail. Although there is no clear evidence in Acts 2 to suggest that Luke's thinking was defined by the Feast of Pentecost, there are several elements that suggest possible reasons why the Holy Spirit should have come down at Pentecost.

Jewish tradition relating to the offering of the firstfruits of the wheat harvest has some striking resemblances to the event of Pentecost in Acts 2. The one hundred twenty disciples in the place might become symbolically the offering of the firstfruits as the beginning of the Church and the conclusion of his earthly ministry. At Pentecost, the ascended Christ as the "firstfruits of those who are asleep" (1 Cor 15:20) sent the Holy Spirit

---

76. Schillebeeckx, "Ascension and Pentecost," 353.

and those gathered on that day became the first fruits of his earthly ministry and of the full harvest of believers to come (cf. 2 Cor 5:5; Eph 1:13–14). Three thousand of them came to the Lord, becoming the firstfruits of the first Christian community. Pentecost became the beginning (the firstfruits) of the Christian mission, the harvest. This might be what Luke emphasized in relation to the offering of the firstfruits on Pentecost.

Since the Feast of Pentecost seems already to have been regarded as the feast of covenant renewal, it is also likely in the time of Jesus to have been regarded as the feast commemorating the lawgiving at Mount Sinai. The evidence of the covenant made with Israel (Luke 1:72; Acts 3:25; 7:8), the concept of the new covenant (Luke 22:20), and the possible reference to Psalm 68 in Acts 2:33, suggest that Luke might have been familiar with the Feast of Pentecost in relation to the lawgiving at Mount Sinai. Philo's exegesis (*Decalogue* 9.33; 11.46–47) also strengthens this view. This makes it a plausibility to associate the Pentecost event in Acts 2 with the Sinaitic covenant. If Pentecost is viewed as part of the fulfillment and renewal of Israel's covenant, the direct allusion to the Year of Jubilee in Luke 4:18–19 as the renewal of the old covenant, it will have a vital role in Israel's restoration. Luke 4:16–30 is indeed the significant beginning, presenting us with a pivotal point in his public ministry and providing an outline for it.

As the logical extension of the Sabbath and the Sabbatical Year, the Year of Jubilee is the time for God to reassert his ownership of the land and its people. The land had been promised and was then given to Israel. This dual tradition of the land—God's divine ownership and God's gift to Israel is based on the theological principle that originated in the redemptive act of the Lord who brought his people out of Egypt and sustained them in their journey to the promised land. It also reminded his people of the fact that they had once been liberated from their captivity in Egypt by the divine power of God, and they were now living in their own land as free citizens who belonged to God.

Although it is still not clear that a Jubilee Year had ever been enacted in the Old Testament, Jesus at the synagogue of Nazareth could have used Jubilee imagery as a way of showing principles involved, or the kind of response required by the arrival of the kingdom of God. If Jesus intended to summon Israel as a whole to celebrate the Year of Jubilee, he would have meant it in both a spiritual and a practical way. We can see that the meaning of the Year of Jubilee is clearly reflected in the ideal

Christian fellowship of Acts 2:42–47. The same principle of the Year of Jubilee underlies the work of the Holy Spirit within the first community of believers. The agreement of the number fifty between the two events should not be overlooked as merely coincidental. In trying to apply the principle of the Year of Jubilee (Lev 25) that was given during the year that Israel camped at Mount Sinai, the church of Acts 2–4 seems to embody those ideal features in its structure, as the Qumran community had also done (1QS I 11f, 5.2, 6; Josephus, *J.W.* 2.122). The Jubilee principle of freedom and release is based on the attitude of complete trust that is practiced in the present, looking forward to the Age that is to come. Thus through the ascension to God and the sending of the Holy Spirit in his Pentecost pilgrimage, Jesus Christ opens the door to the time of the true and actual Jubilee, which is all about coming back to our owner. With the eschatological aspect of the Jubilee legislation, the Pentecost experience plays an essential part in the divine plan of salvation that his Pentecost pilgrimage has brought and will bring, with the descent of the Holy Spirit. Thus Jesus' Pentecost pilgrimage is not only the completion of his earthly ministry, but it also becomes the beginning of his final pilgrimage (his glorious *Parousia*), providing the new pilgrimage model. It is the pilgrimage to God in Heaven, for those who will follow the Way of Jesus. In the Feast of Pentecost God as the Holy Spirit came to Jerusalem (Pss 96:13; 98:9) and made himself known (Pss 48:3; 50:2; 76:1–2; 98:2). In the feast Jesus completed his own purpose to reveal who he was in relation to the Holy Spirit and made the Father's promise known through the medium of the Feast of Pentecost. Thus the gradual progression of the disciples in the knowledge of God has been completed with the descent of the Holy Spirit. For the disciples at Pentecost the symbols and rites of the feast were experienced through the descent of the Holy Spirit in his saving works and expressed through the internal work of the Holy Spirit in relation to the Year of Jubilee. This becomes the message of Jesus' Pentecost pilgrimage for the Lukan community and the readers who will journey to God in the guidance of the Holy Spirit.

7

Summary of Conclusions

IN ISRAEL'S UNDERSTANDING, CREATION and history are inseparably related. Creation is the foundation of the history of Israel. When expulsion from Eden is seen to be *the first journey mankind ever took*, it is understood as a process of rescue rather than of judgment, God's saving grace becomes crystal clear as the narrative of his people unfolds. In the formulation of the history of Israel, Creation, together with historical events (the Exodus, the times of exile), had decisive significance for the historical interpreter. Thus, for Israel, Creation is the calling from God to grasp the reality of God as the Creator and that of mankind as his creatures. Though homeless on this earth, the Israelites were no more than exiles wandering and yearning for a return to the Edenic state; *being with God* was the final destination of pilgrimage, for life outside the garden is *life away from one's true home*.

It may be noted that journey as the main framework of pilgrimage played a significant role as the Abrahamic and Jacob narratives unfolded. The Abrahamic pilgrimage that began with the divine command that brought Abraham out of Ur, concludes on Moriah with Abraham's total appreciation of and submissive response to the true God. Abraham's obedience to God on Moriah as the prototype for Israel in Jerusalem emphasizes how the Abrahamic pilgrimage foreshadows the history of Israel.

Abraham's journey to the promised land concludes with Jacob's journey down into Egypt in the patriarchal story. That was, however, the beginning of the history of the people. "The years of my pilgrimage" (Gen 47:9), Jacob's summary of his life and his fathers' lives, could be the total appreciation of who he was before God and who God in reality really was. In the nomadic wanderings of the patriarchs from Ur to Haran and then southward to the land of Canaan and even down to Egypt, pilgrimage became a crucial necessity to fulfill God's promises for his people. Thus the pilgrimage motif encompassing the journey motif became a distinctive feature of the patriarchal narrative as a whole with a strong theological content.

This pattern is also prominent in the journeys followed in the Exodus and the forty years in the wilderness before Joshua led Israel into the promised land. In Israel's wilderness wanderings like the patriarchs' narratives the *knowing God motif* became the key experience for the Israelites in terms of the several stages of a faith journey. Exodus 19:5, "I brought you to myself," provides the clear reason for the journey to Sinai, which was the most profound theological interpretation of pilgrimage. The destination of the journey was not the mountain or the promised land, but bringing the Israelites on the move to God himself. The Israelites should have known that a life of obedience is a life on the move towards not the land, but God himself. God was the focus and the goal of the Exodus in which the whole physical journey, namely walking, was engaged. This allusion to the "walking in his ways" metaphor offers a fundamental image of the pilgrimage (journey) paradigm.

Since there was still no fixed center of worship and government after the settlement in Canaan, the ark became the symbol of God's guidance and presence in the midst of his people in the period of Judges. David and Solomon bound Israel to Jerusalem by bringing the ark into the city and building the temple around it. In the course of history Jerusalem thus increasingly became the "religious" as well as the political center as the capital of the kingdom. It should, however, be noted that it is understandable that the city could become dangerous when God's protection and blessing were restricted to a particular place and the religious life of Israel was often linked with polytheistic and syncretistic practices, particularly forms of Baal worship. Consequently the fall of Jerusalem was inevitable to end the false confidence and unity of God and place, so that trust in God might be separated from trust in a place.

Through the journey framework, God guided Abraham and Jacob in their lives and led Israel as a nation to the promised land. Again, God brought about the same pattern and process—being carried away to Babylon, sojourn in Babylon, and the return to the promised land—for his idolatrous people to know who he was and to come back to him. Thus the exile and restoration for Israel were not just physical movements, but also a pilgrimage of faith and the rod in God's hand that brought the people to recognize what they were and who he was. After the theological reflection upon the exile and the return, the prophets and Psalms proclaim that the exile and the return were not merely a wandering through the wilderness toward the promised land, but a pilgrimage to the holy mountain, Jerusalem. The return from exile sounded again the pilgrimage motif of a people restlessly seeking the satisfaction of their spiritual hunger in Jerusalem. Thus the unity of God and the city, Jerusalem, was redefined. Having embraced the decisive events in the history of Israel that became the dominant paradigm for Israel's faith, God's *coming* and *making himself known* became reality experienced and visibly expressed through the symbols and rites of the three feasts in Jerusalem.[1]

Jewish literature from the Second Temple period contains many allusions to and information about pilgrimage customs and practices. The presence of the pilgrimage paradigm in a collection of Jewish literature from the Second Temple period spells out how deeply the pilgrimage practice in relation to the three feasts was embedded in the everyday life of the Israelites.

The previous observation displays the characteristics of the pilgrimage paradigm that can be listed under three headings: the journey motif, "walk and way" metaphor, the knowing God motif.

1. The journey motif is one of the dominant literary patterns of the whole Bible. The physical journey became the outward visible procedure through which God brought about his providence and fulfilled his promise for his people. The literal journey as walking towards the promise was the prerequisite of bringing the promise into reality. Since pilgrimage as physical movement is closely intertwined with God's way of transforming his people, namely, discipleship, Israel's physical journeys, the Exodus, the exile, and the return, are to be understood as a theological paradigm for the nation on pilgrimage.
2. The journey motif displays a strong spiritual emphasis reflecting both a physical and literal aspect of it in terms of "walk" before him and "way" metaphor. In a very real sense the *walking* and *way* metaphor becomes a metaphor for life. The walk and way metaphor

---

1. See Mowinckel, *Psalms in Israel's Worship*, 1:136–44.

emerges from allusion to Israel's journey including the wilderness period, the destruction of Jerusalem, the cessation of the sacrificial cult and of the monarchy, and the experience of the exile, which supplied the contours of the larger Judaic framework.

3. The primary image of pilgrimage in Israel is that of drawing near to God or knowing God. The knowing God motif as the key experience for the Israelites becomes one of the main themes of the Exodus. This is seen first in the Lord's encounter with Abraham and Jacob. For the Israelites the Exodus was not mere rescue, but an experience of knowing God (Exod 6:7). In the long story of Israel from the Abrahamic pilgrimage to the return to Jerusalem from Babylon we can trace the interlocking relationship between pilgrimage as physical movement and transformation into faith's pilgrimage, namely, knowing God through encounter with God on the way (Exod 3:1; 4:17). From the viewpoint of the knowing God motif his revelation was progressive and the understanding of God drawn upon the perception of his people was gradual.

We have seen that the gospels of Luke and John were continually linking the three pilgrimage feasts with Jesus' ministry in Jerusalem, and have established that the three feasts of pilgrimage had a profound effect on Jesus himself and the Gospel writers' thinking. It is supported by Lightfoot's comment that Jesus went to (was at) Jerusalem only "in connection with a festival."[2] Due to the great symbolic significance of the Passover it was historicized to commemorate the Exodus. In Luke and the Fourth Gospel the journey motif is carefully shaped into the Passover pilgrimage paradigm in relation to Jerusalem, particularly the temple. Thus the temple and Jerusalem festivals are closely woven into the plot of the narrative in the gospels of Luke and John.

Through Jesus' Passover pilgrimage at the age of twelve in which Luke emphasizes that the child was not redeemed but rather consecrated to the service of God, Luke anticipates the unfolding redemptive events of his ministry to follow. For Luke it explains Jesus' strong sense of identity and why it was that Jesus felt he belonged to the Lord as well as recognizing himself as sent by the Father to reveal and to do his will. In the Fourth Gospel the cleansing of the temple in Jesus' Passover pilgrimage is at the heart of the pilgrimage paradigm, *the destination of pilgrimage*

---

2. Lightfoot, *St. John's Gospel*, 148.

and *knowing God through the encounter with Jesus*. From the very beginning of the Gospel the narrative makes it clear that the Word of God should carry on God's journey for completing his mission of making the Father and himself known. While Jesus challenged Israel's abuse of the temple, he told Israel that its temple belonged to him (John 2: 21), for he as the Son of God, the Davidic King, and the Messianic Priest, was responsible for the temple (Ezek 45). He is also the new Temple. So to go on pilgrimage is to come to Jesus.[3] The goal of pilgrimage has been transformed christologically.[4]

While the Feast of Passover was historicized in remembrance of the Exodus event, the Feast of Tabernacles was associated with the wilderness wandering of Israel. Like the Passover celebration, the Israelites might have developed the Feast of Tabernacles, having encountered and adopted both a nomadic and sedentary lifestyle. The Feast of Tabernacles suggests that a New Year festival had a special connection with the rainy season, which closed the agricultural year and opened the new one. Although some of the original ideas have remained right down to the Second Temple period, all of these symbols and rites of the feast were gradually reinterpreted in the context of the evolving history of the Israelites. In Jesus' Tabernacles pilgrimage the feast was imbued with new sense and further significance. Jesus transformed the water and light rituals of the Tabernacles, proclaiming himself to be the light and water of the world. This confirms a strong probability that Jesus thought about the meaning of the feast and meaning of his pilgrimage when he planned his journey to Jerusalem and decided to go for the Feast of Tabernacles. He acknowledged the great symbolic representation of the feast, through which he had to reveal who he was and so he claimed himself to be the completion of the feast.

Thus the location of worship is no longer relevant, because true worship must be in keeping with Christ, not with a place (John 14:6, 16, 25–26). As in the Feast of Tabernacles Jesus replaces two ritual symbols: water (7:37) and light (8:58), at Passover he becomes the sacrifice of the feast (19:31–37), dismissing the importance of Holy Places including the real estate of Judea, Samaria, or Galilee. The journeys to Jerusalem that are precipitated by an impending Jewish festival (2:13; 5:1; 7:2, 10; 11:55; 13:1) and the pilgrimage feasts that the Fourth Gospel gives close

3. Lincoln, "Pilgrimage," 39.
4. Ibid.

attention to, strongly suggest that Jerusalem and the pilgrimage feasts had an important place in his ministry. However, this is not because of the significance of the feasts or Jerusalem, but because of the fact that it should be made known that Jesus Christ, who is the Holy Place, is the true destination of each person's pilgrimage and the completion of the pilgrimage feasts. Christology could not be clearer in answering the Jewish yearning for place.

For Luke it is, however, Jerusalem as the place of the temple that is highlighted. The temple as the true goal of Jesus' pilgrimage in Luke is more than the place where Jesus' journey ends.[5] For Luke Jesus' Passover pilgrimage to Jerusalem was a way to show what kind of Messiah he was. The stress on Jerusalem, the place where he must suffer, is heightened by his awareness as the Suffering Messiah. "The Way" began when Jesus made the decisive choice to head toward Jerusalem (Luke 9:51). Thus the disciples of Jesus had to come to terms with the fact that he was going to the Father via the cross. This model enabled his disciples to come to terms with his death not as defeat but as achievement, and to see the whole "Way" of Jesus. By showing that the death of Christ coincided with Passover (John 18:14, 28) John demonstrates that the association of the Lamb of God with Passover identifies the lamb as a paschal sacrifice (John 19:36). Jesus also reinterpreted the symbols of the Passover and gave them new meaning, identifying the bread with the body of Jesus and relating the cup to the new covenant in his blood. Jesus revealed his coming death and his own suffering and gave bread and wine "as a new mode of celebrating Israel's feast of deliverance."[6] So his body and blood replaced the Passover lamb that was the Passover sacrifice. The meaning of Passover has been transformed christologically. The connection of this reinterpreted Passover with the reference to Jesus' death could not be clearer in the context of his action on the cross. This confirms a strong probability that Jesus thought about the meaning of the feast and meaning of his pilgrimage when he planned his journey to Jerusalem and decided to go for the Feast of Passover. He acknowledged the great symbolic representation of the feast, through which he had to reveal who he was and so he claimed himself to be the completion of the feast. Like the Tabernacles pilgrimage the revelation of Jesus became the message of his Passover pilgrimage with all the rich experiences contained in the

---

5. Dawsey, "Jesus' Pilgrimage to Jerusalem," 226.
6. Fitzmyer, *Luke X-XXIV*, 1392.

feast. Thus his Passover pilgrimage offers the underlying dynamic of the feast, the knowing God motif. Nolland confirms that Jesus who is no longer present in his historical ministry will make himself known and confer ever afresh to the disciple community the benefits of his passion.[7] This is what the Lukan Gospel intends and the readers who journey with Jesus should note in his Passover pilgrimage.

Although Jesus repeatedly spoke of being lifted up, of being betrayed, and of dying, the disciples could not apprehend his mission. Jesus was, however, ready for this misunderstanding. Thus Jesus asked the Father to give to the disciples the Spirit (John 14:16-17) who is the One whereby the Father and the Son are present with and in the believers. The Holy Spirit will be given only as a result of Christ's death, resurrection, and exaltation. The entire section of John 14 envisions that the giving of the Spirit is conditioned by his departure (John 7:39; 16:7). The descent of the Holy Spirit is closely connected with what preceded: the passion, resurrection, and ascension. Only by entering into glory was Jesus' pilgrimage completed and the Spirit bestowed upon his disciples (John 15:26). The ascension, Jesus' pilgrimage to God, is presented in Luke and John as the climax and fulfillment of his whole pilgrimage— namely his earthly ministry. This means that Jesus' final Passover pilgrimage made the Pentecost pilgrimage indispensable.

Luke is the only writer to pass on to us the descent of the Holy Spirit connected with the Feast of Pentecost. As the Feast of Passover and the Feast of Tabernacles were historicized in remembrance of the Exodus event, including the wilderness wandering of Israel, in later Judaism the Feast of Pentecost was associated with the events of Mount Sinai and the patriarchs, and given a further historical meaning. Since the Feast of Pentecost seems already to have been regarded as the feast of covenant renewal, it is also likely in the time of Jesus to have been regarded as the feast commemorating the lawgiving at Mount Sinai.

The evidence of the covenant made with Israel (Luke 1:72; Acts 3:25; 7:8), the concept of the new covenant (Luke 22:20), and the possible reference to Psalm 68 in Acts 2:33, suggests that Luke might have been familiar with the Feast of Pentecost in relation to the lawgiving at Mount Sinai. Philo's exegesis (*Decalogue* 9.33; 11.46-47) also strengthens this view. This opens a plausibility to associate the Pentecost event in Acts 2 with the Sinaitic covenant. If Pentecost is viewed as part of the fulfill-

---

7. Nolland, *Luke 18:35—24:53*, 1056.

ment and renewal of Israel's covenant, the direct allusion to the Year of Jubilee in Luke 4:18–19 as the renewal of the old covenant, will have a vital role in Israel's restoration. Luke 4:16–30 is indeed the significant beginning, presenting us with a pivotal point in Jesus' public ministry and providing an outline for it. If Jesus intended to summon Israel as a whole to celebrate the Year of Jubilee, he would have meant it in both a spiritual and a practical way. We can see that the meaning of the Year of Jubilee is clearly reflected in the ideal Christian fellowship of Acts 2:42–47. The same principle of the Year of Jubilee underlies the work of the Holy Spirit within the first community of believers. The Jubilee principle of freedom and release is based on the attitude of complete trust that is practiced in the present, looking forward to the Age that is to come. Thus through the ascension to God and the sending of the Holy Spirit in his Pentecost pilgrimage, Jesus Christ opens the door to the time of the true and actual Jubilee, which is all about the final journey, going back to our owner. Since the very beginning of Genesis, life outside the garden has been for his people *life away from their true home*. They are no more than exiles wandering and yearning for a return to the Edenic state *being with God*, the final destination of pilgrimage.

Our study has established that the three pilgrimage feasts had a profound effect on Jesus himself and the writers' thinking. We have concluded that throughout the Bible the physical journey became the outward visible procedure through which God brought about his providence and fulfilled his promise for his people. Since pilgrimage to the temple in Jerusalem was to meet with God, the three pilgrimage feasts at the time of Jesus became opportunities to come to God, to meet with, and learn from him. Jesus made his journeys to Jerusalem only in relation to pilgrimage feasts. Jesus, having fully understood the meaning of each feast, fulfilled his earthly ministry through physical pilgrimages for the feasts of Passover and Tabernacles and one pilgrimage, heavenly journey, for the Feast of Pentecost. Jesus' pilgrimage to Jerusalem was to reveal who God the Father, God the Son, and God the Spirit were in the light of the three pilgrimage feasts. Those who participated in a pilgrimage with Jesus experienced the divine blessing *God's coming and making himself known* through Jesus the Son of God. In terms of beneficiary, Jesus' pilgrimages to Jerusalem were for the disciples, the people Jesus encountered, and the readers of the Gospels also make a gradual progression toward the full comprehension of who God, Jesus, and the

Spirit are. Since Jesus' making himself known is the main agenda from the very beginning of his pilgrimages in relation to the feast, each pilgrimage of Jesus to Jerusalem contributed to the revelation of his earthly campaign or ministry. It is contended, therefore, that Jesus' pilgrimages to Jerusalem were always purpose driven in terms of the meaning of each pilgrimage feast, becoming modes of instruction for the people he encountered and the readers of the Gospels.

If such can be constructed, what is certain is that the open-ended ending of the Pentecost pilgrimage suggests that the message of the pilgrimage paradigm in Jesus Christ would continue in a significant way. Thus, it is the model of the pilgrimage paradigm that is present in the rest of the New Testament. Although more work remains to be done in all areas, an attempt has to be made to establish the implications for pilgrimage of those of the Pauline epistles, 1 Peter, and Hebrews. As has been demonstrated, there is a realized aspect to the pilgrimage of God's people, which becomes a metaphor for the journey of Christian living and the eschatological pilgrimage of the nations taking place in the conversion of Gentiles. In particular, despite the ample imageries and pastoral implications for pilgrimage there is no space here to attempt to reflect upon the theme in the Pauline epistles.

Since the present study does not make any attempt to reach a final consensus, it is hoped that this limited study will provoke others to discuss further the pilgrimage paradigm.

Appendix

Pilgrimage in Other Ancient Texts

The pilgrimage paradigm will now be examined for its presence in Jewish literature from the Second Temple period.

APOCRYPHA

Tobit (250 BCE–175 BCE)

*I*TOBIT HAVE WALKED *all the days of my life in the way of truth and justice, and I did many alms deeds to my brethren, and my nation, who came with me to Nineve, into the land of the Assyrians* (Tob 1:3).[1] Tobit was a Jew of Galilee who is said to have lived in the eighth century BCE. The book of Tobit introduces his relationship with God and his fellow Jews by using the walking metaphor. In this case, the metaphor relates to walking with God as the pattern of obedience. The frequent use of the Hebrew root הָלַךְ—"to walk and go" in Genesis 12:1; 13:17; 17:1; 22:2; 24:40, and 48:15—demonstrates its significance for describing Abraham's relationship with God. The book of Tobit presents Tobit's life as a pious and Torah-observant journey. Despite the idolatrous practices of the Northern Kingdom and her breaking away from Jerusalem in favor of the alternate temples of Jeroboam, the book of Tobit emphasizes that he made frequent pilgrimages to Jerusalem to observe the appointed festivals. *But I alone went often to Jerusalem at the feasts, as it was ordained unto all the people of Israel by an everlasting decree* (Tob 1:6). However, Tobit and his family were taken as captives to Nineveh during the reign

---

1. All texts are taken from *The New English Bible: the Apocrypha*.

of Shalmaneser (about 721 BCE). In exile, Tobit maintained his faithfulness towards God and his fellow Jews. As one of his acts of charity he buried fellow Jews who had been killed by Sennacherib. For this reason he became a fugitive. With the help of Ahikar, his nephew, he returned home. Shortly afterwards the family celebrated the Feast of Pentecost. *Now when I was come home again, and my wife Anna was restored unto me, with my son Tobias, in the feast of Pentecost, which is the holy feast of the seven weeks . . .* (Tob 3:10). Due to the restriction on access to the temple in Jerusalem, the Feast of Pentecost was observed at home. Tobit sent his son, Tobias, to invite the righteous poor to dine with them. However, his good will again turned into disaster, when sparrows muted warm dung into his eyes and blinded him (Tob 2:10).

On one occasion Tobit believed that he was at death's door and instructed his son, Tobias, to go to Media in order to collect the money that he had left in trust with Gabael. Tobit found Azarias, the angel Raphael in disguise, whom God had sent to help Tobias to give safety and guidance on the journey (Tob 5:4). *Then said he to Tobias, prepare thyself for the journey, and God send you a good journey. And when his son had prepared all things for the journey, his father said, Go thou with this man, and God, which dwelleth in heaven, prosper your journey, and the angel of God keep you company* (Tob 5:16). The author of Tobit certainly theologizes the meaning of the journey. God had guided Abraham and Jacob in their lives through their journeys and had led Israel as a nation to the promised land. For Abraham, Jacob, and then Israel the beginning of the journey did see the fulfillment of the promise. Yet the literal journey as representing a movement towards the promise was for them the essential thing in terms of bringing the promise to fulfillment. The author of Tobit brought a similar significance. As Psalm 121 praises God who is the help of the pilgrim making a journey to his home or to the Holy City, so Tobit believes that God will not only protect him on his journey from all harm, but will also be journeying with him. Tobit was convinced that God would bless Tobias's journey, as he had blessed Abraham, Jacob, and Israel through their journeys. David deSilva claims that the author of Tobit drew upon the narratives of Genesis 24 and 29, two journeys undertaken to procure a wife, in describing Tobias's journey.[2] Tobit's instruction with regard to the selection of a wife from

---

2. DeSilva, *Introducing the Apocrypha*, 73.

among his kin (Tob 4:12–13) clearly indicates that getting a wife was one of the reasons for Tobias's journey.

On the way to Media they reached Ecbatana and met Sarah who had lost seven bridegrooms in succession. Tobias immediately fell in love with her. Having realized what had happened to Sarah's previous seven husbands, by following the instruction given by Azarias, Tobias expelled Asmodeus, a demon who had successively slain Sarah's bridegrooms on their wedding nights. After the fourteen-day wedding feast, Tobias, Sarah, and Azarias returned home with the money from Gabael and the property that Raguel, Sarah's father, divided with his son-in-law. He also restored Tobit's sight with fish's gall. The narrative closes with Tobit's deathbed speech, which instructed Tobias and his family to leave Nineveh ahead of its imminent destruction.

The whole story of Tobit brings together two very different people in different places through a journey and is structured within the journey framework. The narrative employs the language and imagery of pilgrimage (pilgrimage feast), and the journey implies that the narrative of Tobit is deeply concerned with the problem of exile and is convinced of the future in terms of a restoration of Zion (Tob 13:2, 5–6, 16–17; 14:5).[3] The journey of Tobias, which is artfully structured in the narrative, probably shows that the journey of exile as the punishment of God (Tob 13:5, 9; 14:4) is not the end of history, but a means of bringing the promise into actualization, including knowing who God is through his protection and guidance, and returning to the promised land of blessing. The outcome of Tobias's journey presents this expectation.

Baruch (200 BCE—50 BCE)

[I]n the land of captivities they shall remember themselves and shall know that I am the Lord their God: for I will give them a heart . . . And I will make an everlasting covenant with them to be their God, and they shall be my people: and I will no more drive my people Israel out of the land that I have given them (Bar 2:30, 35). Coming to know the Lord as their God, Baruch sums up the conclusion of repentance for the people (Bar

---

3. The main actor of this narrative bases his life upon what came to be called *almsgiving*. The connection between Tobit and the New Testament concerning teaching is almsgiving. Raphael defines that the life of the righteous is based on prayer, almsgiving, and fasting (Tob 12:8). Jesus also assumes that prayer, fasting, and almsgiving are part of life for his followers (Matt 6:1–21).

2:31–34).[4] As a result of heartfelt repentance, God will bring them to the promised land, restoring the covenant relationship and promising no more journey for the people (God will never again drive his people, Israel, out of the land). At the bank of the River Jordan, Deuteronomy reviews the wilderness wandering as a journey that made the Israelites come to the stage of acknowledgement that the Lord was God and there is no one besides him. *During the forty years that I led you through the desert, your clothes did not wear out, nor did the sandals on your feet. You ate no bread and drank no wine or other fermented drink. I did this so that you might know that I am the Lord your God* (Deut 29:5–6). Deuteronomy confirms this *knowing God motif* as the key experience for the Israelites, as previously seen in the Abrahamic and Jacob narrative as well as in Exodus. In the same manner Baruch also provides a framework for understanding the nation's exile and restoration. Thus the physical journey, namely walking, became the outward visible procedure through which God brought about his providence. This traveling by foot, or walking, has emerged as a fundamental image of spirituality in the form of the pilgrimage (journey) motif. This is evident in Baruch.

For if thou hadst walked in the way of God (Bar 3:13). *And hold her fast will live, and those who forsake her will die. Turn, O Jacob, and take her; walk toward the shining of her light* (Bar 4:1). *They knew not his statutes, nor walked in the ways of his commandments* (Bar 4:14). *That Israel may go (walk) safely in the glory of God* (Bar 5:7). As Deuteronomy aligns the "walk" imagery with the covenant relationship, Baruch links the "walking" metaphor with the "way of God" (Bar 3:13). For Baruch the event of exile was to chasten Israel who had departed from walking with God in obedience. It is, as deSilva points out, certain that Deuteronomy's theology of suffering provides a framework for understanding national misfortunes.[5] Baruch also personifies Jerusalem in focusing on Jerusalem as he does (Bar 4:5—5:9) and encourages Israel to return to walk in the way of God, namely Israel's wholehearted commitment to God's requirements, so that God may deliver them from the oppressor. *Take a good heart, O Jerusalem* (Bar 4:30). Considering the possibility that Baruch might be written in Babylon in the fifth year, on the seventh day of the fifth month, the date on which the Chaldeans captured Jerusalem and

---

4. Baruch, the close companion of the prophet Jeremiah (Jer 32:12; 36:4; 51:59), is recognized as a "scribe" in the book of Jeremiah (Jer 36:26, 32).

5. DeSilva, *Introducing the Apocrypha*, 210.

set the temple and city on fire, it is no wonder that Baruch details and reflects upon the crucial events of the fall of Jerusalem and the destruction of the temple of Jerusalem, as do the books of Jeremiah, Ezekiel, and Isaiah.[6] *And thy children gathered from the west unto the east, by the word of the Holy One, rejoicing in the remembrances of God. For they departed from thee on foot, and were led away of their enemies . . . For God hath appointed that every high hill, banks of long continuance, should be cast down, and valleys filled up, to make even the ground. That Israel may go (walk) safely in the glory of God* (Bar 5:5–7). Baruch envisages her children (the pilgrims) making a journey to Jerusalem. Jerusalem as the image of mother eagerly anticipates the return of her children, the pilgrims returning to Jerusalem. As Psalm 121 praises God who would keep the pilgrim's life from all harm, Baruch believes that the pilgrim's journey is under the vigilant watch of God. Baruch ends with the hope for Jerusalem, envisaging the Holy City reestablished.

First Esdras (second century BCE ?)[7]

The first book of Esdras has a close relationship with 2 Chronicles 35:1—36:23, and with the whole of Ezra and Nehemiah 7:73—8:12. Due to the extent of overlap, three options have been suggested.[8] The probability is generally supported that 1 Esdras used Ezra-Nehemiah as a source. The first book of Esdras begins with the celebration of Passover in the Jerusalem Temple in the reign of Josiah. Exodus 12 indicates that the Passover was originally a family observance. However, after the Northern Kingdom was destroyed as a result of the Assyrian invasion, Passover became a national observance. Hezekiah invited "all Israel" to come to the temple in Jerusalem for the celebration of Passover (2 Chr 30:1–5). The Chronicler shows that Israel united under the temple of the Lord in Jerusalem, and sees a theological implication that people from both

---

6. There is no internal evidence that points decisively to some specific date on which Baruch was written.

7. Determining the date of 1 Esdras is difficult, since it is primarily interested in reflecting on past history rather than providing clues to grasp the situation of the author. Thus deSilva believes that determination of date has rested on an examination of the vocabulary of the book, which appears to have much in common with the vocabulary of other second-century BCE works. See deSilva, *Introducing the Apocrypha*, 284.

8. The three options are as follows: (1) First Esdras was used as a source by the author of Ezra-Nehemiah; (2) 1 Esdras and Ezra-Nehemiah are both dependent on the original Chronicler's work; (3) 1 Esdras used Ezra-Nehemiah as a source.

Israel and Judah restored the broken community. For the Chronicler Passover was, therefore, a means of uniting people of all Israel, particularly the remnant.[9] The Chronicler enters into details regarding Josiah's Passover celebration (2 Chr 35) to which a brief reference is made in 2 Kings 23:21-23. He emphasizes that Passover had not been observed since the days of the prophet Samuel (2 Chr 35:18). For Passover was not a pilgrimage feast held at Jerusalem until Josiah's Passover. From the time of Josiah (640-609 BCE) until the destruction of the temple in 70 CE, Passover was a pilgrimage feast held at Jerusalem.[10]

Take your places in the temple as Levites in the prescribed order of your families in the presence of your brother Israelites; sacrifices for your brothers. Observe the Passover according to the ordinance of the Lord which was given to Moses (1 Esd 1:5-6). This abrupt beginning with a description of Passover under the reign of King Josiah implies its significance in the plot of 1 Esdras. It is, in fact, one of the most distinctive features of 1 Esdras that the narrator shows a greater interest in the observance of the feasts of Passover and Tabernacles in relation to the temple in Jerusalem. First Esdras consists of three different occasions (1 Esd 2:1-15; 5:7-43; 8:1-67) when Jewish exiles returned to Jerusalem—one in 538 BCE or soon after, headed by Sheshbazzar (2 Chr 36:22-23; Ezra 1:1-11); one in 520 BCE, headed by Zerubbabel (Ezra 2:1-67; Neh 7:6-69); and one in 397 BCE, headed by Ezra (Ezra 7:1—8:36).

For each occasion the observance of Passover and Tabernacles in relation to the temple at Jerusalem provides the main framework for the narrative (1 Esd 1:1-22, Passover: 5:47-73, Booths: 7:1-15, Passover: 9:55-?). *They observed the Feast of Tabernacles as enjoined in the law, and the proper sacrifices day by day; and thereafter the continual offerings, and sacrifices on Sabbaths, at new moons, and on all solemn feasts* (1 Esd 5:51-52). *The Israelites who had returned from exile kept the Passover on the fourteenth day of the first month.... All those Israelites participated who had returned from exile and had segregated themselves from the abominations of the peoples of the land to seek the Lord. They kept the Feast of Unleavened Bread for seven days, rejoicing before the Lord* (1 Esd 7:10, 13, 14).

---

9. The Chronicler mentions "men of Israel . . . who lived in the towns of Judah" (2 Chr 31:6) and "the people of Manasseh, Ephraim and the entire remnant of Israel" who join with "the people of Judah and Benjamin and the inhabitants of Jerusalem" (2 Chr 34:9).

10. Except for the period between 587 and 517/16 BCE.

Unlike Ezra, 1 Esdras 7:13 highlights the returnees who observed the feast, keeping marriage purity.[11] However, fifty years after the first returnee, 1 Esdras 9:4 designates the returnees as those who had returned from the captivity, mentioning nothing about those who had married heathen women (outside the family of Israel). As deSilva points out, 1 Esdras becomes less exclusive as the narrative comes to the end.[12] Nevertheless, the final episode of the narrative ends with the national repentance and elimination of non-Israelitish elements. In relation to the question of who can observe the pilgrimage feast and the boundary of "true Israel," 1 Esdras provides a precedent for those who made pilgrimage until the destruction of the temple in 70 CE.

In particular Ezra is introduced with a description of preparing for the journey from Babylon to Jerusalem. The safety of the journey is the main concern here. *There I made a vow that the young men should fast before our Lord to beg him to give us a safe journey for ourselves, our children who accompanied us, and our pack-animals. I was ashamed to ask the king for an escort of infantry and cavalry against our enemies; for we had told the king that the strength of our Lord would ensure success for those who looked to him. So once more we laid all these things before our Lord in prayer and found him gracious* (1 Esd 8:50–53). The pilgrim on his journey to Jerusalem, the dwelling place of God, can have great confidence that God, the keeper of Israel, will be his help and will keep him safe and secure because he trusts in God. The message of Psalm 121, a song of ascent, may be summed up in this way: "We left the river Theras on the twelfth day of the first month, and under the powerful protection which our Lord gave us we reached Jerusalem. He guarded us against every enemy on our journey, and so we arrived at Jerusalem" (1 Esd 8:61–62). As Ezra contemplated his journey with the returnees, he looked towards the route and final destination with both trepidation and anticipation. Ezra noted that God was there to guide and protect the returnees from danger encountered in the journey and that the final resting place was Jerusalem itself.

---

11. "The returnees and all who had joined them and separated themselves from the pollutions of the nations of the land" (Ezra 6:21). This verse clearly designates the two groups. For that reason deSilva claims that the Hebrew Ezra is certainly less exclusive. See deSilva, *Introducing the Apocrypha*, 291.

12. Ibid., 291–92.

PSEUDEPIGRAPHA

The motif of the journey to heaven is a vitally important phenomenon in the apocalypses. Apocalypses are typical of the Pseudepigrapha. Five figures in the Bible ascended to heaven: Enoch (Gen 5:24); Elijah (2 Kgs 2:1–12); Jesus (Luke 24:51; Acts 1:9); Paul (2 Cor 12:2-4); and John (Rev 4:1). The Jewish apocalyptic movement is frequently associated with famous figures drawn from the past, like Enoch, Abraham, and Levi. The famous figures as revealers of mysteries through heavenly journeys firmly fix 1 Enoch, Testaments of Abraham and Levi, and 3 Baruch in Pseudepigrapha, in the context of journey expectation. This aspect of the apocalyptic literature is the characteristic that makes the apocalyptic literature unique among Jewish literature. That the authors of the apocalyptic literature chose to convey the mysteries of God by means of a heavenly journey demonstrates the diversity of the use of the journey motif. It is noticeable that the motif of the otherworldly journey was widespread in the Hellenistic-Roman world.[13] Thus the thoroughly Jewish character of apocalypticism as it developed in Pseudepigrapha should be recognized in its Hellenistic Judaism context that was a product of its age.

The earliest Jewish apocalyptic movement is associated with the figure of Enoch. First Enoch embraces a series of vision accounts. While the emphasis is on the visionary experience of Enoch, it provides an example of the heavenly journey type often in an elaborated form.

First Enoch (second century BCE—first century CE)

Enoch walked with God; and he was not, for God took him (Gen 5:24). Genesis ascribes *walking with God* to Enoch and Noah. Enoch walked with God, setting a typological precedent. The invitation to walk with God is accompanied by eternal life. Enoch's life affirms that those who "walk with God" (Gen 5:22, 24) will experience life, not death. Thus Enoch's life, namely *walking with God*, was a preparation for being taken to God without tasting death. *Walking with God* denotes the intimate fellowship with God in considering the intimacy of Eden where God walked in the garden. The motif of *walking with God*, which is so embedded in Genesis, has become a fundamental image of pilgrimage and

---

13. Collins, "Apocalypses and Apocalypticism," 285.

journey metaphor in the tradition of the Israelites. Westermann, therefore, claims:

> The old tradition understood the words in the sense that Enoch stood in a direct and immediate relationship to God, (F. Delitzsch refers correctly to 3:8), and so was entrusted with God's plans and intentions. This is the starting point for the significance that the figure of Enoch had in a tradition that began early and reached its fullness only in the Apocalyptic Literature.[14]

It is no wonder that the walk metaphor is vividly embedded in 1–3 Enoch and 1–3 Baruch. Evidence in 1 Enoch 91–107 indicates that the narrative assumes God's imminent judgment and eternal blessing to the righteous who walk in the way of righteousness (1 En. 91:4, 19; 94:3–4; 99:10).

But walk in righteousness, my children, it shall lead you in the good paths: and righteousness shall be your friend (1 En. 91:4). *Now listen to me, my children, and walk in the way of righteousness, and do not walk in the way of wickedness, for all those who walk in the ways of injustice shall perish* (1 En. 91:19). *Do not walk in the evil way, or in the way of death! . . . Walk in the way of peace so that you shall have life and be worthy!* (1 En. 94:3–4).[15] Helfmeyer sees in the expression (Gen 5:22, 24) the meaning of *walking with God* as more than to "live a life pleasing to God"; it means "intimate companionship" with God, like that expressed in the divine revelations to Noah and perhaps also to Enoch.[16] It certainly means more than his virtuous way of life. It seems that 1 Enoch does not speak of *walk in the way* in the same way as Helfmeyer sees it. First Enoch, however, retains the image of the way (the paths of righteousness) in passages that speak of walking in the upright, blameless way, as is expressed in 1 Kings 8:36, Isaiah 57:2, Jeremiah 6:16, Psalm 101, and Proverb 8:20. A different sense is found in 2 Enoch. *Do not turn away from God. Walk before his face . . .* (2 En. [J] 2:2) *. . . and who walk without a defect before the face of the Lord* (1 En. [J] 9:1). *Enoch teaches his sons and all the elders of the people how they should walk with fear and trembling in front of the Lord* (2 En. [J] 66:1). In 2 Enoch *walk in the way* is replaced by *walk before his face*. Although these passages do not speak

---

14. Westermann, *Genesis 1–11*, 358.
15. All texts are taken from Charlesworth, *Old Testament Pseudepigrapha*.
16. Helfmeyer, "הָלַךְ," 394.

explicitly of walking in the ways of God, their context shows clearly that what is meant is conduct according to the will of God.

In 1 Enoch, who stands as a symbol of life with God forever without tasting death, is offered heavenly journeys (*1 En.* 12–36). *And behold I saw the clouds: And they were calling me in a vision; and the fogs were calling me to desire, and in the vision, the winds were causing me to fly and rushing me high up into heaven* (*1 En.* 14:8). As the title typified by the vision form indicates, 1 Enoch is typical of the apocalypses.[17] As the vision in the apocalypses is not published under its writer's name, but is attributed to a famous figure drawn from the past, a description of ascent is given in the vision form under the name of Enoch.

For Enoch the heavenly journey functions "as a foretaste or anticipation of a final or permanent ascent to heavenly life."[18] On the basis of his revealed knowledge of heaven, Enoch addressed certain instructions (*1 En.* 94–104) to his children. The already existent heavenly realities are an assurance of salvation for Enoch's instruction. Enoch's ascent in chapter 14 clearly indicates that judgment is the reason for Enoch's ascent as a central feature in the heavenly journeys.[19] First Enoch 12–16 relates a journey to the throne of God that climaxes in a word of judgment against the rebellious watchers. That places of punishment (Hades) and reward (paradise) are met in the heavens is a facet of most of the heavenly journeys.[20] Thus *walking with God* in Enoch's instruction carries with it a sense of walking towards an Enoch-like destination, as "life on the move towards the land," was for the Israelites as a nation, a life of obedience.[21] In chapters 17–19 Enoch was led on a cosmic tour by angels. This angel-guided journey is a typical prototype for the heavenly journey.

The direction of his journey is towards the west. In chapters 21–36 Enoch retraces his journey from the far northwest eastward to three gates of heaven in the north, west, and south through Jerusalem, the center of the earth. Thus, the goal of the journey, namely pilgrimage, for Enoch was no longer the earthly Jerusalem, but the heavenly Jerusalem, which he had already accessed. The spatial, horizontal, and vertical aspects of

---

17. Ezekiel 40–48 resembles the heavenly journeys of the apocalypses in form. Paul's own experience of ascent to Paradise (2 Cor 12:2–4) is a striking example in the NT.

18. Tabor, "Heaven, Ascent to," 93.

19. Dean-Otting, *Heavenly Journeys*, 63.

20. Ibid., 66.

21. Millar, *Now Choose Life*, 73.

Enoch's heavenly journey, including the point of departure and direction of the journey, indicate that this narrative is structured within the journey framework. Now 1 Enoch is telling its readers that the journey motif, which becomes the framework of the heavenly journeys, is already part of the biblical work, and is firmly rooted in biblical Judaism.

Testaments of the Twelve Patriarchs—Testament of Levi (second century BCE)

Like Enoch (1 *En.* 14), Levi makes his journey during a deep sleep (2:5). While Enoch's concern is with the fallen watchers, Levi sees the evil of the whole world and longs to be separated from it in order to be with God. The angel declares that Levi will have a place in the heavens.

You shall stand near the Lord, and you shall be his priest and you shall tell forth his mysteries to men. You shall announce the one who is about to redeem Israel. Through you and Judah the Lord will be seen by men, [by himself saving every race of humankind]. Your life shall be from the Lord's provision; he shall be to you as field and vineyard and produce, as silver and gold (T. Levi 2:10–12). *Because You shall stand near the Lord.* This passage indicates that God is the focus and the goal of the heavenly journey of Levi. The destination of the journey is bringing Levi to God himself. The idea of *being with God as his partner*, in particular, binds it to the creation narrative. God's presence was the central aspect of the garden. However, life outside the garden for humankind is not meant to be without God. If that is the case, life outside the garden would not have existed, for God is the source of life. God still remains in relationship with mankind, leaving hopeful signs for the future. Therefore, life outside the garden is better viewed not as life without God, but as "life away from one's true home."[22] The promised land is not utopia for the Israelites, for they are on their way to "the garden of the Lord" (Gen 13:10). They are no more than exiles wandering and yearning for a return to the Edenic state, the final destination of pilgrimage.

And you shall tell forth his mysteries to men. You shall announce the one who is about to redeem Israel (T. Levi 2:10). The emphasis on Levi as revealer of mysteries could be understood in the context of messianic expectation. For this reason Mary Dean-Otting believes that this aspect of the Testament of Levi is the characteristic that makes the Testament of

---

22. Birch, *Theological Introduction*, 51.

Levi unique among the heavenly journey texts.[23] The one who was taken into heaven and to whom mysteries were revealed becomes a declarer of mysteries and a teacher for the implication of mysteries. *And now, my children, I command you: Fear the Lord your God with your whole heart, and walk according to his law in integrity* . . . (T. Levi 13:1). As 1 and 2 Enoch indicate that the goal of Enoch's journey is to learn, thereafter, teach, the didactic role is one of striking developments that emerges as a result of the heavenly journey context. *Walking with God* as one of the main didactic teachings is also maintained in the Testament of Levi.

Third (Greek Apocalypse of) Baruch (first–third century CE) and Jubilees (second century BCE)

Lord, why have you set fire to your vineyard and laid it waste? Why have you done this? And why, Lord, did you not requite us with another punishment, but rather handed us over to such heathen so that they reproach us saying, "Where is their God?" (3 Bar. 1:2). Third Baruch that has the most highly developed texts of the heavenly journey begins with the question that occupies the rest of the book, "Where is their God?" This question reflects the growing perplexity at the destruction of Jerusalem and the temple. Third Baruch presents the heavenly journey in response to the question posed in the opening paragraph. As an answer to the question, God's power and concern is revealed in the course of the heavenly journey that takes place in a sleeping vision (3 Bar. 17:3). As usual the angel is sent to act as a guide to Baruch in the revelation of the mysteries of God.[24]

And taking me, he led me up to the first heaven and showed me a very large door. And he said to me, "Let us enter through it." And we entered as on wings about the distance of 30 days' journey (3 Bar. 2:2). Like 1 Enoch and the Testament of Levi, the journey in 3 Baruch is concerned with a revelation of the mysteries of God. The journey is once again the outward visible procedure through which God brought about his providence. In the same way that the knowing God motif became one of the main concerns for the Israelites in the Exodus (as it was in the Abrahamic and Jacob narrative), *knowing the mysteries of God* becomes the key experience for the heavenly journey. The theme of judgment and

---

23. Dean-Otting, *Heavenly Journeys*, 89–90.
24. In Ezekiel this angel guided-tour type of revelation is also found.

reward, a facet of most of the heavenly journeys, familiar to us from 1 Enoch and the Testament of Levi, is also detected here in the role of the archangel Michael.

As the title indicates, Martyrdom and Ascension of Isaiah (second century BCE–fourth century CE) is another typical example of the heavenly journey. In Isaiah's vision, he describes his journey up through the seven heavens (*Mart. Ascen. Isa.* 7:1—9:26). In the last part of the vision Isaiah sees the descent of "the Lord" through the seven heavens, his birth, life, death, resurrection and ascension (*Mart. Ascen. Isa.* 10:7—11:33).[25] In Testament of Abraham the heavenly journey serves as a vehicle to highlight issues of divine justice and mercy, rather than being the central role in the book. Martyrdom and Ascension of Isaiah and Testament of Abraham do share many features with the heavenly journeys of 1 Enoch, Testament of Levi, and 3 Baruch.

In History of the Rechabites (first to fourth century CE), God answered Zosimus's prayer for meeting the blessed one. Thus to see the blessed one he was able to journey over the great ocean and a dense cloud to an island where there is an intermediate state between the corruptible world and the heavenly realm (*Hist. Rech.* 1–3). The blessed ones are the Rechabites who departed from Jerusalem in the time of Jeremiah by the help of the angels of God (*Hist. Rech.* 8–10). To convey this unique thought in biblical and quasi-biblical literature a journey framework is adopted as a vehicle.

According to Jubilees (second century BCE) Abraham is the first to celebrate the Feast of Tabernacles *Sukkot* (*Jub.* 16:20–31). Jubilees relates how Abraham was rejoicing over and over again the promise of Isaac, characterizing *Sukkot* as the festival of joy. Levi, the son of Jacob, fulfilled the promise to Abraham and he and his sons were given the priesthood of God (*Jub.* 32:1–9). Jacob with Isaac and Rebecca came to Bethel for pilgrimage (*Jub.* 31) and celebrated the festival for his son Levi (*Jub.* 32). Having recounted Exodus 19–24, Jubilees closely links the Festival of Weeks with the covenant made at Mount Sinai. According to Jubilees, the Festival of Weeks was closely related to the renewal of the covenant and the Torah (*Jub.* 1:1), and had been celebrated in heaven from the day of creation on, and was the festival that Noah and his family first observed on earth (*Jub.* 6:18).[26] The covenant with Abraham, his circumcision, was

---

25. For this reason, chapters 6–11 are believed to be a Christian work.
26. Chapter 7 deals with the Festival of Weeks in Jubilees in detail.

made (*Jub.* 15:1; cf. 14:20) and Abraham died on this festival (*Jub.* 22:1). Jubilees 49 also deals with the Feast of Passover.[27]

DEAD SEA SCROLLS

There appears to be the same association between the Festival of Weeks and covenantal renewal ceremony in the Dead Sea Scrolls, despite the fact that there is no mention that this ritual was performed on the feast. Considering the close relation between the Qumran texts and Jubilees, it is likely that the Qumran community used the Festival of Weeks as the occasion for their annual covenantal ceremony in which they admitted new members and renewed the covenant (1QS I 16—2.18). Although the terms for the journey metaphor are not found, it can be readily appreciated just how central the *walk* הֹלֵךְ and *way* דֶּרֶךְ metaphor was to the authors of the Qumran manuscripts.[28] In a very real sense the *walking and way* metaphor becomes a metaphor for life itself. The walk and way metaphor emerges from allusions to Israel's journey, including the wilderness period, the destruction of Jerusalem, the cessation of the sacrificial cult and of the monarchy, and the experience of the exile that supplied the contours of the larger Judaic framework.

The Dead Sea Scrolls reflects a distinct use of הֹלַךְ (117 times [64 times in the rules; 11 times in hymns and poems; 10 times in calendars, liturgies, and prayers; 17 times in apocalyptic works; 7 times in Bible interpretation; 8 times in biblically based apocryphal works; and once in miscellanea]) and דֶּרֶךְ (75 times [35 times in the rules; 19 times in hymns and poems; 5 times in calendars, liturgies, and prayers; 14 times in apocalyptic works; 4 times in Bible interpretation, and once in miscellanea]), particularly for the movements of human life, the ethical ideal of human activity. Thus the Dead Sea Scrolls clearly indicate that the walk and way metaphor was deeply embedded in the life of Israel before the proclamation of Jesus Christ. For the metaphor is found everywhere in the Dead Sea Scrolls, in one form or another, shaping the way they saw themselves and the future.

It was taken for granted that the standards and sanctions of morality were firmly grounded in religious faith (the relationship with God).

---

27. Aristobulus (second century BCE) deals with astronomical characteristic of the date of Passover.

28. The term for journey is mentioned only once in the sense of travel of any distance being forbidden on holy days of rest (CD X 20).

Therefore, for the community the mainspring of the ethical ideal derived from a sense of the inner spiritual qualities rather than external qualities. According to the Manual of Discipline, the inner spiritual qualities must be cultivated, and then expressed in moral action. The individual aspect of the theology and ethics of the Qumran community cannot be appreciated without an understanding of their belief that God had called them into being, had chosen and redeemed them as a community. Thus the ethical ideal was community shaped. The essence of the ethical ideal was corporate. The community rule emphasizes the significance of walking together, " . . . so that in the midst of the men of the Community they may walk perfectly together in all that has been revealed to them" (1QS IX 19).[29] In the same way the opening section of Damascus Document stresses the fact that the exile was a result of sin that Israel as a whole had committed. *For when they were unfaithful and forsook Him, He hid His face from Israel and His Sanctuary and delivered them up to sword* (CD I 3-4).

Having made the point, we must emphasize that such a community-orientated ethic did not diminish the responsibility of the individual. In the very real sense of the responsibility of the individual, the walk and way metaphor can be viewed as a metaphor for life as a journey and for the practice of morality in the community. It appears that at Qumran he who walks on the good way obtains the rest of salvation. God's eyes were upon all the movements (ways and walking) of his people. He was able to see the movements in their heart and mind. The community, therefore, appealed to God's people to walk in his ways in order to establish a relationship with him. Particularly drawing a parallel between "walking in the light" and "walking in the darkness" (negative expressions: 1QS I 25, 1QS II 12, 1QS IV 12, 1QS V 11, 1QS V 5, 1QS VII 19, 1QS IX 10, 1QS XI 10), the Dead Sea Scrolls urge its community to walk in the light, and not in the darkness. There is a dynamic equivalent of this contrast in John 8:12: "Whoever follows me will never walk in darkness, but will have the light of life." In a very real sense in the history of Israel the new going down to Egypt in fulfillment of God's warning of judgment (CD VII 9-15) reflects *walking in the darkness*, whereas the return that led to a lengthy wilderness wandering (1QS VIII 12-14) was oriented towards *walking in the light*.

---

29. All texts are taken from Vermes, *Complete Dead Sea Scrolls*.

The terms *way* and *walk* do not stand alone as the defining feature of the community. They are yoked with the term *perfect* תְּמִים. The term *perfect* is often used with the term *way* (1QS IV 22, IX 2, 5) or *walk* (1QS I 8, VIII 1, IX 6, 9, 19) and sometimes with both (1QS II 2, III 9, VIII 18, 20, IX 8). *The sons of heaven to the perfect of way* (1QS IV 22). *As for the property of the men of holiness who walk in perfection . . .* (1QS IX 9). *And the Priests shall bless all the men of the lot of God who walk perfectly in all His ways* (1QS II 2). However, the meaning of "perfect" is still perplexing. If von Rad's point is taken on Genesis 6:9 and 17:1, *perfect* תְּמִים can be considered as the relational concept *the condition of a man pleasing to God*.[30] Moral faultlessness should, however, be on the agenda in the Dead Sea Scrolls, considering all the practical implications given. The image of *way* and *walk* speaks of walking in the good and blameless way (1QS II 2, 1QS III 10, 1QS V 10, 1QS V 20, 1QS VIII 4, 1QS VIII 20, 1QS IX 9, 1QS IX 11, 1QS IX 19), as the concept is retained in 1 Kings 8:36, Isaiah 57:2, Jeremiah 6:16, Psalm 101:6, and Proverbs 8:20. The community rule indicates that there are two ways for each man to choose: "walk in the spirit of truth or injustice and the ways of light or darkness" (1QS III 19–20). Although E. P. Sanders claims that salvation in Qumran thought simply means joining the sect, namely the covenant, due to the absence of soteriology in the teaching of the community,[31] the thanksgiving hymns in the Dead Sea Scrolls clearly points out that the Holy Spirit is the medium to make it possible for humanity to walk in the perfect way that leads to salvation. *The way of man is not established except by the spirit which God created for him to make perfect a way for the children of men* (1QH XII 32). By continuously challenging their people to choose to walk in the spirit of truth and the ways of light the community tried to distinguish itself from the outside world, calling themselves, "the Repenters of Israel" (CD IV 2, VI 5, VIII 16, XIX 29) and "the comers into the New Covenant" (CD VI 19, VIII 21, XIX 33). In this context, the distinctive *walk* and *way* was developed as *in his way*, the true way, in the community to interpret the Torah and the prophets (CD III 16–17, VI 2–11, VII 15–21).

It is, in particular, noticeable that the Qumran community (the Essenes) were known as "the Way" and the first Christians were also

---

30. Von Rad, *Genesis*, 126.

31. E. Sanders, "Covenant as a Soteriological Category," 40.

designated "The Way" (Acts 9:2; 19:9, 23; 22:4; 24:14, 22).[32] They were those who followed Jesus Christ. We also find Isaiah crying out in the strong messianic prophecy with the *walk and way* metaphor. *And a highway will be there; it will be called the Way of Holiness. The unclean will not journey on it; it will be for those who walk in that Way; wicked fools will not go about on it* (Isa 35:8). *Walk and way* are found everywhere in the Dead Sea Scrolls that tell how deeply the *metaphor* was embedded in the life of the community. With the perspective emerging from Israel's journey, including the wilderness period, the community saw themselves on the journey to the Way of Holiness. The community thus separated itself from unjust men and went into the wilderness to prepare the way for God's coming by studying the law of Moses. *And when these become members of the Community in Israel according to these rules, they shall separate from the habitation of unjust men and shall go into the wilderness to prepare there the way of Him; as it is written, Prepare in the wilderness the way of . . . make straight in the desert a path for our God. This path is the study of the Law which He commanded by the hand of Moses, that they may do according to all that has been revealed from age to age, and as the prophets have revealed by His Holy Spirit* (1QS VIII 13–15). The Dead Sea Scrolls, therefore, invest this metaphor with great depth of meaning and significance, envisaging the *walk* and *way* as the internalizing of the Torah.

PHILO

Echoes of the pilgrimage paradigm are—fragmentary as it may be—detectable in Philo's writings. The story of Abraham's migration in Philo's writings reflects significant literal and spiritual meaning to the journey Abraham took. Philo considers how Abraham's migration, the experience of his physical journey, relates to the spiritual. *God, wishing to purify the soul of man, first of all gives it an impulse towards complete salvation, namely, a change of abode, so as to quit the three regions of the body, the outward sense and speech according to utterance; for his country is the emblem of the body, and his kindred are the symbol of the outward sense, and his father's house of speech* (Migration 1:2).[33] Philo states that

---

32. It is still puzzling that the Essenes are never mentioned by name in the New Testament, nor in the Qumran literature.

33. Yonge, *Works of Philo*, 253. All quotations are taken from Yonge, *Works of Philo*.

a journey, *a change of abode*, is a means for God to purify the soul of man. God initiates journeys according to his sovereign plan. A driving force to journey, *an impulse towards a change of abode*, to purify our soul causes the tension between our rest, a tendency to cling to *status quo*, and our journey—that is to leave the three regions of the body (the country, the kindred, the father's house).

In Special Law 1 Philo again confirms that he who manages to quit his country, his friends, and his relations would make a pilgrimage to the temple. *He does not permit those who desire to perform sacrifices in their own houses to do so, but he orders all men to rise up, even from the furthest boundaries of the earth, and to come to this temple, by which command he is at the same time testing their dispositions most severely; for he who was not about to offer sacrifice in a pure and holy spirit would never endure to quit his country and his friends, and relations, and emigrate into a distant land, but would be likely, being under the influence of a more powerful attraction than that towards piety, to continue attached to the society of his most intimate friends and relations as portions of himself, to which he was most closely attached* (Spec. Law 1, XII 68-69). Philo must have made the pilgrimage himself in order to pray and make sacrifices. *At the time when I was on my journey towards the temple of my native land for the purpose of offering up prayers and sacrifices therein* (Providence 2, 64). He reports his encounters on the way to Jerusalem. *And the most evident proof of this may be found in the events which actually took place. For innumerable companies of men from a countless variety of cities, some by land and some by sea, from east and from west, from the north and from the south, came to the temple at every festival . . .* (Spec. Law 1, XII 69). We also note that in Special Law 2 the Passover is interpreted as a symbol of the journey from body to spirit in connection with the purification of the soul.[34] Thus Philo believes that the tension between our rest and our journey is a continuing and necessary element, for humans need to be set free in order to depart from the three regions of the body and outward senses that represent home *a comfort zone*. Home seems to be better than a journey. The home, however, leads to spiritual blindness,

---

34. Ibid., 582. Philo mentions ten festivals in Special Law 2. Philo finds the real meaning of Sabbath and festivals not in their commemoration of some events in Jewish history, but in their mystic symbolism. Three festivals (Passover, Pentecost, and Tabernacles) in connection with pilgrimage are dealt with in depth in chapters 5, 6, and 7.

whereas a journey brings future, which leads to true rest, the full comprehension of God.

Then, opening the road for itself, and hoping by travelling along it to arrive at a notion of the father of the universe, so difficult to be understood by any guesses or conjectures, when it has come to understand itself accurately, it will very likely be able to comprehend the nature of God; no longer remaining in Charran, that is in the organs of outward sense, but returning to itself. For it is impossible, while it is in the state of motion, in a manner appreciable by the outward sense rather than by the intellect, to arrive at a proper consideration of God (*Migration* 35:195). For Israelites the Exodus was not mere rescue, but an experience of knowing God. This was seen first in the Lord's encounter with Abraham and Jacob. Philo believes that knowing God through the encounter with God on the way *was* the key experience for Abraham. The journey for Abraham led him to discover who God was. Thus journey, pilgrimage, is not just a physical movement, but also a faith movement that encompasses *knowing God* and *obedience to God as a consequence of knowing God*. Those who take a journey and labor to go through with the journey will be given the prize of victory, *a proper consideration of God = knowing who God is*. The primary reason to journey for Abraham was to know God as it was to Israelites in the wilderness. *Then you will know that I am the Lord your God* (Exod 6:7).

Philo clearly confirms this in *On the Virtues. Moreover, after the lawgiver has established commandments respecting one's fellow countrymen, he proceeds to show that he looks upon strangers also as worthy of having their interests attended to by his laws, since they have forsaken their native land and their national customs, and the sacred temples of their gods, and the worship and honor which they had been wont to pay to them, and have migrated with a holy migration, changing their abode of fabulous inventions for that of the certainty and clearness of truth, and of the worship of the one true and living God. Accordingly, he commands the men of his nation to love the strangers, not only as they love their friends and relations, but even as they love themselves . . .* (*Virtues* 20:102–104). In chapter 1 the Abrahamic pilgrimage is outlined as the transformation that Abraham underwent from the stage of having a relationship with a personal god to that of having the relationship with the one true and living God. Philo, having interpreted Abraham as the prototype of proselytes, elucidates proselytes in the new sense of migration from his native country and its polytheism to the place of discovering the one true and living God. We see that the one true God had patiently and diligently waited until Abraham came to the stage where he finally and fully recognizes the one true God. Until then, Abraham's journey had to go on.

This same principle may also apply missiologically. *And the most visible proof of this migration in which the mind quitted astronomy and the doctrines of the Chaldaeans, is this. For it is said in the Scriptures that the very moment that the wise man quitted his abode, "God appeared unto Abraham," to whom, therefore, it is plain that he was not visible before, when he was adhering to the studies of the Chaldaeans, and attending to the motions of the stars, not properly comprehending any nature whatever, which was well arranged and appreciable by the intellect only, apart from the world and the essence perceptible by the outward senses. But after he changed his abode and went into another country he learnt of necessity that the world was subject, and not independent; not an absolute ruler, but governed by the great cause of all things who had created it, whom the mind then for the first time looked up and saw* (Abraham 27:77–78). Internalizing journey in a missiological sense, Philo sees that the reason to change abode is to leave his educational and cultural background that has founded his worldview, the studies of the Chaldaeans, and attending to the motions of the stars. For the conception based on his background is a hindrance to seeing God properly. Thus the change of abode is to escape from the background, to change his worldview, so that he may fully apprehend and see the God who is the absolute rule of the world. For Abraham the journey, the change of abode, was the empowering of the mind to apprehend the God who was beyond both material and immaterial natures and had created both. It appears that the change of abode, journey, guarantees homecoming too. To Philo only those who take a journey, wrestling and laboring with outward senses, are given the prize of homecoming.

And for this reason the following scripture has been given to men, "Return to the land of thy father and to thy family, and I will be with thee;" which is equivalent to saying, you have been a perfect wrestler for me, and you have been thought worthy of the prize and crown of victory, virtue having been the establisher of the contest and prospering to give prizes of victory; and now get rid of your fondness for contention, that you may not be always laboring but that you may be able to enjoy the fruit of your labors, which will never happen to you if you remain here dwelling among the objects of the eternal senses . . . (Migration 5:27–28). Return to the land of thy father and to thy family, and I will be with thee. Hebrews interprets this homecoming in connection with the heavenly place. The goal of pilgrimage (journey) for Hebrews is not the earthly Jerusalem, but the heavenly Jerusalem. For Philo the conclusive pinnacle of journey was homecoming and the completion of the promise, "I will be with thee"—"I will be their God" (Gen 17:8) that God made with Abraham and Jacob. The promise was also the continuous reminder to the people of God of his presence with them (Exod 25:8). Philo, however, clearly states that nothing will happen unless he leaves the *status quo*. For Philo the Abraham narrative teaches that a response to God involves a wholehearted commitment including the change of abode and making a journey from the inner being. God patiently and diligently waited until Abraham, Jacob, and the people of God on the journey came to the stage of full appreciation of God. By fully grasping God they realized that the primary destination of the journey was God himself who was their God. *I bore you on eagles' wings and brought you to myself* (Exod 19:4). Looking at Abraham's narrative offering a story centered around a journey, Philo saw a clear typological link between Abraham's journey and Israel's and offered the literal, allegorical, and spiritual meaning of the journeys of Abraham. Thus in Philo Abraham as the founder of the nation becomes a perfect example for Israel.

Due to his Hellenistic speculation, we tend to treat Philo's ideas as unique, not taking his theory as being truly representative of Jewish thought. However, as far as the pilgrimage paradigm is concerned, his missiological background, *the Hellenistic influence with Jewish background*, might have led him to offer the above interpretation.

JOSEPHUS

Unlike Philo, there is no evidence to show how Josephus saw the change of abode, the journey, in relation to migration and pilgrimage. Louis Feldman, however, traces the way Josephus, a Diaspora Jew, viewed the exile. On the supposition that Josephus had two audiences (his fellow Jews and the Romans) in mind when wrote his writings, Feldman suggests that his deepest felt sentiments, as seen in his *The Life*, are to view the Diaspora positively, and in sharp contrast to Philo (*Rewards* 29.165), who envisages an ingathering of the exiled Jewish people, he clearly regarded the exile as "everlasting and never foresees an end to it."[35]

In his writings Josephus shows that the pilgrimage practice exerted a great impact on the Jews. Seeing himself as a Diaspora Jew, he seems to place pilgrimage to the Second Temple in a primary setting. *Let there be then one city of the land of Canaan . . . Let there also be one temple therein, and one altar, not reared of hewn stones, but of such as you gather together at random . . . And let there be neither an altar nor a temple in any other city; for God is but one, and the nation of the Hebrews is but one* (Ant. 4.200). *There ought also to be but one temple for one God; for likeness is the constant foundation of agreement* (Ag. Ap. 2.193).[36] *One temple for one God.* With these words the Jewish historian, Josephus, testifies in effect that during the time of the Second Temple, pilgrimage to Jerusalem was one of the most widespread religiously motivated movements of the people. At the heart of the festivals the temple in Jerusalem stood. Josephus indicates that within the Jewish community the Second Temple played a very powerful unifying part, motivating several aspects of pilgrimage to it.

According to Josephus, pilgrimage to the temple in Jerusalem was often undertaken by whole towns or by large numbers of people from many cities on the three feasts of Passover, Pentecost, and Tabernacles. *But when Cestius had marched from Antipatris to Lydda, he found the city empty, of its men, for the whole multitude were gone up to Jerusalem to the feast of tabernacles* (J.W. 2.515). Josephus affirms that a countless number of pilgrims came from Galilee, Edom, Jericho, as well as Transjordan. The Jews said this Pentecost (i.e., the fiftieth day) was at hand, ". . . *Wherefore an immense multitude ran together, out of Galilee, and Idumea, and Jericho, and Perea . . .*" (J.W. 2.42-43). *The great part of whom were indeed of the same nation [with the citizens of Jerusalem], but not belonging to the city itself; for they were come up from all the country to the feast of unleavened bread* (J.W. 6.421-22). Josephus indicates that the amount of time necessary for a sixty-five-mile journey from the south of Galilee to Jerusalem was a three-day journey. *It was absolutely necessary for those that go quickly [to Jerusalem] to pass through that country; for in that road you may, in three day's time go from Galilee to Jerusalem* (Life 269). Thus a three-day journey to celebrate a festival to God in Exodus

---

35. Feldman, "Concept of Exile," 172. On this point Feldman quotes Wolfson.
36. All quotations are taken from Whiston, *Josephus*.

3:18 and 5:1 probably echoes the standard length for a pilgrimage journey. For the three-day journey from Galilee to Jerusalem the pilgrims had to go through Samaria (*Life* 269). However, due to the complexities with the Samaritans (*J.W.* 2.223-32; *Ant.* 20.118), alternative routes—the Jordan Valley, the Jericho-Jerusalem route, or the Mount Ephraim-Antipatris-Jerusalem route—were followed.[37]

The pilgrimage was not limited to Jews in Israel. There is a text in Josephus that speaks of the Diaspora Jews and foreigners from beyond the Euphrates who made a four-month's journey with a great effort in order to offer their sacrifices to God in the temple. *For still some there have been, who have come from the parts beyond Euphrates, a journey of four months, through many dangers and at great expenses, in honor of our temple . . .* (*Ant.* 3.318). Though it was hardly the case that everyone in the Diaspora or even in the land of Israel made a pilgrimage to the temple in Jerusalem, the number of Jewish pilgrims to the temple figured by Josephus was 2,565,000 pilgrims (*J.W.* 6.423-26). The governor, Cestius, counted 256,500 paschal lambs at one Passover festival. Allowing ten people to one lamb, this would make 2,565,000 pilgrims. Josephus relates that the riots against the Roman government often erupted during the feasts (*J.W.* 1.88; 2.224). Considering the size of Jerusalem the question of how it could accommodate such a great multitude is raised. In his description of how the people raised a sedition against Archelaus, Josephus affirms that the pilgrims slept in the city itself or in tents around the city (*Ant.* 17.213-17). Although it is not certain that Jerusalem with surrounding area was spacious enough for those immense multitudes to sojourn, Josephus shows that the pilgrims were received by the Jerusalemites with warm hospitality.

Let those that live as remote as the bounds of the land which the Hebrews shall possess, come to that city where the temple shall be, and this three times in a year, that they may give thanks to God for his former benefits, and may entreat him for those they shall want hereafter; and let them, by this means, maintain a friendly correspondence with one another by such meetings and feastings together—for it is good thing for those that are of the same stock, and under the same institution of laws, not to be unacquainted with each other; which acquaintance will be maintained by thus conversing together, and by seeing and talking with one another, and so renewing the memorials of this union; for if they do not thus converse

---

37. Safrai and Stern, *Jewish*, 901.

together continually, they will appear like mere strangers to one another (*Ant.* 4.203–204). This source clearly indicates that pilgrimage was a corporate event for those who joined it. Philo of Alexandria also emphasizes that the pilgrimage practice reinforced the corporate identity of the people of God following the building of a friendship and a compelling certainty of unity in the one God. *Ties of friendship are created between those who did not know each other before, and the sacrifices and libations are occasions of emotional exchange which provide the strongest certainty that all are of one mind* (*Spec. Law* 1, 68). Since the object of the pilgrimage was, as Josephus stresses, to bring about friendship and congregate together for discussions and festive meals in common, the pilgrimage was not only an individual experience but also a corporate experience of the people of God. Thus the encounter with God and yearning for salvation, the aims of pilgrimage, through offering a sacrifice were preceded by fellowship with the people of God on the way to Jerusalem and in the city.

There was also on the other side one southern and one northern gate, through which was a passage into the court of the women . . . This place was allotted to the women of our own country, and of other countries, provided they were of the same nation (*J.W.* 5.199). The evidence that the pilgrimage to the temple was not joined only by men but also large numbers of women including many from the Diaspora suggests that the whole family might have often taken part in pilgrimage. Together with the evidence, the fact that pilgrimage to the temple was often participated in by whole towns or by large numbers of people (*J.W.* 2.515), reinforces the corporate aspect of pilgrimage from the very beginning. This source also alludes to the fact that the pilgrims probably came to a decision to take part in pilgrimage by corporate initiation rather than by individual initiation or determination.

RABBINIC LITERATURE

The Rabbinic literature is an enormously complex collection of traditional liturgies and prayers, legal writings (Mishnah, Tosefta, Palestinian, and Babylonian Talmud), and biblical expositions (Midrashim and Targumim). The pilgrimage practice found in the legal writings confirms a continuity of the tradition in and after Second Temple times.

All are liable for an appearance offering [before the Lord] (Exod 23:14; Deut 16:16) *except a deaf-mute, an idiot, a minor . . . (m. Hag. 1:1).*[38] Three times in the year were the Israelites commanded to go on pilgrimage: on the Feast of Unleavened Bread, on the Feast of Weeks and on the Feast of Booths (*b. Hag.* 7a). Although there are clear indications (*m. Hag.* 1:1; *b. Hag.* 2a, 2b, 7b) that various individuals were exempted from the pilgrimage practice, the Mishnah and Talmud, as in Exodus 23:17 and Deuteronomy 16:16, speak of the obligation to make a pilgrimage. In particular, the Babylonian Talmud confines the practice to those who possessed land. *For R. Ammi said: Every man who owns land must make the Festival pilgrimage (b. Pesah. 8b).*[39] H. Freedman supplies an additional note on this. For him the fact confirms that the Almighty assures the pilgrim that his land will be safe in his absence, which proves that the command refers only to those who possess land.[40] The Mishnah and Babylonian Talmud seem to view the pilgrimage practice as an important religious responsibility. However, Pesahim 1:1 in the Mishnah suggests that making a pilgrimage three times a year is not an absolute requirement but a positive command that is encouraged. *These are the things for which no measure is prescribed: Pesah, First fruit, the Festal Offering, deeds of loving-kindness and the study of the Law (m. Pesah. 1:1).*[41] Having considered that making a pilgrimage three times a year was not a viable obligation for ordinary people, it was quite probable that people might have gone to the temple in Jerusalem every year or once in several years, or even only once in a lifetime. Typically it could be only once in their lifetime for many in the Diaspora. On this point there is enough evidence in the Scriptures. Luke writes that Jesus' parents made a pilgrimage to Jerusalem once every year. The fact that the Synoptic Gospels record only one visit of Jesus to Jerusalem on Passover confirms that Jesus did not make the pilgrimage on each feast every year, although John's Gospel mentions several pilgrimages of Jesus.

Although Tosefta allows individuals or families in "caravans" to make a pilgrimage to Jerusalem by themselves (*t. Bikkurim* 2:12), the Babylonian Talmud emphasizes the corporate aspect of the pilgrimage

38. All quotations for the Mishnah are taken from Neusner, *Mishnah*.
39. Freedman, "Pesahim," 36.
40. Ibid.
41. Deuteronomy 16 provides that all male Israelites shall appear thrice a year in the temple.

practice, asking the male pilgrims to form a group for their journey. *They must not appear in divisions, for it is said: All thy males . . .* (*b. Hag.* 7a).

Josephus also describes the pilgrimage participation by whole towns or by large numbers of people from many cities (*J.W.* 2.515). There must have been a safety concern to reduce any risk involved on their journey. The corporate aspect of the pilgrimage practice tells that what was happening among the group on the way to the temple was a meaningful process prior to an appearance offering before the Lord. As they journeyed closer to Jerusalem, the importance of family ties, as Edward Reeves points out, might have broken down in favor of more general societal ties.[42]

The Mishnah (*m. Bikkurim* 3:2-5) shows how pilgrims traveled to the temple for Booths (Tabernacles). *[The men of] all the smaller towns that belonged to the Maamad gathered together in the town of the Maamad . . .* (*m. Bikkurim* 3:2). Villagers would assemble in their towns and then go to the main town in the district for the night. On the next day they would journey with their offerings of fruits to Jerusalem. After gathering in Jerusalem, pilgrims would proceed to the temple. *Early in the morning the officer [of the Maamad] said, Arise ye and let us go up to Zion unto the Lord our God. They that were near [to Jerusalem] brought fresh figs and grapes . . . The flute was played before them until they drew nigh to Jerusalem. When they had drawn nigh to Jerusalem they sent messengers before them and bedecked their First-fruits* (*m. Bikkurim* 3:3-5). The Mishnah provides a vivid picture for procession that pilgrims would be met by the music of the flute until they reached the Temple Mount. The Mishnah also reports how Passover was celebrated in Jerusalem (*m. Pesah.* 5.5-10). In the process the priests were to take the sacrificial portions of the lamb for burnt offerings and return the rest to the people. After nightfall the people roasted their offerings, and the seder meal took place after the sacrifice (Matt 26:27-30).

As the entire family including sons and daughters participated in the pilgrimage, women also participated in the festal rejoicing of the family offerings, but were not obliged to offer sacrifices at the pilgrimage apart from the times when it was incumbent upon them to do so (*b. Hag.* 6b; *b. Pesah.* 89a). The Mishnah hints that the pilgrims remained in Jerusalem until the end of feast-days throughout all the feasts (*m.*

---

42. Reeves remarks that pilgrimage breaks down the importance of family ties in favor of more general societal ties. See Reeves, *Hidden Government*, 54.

ZebaHim 11:7; b. ZebaHim 97a). During the whole period, the pilgrims would interact with teachers of law, prophets, and scholars, and avail themselves of the public of Jerusalem, making friendships with them. Psalm 15 seems to reflect this picture of the temple courts. A religious leader asks the pilgrim questions and then responds to the pilgrim with an appropriate promise. Luke also speaks of Jesus interacting with the people in the temple courts for the Feast of Passover (Luke 2:45–47).

Conclusion

The Second Temple period was an age of definition for Judaism. In Judaism, of course, the Second Temple period was a time of sects and heresies and divisions and splits and schools of all sorts as Judaism tried to figure out exactly what Judaism was. Thus a study of the New Testament and of early Christianity without an intimate knowledge of Jewish sources might lead to inaccurate and fragmentary results. Jewish literature from the Second Temple period contains many allusions to and information on pilgrimage customs and practices. Jewish literatures from the period examined shows the presence of the pilgrimage paradigm. Baruch in the Apocrypha is a classic example of the claim.

The whole story of Tobit brings together two very different people in different places through a journey and is structured within the journey framework. The fact that the narrative employs the language and imagery of pilgrimage (pilgrimage feast) and journey implies that the narrative of Tobit is deeply concerned with the problem of exile and is convinced of the future in terms of a restoration of Zion (Tob 13:2, 5–6, 16–17; 14:5). Thus the literal journey as walking towards the promise was the prerequisite of bringing the promise into reality. The journey of Tobias, which is artfully structured in the narrative, probably shows that the journey of exile as the punishment of God (Tob 13:5, 9; 14:4) is not the end of history, but a means of bringing the promise into actualization, including knowing who God is through his protection and guidance, and returning to the promised land of blessing. The outcome of Tobias's journey presents this expectation. In the same manner, Baruch also provides a framework for understanding the nation's exile and restoration. The physical journey, namely walking, became the outward visible procedure through which God brought about his providence. Therefore, in 1 Esdras, Ezra contemplated his journey with the returnees and looked towards the route and final destination with both trepidation and anticipation. Ezra confirmed that God was there to guide and protect the returnees from danger encountered on the journey and that the resting place of the final journey was Jerusalem.

First Enoch, Testaments of Abraham and Levi, and 3 Baruch in the Pseudepigrapha present the famous figures as revealers of mysteries through the heavenly journeys in the context of journey expectation. This aspect of apocalyptic literature is the characteristic that makes apocalyptic literature unique among Jewish literature. That the authors of apocalyptic literature chose to convey the mysteries of God by means of a heavenly journey demonstrates the diversity of the use of the journey motif. Although the terms for pilgrimage or journey metaphor are not found in the Dead Sea Scrolls, it can readily be appreciated just how central the *walk* הָלַךְ and *way* דֶּרֶךְ metaphor was to the authors of the Qumran manuscripts. In a very real sense the *walking and way* metaphor becomes a metaphor for life. The *walk and way* metaphor emerges from allusion to Israel's journey including the wilderness period, the destruction of Jerusalem, the cessation of the sacrificial cult and of the monarchy, and the experience of the exile, which supplied the contours of the larger Judaic framework. Philo sums up the reason why God has used a physical journey to reveal his will and change his people, showing how Abraham's physical journey, the change of abode, relates to the spiritual meaning of journey, and seeing a clear typological link between Abraham's journey and Israel's journey. In his writings Josephus shows that the pilgrimage practice exerted a great impact on the Jews. Seeing himself as a Diaspora Jew, he seems to place pilgrimage to the Second Temple in a primary setting. Having provided a whole picture of the pilgrimage practice in the Second Temple period, Josephus and the rabbinic works clearly report how deeply the pilgrimage practice in relation to the three feasts was embedded in the everyday life of the Israelites.

The presence of the pilgrimage paradigm in a collection of Jewish literature from the Second Temple period indicates that we should not overlook the available Jewish sources in arriving at a more precise understanding of the origins of Christianity.

Bibliography

Abraham, I. "Hagigah." In *The Babylonian Talmud: Seder Mode,* edited by I. Epstein. Vol. 2. London: Soncino, 1938.
Ackroyd, Peter. *Exile and Restoration.* London: SCM, 1968.
Alders, G. Charles. *Genesis.* Vol. 1. Grand Rapids: Zondervan, 1981.
Alexander, T. Desmond. *From Paradise to the Promised Land: An Introduction to the Pentateuch.* Carlisle: Paternoster & Baker, 2002.
Andersen, Øivind, and Vernon. K. Robbins. "Paradigms in Homer, Pindar, the Tragedians and the New Testament." In *The Rhetoric of Pronouncement, Semeia* 64, edited by Vernon K. Robbins. Missoula, MT: Scholars, 1994.
Anderson, A. A. *2 Samuel.* Dallas: Word, 1989.
Anderson, Bernhard W. *Contours of Old Testament Theology.* Minneapolis: Fortress, 1999.
———. *Creation in the Old Testament.* London: SPCK, 1984.
———. *From Creation to New Creation.* Minneapolis: Fortress, 1994.
Armstrong, Karen. *In the Beginning: A New Interpretation of Genesis.* New York: Ballantine, l996.
Ashbey, Godfrey. "The Lamb of God." *JTSA* 21.1 (Dec 1977) 63–65.
Baban, Octavian. "Luke's 'on the Road' Encounters as Narrative Mimesis: A Contribution to the Study of Luke's Theology of the Way, The Narrative Anatomy and Function of Luke's Post-Easter Hodos Encounters." PhD diss., London: Brunel University, 1998.
Bailey, Kenneth E. *Poet and Peasant: A Literary-cultural Approach to the Parables in Luke.* Grand Rapids: Eerdmans, 1976.
Baker, Joshua, and Earnest W. Nicholson, eds. and trans. *The Commentary of Rabbi 22.* Cambridge: Cambridge University Press, 1973.
Barker, David G. "The Lord Watches Over You: A Pilgrimage Reading of Psalm 121." *BSac* 152.606 (Apr 1995) 163–81.
Barr, James. *The Concept of Biblical Theology: An Old Testament Perspective.* Philadelphia: Fortress, 1999.
———. *The Garden of Eden and the Hope of Immortality: The Read-Tuckwell Lectures for 1990.* London: SCM, 1992.
Barrett, Charles K. *The Acts of the Apostles.* Vol. 1, Acts 1–14. London: T&T Clark, 2004.
———. *Essays on John.* Philadelphia: Westminster, 1982.
———. *The Gospel According to St. John: An Introduction with Commentary and Notes on the Greek Text.* London: SPCK, 1978.
Barth, Christopher, and Geoffrey W. Bromiley, eds. *God With Us: A Theological Introduction to the Old Testament.* Grand Rapids: Eerdmans, 1991.

Bartholomew, Craig, and Fred Hughes, eds. *Explorations in a Christian Theology of Pilgrimage*. Hants: Ashgate, 2004.
Bassler, Jouette M. "The Galilean: A Neglected Factor in Johannine Community Research." *CBQ* 43.2 (Apr 1981) 243–57.
Batey, Richard. *New Testament Issues*. New York: Harper & Row, 1970.
Beasley-Murray, George R. *John*. Word Biblical Commentary 36. Waco, TX: Word, 1987.
Beck, Brian E. *Christian Character in the Gospel of Luke*. London: SPCK, 1989.
Bergsma, John S. "Once again, the Jubilee, Every 49 or 50 Years?" *VT* 55.1 (2005) 121–25.
Bernard, John H. *A Critical and Exegetical Commentary on the Gospel according to St. John*. Vol. 1. Edinburgh: ICC, 1962.
Billington, Anthony. *Mission and Meaning: Essays presented to Peter Cotterell*. Carlisle: Paternoster, 1995.
Birch, Bruce C., et al. *A Theological Introduction to the Old Testament*. Nashville: Abingdon, 1999.
Blocher, Henri. *In The Beginning: The Opening Chapters of Genesis*. Leicester: InterVarsity, 1984.
Blomberg, Craig L. "Midrash, Chiasmus, and the Outline of Luke's Central Section." In *Gospel Perspectives: Studies in Midrash and Historiography*, edited by R. T. France and David Wenham, vol. 3, 217–61. Sheffield: JSOT, 1983.
Blosser, Don W. "The Sabbath Year Cycle in Josephus." *HUCA* 52.01 (2004) 129–39.
Bock, Darrell L. *Luke, volume 1:1:1—9:50*. Grand Rapids: Baker, 2004.
———. *Luke, volume 2:9:51—24:53*. Grand Rapids: Baker, 2004.
———. *Proclamation From Prophecy and Pattern: Lucan Old Testament Christology*. JSNT 12. Sheffield: Sheffield Academic Press, 1987.
Boice, James Montgomery. *Genesis: An Expositional Commentary*. Edinburgh: B. McCall Barbour, 1982.
Borchert, Gerald L. *John 1–11*. New American Commentary 25A. Nashville: Broadman & Holman, 1996.
Bratcher, Robert G., and William D. Reyburn. *Psalms*. New York: United Bible Societies, 1976.
Brooke, George J., ed. *Temple Scroll Studies: Papers presented at the International Symposium on the Temple Scroll*. Journal for the Study of the Pseudepigrapha: Supplementary Series 7. Sheffield: Sheffield Academic Press, 1989.
Brooks, R., ed. *Reconciliation and Hope, New Testament Essays presented to L. L. Morris on his 60th birthday*. Carlisle: Paternoster, 1974.
Brown, Raymond E. *The Birth of the Messiah: A Commentary on the Infancy Narratives in the Gospels of Matthew and Luke*. London: Geoffrey Chapman, 1993.
———. *The Gospel according to John I–XII*. New York: Doubleday, 1966.
———. *The Gospel according to John XIII–XXI*. New York, Doubleday, 1970.
———. "Johannine Ecclesiology—The Community's Origin." *Interpretation* 31 (1977) 379–93.
Bruce, Frederick F. *The Acts of the Apostles*. Grand Rapids: IVP, 1990.
———. *The Book of Acts*. Grand Rapids: Eerdmans, 1988.
Brueggemann, Walter. *First and Second Samuel*. Louisville: John Knox, 1990.
———. *Genesis*. Interpretation: A Bible Commentary for Teaching and Preaching. Atlanta: John Knox, 1982.

———. *Ichabod Toward Home: The Journey of God's Glory.* Grands Rapids: Eerdmans, 2002.

———. *The Land, Place as Gift, Promise, and Challenge in Biblical Faith.* Philadelphia: Fortress, 1977.

———. *Theology of the Old Testament: Testimony, Dispute, Advocacy.* Minneapolis: Fortress, 1997.

Brumberg-Kraus, Jonathan. "'Not by Bread Alone . . .': The Ritualization of Food and Table Talk in the Passover Seder and in the Last Supper." *Semeia* 86.1 (1999) 165–91.

Bultmann, Rudolf K. "γινώσκω." In *TDNT* 1 (1977) 689–719.

———. *The Gospel of John: A Commentary.* Oxford: Basil Blackwell, 1971.

Burge, Gary M. *Interpreting the Gospel of John.* Guides to New Testament Exegesis. Grand Rapids: Baker, 1992.

———. *John.* NIV Application Commentary. Grand Rapids: Zondervan, 2000.

———. "Territorial Religion and the Vineyard of John 15." In *Jesus of Nazareth: Lord and Christ: Essays on the Historical Jesus and New Testament Christology*, edited by Joel B. Green and Max Turner, 384–96. Grand Rapids: Eerdmans, 1994.

Busey, Robert S. "Between Text and Sermon, Luke 22:7–23." *Interpretation* 52.1 (Jan 1998) 70–73.

Caird, George B. *The Gospel of St. Luke.* Baltimore: Penguin, 1963.

Calvin, John. *Genesis* (1563). Edinburgh: Banner of Truth, 1965.

Caragounis, Chrys C. "Jesus, his Brothers and the Journey to the Feast." *SEA* 63 (1998) 177–87.

Carroll, Thomas K. "The Council and the Jubilee." *DRev.* 413 (2000) 235–42.

Carson, David A. *The Gospel according to John.* Leicester: IVP, 1991.

Casey, Maurice. *Is John's Gospel True?* London: Routledge, 1996.

———. "Method in our Madness and Madness in their Methods: Some Approaches to the Son of Man Problem in Recent Scholarship." *JSNT* 42 (1991) 17–43.

Casperson, Lee W. "Sabbatical, Jubilee, and the Temple of Solomon." *VT* 53.3 (2003) 283–96.

Cassem, N. H. "A Grammatical and Contextual Inventory of the Use of Kosmos in the Johannine Corpus with some Implications for a Johannine Cosmic Theology." *NTS* 19 (1972) 81–91.

Cassuto, Umberto. *A Commentary on the Book of Genesis, Part 1: from Adam to Noah, Genesis I–VI 8.* Jerusalem: Hebrew University Magnes Press, 1961.

———. *A Commentary on the Book of Genesis, Part 2: From Noah to Abraham, Genesis VI 9–XI 32.* Jerusalem: Hebrew University Magnes Press, 1992.

Ceresko, Anthony R. "Psalm 121: Prayer of a Warrior?" *Biblica* 70.4 (1989) 496–510.

Charlesworth, James H., ed. *The Old Testament Pseudepigrapha, Volume 1 Apocalyptic Literature and Testaments.* London: Doubleday, 1983.

———. *The Old Testament Pseudepigrapha, Volume 2 Expansions of the Old Testament And Legends, Wisdom and Philosophical Literature, Prayers, Psalms, and Odes, Fragments of Lost Judeo-Hellenistic Works.* London: Doubleday, 1985.

Childs, Brevard S. *The Book of Exodus.* London: SCM, 1974.

Christensen, Duane L. *Deuteronomy 1–11.* Word Biblical Commentary 6A. Dallas: Word, 1991.

Clements, Ronald E. *Deuteronomy.* Old Testament Guides. Sheffield: JSOT, 1989.

———. *Old Testament Theology: A Fresh Approach.* London: Marshall, Morgan & Scott, 1978.

Clifford, Richard J. *The Cosmic Mountain in Canaan and the Old Testament*. Harvard Semitic Monographs 4. Cambridge: Harvard University Press, 1972.

Cohen, Shaye J. D. *Josephus in Galilee and Rome: His Vita and Development as a Historian*. Leiden: Brill, 1979.

Collins, John J. "Apocalypses and Apocalypticism (Early Jewish Apocalypticism)." In *ABD* 1, edited by David Noel Freedman, 282–283.

Comfort, P. W., and W. C. Hawley. *Opening the Gospel of John*. Wheaton: Tyndale, 1994.

Conzelmann, Hans. "φῶς." In *TDNT* 9 (1977) 310–358.

———. *The Theology of St. Luke*. London: SCM, 1960.

Crehan, Joseph H. "St. Peter's Journey to Emmaus." *CBQ* 15.4 (Oct 1953) 418–26.

Crespy, Georges. "The Parable of the Good Samaritan: An Essay in Structural Research." *Semeia* 2 (1974) 27–50.

Cribbs, F. Lamar. "St. Luke and the Johannine Tradition." *JBL* 90.4 (Dec 1971) 422–50.

Crossan, John Dominic. *The Birth of Christianity: Discovering What Happened in the Years Immediately After the Execution of Jesus*. New York: HarperCollins, 1998.

Cullman, Oscar. *Salvation in History*. Translated by Sidney G. Sowers. London: SCM, 1965.

Curtis, Edward M. "Structure, Style and Context as a Key to Interpreting Jacob's Encounter at Peniel." *JETS* 30:2 (June 1987) 129–37.

Daly, Robert J. "The Soteriological Significance of the Sacrifice of Isaac." *CBQ* 39.01 (2004) 45–75.

Danby H. *The Mishnah*. Oxford: Clarendon, 1933.

Davies, G. Henton. "Vows." In *IDB* 4. Edited by Keith R. Crim and George A. Buttrick, 792–93. Nashville and New York: Abingdon Press, 1976.

Davies, P. R., and B. D. Chilton. "The Aqedah: A Revised Tradition History." *CBQ* 40.04 (2004) 514–46.

Davies, W. D. *The Gospel and the Land: Early Christianity and Jewish Territorial Doctrine*. Sheffield: JSOT, 1994.

Davis, J. H. "The Purpose of the Central Section of St. Luke's Gospel." *SE* 2 (1964) 164–69.

Dawsey, James M. "Jesus' Pilgrimage to Jerusalem." *PRSt* 14.3 (Fall 1987) 217–32.

Dean-Otting, Mary. *Heavenly Journeys: A Study of the Motif in Hellenistic Jewish Literature*. New York: Verlag Peter Lang, 1984.

Deasley, Alex. *The Shape of Qumran Theology*. Carlisle: Paternoster, 2000.

De Lange, Harry M. "The Jubilee Principle: Is it relevant for Today?" *ER* 38.4 (Oct 1986) 437–43.

deSilva, David A. *Introducing the Apocrypha: Message, Context, and Significance*. Grand Rapids: Baker, 2002.

De Vaux, Roland. *Ancient Israel: Its Life and Institutions*. London: Darton, Longman & Todd, 1978.

———. "Jerusalem and the Prophets." In *Interpreting the Prophetic Tradition*, edited by Harry M. Orlinsky, 275–300. New York: Ktav, 1969.

Denaux, Adelbert, ed. *John and the Synoptics*. Leuven: Leuven University Press, 1992.

Dillard, Raymond B. *2 Chronicles*. Word Biblical Commentary 15. Dallas: Word, 1998.

Dillon, Matthew. *Pilgrims and Pilgrimage in Ancient Greece*. London: Routledge, 1997.

Dodd, C. H. "The Fall of Jerusalem and the Abomination of Desolation." *JRS* 37 (1947) 47–54.

———. *Historical Tradition in the Fourth Gospel*. Cambridge: Cambridge University Press, 1963.

———. *The Interpretation of the Fourth Gospel*. Cambridge: Cambridge University Press, 1968.

Dodd, C. H. ed. *The New English Bible with the Apocrypha*. Oxford and Cambridge: Oxford University Press and Cambridge University Press, 1970.

Drury, John. *Tradition and Design in Luke's Gospel: A Study in Early Christian Historiography*. Atlanta: John Knox, 1977.

Dugid, Ian M. "A Note on the Allure of Egypt in the Abraham Cycle." *WTJ* 56 (Fall 1994) 419–21.

Dumbrell, William J. *Covenant and Creation: A Theology of the Old Testament Covenants*. Carlisle: Paternoster, 2002.

———. "Genesis 2:1–17: A Foreshadowing of the New Creation." In *Biblical Theology, Retrospect and Prospect*, edited by Scott J. Hafemann. Leicester: Apollos, 2002.

Dunn, James. *Jesus and the Spirit: A Study of the Religious and Charismatic Experience of Jesus and the First Christians as Reflected in the New Testament*. London: SCM, 1975.

———. "Paul's Understanding of the Death of Jesus." In *Reconciliation and Hope, New Testament Essays on Atonement and Eschatology Presented to L. L. Morris on his 60th birthday*, edited by Robert Banks, 125–41. Carlisle: Paternoster, 1974.

Dupont, J. "Ascension du Christ et don de 1'Espirit d'après Actes 2:33." In *Christ and Spirit in the New Testament*, edited by B. Lindars and S. S. Smalley, 219–28. Cambridge: Cambridge University Press, 1973.

Durham, John I. *Exodus*. Word Biblical Commentary 3. Waco, TX: Word, 1987.

Eaton, John H. *Kingship and the Psalms*. Sheffield: JSOT, 1986.

Edersheim, Alfred. *The Temple: Its Ministry and Services As They Were at the Time of Jesus Christ*. London: James Clarke, 1959.

Egelkraut, Helmuth L. *Jesus' Mission to Jerusalem: A Redaction Critical Study of the Travel Narrative in the Gospel of Luke, Lk. 9:51—19:48*. Frankfurt: Lang, 1976.

Eichrodt, Walther. *The Theology of the Old Testament*. Vol 1. London: SCM, 1969.

Ellis, E. Earle. *The Gospel of Luke*. New Century Bible Commentary. Grand Rapids: Eerdmans, 1981.

Engnell, Ivan. *Critical Essays on the OT*. London: SPCK, 1970.

Enns, Peter. *Exodus*. NIV Application Commentary. Grant Rapids: Zondervan, 2000.

Enslin, Morton S. "Luke and Samaritans." *HTR* 36.4. (Oct 1943) 277–97.

Epstein, Isidore, ed. *The Babylonian Talmud: Volume I–VI*. London: Soncino, 1938.

Evans, Christopher F. "The Central Section of St. Luke's Gospel." In *Studies in the Gospels: Essays in Memory of R. H. Lightfoot*, edited by D. E. Nineham, 37–53. Oxford: Basil Blackwell, 1955.

———. *St. John's Gospel: A Commentary*. Oxford: Oxford University Press, 1983.

Farmer, William Reuben. *Maccabees, Zealots, and Josephus: An Inquiry into Jewish Nationalism in the Greco-Roman Period*. New York: Columbia University Press, 1956.

Feldman, Louis H. "The Concept of Exile in Josephus." In *Exile: Old Testament, Jewish and Christian Conceptions*, edited by James M. Scott, 145–72. Leiden: Brill, 1997.

Filson, Floyd V. "The Journey Motif in Luke-Acts." In *Apostolic History and the Gospel: Biblical and Historical Essays Presented to F. F. Bruce*, edited by W. Ward Gasque and Ralph P. Martin, 68–72. Exeter: Paternoster, 1970.

Finlayson, R. A. "Pilgrimage." In *The New Bible Dictionary*, edited by J. D. Douglas et al, 997–98. London: InterVarsity, 1962.

Fitzmyer, Joseph A. *The Acts of the Apostles: A New Translation with Introduction and Commentary*. London: Doubleday, 1998.

———. "The Ascension of Christ and Pentecost." *TS* 45.3 (Sept 1984) 409–40.

———. *The Gospel According to Luke I–IX*. Anchor Bible 28. New York: Doubleday, 1981.

———. *The Gospel According to Luke X–XXIV*. Anchor Bible 28A. New York: Doubleday, 1983.

———. *Luke the Theologian*. London: Chapman, 1989.

———. *The Semitic Background of the New Testament*. Grand Rapids: Eerdmans, 1997.

Fishbane, Michael. *Biblical Interpretation in Ancient Israel*. Oxford: Clarendon, 1985.

Flender, Helmut. *St. Luke: Theologian of Redemptive History*. Translated by Reginald Fuller and Ilse Fuller. Philadelphia: Fortress, 1967.

Flusser, David. *Judaism and the Origins of Christianity*. Jerusalem: Hebrew University Magnes Press, 1988.

Fokkelman, J. P. *Narrative Art in Genesis*. Assen, Amsterdam: Van Gorcum, 1975.

France, R. T., and David Wenham, eds. *Gospel Perspectives: Studies in Midrash and Historiography*, vol. 3. Sheffield: JSOT, 1983.

Freedman, H. "Pesahim." In *The Babylonian Talmud: Seder Mode*, edited by I. Epstein. Vol. 2. London: Soncino, 1938.

Fretheim, Terence E. *Exodus*. Interpretation: A Bible Commentary for Teaching and Preaching. Louisville: John Knox, 1991.

Freyne, Sean. *Galilee: From Alexander the Great to Hadrian 323 BCE to 135 CE: A Study of Second Temple Judaism*. Wilmington, DE: Michael Glazier, 1980.

———. "Galilee-Jerusalem Relations according to Josephus's Life." *NTS* 33 (1987) 600–09.

———. "The Geography of Restoration: Galilee-Jerusalem Relations in Early Jewish and Christian Experience." *NTS* 33 (1987) 289–311.

Garrett, Susan R. "Exodus from Bondage: Luke 9:31 and Acts 12:1–24." *CBQ* 52.4 (Oct 1990) 656–80.

Gartner, Bertil. *The Temple and the Community in Qumran and the New Testament: A Comparative Study in the Temple Symbolism of the Qumran Texts and the New Testament*. Cambridge: Cambridge University Press, 1965.

Gasque, W. Ward, and Ralph P. Martin, eds. *Apostolic History and the Gospel, Biblical and Historical Essays Presented to F. F. Bruce on his 60th birthday*. Exeter: Paternoster, 1970.

Gerlach, Karl. *The Antenicene Pascha*. Leuven: Peeters, 1998.

Giblin, Charles H. "Suggestion, Negative Response, and Positive Action in St. John's Portrayal of Jesus (John 2.1–11; 4.46–54; 7.2–14; 11.1–44)." *NTS* 26 (1980) 197–211.

Gileadi, Avrahan, ed. *Israel's Apostasy and Restoration*. Grand Rapids: Baker, 1988.

Gill, David. "Observation on the Lukan Travel Narrative." *HTR* 63 (1970) 199–221.

Goldingay, John. *Theological Diversity and the Authority of the Old Testament*. Carlisle: Paternoster, 1995.

Goodenough, Erwin R. *An Introduction to Philo Judaeus*. Oxford: Basil Blackwell, 1962.

Goppelt, Leonhard. *Apostolic and Post-Apostolic Times*. Grand Rapids: Baker, 1970.

———. *Typos: The Typological Interpretation of the Old Testament in the New*. Grand Rapids: Eerdmans, 1982.

Goulder, Michael D. *The Psalms of the Return (Book V, Psalms 107-150): Studies in the Psalter, IV*. Sheffield: Sheffield Academic Press, 1998.
Green, Joel. *The Gospel of Luke*. New International Commentary on the New Testament. Grand Rapids: Eerdmans, 1997.
Green, Joel B., and Max Turner, eds. *Jesus of Nazareth: Lord and Christ, Essays on the Historical Jesus and New Testament Christology*. Grand Rapids: Eerdmans, 1994.
Gunkel, Hermann. *The Legends of Genesis: The Biblical Saga and History*. New York: Schocken, 1964.
Hafemann, Scott J., ed. *Biblical Theology: Retrospect and Prospect*. Leicester: Apollos, 2002.
Hamerton-Kelly, Robert, and Robin Scroggs, eds. *Jews, Greeks and Christians*. Leiden: Brill, 1976.
Hamilton, Victor P. *The Book of Genesis, Chapters 1–17*. New International Commentary on the Old Testament. Grand Rapids: Eerdmans, 1990.
———. *The Book of Genesis, Chapters 18–50*. New International Commentary on the Old Testament. Grand Rapids: Eerdmans, 1995.
Haran, Menahem. *Temples and Temple-Service in Ancient Israel: An Inquiry into the Character of Cult Phenomena and the Historical Setting of the Priestly School*. Oxford: Clarendon, 1978.
Hasting, Adrian. *Prophet and Witness in Jerusalem: A Study in the Teaching of Saint Luke*. London: Longman, 1958.
Hauck, R., and S. Schulz. "πορεύομαι." In *TDNT* 6 (1977) 566–579.
Heimerdinger, Jean-Marc. "The God of Abraham." *VE* 21 (Apr 1992) 41–55.
Helfmeyer, F. J. "הָלַךְ." In *TDOT* 3 (1978) 388–403.
Hempel, Charlott. *The Damascus Texts*. Sheffield: Sheffield Academic Press, 2000.
Hendriksen, William. *Exposition of the Gospel According to Luke*. Grand Rapids: Baker, 1978.
———. *The Gospel of John*. Geneva Series Commentary. London: Banner of Truth, 1969.
Hengel, Martin. *The Charismatic Leader and His Followers*. Edinburgh: T&T Clark, 1981.
———. "φάτνη." In *TDNT* 9 (1977) 49–55.
Hertig Paul. "The Jubilee Mission of Jesus in the Gospel of Luke: Reversals of Fortunes." *Missiology* 26.2 (Apr 1998) 167–79.
Hess, Richard S., and David T. Tsumura, eds. *I Studied Inscriptions from Before the Flood: Ancient Near Eastern, Literary, and Linguistic Approaches to Genesis 1–11*. Sources for Biblical and Theological Study, vol. 4. Winona Lake: Eisenbrauns, 1994.
Hoffmeier, James K. "The Wives Tales of Genesis 12, 20 & 26 and the Covenants at Beer-Sheeba." *Tyndale Bulletin* 43.1 (1992), 81–99.
Holland, Tom. *Contours of Pauline Theology: A Radical New Survey of the Influences on Paul's Biblical Writings*. Ross-Shire: Mentor, 2004.
Houtman, Cornelis. *Exodus*. Historical Commentary on the Old Testament. Vols. 1 and 2. Kampen: Kok, 1993–1996.
———. *Exodus*. Historical Commentary on the Old Testament. Vol. 3. Leuven: Peeters, 2000.
Howard, J. K. "Passover and Eucharist in the Fourth Gospel." *SJT* 20 (1967) 329–37.
Janin, Hunt. *Four Paths to Jerusalem: Jewish, Christian, Muslim, and Secular Pilgrimages, 1000 BCE to 2001 CE*. London: McFarland & Company, 2002.

Jeremias, Joachim. *Jerusalem in the Time of Jesus*. London: SCM, 1969.
Johnson, Luke Timothy. *The Gospel of Luke*. Sacra pagina 3. Collegeville, MN: Michael Glazier, 1991.
Joyce, Paul. *Divine Initiative and Human Response in Ezekiel*. Sheffield: JSOT, 1989.
Kaiser, Walter C. *Toward an Old Testament Theology*. Grand Rapids: Zondervan, 1991.
Kaufmann, Yehezkel. "The Biblical Age." In *Great Ages and Ideas of the Jewish People*, edited by Leo W. Schwarz, 53–56. New York: Random, 1956.
Keener, Craig S. *The Gospel of John: A Commentary*. Vol 2. Peabody, MA: Hendrickson, 2003.
Keet, Cuthbert C. *A Study of the Psalms of Ascents: A Critical and Exegetical Commentary upon Psalms CXX to CXXXIV*. London: Mitre, 1969.
Kellerman, Diether. "גּוּר." In *TDOT* 2 (1986) 439–49.
Kesich, Veselin. "Resurrection, Ascension and the giving of the Spirit." *GOTR* 25.3 (Fall 1980) 249–60.
Kim, Deuk Joong. *The Theology of St. John*. Seoul: Concordia, 1994.
Kim, Kyoung-Jin. *Stewardship and Almsgiving in Luke's Theology*. Sheffield: Sheffield Academic Press, 1998.
Kirkpatrick, Alexander Francis. *The Book of Psalms*. Cambridge Bible for Schools and Colleges. Cambridge: Cambridge University Press, 1906.
Kittel, Rudolf. ed. *Biblia Hebraica*. 3rd ed. Stuttgart: Württembergische Bibelanstalt, 1937.
Kline, Meredith G. "Investiture with the Image of God." *WTJ* (1977/XL/1) 39–62.
Knox, W. L. *The Acts of the Apostles*. Cambridge: Cambridge University Press, 1948.
Konkel, A. H. "גּוּר." In *NIDOTTE* 5 (1997) 836–39.
Köstenberger, Andreas J. *John*. Baker Exegetical Commentary on the New Testament. Grand Rapids: Baker, 2004.
Krahmalkov, Charles R. "Exodus Itinerary Confirmed by Egyptian Evidence." In *BAR* 20.5 (Sept/Oct 1994), 55–79.
Kraus, Hans-Joachim. *Worship in Israel: A Cultic History of the Old Testament*. Oxford: Basil Blackwell, 1966.
Kugel, James L. *The Bible As It Was*. Cambridge and Massachusetts: Belknap Press, Harvard University, 1997.
Kugler, Robert A. *The Testaments of the Twelve Patriarchs*. Sheffield: Sheffield Academic Press, 2001.
Laney, J. Carl. *John*. Moody Press Commentary. Chicago: Moody, 1992.
LaSor, William Sanford, et al. *The Dead Sea Scrolls and the Christian Faith*. Chicago: Moody, 1962.
———. *Old Testament Survey: the Message, Form, and Background of the Old Testament*. Grand Rapids: Eerdmans, 1996.
Lee, Dorothy A. *The Symbolic Narratives of the Fourth Gospel: The Interplay of Form and Meaning*. Sheffield: JSOT, 1994.
Lee, Edwin Kenneth. *The Religious Thought of St. John*. London: SPCK, 1950.
Liefeld, Walter L. *Luke*. Expositor's Bible Commentary. Grand Rapids: Zondervan, 1984.
Lightfoot, Robert Henry. *Locality and Doctrine in the Gospels*. London: Harper Bros., 1938.
———. *St. John's Gospel: A Commentary*. Oxford: Oxford University Press, 1956.

Lincoln, Andrew T. "Pilgrimage and the New Testament." In *Explorations in a Christian Theology of Pilgrimage*, edited by C. Bartholomew and F. Hughes, 29-49. Hants: Ashgate, 2004.
———. "Theology and History in the Interpretation of Luke's Pentecost." *ExpTim* 96 (1985) 204-9.
Lindars, Barnabas. *Behind the Fourth Gospel*. London: SPCK, 1971.
———. *The Gospel of John*. New Century Bible Commentary. Greenwood: Attic, 1972.
———. *John*. New Testament Guides. Sheffield: Sheffield Academic Press, 1990.
Lindars, Barnabas, and Stephen S. Smalley, eds. *Christ and Spirit in the New Testament: Studies in honour of Charles Francis Digby Moule*. Cambridge: Cambridge University Press, 1973.
Litwak, Kenneth Duncan. *Echoes of Scripture in Luke-Acts*. London: T&T Clark, 2005.
Lohmeyer, Ernst. *Galiläa und Jerusalem*. Gottingen: Vandenhoeck & Ruprecht, 1936.
Lohse, Eduard. "πεντηκοστή." In *TDNT* 6 (1977) 44-53.
Lotowitz, Meir Z., and Nosson Scherman, trans. *Genesis: A New Translation with a Commentary Anthologized from Talmudic, Midrashic and Rabbinic Sources*. New York: Mesorah, 1977, 1986.
MacRae, George W. "The Meaning and Evolution of the Feast of Tabernacles." *CBQ* 22.3 (Jul 1960) 251-76.
Maddox, Robert. *The Purpose of Luke-Acts*. FRLANT 126. Göttingen: Vandenhoeck & Ruprecht, 1982.
Mann, Jacob. "Rabbinic Studies in the Synoptic Gospels." *HUCA* 1.01 (2004) 323-29.
Marshall, I. Howard. *Acts*. Tyndale New Testament Commentary. Leicester: IVP, 1980.
———. *The Gospel of Luke: A Commentary on the Greek Text*. Exeter: Paternoster, 1978.
———. *Luke: Historian and Theologian*. Grand Rapids: Zondervan, 1970.
———. "The Significance of Pentecost." *SJT* 30 (1977) 347-69.
Marxen, Willi. *Mark the Evangelist: Studies on the Redaction History of the Gospel*. Nashville: Abingdon, 1969.
Mason, Steve. *Josephus and the New Testament*. Peabody, MA: Hendrickson, 2003.
Matera, Frank J. "Jesus' Journey to Jerusalem (Luke 9:51—19:46): A Conflict with Israel." *JSNT* 51 (Sept 1993) 57-77.
May, H. G. "The Ark—Miniature Temple." *AJSL* 52 (1936) 215ff.
McConville, J. Gordon. *Deuteronomy*. Apollos Old Testament Commentary. Leicester: Apollos, 2002.
———. "Pilgrimage and 'Place': an Old Testament View." In *Explorations in a Christian Theology of Pilgrimage*, edited by C. Bartholomew and F. Hughes, 17-28. Hants: Ashgate, 2004.
McKane, William. *Studies in the Patriarchal Narratives*. Edenburgh: Handsel, 1979.
McLaren, James S. *Turbulent Times?: Josephus and Scholarship on Judea in the First Century CE*. Sheffield: Sheffield Academic Press, 1998.
Meagher, John C. "John 1:14 and the New Temple." *JBL* 88.1 (Mar 1969) 57-68.
Meeks, Wayne A. "Galilee and Judea in the Fourth Gospel." *JBL* 85 (1966) 159-69.
———. "The Man From Heaven in Johannine Sectarianism." *JBL* 91 (1972) 42-72.
Merrill, Eugene H. "Pilgrimage and Procession: Motifs of Israel's Return." In *Israel's Apostasy and Restoration*, edited by Avrahan Gileadi, 261-72. Grand Rapids: Baker, 1988.

Metzger, Bruce M. *An Introduction to the Apocrypha*. New York: Oxford University Press, 1957.
Millar, J. Gary. *Now Choose Life: Theology and Ethics in Deuteronomy*. Leicester: Apollos, 1998.
Moberly, R. W. L. *The Bible, Theology and Faith: A Study of Abraham and Jesus*. Cambridge: Cambridge University Press, 2000.
———. *The Old Testament of the Old Testament: Patriarchal Narratives and Mosaic Yahwism*. Minneapolis: Fortress, 1992.
Moessner, David P. "Luke 9:1–50: Luke's Preview of the Journey of the Prophet Like Moses of Deuteronomy." *JBL* 102 (1983) 575–605.
Moloney, Francis J. *The Gospel of John*. Sacra pagina 4. Collegeville, MN: Liturgical, 1998.
Moore, Thomas S. "'To the End of the Earth': The Geographical and Ethnic Universalism of Acts 1:8 in Light of Isaianic Influence on Luke." *JETS* 40.3 (Sept 1997) 389–99.
Morris, Leon. *The Gospel According to John*. New International Commentary on the New Testament. Rev. ed. Grand Rapids: Eerdmans, 1995.
Motyer, Stephen. *Your Father the Devil?: A New Approach to John and 'the Jews.'* Carlisle: Paternoster, 1997.
Moule, Charles F. D. "The Post-Resurrection Appearances in the Light of Festival Pilgrimages." *NTS* 4 (1958) 58–61.
Mowinckel, Sigmund. *Psalmenstudien V*. 1921–24. Reprint, Amsterdam: P. Schippers, 1966.
———. *The Psalms in Israel's Worship*. Translated by D. R. AP-Thomas. 2 vols. Oxford: Basil Blackwell, 1962.
Mowvley, Henry. "John 1:14–18 in the Light of Exodus 33:7—34:35." *ExpTim* 95 (1984) 135–37.
Neusner, Jacob. *The Mishnah: A New Translation*. New Haven and London: Yale University Press, 1988.
Neusner, Jacob, ed. *Christianity, Judaism and Other Greco-Roman Cults: Part One*. Leiden: Brill, 1975.
———. *Christianity, Judaism and other Greco-Roman Cults: Studies for Morton Smith at Sixty*. Vol. 1. Leiden: Brill, 1975.
Neusner, Jacob, and William Scott Green, eds. *Dictionary of Judaism in the Biblical Period: 450 BCE to 600 CE*. Peabody, MA: Hendrickson, 1999.
Newman, Barclay M., and Eugene A. Nida. *A Translator's Handbook on the Gospel of John*. New York: United Bible Societies, 1980.
Ng, Wai-Yee. *Water Symbolism in John*. New York: Peter Lang, 2001.
Nickelsburg, George W. E. *Jewish Literature between the Bible and the Mishnah*. London: SCM, 1981.
Nineham, Dennis E., ed. *Studies in the Gospels: Essays in Memory of R. H. Lightfoot*. Oxford: Basil Blackwell, 1955.
Nolland, J. *Luke 1–9:20*. Word Biblical Commentary 35a. Dallas: Word, 1989.
———. *Luke 18:35–24:53*. Word Biblical Commentary 35c. Waco, TX: Word, 1989.
Noth, Martin. *Exodus: A Commentary*. Old Testament Library. London: SCM, 1962.
———. *A History of Pentateuchal Traditions*. Atlanta: Scholars, 1981.
Pao, David W. *Acts and the Isaianic New Exodus*. Grand Rapids: Baker, 2002.
Parente, Fausto, and Joseph Sievers, eds. *Josephus and the History of the Greco-Roman Period: Essays in Memory of Morton Smith*. New York: Brill, 1994.

Parker, Pierson. "Two Editions of John." *JBL* 75 (1956) 303-14.
Parsons, Mikeal C. *The Departure of Jesus in Luke-Acts: The Ascension Narrative in Context*. Sheffield: Sheffield Academic Press, 1987.
———. "The Text of Acts 1:2 Reconsidered." *CBQ* 50.1 (Jan 1988) 58-71.
Pedersen, Johannes. *Israel: Its Life and Culture*. London: Oxford University Press, 1959.
Percy, Martyn. *Calling Time: Religion and Change at the Turn of the Millennium*. Sheffield: Sheffield Academic Press, 2000.
Pfeiffer, Charles F. *The Dead Sea Scrolls and the Bible*. Grand Rapids: Baker, 1969.
Pfeiffer, Robert H. "Image of Yahweh." *JBL* 45 (1926) 211-22.
Prior, Michael. *Jesus the Liberator: Nazareth Liberation Theology (Luke 4:16-30)*. Sheffield: Sheffield Academic Press, 1995.
Pritchard, John. "Jesus and Jubilee." *ER* 26.2 (Apr 1999) 52-59.
Prosic, Tamara. "Passover in Biblical Narratives." *JSOT* 82 (1999) 45-55.
Pryor, John W. *John: Evangelist of the Covenant People: The Narrative and Themes of the Fourth Gospel*. London: Longman & Todd, 1992.
Rajak, Tessa. *Josephus: The Historian and His Society*. London: Duckworth, 1983.
Reeves, Edward B. *The Hidden Government: Ritual, Clientalism, and Legitimation in Northern Egypt*. Salt Lake City: University of Utah Press, 1990.
Reicke, Bo. "Instruction and Discussion in the Travel Narrative." *SE* 1 (1959) 206-16.
Reicke, Bo, and Georg Bertram. "παρίστημι." In *TDNT* 5 (1977) 837-41.
Resseguie, James L. "Point of View in the Central Section of Luke (9:51—19:44)." *JETS* 25.1 (Mar 1982) 41-47.
Ridderbos, Herman. *The Gospel of John: A Theological Commentary*. Cambridge: Eerdmans, 1992.
Rigsby, R. O. "Jacob." In *DOT* (2003) 461-67.
Ringe, Sharon. H. *Jesus, Liberation, and the Biblical Jubilee: Images for Ethics and Christology*. Philadelphia: Fortress, 1985.
———. "Luke 9:28-36: The Beginning of an Exodus." In *Semeia* 28 (1983) 85-99.
Robbins, Vernon K., ed. *Semeia 64: The Rhetoric of Pronouncement*. Missoula: Scholars, 1994.
Robinson, John A. T. *Redating the New Testament*. London: SCM, 1981.
Robinson, W. C. "The Theological Context for Interpreting Luke's Travel Narrative (9:55ff)." *JBL* 79 (1960) 20-31.
Rodgers, Margaret. "Luke 4:16-30: A Call for a Jubilee Year?" *RTR* 40 (1981) 72-82.
Rogerson, J. W. "The Hebrew Conception of Corporate Personality: A Re-Examination." *JTS* 21 (1970) 1-16.
Ronning, John. "The Naming of Isaac: The Role of the Wife/Sister Episodes in the Redaction of Genesis." *WTJ* 53 (1991) 1-27.
Ross, Allen P. "Jacob's Vision: The Founding of Bethel." *BSac* 142.567 (July 1985) 234-37.
Rost, Leonhard. "*Weidewechsel und aldisraelitischer Festkalender*" *ZDPV* 66 (1943) 205-16.
Rowley, Harold Henry. *The Re-discovery of the Old Testament*. London: James Clarke, 1945.
Ryrie, Charles C. "The Significance of Pentecost." *BSac* 112.448 (Oct 1955) 330-39.
Safrai, S., and M. Stern, eds. *The Jewish People in the First Century: Historical Geography, Political History, Social, Cultural and Religious Life and Institutions*. Compendia Rerum Iudaicarum ad Novum Testamentum. Amsterdam: Van Gorcum, 1976.

Sanders, Ed Parish. "The Covenant as a Soteriological Category and the Nature of Salvation in Palestinian and Hellenistic Judaism." In *Jews, Greeks and Christians*, edited by Robert Hamerton-Kelly and Robin Scrogg, 11–44. Leiden: Brill, 1976.

———. *Judaism: Practice and Belief, 63 BCE–66 CE*. London: SCM, 1992.

Sanders, J. A. "From Isaiah 61 to Luke 4." In *Christianity, Judaism and Other Greco-Roman Cults: Studies for Morton Smith at Sixty*, Part 1, *New Testament*, edited by J. Neusner, 75–106. Leiden: Brill, 1975.

Sarna, Nahum M. *Exploring Exodus: The Origins of Biblical Israel*. New York: Schocken, 1996.

———. *Genesis*. JPS Torah Commentary. Philadelphia: Jewish Publication Society, 1989.

Schillebeeckx, Edward. "Ascension and Pentecost." *Worship* 35 (1960) 336–63.

Schlatter, A. *Der Evangelist Johannes*. Stuttgart: Calwer, 1930.

Schnackenburg, Rudolf. *The Gospel According to St. John: Commentary on Chapters 5–12*. Vol. 2. London: Burns & Oates, 1979.

———. *The Gospel According to St. John: Introduction and Commentary on Chapters 1–4*. Vol. 1. Translated by Kevin Smith. New York: Crossroad, 1987.

Schwarz, Leo W., ed. *Great Ages and Ideas of the Jewish People*. New York: Random, 1956.

Schweizer, Eduard. *The Good News According Luke*. Translated by David L. Green. London: SPCK, 1984.

Scobie, Charles H. H. "The Origin and Development of Samaritan Christianity." *NTS* 19 (1973) 390–414.

Scott, James M., ed. *Exile: Old Testament, Jewish and Christian Conceptions*. Leiden: Brill, 1997.

Scroggs, Robin, and Robert Hamerton-Kelly, eds. *Jews, Greeks and Christians*. Leiden: Brill, 1976.

Seesemann, Heinrich. "πατέω." In *TDNT* 5 (1991) 940–45.

Segal, J. B. *The Hebrew Passover: From the Earliest Times to AD 70*. London: Oxford University Press, 1963.

Segovia, Fernando F. "The Journey(s) of Jesus to Jerusalem." In *John and the Synoptics*, edited by Adelbert Denaux, 535–41. Leuven: Leuven University Press, 1992.

———. "Journey(s) of the Word of God: A Reading of the Plot of the Fourth Gospel." *Semeia* 53 (1991) 23–54.

Shanks, Hershel, ed. *Understanding the Dead Sea Scrolls: A Reader from the Biblical Archaeology Review*. London: SPCK, 1993.

Shepherd, William H., Jr. *The Narrative Function of the Holy Spirit as a Character in Luke-Acts*. Society of Biblical Literature Dissertation Series 43. Atlanta: Scholars, 1994.

Sheriffs, Deryck. "Faith." In *DOT* (2003) 281–85.

———. *The Friendship of the Lord: An Old Testament Spirituality*. Carlisle: Paternoster, 1996.

———. "Moving on With God: Key motifs in Exodus 13–20." *Themelios* 15.2 (1990) 49–60.

Sloan, Robert. *The Favorable Year of the Lord: A Study of Jubilary Theology in the Gospel of Luke*. Austin, TX: Schola, 1977.

Sloyan, Gerard S. *John*. Interpretation: A Bible Commentary for Teaching and Preaching. Atlanta: John Knox, 1988.

Smalley, Stephen. *John, Evangelist and Interpreter*. Exeter: Paternoster, 1978.
Smith, Charles W. F. "Tabernacles in the Fourth Gospel and Mark." *NTS* 9 (Jan 1963) 10–46.
Smith, Mark S. *The Pilgrimage Pattern in Exodus, with contributions by Elizabeth M. Bloch-Smith*. Sheffield: Sheffield Academic Press, 1997.
Smith, Robert Houston. "Exodus Typology in the Fourth Gospel." *JBL* 81.4 (Dec 1962) 329–42.
Stanley, D. M. "The Feast of Tents: Jesus' Self-Revelation." *Worship* 34.1 (1959) 20–27.
Stibbe, Mark W. G., ed. *The Gospel of John as Literature: An Anthology of Twentieth-Century Perspective*. Leiden: Brill, 1993.
———. *John*. Sheffield: JSOT, 1993.
Stigers, Harold G. *A Commentary on Genesis*. Grand Rapid: Zondervan, 1978.
Stone, Michael E. *Jewish Writings of the Second Temple Period: Apocrypha, Pseudepigrapha, Qumran Sectarian Writings, Philo, Josephus*. Philadelphia: Fortress, 1984.
Story, Cullen I. K. "The Bearing of Old Testament Terminology on the Johannine Chronology of the Final Passover of Jesus," *NovT*. 31.4 (1989) 316–24.
Stott, John. *The Message of Acts: To the End of the Earth*. Leicester: IVP, 2005.
Strauss, David Friedrich. *The Life of Jesus Critically Examined*. London: SCM, 1972.
Strauss, Mark L. *Davidic Messiah: The Promise and its Fulfillment in Lukan Christology*. Sheffield: Sheffield Academic Press, 1995.
Tabor, James D. "Heaven, Ascent to." In *ABD* 3 (1997) 91–94.
Talbert, Charles H. "The Way of the Lukan Jesus: Dimensions of Lukan Spirituality." *PRSt* 9.3 (Fall 1982) 237–49.
Tasker, R. V. G. *The Gospel According to St. John*. Leicester: IVP, 1999.
Tisera, Guido. *Universalism According to the Gospel of Matthew*, European University Studies Series 23, Theology, vol. 482. New York: Lang, 1993.
Tolbert, Mary Ann, ed. *Semeia* 28: *The Bible and Feminist Hermeneutics*. Missoula: Scholars, 1983.
Trocmé, André. *Jesus and the Nonviolent Revolution*. Pennsylvania: Herald, 1973.
Turner, Laurence A. *Announcements of Plot in Genesis*. Sheffield: JSOT, 1990.
Turner, Max. *Power from on High: The Spirit in Israel's Restoration and Witness in Luke's Acts*. Sheffield: Sheffield Academic Press, 1996.
Ulfgard, Hakan. *The Story of Sukkot: The Setting, Shaping, and Sequel of the Biblical Feast of Tabernacles*. Tübingen: Mohr Siebeck, 1998.
Unger, Merrill F. "The Significance of Pentecost." *BSac* 122.486 (Apr/Jun 1965) 169–77.
Urdang, Laurence. *The Random House Dictionary of the English Language*. New York: Random, 1983.
VanderKam, James C. "Covenant and Pentecost." *CTJ* 37.2 (Nov 2002) 239–54.
———. *The Dead Sea Scrolls Today*. London: SPCK, 1994.
———. "The Temple Scroll and the Book of Jubilees." In *Temple Scroll Studies: Papers presented at the International Symposium on the Temple Scroll*. Journal for the Study of the Pseudepigrapha: Supplementary Series 7, edited by George J. Brooke, 211–36. Sheffield: Sheffield Academic Press, 1989.
———. "Weeks, Festival of." *ABD* 6 (2002) 895–97.
Vanderlip, D. George. *Christianity According to John*. Philadelphia: Westminster, 1975.
Van Seters, John. *Abraham in History and Tradition*. New Haven, CT: Yale University Press, 1975.

Veijola, Timo, ed. *The Law in the Bible and its Environment*. Gottingen: Vanhenhoeck & Ruprecht, 1990.

Vermes, Geza. *The Complete Dead Sea Scrolls in English*. London: Allen Lane Penguin, 1997.

Verseput, Donald J. "Jesus' Pilgrimage to Jerusalem and Encounter in the Temple: A Geographical Motif in Matthew's Gospel," *NovT* 36.2 (1994) 105–21.

Vincent, John J. *Stirrings*. London: Epworth, 1976.

Vischer, Lukas. *Jubilee Challenge, Utopia or Possibility?: Jewish and Christian Insight*. Geneva: WCC, 1997.

von Rad, Gerhard. *Genesis: A Commentary*. Translated by John Bowden and J. H. Marks. London: SCM: 1972.

———. *Old Testament Theology, Vol 1, The Theology of Israel's Historical Traditions*. London: Westminster John Knox, 1962.

———. *Problem of the Hexateuch*. London: SCM: 1984.

Vriezen, Th. C. *An Outline of the Old Testament Theology*. Wageningen, Holland: Veennam & Zonen N. V., 1960.

Wagenaar, Jan A. "Passover and the First Day of the Festival of Unleavened Bread in the Priestly Festival Calendar." *VT* 54 (2004) 250–68.

Walker, Peter W. L. *Jesus and the Holy City: New Testament Perspectives on Jerusalem*. Grands Rapids: Eerdmans, 1996.

Waltke, Bruce K. *Genesis*. Grand Rapids: Zondervan, 2001.

Walton, John H., and Victor H. Matthews. *The IVP Bible Background Commentary: Genesis–Deuteronomy*. Downer's Grove: IVP, 1997.

Watson, Paul. "The Tree of Life." *ResQ*. 23.4 (1980) 232–38.

Watts, Rikki E. *The Influence of the Isaianic New Exodus on the Gospel of Mark*. WUNT 2.88. Tubingen: Mohr Siebeck, 1997.

Weinert, Francis D. "The Parable of the Throne Claimant (Luke 19:12,14–15a, 27) Reconsidered." *CBQ* 39 (Oct 1977) 505–14.

Weinfeld, Moshe. "Sabbatical Year and Jubilee in the Pentateuchal Laws." In *The Law in the Bible and its Environment*, edited by Timo Veijola, 39–62. Gottingen: Vanhenhoeck & Ruprecht, 1990.

Weiser, Artur. *The Psalms: A Commentary*. Old Testament Library. Philadelphia: Westminster, 1962.

Wellhausen, Julius. *Prolegomena to the History of Israel*. London: A & C Black, 1895.

Wenham, Gordon J. *Genesis 1–15*. Word Biblical Commentary. Vol. 1. Waco, TX: Word, 1987.

———. *Genesis 16–50*. Word Biblical Commentary. Vol. 2. Waco, TX: Word Books, 1987.

———. "Sanctuary Symbolism in the Garden of Eden Story." In *I Studied Inscriptions from before the Flood: Ancient Near Eastern, Literary and Linguistic Approaches to Genesis 1–11*, edited by Richard S. Hess and David T. Tsumura, 399–404. Winona Lake: Eisenbrauns, 1994.

Westermann, Claus. *Creation*. London: SPCK, 1977.

———. *Genesis 1–11*. A Continental Commentary. Minneapolis: Fortress, 1994.

———. *Genesis 12–36*. A Continental Commentary. Minneapolis: Augsburg, 1985.

———. *The Living Psalms*. Grand Rapids: Eerdmans, 1984.

Whiston, William, trans. *Josephus: The Complete Works*. Nashville: Thomas Nelson, 1998.

Williams, Wilbur G. *Genesis: A Commentary for Bible Students*. Bellingham: Wesleyan, 2000.

Williamson, P. R. "Abraham." In *DOT* (2003) 8–17.

Willoughby, Robert. "The Concept of Jubilee and Luke 4:18–30." In *Mission and Meaning: Essays presented to Peter Cotterell*, edited by Anthony Billington, 41–55. Carlisle: Paternoster, 1995.

Wilson, Stephen G. *The Gentiles and the Gentile Mission in Luke-Acts*. Cambridge: Cambridge University Press, 1973.

Wise, Michael, et al. *The Dead Sea Scrolls*. London: HarperCollins, 1996.

Wise, M. O. "Feasts," in *DJG* (1992) 234–41.

Wohlgemut, Joel R. "Where Does God Dwell? A Commentary on John 2:13–22." *Direction* 22.2 (Fall 1993) 87–93.

Wolfson, Harry A. *Philo: Foundations of Religious Philosophy in Judaism, Christianity, and Islam*. Cambridge: Harvard University Press, 1961.

Woll, D. Bruce. "The Departure of 'The Way': The First Farewell Discourse in the Gospel of John." *JBL* 99/2 (1980) 225–39.

Wood, Pape William. "John 2:13–22." *Interpretation* 45.1 (Jan 1991) 59–63.

Wright, Christopher J. H. "Jubilee, Year of." In *ABD* 3 (1992) 1025–1030.

Wright, Nicholas Thomas. *The Climax of the Covenant: Christ and the Law in Pauline Theology*. Edinburgh: T&T Clark, 1991.

———. *Jesus and the Victory of God*. London: SPCK, 1999.

Yee, Gale A. *Jewish Feasts and The Gospel of John*. Wilmington: Michael Glazier, 1989.

Yoder, John Howard. *The Politics of Jesus*. Grand Rapids: Eerdmans, 1972.

Yonge, Charles Duke. *The Works of Philo*. Peabody, MA: Hendrickson, 1997.

Index of Names and Subjects

agricultural life, 94
alien, 15, 16, 23, 119, 187
Anderson, A., 69, 70, 71
Anderson, Bernhard, 19
anticipation, 142, 215, 218, 236
Ark narrative, 69, 70
Ascension, xiii, 146, 149, 165, 167–72, 178, 179, 183, 188, 193, 196–98, 205, 206, 221
Ascent, 167–69, 183, 196, 215, 218
Jesus' ascent to God, 196

Baban, Octavia, 148
Babylonian gods, 10
Barth, Christopher, 9
Barrett, Charles, 109, 110, 112, 127, 128, 130, 133, 169, 194
Beasley-Murray, George, 110, 136
being with God, xiii, 9, 44, 199, 206, 219
  being with, 5, 6, 23, 24, 32
Bernard, John, 127
Blomberg, Craig, 144
Blosser, Donald, 193
Bock, Darrell, 44, 98, 103
Brown, Raymond, 97, 107, 111, 128
Brueggemann, Walter, 6, 7, 32, 40, 67
Bultmann, Rudolf, 136, 139, 154

Caragounis, Chrys, 127
Carson, David, 109, 111, 113, 127, 130
Cassuto, Umberto, 2, 9, 11, 12, 17, 19, 31, 42, 52, 65
cause-effect relationship, 12
Ceresko, Anthoney, 81
Childs, Brevard, 50

Clements, Ronald, 62, 63
Conzelmann, Hans, 135, 145, 152, 178
corporate personality, 7, 58
cosmic journey of the Word of God, 106
Creation, 44, 49, 123, 124, 125, 133, 137, 141, 176, 199, 219, 221
Cribbs, F. Lamar, xiv

Davies, W.D., 12
Dawsey, James, 152
Dead Sea Scroll, 139, 177, 179, 195, 222–25, 236
Dean-Otting, Mary, 219
death, 7–8, 26, 44, 63, 64, 91, 96, 134, 139, 146, 147, 149, 151, 152, 156, 157, 158, 159, 163, 166, 172, 179, 194, 204, 205, 210, 216
departure, 33, 52, 106, 146, 150, 151, 163, 166, 170, 171, 172, 196, 205, 219
descent of the Holy Spirit, 167, 171, 172, 179, 180, 194, 195, 196, 198, 205
De Vaux, Roland, 70, 90
discipleship paradigm, 76
Dobschutz, E. Von, 181
Dodd, C. H., 110, 159, 160, 162
Dunn, James, 158, 180, 181
Durham, John, 49, 50, 52, 53

eating and walking, 51
Eichrodt, Walter, 55, 66, 68, 72, 84, 85
Ellis, E. Earle, 144
Enns, Peter, 49
eschatological blessings, 142
enthronement of God, 124, 140

254 Index of Names and Subjects

enthronement Psalms, 125, 140
Eugene, Merrill, 69, 71
Evans, C., 110, 150
exile, 58, 66–86, 87, 122, 148, 189, 199, 201, 202, 206, 210, 211, 212, 214, 219, 222, 223, 229, 230, 235, 236
Exodus, vii, xiv, 1, 10, 17, 43, 44–60, 65, 74, 77, 78, 81, 82, 85, 87, 89, 90, 92, 93, 94, 96, 97, 100, 112, 114, 115, 121, 123, 124, 135, 140, 147, 148, 150, 151, 152, 156, 172, 175, 195, 199, 200–3, 205, 220, 227
expiatory sacrifice of the Lamb, 158
Expulsion, 6–10, 24, 44, 49, 199
   from judge's point of view, 9, 49
   from rescuer's point of view, 10, 49

face-to-face encounter, 39
Fall, 8, 44, 72, 76, 77, 85, 93, 200, 213
fear of the Lord, 53, 56, 57
fear of God, 10, 25, 28, 29, 30, 53, 56, 100
Feast
   three pilgrimage feasts, xii, xiii, 88, 119, 126, 173, 202, 206
   Feast of Passover, xiv, 51, 87–116, 89, 100, 108, 121, 123, 125, 126, 140, 143-166, 144, 145, 151, 156, 166, 171, 195, 203, 204, 205, 222, 235
   Feast of Pentecost, xiv, 100, 167–98, 172, 173, 175, 177, 179, 181, 182, 183, 195, 196, 197, 198, 205, 206, 210
   Feast of Tabernacles, xiv, 88, 100, 101, 117–42, 118, 119, 120, 122, 123, 124, 125, 126, 127, 128, 130, 133, 134, 135, 136, 137, 140, 141, 142, 164, 195, 203, 205, 214, 221, 230
   festal experience, 83, 104, 105, 112, 116, 125, 140, 161
message of the festival, 104
Feldman, Louis, 229
first journey, 10, 44, 199
firstborn son, 91, 94, 96, 98
   as a family representative, 98
   as becoming the redeemer, 98
first fruit, 90, 175, 197, 233, 234

Fitzmyer, Joseph A., 97, 104, 146, 150, 171, 178, 185
Fretheim, Terence, 49
focus shift, 7–8

garden of Eden, 2, 3, 4, 6, 8, 9, 10, 17, 44, 49
Garrett, Susan, 152
Gerhard Kittel, xii, xvii
Gill, David, 152
God's coming, 105, 116, 124, 131, 140, 142, 201, 206, 225
Goppelt, Leonard, 132, 183
gradually growing awareness, 113
Green, Joel, 155
Gunkel, Herman, 37, 39

Haenchen, E., 179
halak, 21, 87, 121
Hamilton, Victor, 7, 9, 26, 36, 37, 43
Haran, Menahem, 93, 100, 101
Hasting, Adrian, 146
Helfmeyer, F. J., 2, 17, 21, 87, 129, 217
Hengel, Martin, 154
Holland, Tom, ix, xii, 91, 98, 99, 103, 115, 158
homelessness of Jesus, 153–55, 165
Hooke, S. H., 122
Houtman, Cornelis, 49, 91
Howard, J.K., 158

incipient monotheism, 57
internalizing of the Torah, 82, 225
Israel's monotheism, 57
Israel's monotheistic faith, 77

Jacob's journey, 12, 30–45
Jesus' ascension to the Father, 167, 196
Jesus' glorification, 134
Jesus' self-consciousness, 142
Jesus' self understanding, vii, xiii
Jesus' self-revelation, 131, 137
Jesus' way, 169, 172, 196
Johnson, L. T., 156, 185
Josephus, xi, 14, 88, 99, 100, 101, 102, 103, 126, 172, 175, 177, 192, 198, 229–36

Journey
  destination of the journey, 54, 64, 85, 200, 219, 229
  goal of the heavenly journey, 219
  journey motif, vii, xii, xiii, 31, 45, 80, 93, 106, 107, 108, 116, 145, 148, 200, 201, 202, 212, 216, 219, 236
  journey framework, xiii, 43, 45, 84, 86, 107, 116, 144, 148, 200, 211, 219, 221, 235
  rescuer's point of view, 10, 49
  journey pattern, 52
  journey themes, 76
  journey to Jerusalem, vii, xiv, 80, 96, 107, 113, 117, 126, 136, 141, 144, 145, 150, 151, 152, 155, 163, 164, 195, 203, 204, 213, 215
  internalizing of the journey, 82, 228
  physical act of walking, 18
  physical journey, 11, 54, 77, 85, 86, 87, 113, 200, 201, 206, 212, 225, 235, 236
  physical reality, 82
Jubilee
  fulfilment of Jubilee, 194
  Jubilee legislation, 187, 188, 189, 193, 194, 198
  Jubilee model, 194
  true and actual Jubilee, 193, 194, 198, 206
  Year of Jubilee, xi, 182–95, 197, 198, 206

Kaiser, Water, 66, 67
Kaufmann, Yehezkel, 77
Keet, Cuthbert, 79
Kellerman, Diether, 16
Kesich, Veselin, 169
knowing God motif, xiii, 50, 62, 63, 85, 116, 125, 135, 140, 142, 157–64, 200, 201, 202, 205, 212, 220
knowing who God is, xiii, 50, 62, 63, 85, 116, 125, 135, 140, 142, 157–64, 200, 201, 202, 205, 212, 220
Köstenburger, Andreas, 106, 108, 110, 111
Kraus, Hans-Joachim, 122, 123
Kugel, James L., 14, 38

Liefeld, Walter, 154, 180
life on the move towards the land, 64, 85, 200, 218
light and darkness, 138
Lightfoot, Robert, 126, 202
light motif, 122
Lightfoot, Robert, 126, 202
Lincoln, Andrew, 112
Lohse, Edward, 175, 177

making himself known, 83, 88, 104, 105, 116, 124, 130, 131, 140, 141, 142, 201, 206, 207
Marshall, I. Howard, 100, 102, 144, 145, 154
May, H. G, 70
McConville, J. Gordon, 62, 82
MacRae, George, 122, 123
Millar, Gary, 63, 64
Moberly, R.W.L., 10, 15, 28, 29
Moessner, David, 151
Moloney, Francis, 127
Motyer, Stephen, 129
monotheism, 19, 41, 58, 63, 77
Morris, Leon, 111, 127, 130
Mount Sinai, xiv, 50, 54–59, 124, 175–77, 182–83, 191, 192, 193, 195, 197, 198, 205, 221
Mowinckel, Sigmund, 81, 83, 90, 104, 122, 123, 124, 125, 140
my covenant, 23, 54

new heart, 74–76
new spirit, 74–76
New Year celebration, 124
Nolland, John, 97, 156, 157, 205
nomadic lifestyle, 90, 123
North, Robert, 188

O'Donovan, Oliver, 58
One true God, 14, 15, 34, 57, 61, 62, 130, 135, 228
ontological change, 7–8
original sin, 7, 44

Pao, David, 185
Paskal ritual, 90

Paschal sacrifice, 158, 165, 204
Passover
  Passover pilgrimage, 87–116, 143–66, 202, 204, 205
  Passover meal, 51, 92, 156
Pentecost
  Jesus' Pentecost pilgrimage, 194–95, 196, 198
  Pentecost experience, 194, 198
  message of, 194
  120 and 12×10, 180–81
personal god, 14–15, 18, 19, 26, 34, 227
Philo, 99, 101, 125, 165, 175, 177, 183, 197, 205, 225–29, 236
pilgrimage
  Abrahamic pilgrimage, 10–30, 11, 12, 20, 27, 28, 44, 54, 65, 77, 83, 86, 199, 202, 227
  destination of , xiii, 9, 27, 44, 49, 112, 113, 115, 160, 199, 202, 206, 219
  faith pilgrimage, 27, 53
  goal of, 20, 79, 112, 113, 116, 203, 229
  his own way of , 114, 129
  Jesus' final pilgrimage, 145, 151, 171, 179, 194, 198
  Jesus' pilgrimage, xii, xiv, 88, 104, 107, 142, 144, 145, 152, 161, 163, 164, 166, 172, 173, 196, 204, 205, 206, 207
  national pilgrimage, 71
  pilgrimage experience, 39, 56, 61, 104
  pilgrimage feasts, xiii, xiv, 88, 117, 119, 126, 164, 173, 174, 202, 203, 204, 206
  pilgrimage festivals, 107, 118, 126, 179
  pilgrimage framework, 78, 80, 83, 84, 86, 111, 148
  pilgrimage paradigm, vii, xi, xii, xiii, xiv, 42, 44, 83, 102, 104, 107, 112, 115, 116, 125, 145, 153, 160, 201, 202, 207, 209, 225, 229, 235, 236
  pilgrimage motif, 39, 44, 45, 200, 201
  pilgrimage sites, 67, 71
  pilgrim God, 71
  pilgrim motif, 12

pilgrim people, 66, 71
pilgrim's ascent, 80
theological interpretation of, 54, 85, 112, 200
traditional way of, 114, 129, 141
years of my pilgrimage, 43, 44, 45, 153, 154, 187, 217
polytheistic belief, 19, 26
practical monotheism, 63
presence of God, 3, 5, 34, 48, 71, 78, 106, 111
Prosic, Tamara, 92, 96

rain theme, 122
Reicke, Bo, 153
return, xiii, 17, 31, 73, 76–86
  to Jerusalem, 74
  to the Edenic state, xiii, 9, 44
  to the garden, xiii, 49
  to the Father, 106, 170, 196
Ridderbos, Herman, 110, 114, 128, 130, 132
Ringe, S. H., 150
Robinson, H.W., 58
Robinson, W. C., 151
Robbins, Vernon, 148
Rowley, H.H., 57

Safrai, S., 99, 177, 231
Sanders, E. P., 109, 224
Sanders, J. A., 190
Sarna, Nahum, 46
Schillebeeckx, Edward, 172, 196
Schnackenburg, 110, 111, 128, 137
Schweizer, Edward, 154
Second Temple period, xiii, xiv, 99, 125, 141, 168, 183, 201, 203, 209, 235, 236
sedentary conditions of life, 94
Seesemann, Heinrich, 139
Segal, J.B., 92, 123
Segovia, Fernando, 106, 107
Shepherd, William, 185
Sheriffs, Deryck, 19, 47, 51, 58, 64, 82
Sinai Covenant, 47, 75, 176, 195
status confessionis , 23
suffering Messiah, vii, 145–47, 158, 165, 204

Sukkot, 221

Tabernacles
   Tabernacles pilgrimage, 117–42, 157, 195, 203, 204
Talbert, Charles, 157
temple cleansing incident, 108, 110
The Way, vii, 143, 148–50, 154, 157, 158, 159, 162, 163, 165, 166, 170, 171, 193, 194, 198, 204
   people of the Way, 150
Thackeray, H. St. J., 120
theological program, 11, 42, 77, 86
theophany, 22, 24, 49, 50, 55, 57, 59, 124, 177, 183
   national theophany, 55
   theophanic encounter, 31
tree of the knowledge of good and evil, 5, 6, 8
tree of life, 6, 8, 9
trepidation and anticipation, 215
Turner, Laurence, 20
Turner, Max, 183

Ulfgard, Hakan, 118, 120, 121
Universalism of Luke, 143

VanderKam, James, 174, 176, 193
Vanderlip, D. George, 160, 162
voluntary partnership with God, 5
von Rad, Gerhard, 1, 12, 20, 30, 37, 38, 41, 57, 61, 66, 67, 68, 77, 224

walk and go, 18, 209
walk and way, xiii, 75, 82, 148, 201, 222, 223, 224, 225, 236
walk before him, 21, 201
walk, journey of life metaphor, 82
walking, 3, 15, 18, 21, 51, 54, 63, 64, 75, 82, 83, 85, 93, 139, 149, 200, 201, 209, 212
walking in his ways, 63, 64, 75, 82, 85, 200
walk in darkness, 134, 138, 223
walking in the light, 83, 139, 223
walking metaphor, 64, 83, 209, 212
walking with God, 209, 212, 216, 217, 218, 220
water motif, 141
way into Jerusalem, 150
way out from Jerusalem, 150
Weinfeld, Moshe, 188
Weiser, Artur, 82
Wellhausen, Julius, 91
Wenham, Gordon, 3, 17, 18, 25, 27, 28, 32, 40
Westermann, Claus, 13, 14, 21, 22, 23, 24, 25, 37, 217
wilderness wandering, xiv, 52, 54, 60–62, 66, 85, 121, 123, 140, 195, 200, 203, 205, 212, 223
Williamson, P. R., 14, 20, 44
Wright, C., 189, 194
Wright, N. T., 109, 111, 191

Yee, Gale, 107

Abou the Author

Seung Yeal Lee was Professor of New Testament at Alliance Graduate School and Asian Graduate School of Theology at Manila. After three years in pastoring Jubilee International Fellowship in Manila, he now serves as Pastor of All Nations International Fellowship in Beijing Onnuri Church. His current research interest is in the Year of Jubilee as the fulfilment of the Church and worship.

www.ingramcontent.com/pod-product-compliance
Lightning Source LLC
Chambersburg PA
CBHW070404240426
43661CB00056B/2536